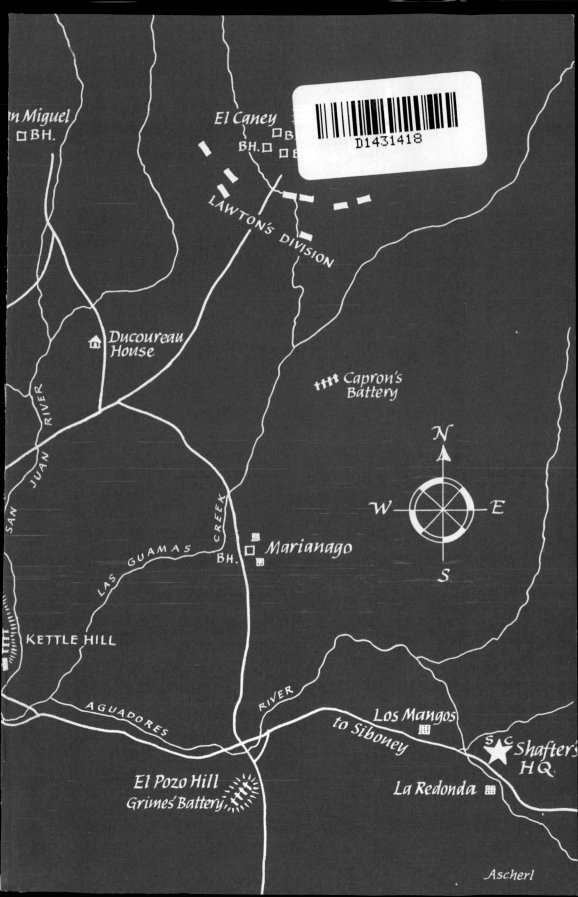

ROOSEVELT'S ROUGH RIDERS

By Virgil Carrington Jones

ROOSEVELT'S ROUGH RIDERS
BIRTH OF LIBERTY
THE CIVIL WAR AT SEA (3 volumes)
EIGHT HOURS BEFORE RICHMOND
GRAY GHOSTS AND REBEL RAIDERS
THE HATFIELDS AND THE MCCOYS
RANGER MOSBY

VIRGIL CARRINGTON JONES

ROOSEVELT'S ROUGH RIDERS

DOUBLEDAY & COMPANY, INC.

GARDEN CITY, NEW YORK

1971

PHOTOGRAPH CREDITS

G. G. Bain, 1.
Collections in the Museum of New Mexico,
2, 3, 84.
Gift to Museum from John Haberl, 4.
U. S. Signal Corps, 5, 6, 9, 11, 12, 13, 14,
19, 24, 26, 27, 29, 30, 31, 32a, 33, 34,
36, 40, 41, 43, 44, 47, 48, 50, 51, 52, 53,
56, 57, 58, 59, 60, 61, 65, 69, 70, 71, 73,
76, 80, 81.
Arizona Pioneers' Historical Society, 7, 8,
17, 74.
Theodore Roosevelt Collection, Harvard College
Library, 10, 15, 16, 20, 21, 22, 23, 25,
38, 39, 46, 49, 62, 63, 64, 68, 72, 77, 78,
79, 82, 83.
Collections of the Library of Congress, 18,
28, 35, 37, 66, 75.
William Dinwiddie, 32b, 45.
U. S. War Dept. General Staff, 42, 54.
William Glackens, 55.
By permission of the Harvard College Library,
67.

CONTENTS

Illustrations follow pages 114, 138, 162, 186, 210, and 234

part one
THE WAR SPIRIT

Chapter 1

FIGHTERS IN FATIGUES

A Cuban insurgent, frantically waving a white banner of welcome, ran out to the end of the high pier at Daiquirí. Below him in the June sun, American soldiers, some white, some black, were beginning to arrive in little boats, ready to pour ashore. Almost all were dressed in the heavy, woolen blue uniforms worn by Northern troops in the Civil War. The exceptions were members of a most unusual regiment known as Rough Riders, a volunteer outfit made up primarily of Westerners. They were allowed to wear, not altogether to their liking, the dusty brown fatigues of the Cavalry, simply because of the prestige and influence of their leaders—Colonel Leonard Wood, former White House surgeon, and Lieutenant Colonel (Teddy) Roosevelt, newly resigned as Assistant Secretary of the Navy.

The Cuban waving the white flag was one of the natives under command of General Demetrio Castillo. Just a short while earlier, this dedicated officer had led his roughneck band into Daiquirí after the Spaniards occupying the squalid seacoast village had departed. They arrived on a scene of general destruction. Behind the flag-waver an ore car of the Spanish-American Iron Company was ablaze. So were machine shops and storehouses, as well as the roundhouse of the little railroad running back to the mines in the mountains. Along a terrace some fifty feet above the water and back of the rocky coastline, untouched by the torch, were about twenty corrugated zinc shacks owned by the mining interests. Also exempt were rows of native huts thatched with palm leaves.

The invaders were confident as they came toward land. But disaster was in the air. No harbor existed. The only protection from the prevailing southeast wind was a slight extension of land to seaward. Part way across an inlet running up into the cove in which the village lay was an iron railroad trestle, built like a modern truss fully forty feet above the water. Designed so that ore from the mines could be loaded by chute directly into vessels, it was too high to be of any service whatever to the invaders. But across from it stood a wooden pier built of cribwork. It was twenty feet wide and connected with shore by a 150-foot tramway on piles along which push-cars could be moved to transfer supplies brought in by ship to the little mining settlement. This would serve their purpose, though not without inconvenience. It was not as high as the trestle, but still so high men would have to wait until their boats crested on waves before they could leap upon it.

The first boat touched shore at 10:24 A.M. It was filled with regulars. They moved fast because they were trained in making landings. On up into the village they ran, leaving death behind, for not all of the thousands who would start for shore that day were as lucky as they.

An odd, bargelike lighter loaded with items the soldiers would need immediately upon landing warped in toward the dock. It was commanded by a seaman with a raspy voice, his cries rising incessantly and annoyingly above the din around the pier.

A New York *World* correspondent was with the vanguard and recorded one of the first tragedies of the war:

> At last it has happened. A boat was overturned. Two men of the 10th Cavalry (colored), tied in blanket rolls and heavy cartridge belts, are in the water. It is horrible to think of them clasped in the arms of their heavy accoutrements, while excitement reigns on the pier head. Lines are thrown; men try to reach down in the water; while over all the hubbub tears the sound of that rasping voice, screaming senselessly to do this and do that.

A hero was on hand. Into the water a fully clothed officer jumped. He swam after the men who had gone out of sight, and for what seemed an interminably long time he was under water. When he surfaced, he was recognized as William O. (Bucky) O'Neill, mayor of Prescott, Arizona, a colorful character serving as captain of one of the Rough Rider troops.

But his efforts were futile. The *World's* newsman added the epitaph:

Well, two of them are gone—killed on the doorstep of Cuba, drowned a moment before they could set foot on that island which had been the subject of their soldierly dreams.

The black troopers—Corporal Edward Cobb of Richmond, Virginia, and Private John English of Chattanooga, Tennessee—had been crushed to death against the pilings. The 10th Cavalry, of which they were a part, as well as the 9th Cavalry, were veteran Negro regiments that were to see their share of battle action in the days ahead. No units of the Army were more experienced. Organized originally from blacks who wanted to remain in service following the Civil War, they were for years stationed along the Rio Grande, in New Mexico, Arizona, Colorado, and the Dakotas. Hunger and cold and privation were as much their enemies as the Indians, bandits, cattle thieves, gunmen, bootleggers, and Mexican revolutionaries. The Comanches, Kiowas, Cheyennes, and Arapahoes, among other tribes, came to recognize them and to give them a name that stuck—the "Buffalo Soldiers" of the Great Plains. History would identify them as a major spearhead in settling the West.

But one of their main claims to fame was that they had crossed the path of an outfit that from its start was destined for greatness. On this June day on the coast of Cuba, in the initial movements of the American invasion of 1898, the Rough Riders had been heard from in a manner that denoted bravery was to them a prerequisite. They would be heard from again and again and again and, in the concerted charge that brought the war to its closing moments, would comprise a major portion of one prong of a two-pronged assault. They would fight, admiring and being admired, alongside the black soldiers.

Besides "Bucky," later to be pictured in stone at Prescott as the most typical of Westerners, there were other celebrities in the ranks of the Rough Riders. There was Benjamin Franklin Daniels, the marshal of Dodge City, an able warrior; Bob Wrenn and Bill Larned, the nation's two top tennis players; Stanley Hollister, champion half-miler; Dudley Dean, identified by sports writers as the "most famous quarterback ever on the Harvard football team"; Craig Wadsworth, leader of cotillions, cross-country rider, and star polo player, as well as many others. In the regiment of about 1200 men were Indians, hunters, trappers, plainsmen, clerks, New York City policemen, socialites, actors, miners, musicians, ranchers, railroad men. They were a hodgepodge of male humanity ranging in age from seventeen to sixty-nine. Some were respectable gentlemen and some were wanted by the law. Never before had there been such an assembly; never again, perhaps, will there be another. In their midst were future governors and members of the United States Congress. And they fought for their country at a time when thousands of other men were streaming toward the Yukon in search of gold.

The regiment existed for only 133 days. Yet it quickly caught the attention of the public and captured its imagination and won its acclaim. For, in battle, its members proved they were no phonies as fighters. In the period of about four and a half months they were together, 37 percent of those who got to Cuba were casualties. Better than one out of every three were killed, wounded, or stricken by disease. It was the highest casualty rate of any American unit that took part in the Spanish-American campaign.[1]

As history has recorded, these men went in as rough riders, but they did their fighting on foot. And they did such a job of it that they made one of their leaders President of the United States.

[1] Official reports show a total casualty list for the Spanish-American War of 2910, including 107 officers and 2803 privates.

Chapter 2

COWBOYS WILL MAKE SPLENDID CAVALRY

Theodore Roosevelt, more than Leonard Wood, deserved credit for the organization of the Rough Riders, officially designated the 1st Volunteer Cavalry, a part of the 5th Corps, the American Army unit sent to Cuba. Member of an affluent family, fate gave him the qualities and the experience necessary to steer and lead such an unusual outfit. As a child, he had suffered from asthma and poor eyesight. In time, his vision was improved by thick spectacles, but it took determination and perseverance to develop the stamina needed for the career he would follow.

Encouraged by his father and through his own aspirations, he learned to box under an ex-prize fighter.[1] He was fond of tennis, horseback riding, walking and climbing, and later took up polo. At eighteen, he entered Harvard, a devotee of natural history, and there continued to be active in athletics. In 1880, the year of his graduation, he began the study of law, got married, and spent his honeymoon in Europe, where he climbed the Matterhorn

[1] Roosevelt's ability to box was a dominant influence throughout his life. By means of it, he gained confidence. He relates this incident in his autobiography, published in New York in 1928 by Charles Scribner's Sons, p. 30: "I felt a great admiration for men who were fearless and who could hold their own in the world, and I had a great desire to be like them. Until I was nearly fourteen I let this desire take no more definite shape than day-dreams. Then an incident happened that did me real good. Having an attack of asthma, I was sent by myself to Moosehead Lake. On the stage coach thither I encountered a couple of other boys who were about my own age, but very much more competent and also much more mischievous. I have no doubt they were good-hearted boys, but they were boys! They found that I was a foreordained and predestined victim, and industriously proceeded to make life miserable for me. The worst feature was that when I finally tried to fight them I discovered that either one singly could not only handle me with easy contempt, but handle me so as not to hurt me much and yet to prevent my doing any damage whatever in return. I made up my mind that I must try to learn so that I would not again be put in such a helpless position."

and Jungfrau. Back home, he joined the 21st District Republican Association, became a leader in politics, and soon was elected to the State Legislature. He was a dynamo.[2] Moreover, his wedded life was so blissful that he built on the shores of Oyster Bay a comfortable home that he named Sagamore Hill. It was typically Rooseveltian, fitted with wide hallways and large fireplaces, and well supplied with trophies of the hunt.

During this period he discovered the West. The climate helped his asthma and the hunting was excellent. He made repeated trips through the country beyond the Red River, in the wild land of the Indian and buffalo.

Roosevelt always came back to New York enthralled by the spirit of the West. The wild freedom of the Bad Lands captivated him. He liked its appeal to the manly instincts and he admired the independence of the people he met. He also became interested in the rifle as a firearm and in time set up a target range at Oyster Bay. He often went there to practice, and occasionally invited guests to shoot. One of these was Baron Hermann Speck von Sternburg, later German Ambassador at Washington. The baron was a professional soldier, an expert marksman, and a capable rider and walker. It was he, in response to his host's enthusiasm about the Western ranchers and cowboys, who suggested what an excellent regiment might be organized among them. This was an idea that Roosevelt did not forget.[3]

During this period, Roosevelt took another step which would prove of value to him. He joined the New York National Guard, and became a member of the 8th Infantry Regiment. He served

---

[2] Roosevelt's gospel of life later was expounded to one of the cowboy members of the Rough Riders: "Get action; do things; be sane; don't fritter away your time; create; act; take a place wherever you are and be Somebody; get action."

[3] Some writers have erroneously given Roosevelt credit for originating the idea of the Rough Riders, but he himself set the record straight. In his autobiography, he states: "It was he [Von Sternburg] who first talked over with me the raising of a regiment of horse riflemen from among the ranchmen and cowboys of the Plains."

However, Roosevelt rightly deserves credit for bringing together the combination of Easterners and Westerners, athletes and cowboys, who made up the Rough Riders. Of this the New York *World* (June 26, 1898) commented:

"In many ways the regiment is an elaborate photograph of the character of its founder, Theodore Roosevelt. At odd times he is ranchman, hunter, politician, reformer, society man, athlete, literateur, and statesman. Only in his complex brain, with its intense versatility, could the idea of forming such a regiment have been born. But its wide knowledge of the ramifications of the social scale told him that the men he wanted were working upon every round of the ladder from the bottom to the top. He knew that the Fifth Avenue clubman had the genuine fighting stuff, as well as the plainsman who carried a dozen notches on his gun. It only needed opportunity to bring it out."

faithfully, and studied the tactics manual as though it were a Bible. Soon he was chosen a company captain.

In 1884, four years after his graduation from college, his mother died suddenly. Within twenty-four hours his wife died in child-birth.[4]

Stunned by this double tragedy, Roosevelt turned his back upon a political career in New York and went West to live, soon acquiring a ranch on the Little Missouri River near Medora, North Dakota, where he built a log home, doing much of the work himself. When it was completed, he settled down to follow ranching and writing as a career.[5] He led a rugged, healthful life, riding the range and following the routine of the cowboys and big-game hunters with whom he came in contact.

At first, he was not wholeheartedly welcomed by the Westerners. His Harvard accent and thick-lensed glasses caused some individuals to consider him a sissy and city slicker, but he changed this impression by his ability to handle his fists. Because of his prominent teeth and strange laugh, the Indians of the area called him "Laughing Horse."[6] They looked upon him as a great hunter.

As he moved about, Baron von Sternburg's suggestion frequently came to mind. He easily envisioned the regiment that might be developed from the hardy men he encountered—sunburned and healthy and accustomed to the outdoors. In the summer of '86, a threat of war with Mexico came about when a newspaper editor who had published an article offensive to that country was arrested on the border. Roosevelt quickly decided the time had come to act upon the German's idea.

He wrote a letter to Henry Cabot Lodge, Harvard graduate, writer, lecturer, whom he had met four years earlier. It was a fortunate meeting, for Lodge quickly developed into a close political ally. Roosevelt's purpose in writing was to report that he had offered to raise some companies of horse riflemen in the event of hostilities and to request that Lodge telegraph at once if war with Mexico became inevitable.

---

[4] The child was named Alice and is now Mrs. Nicholas Longworth of Washington, D.C.

[5] Roosevelt wrote a number of books, the first of which, a history of the naval end of the War of 1812, was started while he was in college. His most outstanding work was a multi-volume history, *The Winning of the West*.

[6] Roosevelt's manner of laughing—"Hah!" with jaws set and teeth bared—remains strong in the recollection of Jesse D. Langdon of Red Hook, New York, one of the last survivors of the Rough Riders.

"Out here," Roosevelt explained, "things are so much behind that I might not hear the news for a week. I haven't the least idea there will be any trouble; but, as my chance of doing anything worth doing seems to grow continually smaller, I intend to grasp at every opportunity that turns up. I think there is some good fighting stuff among these harum-scarum rough-riders out here; whether I can bring it out is another matter."

But the moment was not at hand. Almost as suddenly as it began, the trouble with Mexico ended. When he was convinced the threat was over, Roosevelt wrote Lodge: "If a war had come off, I would surely have had behind me as utterly reckless a set of desperadoes as ever sat in the saddle."

The years Roosevelt spent as a ranchman were his most memorable. "I was never happier in my life," he wrote of them. But the Republicans back East, remembering his spirit in the State Legislature and his behavior at a national convention at which he had spoken from a platform shared with such towering political figures as William McKinley, would not let him rest. In 1886, they successfully pressured him to return to New York City and run for mayor.

After the campaign, a three-man race in which Teddy came in last, he packed off to Europe to take on another bride.[7] Returning to Sagamore Hill, he continued to write, occasionally making trips back to Medora to look after his rather unprofitable ranching interests. His yearning for the study of law had waned. While he was still interested in nature, he was never able to make up his mind to become a naturalist. He frankly admitted he did not know what vocation he would like to follow. He did not consider himself rich, though well to do. Fate made his decision.

Roosevelt's role in politics had brought him into national prominence. When the Republican presidential candidate, Benjamin Harrison, had been placed in office in 1888, he yielded to pressure from Lodge and others and named Roosevelt to membership on the Civil Service Commission, a new and unpopular agency. The appointee came to Washington in May '89, determined to make the provisions of the Civil Service Act a success. For six years he pursued his goal, while politicians and partisan newspapers

[7] Roosevelt's first wife was Alice Hathaway Lee of Massachusetts, one of the radiant members of the young group with which he associated in college; his second, Edith Kermit Carow, a childhood sweetheart.

snapped at his heels. Yet his record was of such distinction that it led to his appointment as head of the New York Police Board.

When Roosevelt moved back to Sagamore Hill in 1895, his thoughts were probably on Washington. Two months earlier, newspapers had reported that an insurrection against the decaying authority of Spain had broken out in Cuba. This was something Americans had hoped would happen. Reports indicated those behind the uprising were prepared for a long struggle.

For generations Spain had dominated the island. Her officers had enslaved the colonials. They had exacted spoils from the Cuban estates. To make matters worse, the economy was generally upset. Once before, in the late '60s, there had been a revolution that lasted ten years. It was ended by a peaceful settlement, but soon a reign of terror had returned. Thousands of families fled to America where they rallied under the leadership of Martí and talked resistance. In Cuba, a new Spanish overlord, General Valeriano Weyler was in control. This officer was commonly referred to as "Butcher" Weyler. He had been sent to Cuba with instructions to crush the revolt. This was the goal he kept in mind. His rule was despotic.

The troubles in Cuba caused heavy losses to American investors. While the United States remained neutral, millions of American dollars were being lost. The press took up the cudgel. Newspapers and magazines mounted editorial campaigns to arouse the public. The insurrection of 1895 was portrayed as a fight on behalf of humanity.

Despite his police activities, Roosevelt took a highly active role in the presidential campaign of 1896. He made numerous speeches on behalf of the party candidate, William McKinley. Shortly after the new President's inauguration, Teddy Roosevelt was named Assistant Secretary of the Navy. Henry Cabot Lodge, then in the United States Senate, helped to pull the strings.

Roosevelt's appointment made him second in power only to the departmental Secretary, John Davis Long. Some people disagreed with McKinley's choice, although Lodge wrote Roosevelt: "The only thing I can hear adverse is a fear that you will want to fight somebody at once."

Roosevelt came back to Washington bursting with energy. His days in the West had restored his health, and he was now a fine physical specimen, with a muscular figure five feet, eight inches in height. His shoulders were broad, legs straight and sinewy, head symmetrical, poised on a powerful neck.

The new Assistant Secretary already had made up his mind about the situation in Cuba: it was intolerable. Since the insurrection in '95, matters had grown steadily worse. Already Americans were joining expeditions and slipping onto the island. Some of these bore arms under such experienced leaders as Generals Calixto García and Maximo Gómez. Food, supplies, and weapons were smuggled to the insurgents. In the meantime, Martí had returned to the island to lead the insurgents in the field and been ambushed and killed. As Roosevelt saw it, war was inevitable. He was convinced that the United States should drive Spain out of the Western Hemisphere and declare itself a world power.

The average American had no idea what Roosevelt was talking about when he said that, in the event of war with Spain, the Philippines should be promptly attacked. The islands were too far away to be considered in connection with hostilities that would center on Cuba. But one official who agreed with him was Commodore George Dewey, president of the Board of Inspection and Survey at Washington. He had served under Admiral David G. Farragut in the Civil War and, as a veteran in the service, recognized that Spain was vulnerable in the Pacific. He openly longed for a command there.

The administration's policy continued to be against any opening of hostilities. McKinley's ambition was to restore business health and bring back good times. In this connection, he sent an envoy, General Stewart L. Woodford, to Madrid. The purpose of Woodford's mission was to open negotiations with the Spanish government with a view toward peace in Cuba.

In the late summer of 1897, Secretary Long went to Maine on vacation. This gave Roosevelt opportunity to spread his ideas. The White House was open to him. Occasionally he dined there and went on afternoon rides with President McKinley, talking volubly of a strong Navy, of the need to attack Manila in the Philippines, and of the fitness of Dewey to lead the squadron in that area.

Meanwhile, the Assistant Secretary was determined to be at the front if war came. One day he wrote General Francis Vinton Greene, head of the New York National Guard, that he would like to go under him, suggesting: "I suppose we should have to raise

a regiment, with you as colonel and me as lieutenant colonel."[8]
About the same time, he wrote Lodge, revealing his thinking
about the way to conduct the war if it came: send the main
American fleet to Cuba at once, place a fleet to harass the coast
of Spain, and throw an expeditionary force into Cuba. "I doubt
if the war would last six weeks so far as the actual phase of it was
concerned," he added.

Roosevelt's enthusiasm for war met strong opposition from the
Navy Secretary. Long was a pacifist, a stout gentleman of sweet
disposition, given to wearing spats. Only a short while back, he
had suffered a nervous breakdown. Not yet completely sure of
himself, he came in as head of the department at a time of unusual stress. The Navy was entrusted with the responsibility of
enforcing American neutrality. Its ships in the Atlantic Squadron
were operating as a police force. Mainly they steamed back and
forth to prevent aid from reaching the insurgents from American
shores. Under administration policy, the United States was to be
kept neutral. Long was horrified at the thought of making the
Navy a vigorous fighting force, something Roosevelt thought essential.

In December, Dewey set sail from San Francisco to take command of the Asiatic Squadron. He had been given instructions to
strike the Spanish at Manila should war come. McKinley still hoped
hostilities could be averted. He even succeeded in obtaining assent
from the Spanish government to send food and clothing to relieve
the Cuban people.

About this time Roosevelt found Washington an attractive place
in which to live. He wrote Lodge: "You will be pleased to hear
that at Washington I finally developed a playmate who fairly
walked me off my legs; a Massachusetts man, moreover, an army
surgeon named Wood."[9]

The "playmate" was the future leader of the Rough Riders. Two
years Roosevelt's junior, he was an ardent lover of sports, especially
sailing small boats off the New England coast in rough weather.
Five feet, eleven inches tall, weighing 180 pounds, he was broad-

[8] While Roosevelt makes mention in this letter of the matter of raising a regiment,
there is no reference to the cowboy and Indian element he had had in mind in '86.
This undoubtedly would not have been the case had he still been in the West. His
sole purpose in writing Greene, it would seem, was to get into the service himself.
[9] Roosevelt was wrong in referring to Wood as "a Massachusetts man," although
the surgeon had at one time resided in that state. His birthplace was Winchester,
New Hampshire.

chested and had powerful shoulders. He also had sledge-hammer
fists, blond hair, and blue eyes. His walk was that of a man of
iron, one who could withstand strain to the highest degree. After
graduation from Harvard Medical School, he spent a year prac-
ticing in Boston, Massachusetts, and then joined the Army as a
contract surgeon. Soon he was tracking Indians out in the South-
western Territories. There he built a reputation as the best boxer in
the American Army and the only white man who could tire out an
Apache on the trail. Records soon were made of his volunteer
leadership in conducting parties over hundreds of miles of Arizona
and Mexican desert to capture such desperadoes as Geronimo and
the Apache Kid. He took part in some of the last campaigns on
the American frontier. A student of the military sciences, an expert
rifle shot, he in every way measured up to the qualifications of a
natural-born soldier. It was no surprise, then, in April 1898, while
training men for the war in Cuba, that he was awarded a Congressional Medal of Honor, mainly for his efforts against Geronimo—
"voluntarily carried dispatches through a region infested with Indians, making a journey of seventy miles in one night and walking
thirty miles the next day."

Wood was the sort of outdoor companion Roosevelt had been
looking for ever since leaving the West. The two often were seen
together, walking or riding or rowing. And now and then passers-by
stopped beside some vacant lot or open field to watch two adults—
and sometimes a third, Senator Lodge—kick a football back and
forth with the grim determination of college athletes.

Wood shared Roosevelt's feeling about the proximity of war.
Although he was kept largely in attendance upon Mrs. McKinley,
who was in poor health, he let it be known that he intended to
serve at the front if hostilities came.

The New Year passed with troubles building up in Cuba. During
the middle of January 1898 a disturbance in Havana caused the
Consul General, Fitzhugh Lee, alarmist nephew of the South's
Robert E. Lee, to call for the battleship *Maine* to be ordered
there for the protection of American citizens. The Spanish Minister
at Washington promptly was informed the vessel was to visit Cuba
as a mark of friendship and national courtesy.

The *Maine* entered the harbor of Havana on the morning of
January 25. Soon there were reassuring reports of the reception
accorded the battleship and her crew. All seemed to be happiness.
Then on the night of February 15, the ship was shattered by an

explosion. It sank, carrying 264 crewmen and two officers to their death.

War fever swept America. Lodge clipped a news report dated from Prescott, Arizona, and sent it to Roosevelt in a letter recalling the trouble with Mexico in '86. The article stated:

> As a result of the sinking of the *Maine* at Havana and the feeling prevailing that war is imminent, initial steps are being taken today in this city to form the first regiment of the Arizona flying cavalry . . . The personnel of the force will be made up principally of cowboys, all of whom are expert marksmen and skilled horsemen . . . The plan was initiated and is being carried forward by Alexander O. Brodie, West Point graduate, and Mayor Wm. O. O'Neill, of this city . . .

Roosevelt responded: "The flurry proved to be nothing, of course, but, by George, if war had come, I'd have been ready. I had all the arrangements made with the Governor of the Territory to raise as many companies of horse riflemen as the War Department would take."[10]

The war fervor spread like wildfire. Offers of enlistment flooded into Washington. In the meantime, America's war-making machinery turned slowly, creaking under the rust that had built up during the thirty-three years the nation had been at peace.

Out of the national capital at this period went a newspaper report that should have been of especial interest to Roosevelt. It announced that the first troops to be ordered to the front would be those stationed in the West, and added: "There is hardly a doubt . . . the government will avail itself of the opportunity to furnish cowboy regiments, as these men, accustomed as they are to withstanding hardships and perfect as they are in horsemanship and in the accurate use of firearms, will make splendid cavalry."

April came. Dandelions bloomed in grassy plots around the Capitol. On the 11th, McKinley sent a message to Congress asking that he be empowered to end the hostilities in Cuba. A resolution to that effect was passed on the 19th. Spain answered by declaring war on the 24th. Next day the United States did the same.

---

[10] It is surprising that Roosevelt at this point apparently had abandoned his dream of leading such a regiment to the front. His correspondence, especially that to Greene and others, reveals that he was interested primarily in helping to raise a regiment rather than to lead one himself. In view of later developments, it is possible that he had withdrawn from the Von Sternburg idea because his association as Assistant Secretary of the Navy with veteran officers of all branches of the service had convinced him of his lack of military experience.

Chapter 3

RAINY SEASON MEANS DEATH

The war already was under way. On the 20th, McKinley had ordered the coast of Cuba blockaded, and next morning Admiral William T. Sampson, chief of the North Atlantic Squadron, took the fleet to sea. Shortly after leaving Key West, it captured two merchant vessels bound for Cuba.

The United States was in a deplorable state of preparation for war.[1] Its standing army was limited by law to 25,000 men. It was made up of twenty-five regiments of infantry and ten of cavalry, all at minimum strength. While considered highly efficient for duties of detached garrison and guard service, its main weakness lay with its officers. They had gained from the Indian wars experience denied the Navy since the Civil War, but few were versed in transporting and encamping large forces of troops. The War Department announced all training camps for the Cuban campaign would be in the South, so as to have the men nearer Cuba and to acclimatize them as much as possible for operations in a semitropical country.

While Roosevelt was primarily interested in getting to war in any capacity, developments during April got him back on course so far as his interest in a cowboy outfit was concerned. One day a colorful character quite familiar with lobbying practices in Washington

---

[1] Secretary of War Alger admitted himself that such a condition existed. In his book, *The Spanish-American War*, p. 455, he states: "It is doubtful if any nation rated as a first power ever entered upon a war of offense in a condition of less military preparation than was the United States in 1898. At that time there were not sufficient *The Spanish-American War*, p. 455, he states: "It is doubtful if any nation rated as addition to the Regular Army as it stood."

The report of the Commission appointed by the President to investigate the conduct of the war states: "One of the lessons taught by the war is that the country should hereafter be in a better state of preparation for war."

came to the White House. He was Judge Jay L. Torrey, president of the Embar Cattle Company of Embar, Wyoming. A rancher, lawyer, old Army captain, and author of a bankruptcy bill pending in Congress, what he wanted was authority to organize twelve troops of cowboys for immediate service.

Torrey's efforts were rewarded. Congress passed a Volunteer Army Bill, one provision of which called for the organization of three regiments from the wild riders and riflemen of the Rockies and Great Plains.[2]

In a matter of hours, Roosevelt was called before Secretary of War Russell A. Alger, white-goateed veteran of the Civil War and former Governor of Michigan. The Assistant Secretary was offered command of one of the three cowboy regiments, but declined to accept, explaining that he was inexperienced in military work.[3] Because of his lack of knowledge of what was required, he explained, he would not be able to equip the regiment quickly enough to get it into the Cuban campaign. However, he said he would be delighted to serve as lieutenant colonel of the regiment if Leonard Wood, a veteran soldier, was appointed colonel. Alger consented.

Torrey in the meantime was already busy organizing the unit he was to command. The third would be led by another colorful character, Colonel Melvin (Milt) Grigsby, Attorney General of South Dakota, a man who had grown up with that state. During the Civil War, he three times was a prisoner, twice escaping. On one of his flights, his face became so darkened by long exposure to the soot of open campfires that he was promptly nicknamed "The Smoked Yank" when he reached friendly Northern troops.[4]

The visit with Alger set off Roosevelt on a campaign of letter writing. One to whom he wrote was William Astor Chanler, cousin of the flamboyant John Jacob Astor, writer, inventor, builder, a

[2] This legislation has been mistakenly accepted by some as the beginning of the idea of a regiment of rough riders. In his excellent book on the regiment, Edward Marshall, newspaper correspondent who was seriously wounded while accompanying it into battle, said that Senator Francis Warren, who sponsored the legislation, "is responsible for the idea." It can be truthfully said that Warren deserved credit for the passage of the legislation, although he had much assistance from other senators.
[3] Roosevelt's hesitation in this instance may have been due to two factors. When he had proposed raising cowboy troops in '86, he was twelve years younger, being only twenty-eight. When offered such a command by Alger, he was almost forty and, in the meantime, had served in a capacity in Washington that enabled him to see and be impressed by the complications and intricacies of military routine.
[4] After the Civil War, he wrote a book about his experiences, entitling it *The Smoked Yank*. It was published by the Regan Printing Company of Chicago in 1891.

man estimated to have a fortune of at least a hundred million dollars. In it, he told of the regiment he had been offered and added: "If I was not limited to Westerners, at least at first, I should feel very much like getting you . . . to get a company of good horsemen and good riflemen to come with me."

Another letter went to a Kentucky author, an old friend, John Fox, Jr. In this correspondence, he gave the first hint that he had in mind actually including some Easterners in the regiment, even though it was to be raised primarily in the Rocky Mountain states.

But the extensive letter writing soon stopped. Newspapers announced that Wood and Roosevelt were working like mad to get their regiment organized, that they were in such a hurry that they were sending messages only by telegraph.

A signal development at this period was the appearance at the White House of the Honorable Joseph Wheeler, congressman from Alabama. He was there by invitation rather than by looks. A thin little man in his early sixties, he weighed barely more than a hundred pounds. His appearance was gnome-like, accentuated by a face full of whiskers that hung half the length of his boyish figure. Clothes swung from him the way they would on a scarecrow. But he still moved and acted with much of the quickness and energy that had marked him as the South's fire-eating cavalry leader, a man of dogged aggressiveness and hard-hitting tactics. Most noticeable about him was a courtesy that was inborn. Friends marveled at the way he scurried like a rabbit to help a woman move a chair or alight from a vehicle. Despite his rank of major general in the Confederate Army, he invariably got to his feet when introduced even to a second lieutenant. Born in Georgia, partly educated in Connecticut, and appointed to West Point from New York, he had served his military apprenticeship in New Mexico fighting Indians.

McKinley told him he had to appoint fifteen major generals and that he wanted him to be one of them.

"I am too old," Wheeler quickly replied.

McKinley had planned his argument. "There must be a high officer from the South," he said. "There must be a symbol that the old days are gone. You are needed."[5]

Others who were present recorded that Wheeler seemed the

[5] A part of this conversation was repeated to fellow officers by General Wheeler while serving in Cuba. See *The Little War of Private Post*, by Charles Johnson Post; Little, Brown and Company, 1960, p. 214.

very antithesis of a fierce cavalry leader. He seemed more like a
boy who had donned false whiskers and sneaked into his grandfather's clothes.

After accepting what was obviously a political appointment,
Wheeler left the White House. At that very moment the American
public was reading a dire warning in the newspapers: a third of
the men selected for the Cuban invasion would die if sent there
during the rainy season.

On April 25, Secretary Long wrote in his diary:

> My Assistant Secretary, Roosevelt, has determined upon re-
> signing, in order to go into the Army and take part in the
> war. He has been of great use; a man of unbounded energy
> and force, and thoroughly honest—which is the main thing.
> He has lost his head to this unutterable folly of deserting the
> post where he is of the most service and running off to ride a
> horse and, probably, brush mosquitoes from his neck on the
> Florida sands . . . And yet how absurd all this will sound, if
> by some turn of fortune he should accomplish some great things
> and strike a very high mark.[6]

[6] Long was haunted by these words to such a degree that he later scribbled a
postscript at the bottom of the page on which they appeared: "Roosevelt was
right, and we, his friends, wrong. His going into the Army led straight to the
presidency."

Chapter 4

VOLUNTEERS ALL

It was as if a mighty clarion sounded to arms throughout the Southwest: Uncle Sam needed cowboys—men accustomed to the outdoors—to fight in Cuba with Wood and Roosevelt. The reaction was widespread. From the ranches, the mines, the plains, the arroyos, the mountains of four Territories—Arizona, New Mexico, Oklahoma, and Indian—most of them came. With rare exception, they were healthy specimens, hard and fearless and confident. Danger to them was a daily matter. It was encountered from horses, the elements, and the lawless renegades of the frontier.

In Arizona, the drive was an anticlimax for Brodie and O'Neill, the first men in the field to become active in forming a cowboy outfit. Enlistees rode in one after another, hurrying to the colors. San Antonio, Texas, it was announced, would be the general rendezvous point.

Spurred by a telegram from Colonel Wood, New Mexico became a mustering center overnight. Santa Fe was named the gathering point for men from Gallup, Albuquerque, Raton, Las Vegas, and Aztec. Recruiting was carried on in the front room of the Governor's office. The city made ready to become, as one local newspaper expressed it, "the scene of war preparations that will stir the blood of every citizen with a desire to join the force and march to the front." Fifteen cowboys, sun-tanned and colorful in their rough clothing, showed up on fine horses from Pecos Valley. It took half a day for two doctors to examine them. Only two were rejected. They had come well recommended, riding in with Charles L. Ballard, large rancher and stock raiser, deputy United States marshal and city marshal of Roswell. People pointed him out: he was the lawman who had broken up the notorious Black Jack Gang of outlaws.

A distinguished figure appeared at the head of a group from Albuquerque. As his proud mount trotted along the street, he was hailed from all sides—Maximiliano Luna, a magic name, a magic figure. Not quite thirty-eight years of age, only a few inches over five feet tall, of direct Spanish descent, courtly and gracious, with dark brown eyes and black hair, he was a talented speaker, accomplished musician, and excellent baseball player. His education had been acquired at the Jesuit College in Las Vegas and at Georgetown University in the District of Columbia, which he attended while his father represented New Mexico Territory in the United States Congress. He himself had served in the Legislative Assembly of the Territory. He was sheriff of Valencia County and an insurance agent. His ancestors were conquistadores, who had reconquered New Mexico and restored it to Spanish rule in 1650. The Lunas had been on the banks of the Rio Grande River since the seventeenth century, some of them grandees and large land owners.

A realistic touch was added to the Santa Fe war fever by the arrival of Captain Thomas P. Ledwidge, a twenty-seven-year-old carpenter from Salem, Illinois. He had joined up with a group of filibusterers in June '96, and fought in Cuba under Generals Gómez, Mateo, and García. Thrice wounded, he showed such gallantry that he was breveted captain. But fever and smallpox disabled him and he had to return to the United States. Now he was ready to go back.

Newspapers announced that the Oklahoma volunteers would rendezvous at Guthrie on May 1, a change from Oklahoma City for reasons of economy and convenience. No word had been received as to when Colonel Wood would arrive to organize the units, as announcements from Washington indicated he would do. However, the War Department issued an official order that each troop should consist of a captain, first lieutenant, second lieutenant, first sergeant, quartermaster sergeant, six sergeants, eight corporals, two farriers and blacksmiths, two trumpeters, one saddler, one wagoner, and sixty-four to seventy-eight privates.

May brought news that stirred American hearts. The month was just breaking when tidings came from the Pacific of a smashing victory in Manila Bay, 7000 miles from the California coast. Dewey,

Roosevelt's choice of leader for the Asiatic theater, had struck the Spanish squadron in the Philippines and soundly defeated it.

This news arrived at a time when the American public, especially along the Atlantic coast, was undergoing considerable alarm. Word had come during April that the Spanish fleet under Admiral Pascual Cervera y Topete had sailed from the Cape Verde Islands in a westward direction. This led to the theory that it was to be used in the relief of Havana. It could also mean—and this was the main cause of concern in the United States—that Cervera planned to attack ports along the Atlantic.

Information about Cervera's movement put an end to a plan that had been simmering in the War Department for weeks. It was a scheme to send 5000 troops to land on the south coast of Cuba to form a junction with Gómez, carrying to him supplies and ammunition. The move was aimed at enabling the insurgents to continue the war against the Spanish until the United States could prepare for a wholesale offensive.

Brigadier General William Rufus Shafter was to lead the expedition. A sixty-three-year-old fat and gouty veteran who looked like three men rolled into one—or, as a quip said, a floating tent—he stood nearly six feet tall, parted his hair in the middle, wore a bushy mustache that drooped at the ends, and had big hands and a big head, the latter covered by a shock of tousled gray hair. When approaching, he lumbered like a bear, but spoke with a voice geared to the proportions of a hummingbird. He was said to have been the first white male child born in Kalamazoo County, Michigan. Once wounded and once captured, he came out of the Civil War a colonel, with a Medal of Honor for bravery displayed in battle in '62 and also with a legendary reputation as one of the best marksmen fighting on the side of the Union. He was profane and proficient, trained to every trick of the trooper's trade, rough in manner and bearing, brave, strong-willed, a fine example of the vanishing breed of hard-boiled regulars. Politics posed for him no attraction. He was without entanglements and without obligations.

Missouri heard of Shafter's assignment with some degree of pride. Oldtimers recalled him as a brakeman on the Hannibal & St. Joseph Railroad. That was before he became a schoolteacher at Breckenridge, Missouri, the job he left to join the Union Army.

Late in April, Shafter had been called from San Francisco to New Orleans and then to Washington, where he was waiting when

Cervera's movements were reported. Immediately the expedition to Cuba was canceled.

This period was the most exhausting Roosevelt had encountered in his career. In addition to his responsibilities as Assistant Secretary, he and Wood were busy night and day with the organization of their regiment. Men were volunteering so fast it was evident there would be no shortage of manpower.

Wood, the veteran soldier, insisted on obtaining for the regiment equipment comparable with that supplied the regulars. He asked for smokeless powder. He also requested .30-caliber Krag-Jorgensen carbines, instead of the old-fashioned .45-caliber Springfields with their black powder of Civil War days. The Krag-Jorgensen, commonly referred to as the "Krag," was a Danish invention with American improvements.

Newspapers already were giving the regiment alliterative nicknames—"Teddy's Terrors," "Wood's Wild Westerners," "Roosevelt's Rangers," "Cavalry Cowpunchers," and "Roosevelt's Rough Riders." The last of these was the most popular. Roosevelt at first resented it, fearing people would get the impression the regiment was to be a hippodrome affair. He candidly admitted that he did not know what nickname would be best, but he pointed out that all would not be from the West, that there would be a number of Knickerbocker and Somerset Club members from New York, as well as Harvard, Princeton, and Yale athletes.

The afternoon of May 4, anyone staring down from Thumb Butte, a granite formation overlooking Prescott, Arizona, would have witnessed a stirring sight. Along the three-mile stretch from Whipple Barracks marched two hundred men, the territory's quota in the regiment of volunteers Wood and Roosevelt were getting together. Dressed in all sorts of clothing and lined up four abreast, they followed along behind the Prescott Band. All wore red and blue hat bands with the lettering "1st U.S. Volunteer Cavalry—Arizona Column."

At the front of the enrollees were the men most responsible for enlisting them—Alexander Oswald Brodie and William O'Neill. They were completely different in character, but both popular throughout the area.

Brodie, a native New Yorker, was forty-eight years old, straight and vigorous as a man of twenty. Of medium size, with broad shoulders and a drooping black mustache, he was by profession a civil and mining engineer. After graduation from West Point, he served for a time in the Army, establishing a reputation as one of the most gallant and experienced Indian fighters in all the West. More recently he had been busy developing the Crown Point Gold Mine in the Castle Creek Mining District of Arizona, a lode he himself had opened. Ore taken from it was running as high as $1000 to the ton of free gold, but, when the war threat came, he ordered the pumps pulled out of the shafts and laid off his miners.[1]

O'Neill, ten years Bodie's junior, was strikingly Irish, six feet, one inch tall, weighing over 200 pounds, with a persuasive voice and manner.[2] His father had been a member of Meagher's famous Irish Brigade in the Civil War and had brought up his son in the schools of the national capital. Stories about Bucky were legion. A lawyer, he had mixed scholarship with the rough life of the West, living at times the life of a student, miner, traveler, cowboy, newspaperman, gambler, and lawyer. It was also said he had come in the garb of a Catholic priest, having lately performed duties of the church in Mexico City. But no matter what his past, his life in Arizona was an open book. He became an inveterate gambler, thereby gaining his nickname for "bucking the tiger" at faro. Then, in 1881, he was converted and thereafter did not tempt fortune. Instead, he developed into quite a writer. He also established a record for such daring that he twice was made Sheriff of Yavapai County. He ran unsuccessfully for Congress, but in '97 was successful in being elected Mayor of Prescott. Already wealthy, having made his fortune in mining, he was considered one of the most successful promoters in the Southwest. He had an active part in the opening of the Grand Canyon of the Colorado and was currently developing two large commercial blocks in Phoenix.

After weeks of beating the bushes for volunteers, the two patriots were now on their way to war. A thunderous applause greeted them and their followers as they moved into Prescott. They

---

[1] Four years after the Cuban campaign, Brodie was elected Governor of Arizona.
[2] There seems to be some confusion over O'Neill's place of birth. Ralph Keithley, in his book, *Buckey O'Neill*, published in 1940 at Caldwell, Idaho, p. 31, refers to his birth at St. Louis, Missouri, on February 2, 1860. The muster roll of the Rough Riders, on file at National Archives in Washington, D.C., however, has this personal information concerning him: "38, 5 ft., 10½ in.; dark brown eyes, dark brown hair; born in Ireland; lawyer; joined April 29, Whipple Barracks; residence, Prescott, Arizona; married."

marched through the Plaza and onto the grounds in front of the bandstand near the courthouse. Waiting there was the Governor of Arizona, Myron H. McCord, and other dignitaries.

McCord was the first introduced. He turned and held aloft a large silk flag. Looking at Major Brodie, he said:

"The patriotic ladies of the Women's Relief Corps of Phoenix have made with their own hands this beautiful flag and commissioned me to present it to you. It is the grand emblem of our country's greatness, and it is more. It is the bearer of the hope and love of the donors who present it—whose hearts will go with you to the end, should fate determine that it shall be carried into the battlefields of Cuba or elsewhere. I have assured them it would be found like the plume of Navarre waving in the front of the battle."

Near the end of the program, the master of ceremonies gave a signal. A young, golden-yellow female mountain lion, with yellow eyes and pink nose, was led out in front of the grandstand. On the part of Robert Brown, local saloonkeeper, the animal was presented as a mascot. Brown at the moment was down at the railroad station hanging mottoes on the sides of the cars that were to transport the volunteers to San Antonio.

In Oklahoma, the territory's quota of troops, many of them Indians, set out by way of the Choctaw Railroad the following day. They had been mustered in by Lieutenant Allyn K. Capron, a capable soldier already tapped by Wood to be adjutant of the Rough Rider regiment. Fifth in a line of military men, he had joined the Army in 1890 and been promoted to second lieutenant in the 7th Cavalry, stationed at Fort Sill. Twenty-six years old, married, a native of Brooklyn, New York, he had spent most of his adult life in the West. There he had become an expert in Indian sign language and had developed into a great rifle shot and hunter.[3]

The New Mexico contingent departed for San Antonio on May 6, creating a scene somewhat similar to that at Prescott. The dif-

[3] Roosevelt wrote of Capron: ". . . On the whole, [he was] the best soldier in the regiment. In fact, I think he was the ideal of what an American Regular Army officer should be . . . Tall and lithe, a remarkable boxer and walker, he looked what he was, the archetype of the fighting man."

ference perhaps lay in the degree of confusion, which was far greater in this territory because it was sending to war fourteen commissioned officers and 342 enlisted men. Business in Santa Fe was suspended for the day. It was said every vehicle in the city was in use.

The procession formed on the Plaza at 3:30 P.M. At the front in a gaily decorated carriage rode Miss Catherine Williams, representing the Goddess of Liberty. A banner on the side of the vehicle boasted: *My brother Owen was with Dewey.*

At the railway station were gathered an estimated 5000 persons, most of them wearing badges and waving flags. A stirring round of speeches sent the men on their way.

Many of the volunteers had paid their own way to Santa Fe, explaining, "We did not enlist for money, but to fight for our country." Prominent among them was Major Henry B. Hersey, who had resigned as Adjutant General of the Territory to go to Cuba. A member of one of Vermont's oldest and most prominent families, he had served since '91 as local weather observer and as a section director of the United States Weather Service.

Another of distinction, the type of man that people turned to stare at wherever he moved, was William H. H. Llewellyn of Las Cruces. Speaker of the New Mexico Legislature and one of the most popular and useful citizens of the area, he was a native of Wisconsin, had served as a special agent of the Department of Justice in Montana and the Dakotas, and still carried four bullets in his body. He had been in charge of the posse that wiped out the Middleton Gang of counterfeiters, cattle thieves, and murderers. At one time, he served as Indian agent, and then was employed as a livestock agent for the Santa Fe Railroad. Along with these duties, he studied law and was admitted to the bar. An experienced miner, cattle and sheep raiser, fruit grower, and agriculturist, he was conversant with irrigation and land laws. Only a few days past he had been appointed to the Bureau of Immigration. Forty-five years old and an excellent specimen of manhood, he still was no match for his nineteen-year-old son, Morgan, also a Rough Rider.

The New York group, promptly dubbed the "Fifth Avenue Boys," included several men of wealth and prominence. Woodbury Kane, a cousin of John Jacob Astor, was older than most of the recruits, a handsome, husky athlete with handlebar mustaches. Over the years he had amassed a reputation as a yachtsman and as one of the best horsemen in the United States and Europe. He also was an outstanding polo player and cross-country rider.[4]

I. Townsend Burden, Jr., muscle-bound football star, was the son of a New York millionaire said to have "money to burn, as well as diamonds to lose." Horace Devereaux, like Kane older than the average, had been an end rush at Princeton about 1880. He was remembered for playing football exceptionally well, even with his head cut open. Wealthy Reginald Ronalds, descendant of the first Pierre Lorillard of tobacco fame, was a Yale football player and the son of a mother who moved in Royal society in London. There were Charles and Henry Bull of the Harvard crew, sons of a New York broker. David M. (Dade) Goodrich of the rubber family was captain of the Harvard crew and one of the most noted college athletes in the country.[5] Kenneth Robinson and Sumner K. Gerard were champion golfers. William Tiffany, Jr., a boyish-looking fellow, bore a name prominent in commercial circles. One of the most outstanding, from the standpoint of reputation and background, was Hamilton Fish, Jr., New York playboy, former captain of the Columbia crew, and grandson of the Secretary of State under President Ulysses S. Grant.

Four men of splendid physique, Philip K. Sweet, Henry H. Haywood, Henry Ebermann, and William Breen, were New York policemen on indefinite leave with full pay. Sweet was an old Indian fighter, having served in the Sioux campaign in 1890 and '91. Haywood, formerly a Cuban ship pilot, had been through six yellow fever epidemics. Ebermann, once a member of the 6th Cavalry, held a medal for gallant conduct in the battle of Pine Ridge during the Civil War. He also had been awarded a sharpshooter's medal.

Roosevelt assembled the recruits in the Army Dispensary Building and delivered a brief speech:

---

[4] Roosevelt wrote of Woodbury Kane: "During the eighteen years that had passed since my graduation, I had seen very little of him, though, being always interested in sports, I occasionally met him on the hunting field, had seen him on the deck of the *Defender* when she vanquished the *Valkyrie*, and knew the part he had played on the *Navajo*, when, in her most important race, that otherwise unlucky yacht vanquished her opponent, the Prince of Wales' *Britannica*."

[5] Goodrich later became Chairman of the Board of the B. F. Goodrich Company of Akron, Ohio.

"Gentlemen: You have now reached the last point. If any one of you doesn't mean business, let him say so now. An hour from now will be too late to back out. Once in, you've got to see it through. You've got to perform without flinching whatever duty is assigned you, regardless of the difficulty or danger attending it. If it is garrison duty, you must attend to it. If it is meeting the fever, you must be willing. If it is the closest kind of fighing, you must be anxious for it. You must know how to ride, how to shoot, how to live in the open. Absolute obedience to every command is your first lesson. No matter what comes, you mustn't squeal. Think it over—all of you. If any man wishes to withdraw, he will be gladly excused, for others are ready to take his place."

He then told them they would be under the command of First Sergeant Thaddeus Higgins of New York City until they got to San Antonio. He motioned toward a tall, straight, gaunt Irishman standing at one side of the room. It was their introduction to one of the best drill sergeants in the business. Only twenty-nine years of age, Higgins had served for ten years in the 6th Cavalry, taking part in two Indian campaigns. Only the preceding spring he had left the service to go to work for the New York Central Railroad.

As they enlisted, the recruits were informed that they were entering the service as plain troopers, that their pay would be thirteen dollars per month, with allowances for rations and clothes.

When Roosevelt left the building, he was met on the stairway by a youth not quite seventeen years of age, but who looked older. He was six feet tall, weighed 180 pounds, and was robust and well-proportioned. His face on one side was badly bruised, and his patched trousers hid a knee that was equally disfigured.

"You're Mr. Roosevelt!" the youth exclaimed.

"Yes," admitted Roosevelt.

"I'm Jess Langdon. I've hoboed by train all the way from North Dakota, and I want to join your Rough Riders."

The youth did not identify himself as the son of W. C. Langdon, an authority on veterinary medicine. Ten years earlier, the father had taken the boy to Roosevelt's ranch near Medora, where he went to inspect cattle for Texas fever. That had been an experience the lad never forgot. While there, Roosevelt picked him up in his arms. The youngster glanced through the thick-lensed glasses—"at eyes that looked like pig's eyes"—and screamed, "Put me down! I'm no baby!"[6]

"Can you ride a horse?" asked Roosevelt.

"I can ride anything that's got hair on it," replied the youth enthusiastically.

"Then go upstairs and tell them I sent you."

The Eastern contingent left Washington over the Baltimore & Ohio Railroad at 10 P.M. May 7. Roosevelt was there to see them off and was approached by Langdon.

"Colonel, I haven't been sworn in yet."

Roosevelt smiled as he noticed the earnest expression on the face of the youth.

"Hah! Well, I'll swear you in personally when I get to San Antonio," he said tolerantly. "Just call on me."

Returning home after watching the troopers depart, Roosevelt wrote intolerantly in his diary before going to bed:

> The delays and stupidity of the Ordnance Department surpass belief. The Quartermaster Department is better, but bad. The Commissary Department is good. There is no management whatever in the War Department. Against a good nation we should be helpless.[7]

[6] This incident was related to the author by Jesse Dyson Langdon during an interview at his home at Red Hook, New York, September 7, 1968. Eighty-seven years old, the veteran, one of five or six Rough Riders still alive at the time, clearly recalled his experience in hoboing across country. This form of transportation was not new to him. He had left home as a boy and had got his fill of hoboing. Then, after a year in college, he had run away again, this time to join the 13th Infantry at Minneapolis, Minnesota, giving his age as nineteen. When he heard of the plan to organize a Rough Rider regiment, he confessed that he was only sixteen and got his release from the 13th. The bruises on his face and knee were received when he jumped from the train in the Washington yards.

[7] This diary was presented by Roosevelt's widow to the Roosevelt Memorial Association after his death. It was a small pocket volume and contained notes in his handwriting both in pencil and ink.

Chapter 5

MILITARY TRAINING IS A CHORE

In 1898, San Antonio was a city of palms, liveoaks, and pecan trees, of five- and six-story buildings and immense parks, of adobe houses and Spanish missions. It was a fast-growing community in a state settled by Spaniards and named for Indians. A large percentage of its population was made up of foreign-born whites, including many Mexicans. Its military importance lay in Fort Sam Houston on Government Hill, one of the nation's principal training posts for cavalry.

Wood arrived on Thursday, May 5, earlier than expected. With him was Major George M. Dunn, the Chevy Chase master of hounds.

At 8 o'clock next morning, a Southern Pacific train with Arizona banners on its sides pulled into San Antonio. It was switched from the main line to the San Antonio & Arkansas Pass track. Then it was shunted out to the Fairgrounds at Riverside Park, a facility about four miles from the city and near the ruins of two old Indian missions beside a little river that wended its way among quaint adobe houses. On hand to greet it was Wood. Much pleased at what he saw, he stood by to watch the men unload, a process newspapers said took no more than two minutes. He was especially interested in the golden yellow lion, by this time generally referred to as "Josephine."

Shortly afterward, Wood headed for Fort Sam Houston, about three miles from the heart of the city, where horses were being rounded up for the regiment. He was surprised on arrival to learn that the prices of range animals suddenly had soared. The trend would change as soon as prospective sellers realized the colonel of the Rough Riders was no slouch when it came to judging horseflesh.

Back at Riverside Park, the Arizona contingent was quartered in the Exposition Hall, a giant, two-story building with a fancy cupola and much other superstructure. Into this great old building near the center of the Fairgrounds, an area surrounded by a high board fence, the men marched, yelling and whooping, each with a blanket looped over his shoulder.

Saturday was devoted to cleaning up the premises and arranging the camp. The floor of Exposition Hall was divided off into company areas. In the southwest corner of the building was located the Commissary Department. Eight tents for officers were erected between the hall and the Fairgrounds entrance.

While the men were busy with their work in the late afternoon, another train chugged up the spur, this one bringing the troops from Oklahoma. As it came to a halt, passengers scuttered off like spiders deserting a ground nest and lined up at attention while a sergeant called the roll. Then they marched off to the barracks in double column, cheered wildly by groups of Arizonians.

Although May 8 was a Sabbath, reveille sounded at 4 A.M. There was still a chill in the air and many of the men were coughing as they rolled out of their blankets. Kitchen fires were already burning. As day broke, attention centered on the dozens of horses brought over from Fort Sam Houston and now staked out in a row in the low prairie in front of Exposition Hall. The problem immediately at hand was that of breaking them to the saddle. This would be done on a volunteer basis.

During the afternoon, all of San Antonio seemed to come for a visit. Thousands of persons in their Sunday best strolled through the park and around the grounds, staring at the strange men and strange costumes.

Monday marked the arrival of the Harvard contingent. After detraining, they rolled their toilet cases, underwear, and similar items in rubber blankets, left their suitcases at the railway station, and headed for the nearby Manger Hotel. There each invested a dollar in a bounteous lunch, after which it was agreed that they would renounce luxurious living until the end of the war. Highly excited, stomachs full, they boarded a rickety trolley and headed out toward Riverside Park.

"I shall never forget," recorded one of the Harvard recruits, twenty-one-year-old Joseph Ogden Wells, "my first view of the sturdy Westerners when we turned the angle in the woods that long May afternoon and tramped into the park . . . The cowboys, hearing the trolley beyond the board fence of the park, had lined up in ranks of welcome at the door of the old fair building which served as barracks."[1]

Full realization that they at last were in the Army overtook them in the late afternoon when a bugler sounded mess call. The notes seemed to pour out in liquid and silvery tones, hauntingly pleasing to the ear. They came from the horn of a professional bugler, Emilio Cassi, bandmaster from Jerome, Arizona. Twenty-seven years old, with brown eyes and black hair, he had been born in Monte Carlo, Monaco, and had lived the life of a soldier of fortune. For years he was first trumpeter of the French regiment of Chasseurs d'Afrique in Algeria, and he also had served in the Italian army.[2]

On May 10, reveille again sounded at 4 A.M. Men stood in line to make a hasty toilet at the hydrants on the Fairgrounds and then messed on bacon, potatoes, and coffee.

Two trains of New Mexicans and another contingent of Easterners, most of them from New York, arrived during the day. A Houston newspaper reporter noted that some of the men from the East had their golf sticks with them.

Wood had the camp well under control. His major interest was the horses. Another concern was the expected arrival of Roosevelt. Although the press reported Teddy coming in on almost every train, he was just this day bidding farewell to his fellow workers at the Navy Department.

Colonel Wood announced on May 11 there would be three squadrons of four troops each, with troop strength at sixty-five, a figure afterward increased.[3] Enough men were on hand to make up the first two of these. The third would be formed of the troops from Indian Territory, still on their way, and of the

[1] Wells, a student before joining the Rough Riders, recorded his experiences in an excellent diary now on file in the library of Harvard University. Because of the brevity of the Cuban campaign, few diaries were kept and few letters were written by the men who took part. The Library of Congress is virtually without either.
[2] Theodore Westwood Miller, another Rider who kept a diary, wrote of Cassi: "A fine-looking fellow and a great character. A typical modern adventurer. He has been in about every country in the world, and has mixtures of French, Spanish, and Mexican blood in him."
[3] Rosters on file at National Archives include more than 1200 names. Some of these may not have seen service, although they were listed as members of particular troops.

leftovers from companies formed from the Oklahoma, New Mexico, and Arizona columns and the "Fifth Avenue Boys."

For squadron commanders, Wood chose Major Brodie to lead the 1st, Major Hersey, the 2nd, and Major Dunn, the 3rd. All three of these man were of superior ability and were older than a vast majority of the other members of the regiment. They were of fine appearance, of athletic build, picked as leaders by a leader. Dunn, in particular, was a thorough tactician and strict drill-master.

During the latter part of the morning, the Westerners prepared to watch what they were sure would be the downfall of one of the "Fifth Avenue Boys." It was whispered about, with much elbow-nudging, that this particular city slicker had got special permission to go into San Antonio and that he was to be allowed to ride one of the horses. The mount chosen, it was noted, was a "Roman-nosed claybank with a retrospective eye." It had been led up to Exposition Hall and tied near the entrance.

The crowd gathered, ready to watch the departure—or downfall. In time, the "tenderfoot" came out, attired in a business suit that came far from blending with a blue flannel shirt and wide-brimmed sombrero.

Spectators pushed together, strangely quiet and excitedly anticipating. There was no hooting or jeering. Smiles on the faces were smug, denoting the "you-should-know-better" attitude of wisdom and experience. Here assembled was a living encyclopedia of horse knowledge, and it recognized a situation. Anyone could see the critter tethered near the Hall was wild and that it would become a volcano of action the moment a foot was put in the stirrup. But apparently not the slicker who had chosen it.

The moment came. With rhythmic ease, he gathered up the reins and swung into the saddle. A practiced heel touched the claybank ever so lightly, quick and commanding. The animal tensed, as though ready to go into a tantrum, but the rider held its head high, signaling authority with a pull of the reins. Instantly there was recognition of the master in the animal's eyes. A hint of a lunge to the side, the slightest bit of a jog with its hind legs, and off it went in a gentle canter.

The horseman raised his sombrero and tipped it gracefully as he moved away. Westerners stared in amazement—and with some degree of disappointment. Things were still too new in camp for them to know that they had been watching Craig Wadsworth, crack polo player and perhaps the best cross-country rider in America.

During drill in the afternoon, it was noticed that the Easterners had some advantage over the Westerners. "Their training in the ballroom makes it easier for them to keep step, wheel, and do similar things," recorded an observer.

The number of horses in camp had increased to 275. By Sunday, it was thought, enough would be on hand to mount the 1st and 2nd Squadrons.

An early reveille on Thursday, May 12, indicated to the men that they were in for another busy day. Truly enough, they were taken on a long extended-order drill, Brodie marching them several miles from the camp and drilling them for two hours. Squadron drill came in the afternoon, followed by the first regimental formation.

A crowd of an estimated 2000 visitors appeared to watch the activities, especially the bronco-bustin'. Word had spread that the Rough Riders were giving exhibitions of horsemanship equal to anything seen in Buffalo Bill's Wild West Show.[4]

Men adept at breaking horses were excused from drill. Among the best of these were Tom Darnell, a red-headed, blue-eyed cowboy from Denver; Jess Langdon, the youth who had hoboed to Washington from North Dakota, and an amazing character from Stillwater, Oklahoma Territory, named William McGinty. "Billy" was only five feet, five inches tall, with blue eyes and sandy hair, young in appearance, although twenty-seven years old. He seemed glued to the backs of the bucking broncos. Another —and perhaps the best all-around horseman in the regiment—was an Alsatian hunter, Frederick Herrig, loyal, simple-minded, a friend of Roosevelt and a man much older than those with whom he served. He and Teddy had hunted deer and mountain sheep.

If Friday the 13th augured ill for the Rough Riders, their misfortune may have been symbolized in the shipment of uniforms that arrived this day. The press reported they were of serviceable brown canvas trimmed with yellow, designating cavalry, but the Riders thought they were more like overalls than uniforms.[5] The

[4] According to Jess Langdon, he and twelve other Rough Riders became a part of Buffalo Bill's Show and put on special acts of horsemanship during the first season after returning from Cuba.

[5] Jess Langdon told the author they definitely were not uniforms. "The only uniforms the Rough Riders got, except the officers," he said, "they got on Long Island after they returned from Cuba. I went home in my old brown jeans—my old stinking

cost to the government, including that for shoes and hat, was reported to be about seven dollars. One newspaper said the uniform "looks like it was cut out with an axe." Whatever their appearance, they were far more comfortable than the heavy flannel uniforms worn by other soldiers.

Arrival of the first shipment of arms on May 14 brought the war nearer. Simultaneously, it was announced that Dr. James Robert Church, son of United States Senate Librarian Alonzo W. Church and formerly contract surgeon at Fort Myer, Virginia, would serve as a surgeon for the regiment. An expert horseman, young and robust, he had played halfback on the Princeton football team and then had served for some time in the West as surgeon of a cavalry troop.

It also was announced during the day that the regiment had accepted for membership a wealthy, crack polo player, Joseph Sampson Stevens of Newport, Rhode Island, only son of the Duchess de Dino of Paris, France. Another addition to the ranks was Albert C. McMillan, marksman of the 7th Regiment and son of a former New York City Park Commissioner.

Late in the afternoon, an informal procession from San Antonio arrived, unannounced, outside the Fairgrounds gate. Included in it were the mayor and other city officials, followed by Professor Carl Beck and his tuneful marching band.

Conservative estimates placed the crowd that strolled through the Fairgrounds and Riverside Park on Sunday, May 15, at 10,000 persons. Long lines of buggies and other horse-drawn vehicles appeared from all directions even before the sun brought the Rough Riders clearly into view.

This was the day that Roosevelt arrived. He came in over the Southern Pacific Railroad at 7:30 A.M. With him was his servant, Marshall, a devoted black who gathered up his several grips and packed them off to the Manger. At camp later in the day, Teddy, dressed in fawn-colored uniform with canary facings, leaped nimbly from a buckboard and began shaking hands. Trumpeter Cassi sounded officers' call, and the crowd surged around.

Before going to his tent next to that of Wood at the west end of the line erected for the officers, Roosevelt was taken on a tour of the Fairgrounds. Comment from Riders who had not seen him

---

brown jeans I wore home. The dye had a very sickening smell. It made us all sick. By golly, it was terrible. And they issued us the damned blue woolen shirts that almost killed us with heat. I wore mine tied around my neck most of the time."

before was far from complimentary. The thick-lensed eyeglasses were his chief detraction.[6]

This day troops were lettered from A to M, with J omitted. Arizonians dominated A, B and C. Eighty of the 104 members of D Troop were from Oklahoma Territory, the remaining twenty-four from ten states and the District of Columbia. New Mexicans were most numerous in E, F, G and H, as well as in I, the hodge-podge troop made up of men from twenty-three states. K was composed mostly of Easterners, although it was another heterogeneous unit. More than half the members of L Troop were from Indian Territory. Thirteen of its twenty-five officers would go down, killed or wounded. M was another chiefly from Indian Territory.

Roosevelt, the human dynamo, sat on May 16 at a small table poring over his mail. All at once, with the suddenness of youth, a shadow spread across the floor of his tent. He looked up. There in the doorway stood Jess Langdon, the veterinarian's son, his figure exaggeratedly straight.

"Colonel, you said you would swear me in when you got to San Antonio."

Caught by surprise, Roosevelt studied a moment before thrusting his hands out significantly. "Hah! So I did. So I did."

In characteristic fashion, he reached spiritedly for a small Bible on the far side of the table.[7] He stood up, grinning. "Come on. Let's go behind the tent where we can have some privacy."

They walked together around the tent and came to a halt close to its back flap. There, the grin still widespread, baring his prominent teeth, Roosevelt extended the Bible. Motioning for Langdon to place one hand on it, with the other raised, he quoted the oath and had the youth repeat it.

"Hah!" he roared. "Now you are a full-fledged Rough Rider."

During the next few hours, Roosevelt worked into the routine of the camp. In their first discussion, Wood proposed that he himself attend to organization and similar details and Teddy direct the drilling.

During the day, horseshoeing activities, a part under contract, went on at a busy pace. Into the camp came two hundred horses from the Concho country near San Angelo, a fine-looking bunch

[6] Tom Hall, who turned out to be a better writer than he was a fighter, was one of the Riders who saw Roosevelt this day. He wrote of him: "He is nervous, energetic, virile. He may wear out some day, but he will never rust out."

[7] Langdon told the author Roosevelt usually kept a Bible within easy reach.

of animals full of spirit, all from three to seven years old and fourteen and a half to fifteen hands high. They had cost an average of thirty dollars per head.

The constant question was when the regiment would leave. Rumor persisted that it would go soon.

People passing along St. Mary's Street during the morning of May 17 watched a Rough Rider officer in full uniform dashing back and forth on a mustang. It was Roosevelt, trying out the first of two horses he had bought for fifty dollars each.

During the middle of the afternoon, the Indian Territory contingent arrived—170 troopers immediately identified as "the fiercest looking lot of men in the camp." With them, accompanied by his wife and daughter, was the man most responsible for getting them together, John R. Thomas, a distinguished federal judge from the West. His son, John R., Jr., was a lieutenant in the troop.

As the Indian Territory men appeared, Roosevelt was putting the 1st and 2nd Squadrons through a series of drills. For three miles out from camp he marched them in the hot sun. On the way back, as they passed a beer garden near Riverside Park, he called for a halt. Turning his horse about, he faced them and announced:

"Captains will let the men go in and drink all the beer they want, and I will pay for it."

Then he shook his fist at the line, gritted his teeth fiercely, and added: "But if any man drinks more beer than is good for him, I will cinch him!"

This gesture by Roosevelt, one of the early evidences of character that made his men admire him, brought a reprimand back in camp. Wood heard of the beer incident and promptly announced to the lieutenant colonel that any officer who would go out and drink with his men was quite unfit to hold a commission. There was no reply.

That night, before tattoo, Teddy came to Wood's tent. "I wish to tell you," he said, "that I took the troops out without thinking of this question of officers drinking with their men and gave them all a schooner of beer. I wish to say, sir, that I consider myself the damnedest ass within ten miles of this camp. Good night."

If the Riders had had complete identifications in plain view, perhaps no place in America would have been more interesting to visitors than the camp at San Antonio. Along its streets walked a cross-section of manhood that gave an insight into the nation's place on the rim of world power. Here represented were individualism and personality, the will to do, and the guts to do it. Balanced against the Easterners with their wealth and poise were characters who had known life at its roughest, had battled the elements, had lived lives largely steered by the ageless demands aimed at self-protection and self-preservation. Youths with rosy cheeks took their places beside men bronzed by Indian ancestry, by the sun and wind, or by all three.

A few minutes at any point around the Fairgrounds would bring to the visitors' attention a kaleidoscopic pattern. Into view might come a skilled packer who had led and guarded trains of laden mules through Indian-infested country toward some outpost of American civilization. Behind him perhaps would appear drivers who had lived through endless days of guiding slow wagon trains across grassy plains, or men who had gained a reputation as Rocky Mountain stage drivers. Present were miners who knew every camp from the Yukon to Leadville, lariat men who year in and year out had driven trail herds from the mesquite brush of the Neuces northward over desolate wastes to the fattening grounds along the Powder and Yellowstone, cowpunchers who could describe brands on herds from Chihuahua to Assiniboine.

These Riders, now in a vacation of luxury, were hardened to the burning heat and bitter cold of the arid plains and pine-clad mountains. They had slept in the open beside their horses. They had cowered from the icy blasts out of the north. And they had lain in the shade of the wagon while the summer was at its peak. In lean-tos, or log cabins, or under the protection of the wagon-sheet, they had lived—sometimes feasting on smoked venison and calf ribs, sometimes, until the next kill, starving on herbs.

Outstanding among them was Ben Daniels, Marshal of Dodge City, considered the toughest town on the continent. He was a large, hawk-eyed man, and somewhere in the past he had lost half an ear—"bitten off," he explained. He was a sharpshooter, and so was Roosevelt's friend, Fred Herrig. Still another was the tall, sinewy, fearless William B. Proffitt from North Carolina, twenty-four years old, son of a Confederate officer, a handsome man of remarkable strength.

From the standpoint of frontier experience, none was more a veteran than Sergeant Sam Rhodes of A Troop, a cowboy, miner, and deputy sheriff from Tonto Basin, Arizona Territory. Thirty-one years old, with light-blue eyes and dark-brown hair, he had never considered it worth while to notch his gun—"ain't enough room." Another in this category was Robert Brown, thirty-eight, of Prescott, nicknamed "Bronco George." His trigger finger had dropped at least five men in "righteous" causes. When a stage driver informed him that Teddy Roosevelt needed his services, he rode up out of Skull Valley, through Devil's Gate and Dead Man's Gulch, and headed for Whipple Barracks. He had a strange cast in one eye and kept his right hand on the handle of his gun at all times. From other directions came "Rocky Mountain Bill" Jenkins of Montana, a deep scar over his right eye left by the claw of a bear; "Dead Shot Jim" Simpson of Albuquerque, said to be able to hit a jackrabbit's eye at a thousand yards from the back of a wild horse, and "Lariat Ned" Perkins of Colorado, artist with a rope.

The list of characters was long, with traits widely varied:

Billy McGinty, who had never walked a hundred yards if there was a horse to ride; Fred Smith, bear hunter and gambler, whose real name was Garfield A. Tod; Sherman Bell, the deputy marshal from Cripple Creek, accepted for service even though bothered by a hernia; Charles Younger, son of Bob Younger of Jesse James's gang, slightly built Westerner afraid of nothing; Walter J. Mc-Cann, Arizona bookkeeper who once had been a buffalo hunter; Tom Darnell, Bill Wood, and Jess Langdon, like McGinty able to ride any horse that came along; Jim Goodwin, Buck Taylor, and Ed Armstrong, all crack shots with rifle or pistol; Warren Crockett, Internal Revenue officer from Georgia.

Into camp this day came Hallett Alsop Borrowe, a name once prominent in gossip columns. Wealthy New Yorker who had stayed abroad most of the time, he became involved while in France with Mrs. J. Coleman Drayton, daughter of Mrs. William Astor, and was challenged by the husband to a duel that never took place. Then he disappeared from sight. Finally he was discovered, working as a car-starter at Newark, New Jersey. With him to Texas he brought his valet.

Much of the excitement during May 18 centered on two automatic, rapid-firing Colt guns brought in by rail.[8] They were set

[8] Some confusion exists as to the actual donors of these guns. All sources agree on Woodbury Kane and Joseph Sampson Stevens, son of the Duchess de Dino of Paris, but some say they were given by Kane and William Tiffany, Jr. In his book, *The Rough Riders*, Roosevelt lists the donors as Kane, Stevens, Tiffany, and one or two others of the New York men.

up in the rear of Roosevelt's tent and immediately became major objects of curiosity. It was said they had cost $10,000 and could shoot 500 bullets a minute.

The day was hot, and made hotter by the invective of Thaddeus Higgins, the drill sergeant. It was noted his profanity was as personal in its application as it was picturesque. This day it was turned on Willie Tiffany, the New York socialite, caught with his hand resting on the muzzle of his gun.

Drill consisted of a ride into the country. A light wind seemed like a blast furnace and sent dust flying in whirling clouds. Back to camp came the men with masks of mud on their faces and their uniforms changed in hue from brown to gray. It gave by-standers an odd feeling to see a column of soldiers move off and then disappear in a cloud of dust.

Camp life was humming. Admiration for Wood and Roosevelt built rapidly. The former was the poker-faced type, reserved, cool, cautious, the trained soldier who did not mix with the rank and file, but who would go to any extreme in his men's behalf. The latter was an extrovert, friendly, bubbling with life, a lover of people. A newspaper noted that he could sit on the ground and eat with a cowpuncher or prospector, and in the same breath turn and address a crowned head. There was no jealousy between them. A sign down at the railroad station read: THIS WAY TO CAMP OF ROOSEVELT'S ROUGH RIDERS, even though the camp was officially named after Wood.

Horses were drawn by number on May 19, and then the first mounted drill was held.

News was broadcast that Cervera's Spanish fleet, last heard of off the Island of Martinique, had now entered Santiago harbor. At Washington, attention centered on Santiago, the city that would be the point of attack. During the day, a fleet under Admiral Winfield Scott Schley left Key West, following after that sent earlier under Sampson.

A carload of tents arrived at San Antonio on May 20. Wood ordered them unloaded immediately. It was a cloudy day, windy and more suited to drilling than stretching canvas, but the work went on regardless. The tents were of the variety commonly referred to as "pup" or "dog," consisting of two pieces four feet wide and six and a half long, buttoned together over a ridge pole about three feet high.

Among arrivals during the day was the Reverend Henry A.

Brown, Oberlin College graduate and rector of the Church of the Advent of Prescott. He would serve as regimental chaplain.

Drill was proceeding satisfactorily, and there was much pride in the speed with which the horses picked up the various formations and commands. Roosevelt took occasion to commend the troopers, telling them he would not be afraid to match them against any regiment in the Regular Army.

During the morning of Sunday, May 22, the troops were assembled in the field south of the grandstand and held at attention for more than an hour while the Articles of War were read to them. Then the Army oath was administered by Roosevelt, much to the chagrin of Jess Langdon, who suddenly realized why there was such a grin on Teddy's face the day he had taken him behind the tent to swear him into the service. Throughout a long life the North Dakotan would talk with praise of a man who, in so patiently honoring impulsive youth, had had the decency to do so in all the privacy available.

On May 23, regimental drill was participated in by all the troops except two in the 3rd Squadron which had not yet received their equipment. When formed, the units were marched out to a prairie near the Mission San Jose. Wood was in command, and newspapers noted that few officers had drilled such a large number of men at one time since the Civil War.

During the late afternoon, attention of the men nearest regimental headquarters was aroused by the sound of shouting. They rushed out of their tents to see Roosevelt dancing in front of Wood, his hat in one hand, the other resting gracefully on his hip. The colonel held a telegram from the War Department inquiring when the 1st Volunteers would be ready to leave. AT ONCE, Wood immediately telegraphed in reply.

Drill on May 24 was more concerted than usual. For the first time since they had come to camp, the troopers were ordered to spur their horses into a gallop. Dust was thick all the way out to Mission San Jose.

Anticipating an early departure, members of the regiment were informed they were to be guests of the mayor of San Antonio at a concert during the evening in nearby Riverside Park. Professor Beck would be there with his famous band, billed as the best in Texas.

Beck had planned a program with special tribute to the Rough Riders. It was a perfect evening for the occasion. The air was pleasant and balmy, and overhead shone a canopy of stars and a golden moon. Tune after tune was played, and finally came the highlight of the evening, the eighth number, listed as "The Cavalry Charge." It had an anvil chorus, and the bandmaster wanted it to be something special. Earlier in the evening, he had rounded up twelve troopers and enlisted their services. At a signal from him, he instructed them, they were to fire into the air the blank cartridges he distributed among them.

Preliminary to starting the chorus, the professor held his baton aloft. Over him a magic spell seemed to fall. He towered, master of his profession. His hair fell back in a flowing wave that came up like a duck's tail at the nape of the neck. In the yellow glow from flickering electric light bulbs, more numerous around the bandstand than elsewhere, his celluloid collar glistened with as much artificiality as a gold tooth. Like water from a sluice, the music burst forth, a crescendo of eager notes. It was evident the bass drummer had a strong arm. Brass and reed vied for honors. The bow tie of a cornetist in the front row signaled the rise and fall of his Adam's apple.

There was frantic rhythm. Notes came out in a whirlwind of harmony, quick and ecstatic, fast, fast, faster. Beck's eyes danced. He reared on tiptoe and fell back upon his heels, swayed by the enthusiasm of the bumptitty-ta-ta beat. He waited for the moment, the moment to start the shooting. It arrived, and he grandiloquently gave the signal with his baton. What followed added no complimentary saga to the history of the Rough Riders. Two thousand shots were fired, it was charged. Women and children— and even some of the men—stampeded.

As the troopers assembled for another lengthy regimental drill on May 25, there was much joshing over what had happened at Riverside Park. Stories were many. It was claimed "gentlemanly cowboys" had cut the electric wires, and one of them, Ham Fish, the New York playboy, was described as gallantly leading an effort to prevent a charge on one of the beer stands, thereby causing attendants to flee in wild confusion.

Roosevelt took occasion during the afternoon to write President McKinley as follows:

> . . . In all the world there is not a regiment I would so soon belong to. The men are picking up the drill wonderfully. They are very intelligent and, rather to my surprise, they are

very orderly—and they mean business. We are ready now to leave at any moment, and we earnestly hope we will be put into Cuba with the very first troops; the sooner the better; at any rate, we want to see active service against the enemy.

At a conference of military advisers in Washington on May 26, the decision was reached to attack Cuba at once. General Shafter was ordered by telegram to BE PREPARED TO LOAD ON TRANSPORTS 25,000 MEN, INCLUDING INFANTRY, FOUR BATTERIES OF LIGHT ARTILLERY, EIGHT SIEGE GUNS, INCLUDING SIEGE MORTARS, AND ONE SQUADRON OF CAVALRY.

Drill at San Antonio on May 27 was punishing. Rough Riders fainted in the hot sun, but the practice sessions went on regardless. Wood wanted to use every moment of daylight.

Just as the men were dispersing after the evening meal, a telegraph messenger made his way to Wood's tent. The purpose of his visit was evident a moment later when the colonel and lieutenant colonel went into a bear hug. Instructions called for the Rough Riders to move to Tampa at once.

May 28 was a day of bustle. Harvard graduate and Indian Territory cowboy worked side by side, sweat pouring freely. The men were told they could take with them only what they could carry in their blanket rolls.

Southern Pacific Railroad officials were informed there were 1060 men in the regiment and that it was equipped with 1258 horses and mules. It was estimated that twenty-five day coaches, two Pullmans, five baggage cars, eight box cars, and sixty livestock cars would be needed. Trains would begin leaving the next afternoon and would be divided into sections, a mile or more apart. The Riders would board them at the Union Stockyards on the railroad about three miles from camp.

Reveille on Sunday, May 29, sounded at 3 A.M., an hour earlier than customary, as it had on a few occasions earlier. Working by lantern and firelight, the men attended to final details. All but a few cooking utensils and the tents had been packed the night before.

Between 8 and 9 A.M., the 1st Squadron under Major Brodie was given orders to saddle up and move to the stockyards, ready to go out on the first section. Roosevelt watched them move away and was proud. "In their slouch hats, blue flannel shirts, brown trousers, leggings and boots, with handkerchiefs knotted loosely around their necks, they looked exactly as a body of cavalry should look," he recorded.

Wood went with the first section. The last of the troopers came into the stockyards at dusk. As there was delay in making up trains, they finally were told to fall out for rest in nearby fields. Roosevelt lay down on the ground among them, without a blanket. Men gathered around, offering accommodations, but the only one he would accept was a nosebag, which he used as a pillow. Admiration for him soared. Those who looked on knew that, as the senior officer present, he could have gone to a hotel and enjoyed the comfort of a bed had he desired.

part two

BY LAND AND BY SEA

Chapter 1

TAMPA!

Theodore Roosevelt, one day to be the 26th President of the United States, rode out of San Antonio at 6 A.M., May 30, on what was described as "a dirty old ramshackle coach." It was part of a long, overcrowded, uncomfortable train comprised of ten coaches, a Pullman, and twelve livestock cars. He was there at his own election, having relinquished his comfortable berth back in the sleeper to an ailing trooper, Charles P. Nicholson of Baltimore, stricken by what was soon diagnosed as measles.

For the troopers untroubled by sickness, it was in the beginning a delightful and unforgettable ride. The route led through country where trees were white with magnolia blossoms and the air filled with fragrance. Behind the chugging locomotive, crowded coaches rocked with the uneven track. Above the noise of the train rose the shouts and songs of the passengers, all swearing vengeance on the Spaniards.

Throughout the day, a hot one, Roosevelt kept constantly busy. Whenever opportunity afforded, he acquired buckets of coffee and had it served to the men. Moreover, preparing for a possible emergency, he bought oats and hay along the way and stored them on the train. From the start, the services of Captain Capron, recognized for his extraordinary energy, executive capacity, and mastery over men, proved invaluable and attested to the thoroughness of his military training.

While Roosevelt and the last section of the Rough Rider trains were en route to Tampa, General Shafter at that point was interpreting an important cipher message from the commander-in-chief of the Army, General Nelson A. Miles, much-wounded veteran of the Union Army and a seasoned Indian campaigner. One part of it would have been of especial interest to the 1st Volunteers. It stated:

> You can take any dismounted cavalry you desire. Limit the animals to the least number required for artillery and transportation, as it is not expected that you will go but a short distance inland.

A wild reception awaited the Riders at every place they stopped. Along the way, Wood wrote his wife:

> New Orleans was very enthusiastic, streets full of people and best of all an American flag in the hands of all. The cost of this war is amply repaid by seeing the old flag as one sees it today in the South. We are indeed once more a united country.

While the Volunteers rolled eastward, excitement increased in Cuban waters. Admiral Sampson drew in with his fleet, joining Schley, and established a tighter blockade off Santiago harbor. Ships were placed in a semicircle six miles from the entrance. At night the area was constantly bathed by searchlights.

Wood reached Tampa on June 2, found General Shafter, and was assigned a camping place with General Wheeler's cavalry division. The colonel was not pleased with what he saw. "On our arrival at Tampa, which was at night," he wrote home, "we found everything confused and in a most frightful mix. Streets packed with soldiers and a foot deep in real beach sand. Confusion, confusion, confusion. War! Why, it is an advertisement to foreigners of our absolutely unprepared condition."[1]

The train bearing Roosevelt and the last section of the Riders arrived on the 3rd, its cars littered with feed and grain. Teddy joined Wood at camp, wearing a uniform that was dirty and unkempt. His fury at railroad officials was vociferous.

In Cuban waters during the hours before dawn, a young lieutenant of the Naval Construction Corps, Richmond Pearson Hobson, performed heroically. Under a hail of fire, he and seven men steered the doomed collier *Merrimac* into the channel of Santiago harbor in an effort to block it, but a shell severed her steering gear and caused her to be sunk before reaching the designated

---

[1] Only three regiments of volunteers were sufficiently prepared by early June to join the forces at Tampa. These were the 71st New York, 2nd Massachusetts, and 1st Volunteer Cavalry. Of the three "cowboy" outfits Congress had authorized, only the Rough Riders would take part in the Cuban campaign, those of Torrey and Grigsby remaining in the United States and failing to advance beyond the training stage.

point. While the effort was a failure, it signified America's determination. Hobson and his crew floundered in the water on a catamaran until they were rescued by a man who happened along in a steam barge. It was Admiral Cervera himself.

The Rough Riders, now all together again, opened their eyes June 4 on a city of complete confusion. For weeks, since the last of April, trains had been pouring into Tampa, sometimes as many as thirty a day, bringing troops and supplies over the only two available rail lines, both single track. As a result, by the first of June there were more than a thousand freight cars parked along sidings all the way to Columbia, South Carolina, some loaded with enough bacon to last 70,000 men ninety days. And what made it worse, invoices and bills of lading were not forwarded promptly, so officers, directing men armed with crowbars, were obliged to break open seals and to hunt from car to car and box to box to ascertain whether they contained clothing, ammunition, horse equipments, commissary stores, or siege guns.

It was an unbearable situation. Some troops came in without uniforms and were forced to drill in citizen's clothes. They did so while fifteen cars loaded with uniforms remained unnoticed for weeks on a siding just twenty-five miles away. Clothing was not the only item. Thousands of rifles badly in demand were out there somewhere, too. So were different parts of the siege train, as well as ammunition it was thought would be badly needed upon landing in Cuba.

The principal cause of confusion was the postal service. Post office facilities at Tampa were so badly overloaded that it was impossible for mail to be assorted and distributed until long after its receipt. Another culprit was the dock, nine miles away at Port Tampa. This was reached by a single-track railroad that was cluttered at periods during the day by excursion trains filled with tourists.

Tampa, on a shallow arm of Tampa Bay, had been selected as the concentration point for the army of invasion mainly because it was the city nearest Cuba with both port and rail facilities. Another influence was the seventy-nine-year-old tycoon, Henry Bradley Plant, builder and promoter most responsible for its becoming a magic city of the Gay Nineties period. He had had enough pull and power to see that it received its share of the business brought on by war. Behind him lay long years of success. A captain's boy on a steamer plying between New York and New Haven in 1838, he had worked up slowly. Eventually, through diligence and good luck, he became an official of the Adams Express Company and finally its manager in the Southern states. There he directed a business that was sold to him at a loss at the start of the Civil War to keep it from falling into the hands of the Confederates. As the war developed, he expanded his holdings, buying with the aid of wealthy associates in the North controlling interest in several flagging railroads in the deep South.

Through foresight, Tampa came to his attention. He was clever enough to see ahead to the day when the United States would do an immense business with Cuba and Central and South America, and he began to prepare for it. One of the things he did was to look about for the most likely spot for port development. Tampa Bay seemed to offer the best possibilities, with Tampa the ideal terminal point to which to build a railroad. He appeared at the place for the first time on December 1, 1883. Since then, progress in the area had come so fast it seemed he was waving a magic wand.

At Port Tampa, he built an immense wharf nearly a mile long, with warehouses close by. He erected Port Tampa Inn, a novel hotel that extended out over the water, making it possible for guests to fish from its windows. A one-track rail line was extended from Tampa. Sidings were laid out along the wharf, with walkways in between. Nearby, as further incentive for tourist travel over the railway, he developed an amusement park called Picnic Island.

Tampa became a boom town almost overnight. The population began to climb steadily, and more and more tourists appeared. Plant at last proposed building a fine hotel. By way of encouragement toward reaching his goal, he got concessions from civic authorities—extension of a street to the site he had chosen and construction of a bridge across the arm of the bay that separated it from the city. On a 60-acre tract acquired for $40,000, the cornerstone of the structure was laid with much pomp and ceremony in 1888. Three years later, its doors were opened. By that time, Tampa's streets had been paved and lighted by electricity.

The hotel was named for Tampa Bay. It was a monstrosity. One newspaper correspondent said it was larger than "the palace which Ismail Pasha built overnight at Cairo." Of dark red Moorish architecture, it was five stories high, spread over six acres, and had nearly 500 rooms. Its porches resembled streets. A walk from the rotunda to the dining room, it was said, was all one needed to work up an appetite. Moorish arches supported the balconies.

Mosque-like curves topped its numerous windows. Towering above it all were huge silver domes and minarets, the latter set off by crescent moons to represent the months of the Moslem year.

Fireproof throughout, the building had concrete floors supported by steel cables and by rails salvaged from some of Plant's railroads when they were converted to standard gauge. Fittings were brought in by the shipload—furniture of ebony and gold, rich tapestries, carpets, huge porcelain vases, statuary from European sources, oil paintings once owned by crowned heads. Much of this was selected by the builder's wife. Encouraged by her doting mate, she took her time touring foreign countries in search of a collection of furnishings that cost more than a million dollars.

Plant's foresight was attuned to the spirit of the Gay Nineties. It was a time for play and relaxation. Accordingly, he built a fine, T-shaped casino on the hotel grounds. In it were club rooms, an auditorium, a swimming pool under a removable floor. As a further attraction, he brought in a golf expert from Scotland to develop a course west of the hotel. Exotic plants were pinpointed over the entire sixty acres. Sweet-smelling blossoms perfumed the air. Peacocks strutted about, adding an animated touch of beauty. Pullman cars of the Florida Express could be brought almost to the very front door.

Once the builder overheard someone remark that the hotel would be more appropriately named "Plant's Folly." No offense was caused. Instead, he commented that it was worth every cent it had cost him just to be able to listen to the majestic music of the German pipe organ installed as one of its attractions.

Undoubtedly, Tampa Bay Hotel was another reason why the city was chosen as a military concentration point. Officers could mix business with pleasure. Its settings and surroundings were lavish, its rates six dollars per day, with bath adjoining.

But the hotel did not harmonize with the community itself. A reporter following the Army pictured the comparison:

> A giant affair of ornamental brick and silver minarets in a city chiefly composed of derelict wooden houses and drifting in an ocean of sand; a dreary city, where the sand has swept the paint from the houses, and where sand swamps the sidewalks and creeps into the doors and windows. It is a city where one walks ankle-deep in sand, and where the names of avenues are given to barren spaces of scrubby undergrowth and palmettoes and pines hung with funeral moss.

Much of Tampa's business was devoted to the cigar industry, many of the products of which were shipped to England. Most of the employees in its factories were Cubans. They were concentrated mainly in and around nearby Ybor City, a straggling, shabby village with a sizable Negro population.

The prosperity stimulated by arrival of twice as many soldiers as there were residents caused the community to change almost with the suddenness of a chameleon. Prices soared. Wrote the correspondent of the Washington *Post:* "The Tampa shopkeepers are making so much money that the city banks will hardly hold it. Even a lemonade man, equipped with a bucket and two cups, can make twenty-five dollars a day." Two young Jewish boys plunged their $300 into red and blue bandannas to be worn around the neck. It became a fad, especially with the Rough Riders, and the youthful merchandizers were on easy street.[2] Red light districts sprang up overnight, especially after the Army shelled out a $175,-000 payroll early in May.

Among those on the scene was Miss Clara Barton, founder and head of the American Red Cross, a busy little lady in her seventy-seventh year, denying by deed and action the charge that she was a "feeble old woman." She was moved to write:

> Tampa became the gathering point of the Army. Its camps filled like magic, first with regulars, then volunteers, as if the fiery touch of Duncraigen had spread over the hills and prairies of America; the great ships gathered in the waters; the monitors, grim and terrible, seemed striving to hide their heads among the surging waves; the transports, with decks dark with human life, passing in and out, and the great monarchs of the sea held ever their commanding sway. It seemed a strange thing, this gathering for war. Thirty years of peace had made it strange to all save the veterans.

It was into this setting the Rough Riders moved. Camps were scattered around the city and over much of the nine miles to Port Tampa, with the main one on a 250-acre tract on Tampa Heights. That assigned the 1st Volunteers was on the Tampa Bay Hotel Road, about two miles from the outskirts. It lay in a flat field,

---

[2] Roosevelt was among those who adopted the fad, also suspending a handkerchief from the back brim of his hat—"à las Havelock," as one observer recorded—as if to circumvent Secretary Long's suggestion of brushing mosquitoes off his neck. The blue polka-dot bandanna later was adopted by the Rough Riders as their hallmark.

without a tree, but surrounded by an extensive forest of scattered pines and palmettoes and by tracts quite marshy in the rainy season.

Joe Wheeler was already on hand, camped a little nearer the hotel. His arrival in Tampa early on the morning of May 13 had been completely without fanfare or even recognition. Dressed in a linen duster, he walked unnoticed through the rotunda of the Tampa Bay Hotel and was assigned a room on the sunny side of the house, where the thermometer climbed to 110 degrees. At lunch that first day, he still escaped notice and was placed at a small table at the back of the dining room, there to wait interminably for service. But "Fightin' Joe" was not long to go unnoticed. He had escaped attention largely because there was little about him to denote a distinguished leader of cavalry, or to point him out as the restless little Southerner who had bedeviled Sherman's supply lines all the way from Atlanta to Nashville.[3]

Days went by before Wheeler appeared in a blue uniform set off by the twin stars of a major general. Then eyes were drawn to him. One of his most impressive characteristics was his extraordinary quickness. "He seemed to take in everything within sight at a single glance," an observer noted, "and to read one's thoughts before the tongue could give expression to them. He grasped ideas when they were only half uttered." A Chicago *Record* newspaper correspondent wrote of him: ". . . the youngest man in the country, the liveliest 'ancient' that every straddled a war horse, and as courtly, gracious, daring and astonishing a general as ever wore shoulder straps." The sixty-two-year-old veteran's headquarters camp was as inconspicuous as its chief occupant. Only a cavalry guidon floating from a low staff and a dozen "A" tents in an irregular line marked its location.

After setting up their camp, Wood and Roosevelt again turned their attention to further preparation for action in the field. In order to rest the horses, drill was on foot. It was very much in style. Through the pines and palmettoes in all directions, as far as they could see, soldiers passed back and forth, in squads, companies, platoons. At one period, Generals Miles and Wheeler cantered up and were given a rousing ovation. The Rough Rider corresponding for the Santa Fe *New Mexican* wrote home about their visit: "Both

[3] Wheeler was the first major general mustered into the volunteer army and the first ex-Confederate to receive a commission into the service of the United States. Two other Southern generals, Fitzhugh Lee and John C. Breckinridge, also served in the Cuban campaign.

are very flattering in their remarks about the 1st United States
Volunteer Cavalry, and unhesitatingly said it is the finest volunteer
regiment they ever saw; also, that never had they known a regiment,
either regular or volunteer, to have learned so much as we in the
one month's service we have seen."

During the drill period on this day, much attention was given to
entrenching procedure. Each man had seven minutes to dig a hole
large enough to crawl into and escape imaginary bullets and shrapnel.

As soon as drill in the hot sun ended, many of the men headed
for a huge board shanty just outside the lines. A sign identified
it as NOAH's ARK and announced that cooling drinks could be had
inside. No public mention was made of the femininity available
there also.

Camped next to the Rough Riders was the 6th Regular Cavalry.
At the moment it seemed comprised of favorite people. Their tents
had board floors, and the camp was a marvel of neatness and
propriety. A band supplied entertainment. Their horses were large,
strong and fat, and they did not seem to drill as much as the
volunteers did. Wood paid no attention to them. He expected to be
in Tampa only a day or two, too short a time to compete with a
Regular Army outfit, so he dispensed with the usual preparations
for a camp. However, he did post a strict guard, barring women
and especially the numerous correspondents and military attachés
of foreign countries who were always present at drill time. Entrance
could be gained only through the guard tent and then by written
permission.

For their part, wherever the Rough Riders moved they were
objects of curiosity, their brown fatigue uniforms of light cloth
bringing many jealous glances from the other troops dressed in
clothing more suitable to winter than the tropical temperatures of
Florida. The New York *World* informed its readers that the "cowboy soldiers" were more courted than "the dozen generals and
other famous folks about Tampa waiting the word to take up the
line of march to the front."

Saturday night was a particular occasion at the Tampa Bay Hotel.
Those of the Rough Riders who could obtain passes and had money
enough to sustain them headed toward it as soon as the chores of
camp were ended. Along the way they met trails of four- and
six-mule wagons hauling provisions, camp equipage, and munitions
of war in the direction of camp and Port Tampa. On a spur

sat seventeen flat cars loaded with fifty prairie wagons. Mounted orderlies trotted past, their eyes to the front, their bodies bent forward with an air of importance and urgency. Everywhere there was an air of war strain, and all of Tampa seemed a part of it. Cuban and American flags hung limply from the façades of restaurants, cigar shops, and private homes.

Supper at the hotel was served sharply at 6 o'clock. When it was over, the guests and visitors drifted about the huge resort in search of rest or amusement. Later in the evening, a nearly full moon climbed over the trees on the eastern side of the hotel. It brought out in soft efflorescence the drifts of white blossoms scattered like fireflies through the dark mass of oleander trees. The pale yellow glow bathed the domes, the Moorish arches, the minarets, the long sides of the entire immense and strangely odd building, an anachronism in a section of Florida blooming with sudden prosperity and modernism.

Down the rows of rocking chairs on the porches a buzz of conversation drifted out onto the spreading lawn. The echo of excited voices came from under the long strings of amazing electric lights so near at hand and so new to everyone. It spread out and flattened and died away in the distance, amid the branches of the professionally placed shrubbery, out where couples strolled hand in hand, occasionally blending together, shielded by the gathered gloom. The peacocks had gone to their roosts.

It was fascinatingly like a massive reunion. On all sides sounded the animated tones of officers who had not seen each other since West Point days, or campaigns on Indian trails, or lonesome days at distant posts. Over it all came the shrill laughter and giggles of wives, daughters, and sweethearts. When the Army first had taken over the hotel, there were no women parading its corridors. This led to the remark that the building looked like a Turkish harem with the occupants left out. Now the scene had changed. Flowing skirts formed a gentle background for the blue and khaki uniforms. Two floors of the building were reserved for officers and their families.

In such a relaxed atmosphere, quips were plentiful:

"Only God knows why Plant built this hotel here, but thank God he did."

"We're gonna lick the Spaniards and make them take Florida back."

Rumors were plentiful, too. One of the most common was that

the American Army would land on the southern coast of Cuba, opposite Havana, and march across the island to attack that city. The great fear of yellow fever caused those who heard it to hope the report was false.

In the Oriental Annex each evening, a band played beneath flourishing palms. Many of the dancers were bright-eyed Cuban señoritas, freshly fled from Havana. Some were members of the best and wealthiest families in Cuba, and their remarkable beauty and handsome gowns attracted general attention. A few spoke English, with that peculiar accent that made conversation with them interesting and fascinating. They came to the hotel with their fathers, their brothers, and their friends.

In another part of the hotel, regimental bands played waltzes and patriotic airs under more rows of incandescent lights. The rotunda was a popular stopping place, for there a bulletin board displayed the latest reports on war developments. Even at night, the pool in the casino was a splash of activity. Men and women, in long, awkward, dripping bathing suits covering everything from neck to knee, cavorted in the delightful coolness of the water.

Celebrities seemed everywhere. Easily spotted was the gawky General Shafter, said to weigh 300 pounds. He was always in complete uniform. Some people looked upon him with veneration, for his reputation was that of a doer, not a worrier. It was known, too, that he had won a battle with yellow fever on the Texas border thirty years back. With him were his wife, daughter, and son-in-law.

Off in another direction was Lieutenant Andrew S. Rowan, tanned and wearing an old panama hat. Just three weeks back he had made his celebrated trip to take a message to García, a junket one day to be immortalized by Elbert Hubbard as an example of blind obedience to orders. O. O. Howard, the Union preacher-general of the Civil War, and Ira Sankey, evangelist, moved about shaking hands and telling everyone that they would be preaching and singing on the morrow. Clara Barton was there talking about the Red Cross. General Fitzhugh Lee, looking like a genial Santa Claus, had a smile and a greeting for all. For a brief period, the browned, smiling, toothy Theodore Roosevelt strolled about with his wife. She had come in from New York during the day to remain with her husband until he sailed. Over and over Teddy remarked to those who stopped to chat, "We shall go wherever we are sent."

Occasional artists, their easels thoughtlessly placed without deference to passing traffic, sketched away at scenes they wished to portray to the public through magazine or newspaper. Photographers were seen only in the daytime.

In a corner of the rotunda, like genial hosts extending hospitality, customarily waited Mr. and Mrs. Plant. The husband evidenced in his dress a preference for comfort over style. He shook hands and had cheery words for all who came along.

Sunday at Tampa was different from those the Rough Riders had passed in Texas. No longer was it a day of rest. Stable police duty assignments were read out immediately after reveille, with watches to consist of two hours on duty and four hours off. The camp was prepared for inspection, conducted by General Wheeler and Colonel Wood. Men stared with strange interest at Wheeler, sitting his horse apparently unaware that he was wearing Yankee blue instead of Confederate gray.

Mrs. Roosevelt came out from the Tampa Bay Hotel for church services and to spend the day with her husband. For her, the hours were full of drills and horseback riding exhibitions.

Now that the camp had begun to settle into routine, free of the mosquitoes so plentiful at San Antonio, newspaper reporters and military attachés from England, Germany, Russia, France, and Japan were allowed to watch. Roosevelt, who already had met some of the correspondents during his service in Washington and New York, began to renew acquaintances. Perhaps the most outstanding of the journalists was Richard Harding Davis, a man who considered himself more historian than news writer, a sort of beau sabreur who wore silk underwear and had special costumes for special assignments.[4] His current dress consisted of a business suit and cork helmet. Some considered him a dude, but not to be overlooked was the fact that he was tall and rather handsome. He also was the model for the popular Howard Chandler Christy drawings.

Davis and Roosevelt were acquainted, but were not particularly friendly. Once while the latter was Police Commissioner of New York, they had had a finger-shaking argument in front of Delmonico's restaurant. Teddy frowned upon the dressiness of the writer, while the writer considered the lieutenant colonel more militant than military.

But Davis recognized in this man and his unique assemblage of

---

[4] Davis wrote his family: "It is as a historian and not as a correspondent that I get on over these men who are correspondents for papers only." *Adventures and Letters of Richard Harding Davis,* p. 234.

cowboys, clubmen, and athletes a better source of news even than Shafter. He was not pleased with the way things were going and had written pieces highly critical of America and its military preparedness.

Besides Davis, the journalistic talent on hand included some top American writers. Stephen Crane, whose *Red Badge of Courage* had won him international fame, was there dressed in a white panama suit. Also present was Frederic Remington, the famous magazine artist and reporter whose paintings were immensely popular at the time.

It was the function of these men to tell the nation what was happening to its Cuban-bound troops at their point of concentration. With the jam growing steadily worse, they had plenty to convey. So did the foreign representatives, who wrote their governments that America's army of invasion was an armed mob, that the Quartermaster Department had gone to pieces. Roosevelt secretly would have had a tendency to agree with the attachés' opinion. He wrote in his diary on this date: "No words can paint the confusion. No head, a breakdown of both the railroad and military systems of the country."

Port Tampa was a basis for some of the charges. Work there was pursued night and day in a madhouse of confused activity. It was evident Plant had not had such a large operation in mind when he developed the port. Interested only in the small steamers of the shipline he owned, he had dredged a narrow channel with 21-foot depth along a tongue of land that served as a pier. Wharfage facilities provided by him served his purpose, but they were not designed to handle the vast quantities of supplies needed by an army of 25,000 men. Eight vessels could lie in the channel at one time, but there was space for only two at the pier. Additional railroad tracks were laid to serve in the emergency, but even with expanded rail lines over which to move the cars of freight, most of the loading still must be done by stevedores. Food and supplies had to be lugged across fifty feet of sand and up a steep ramp into the vessels. Since invoices were in most instances not available, thus making it impossible to assemble complete cargoes at one time, it often was necessary to move a transport away from the wharf and then bring it back one or more times to complete the loading.

But in spite of the cramped and disorganized conditions under which the activity at Port Tampa was conducted, all the ships were coaled, watered, and policed by June 1.[5] Then attention was centered on the installation of bunks and stalls and the loading of commissary stores, wagons, guns, ammunition, and caissons. Animals would be left ashore as long as possible.

Through respect for his distinguished friend while his wife was visiting him, Wood relieved Roosevelt of as much responsibility as he could. This permitted the latter to spend more time away from camp. With the added freedom, he arranged an old home occasion for supper at the Tampa Bay Hotel Sunday night, inviting as guests the two young Scotchmen, Bob Ferguson and Kenneth Robinson, both intimate family friends. But they made the mistake of wearing uniforms, thus denoting their inferior rank, and Teddy wrote his sister, Corinne[6], that the gathering was "to the great scandal of the Regular Army officers as I afterwards found."

As this day was the Sabbath, no dancing took place at night in the ballroom of the hotel. Instead, a large crowd gathered around the east veranda to listen to a concert by the 6th Infantry Band. The war spirit was overwhelming.

Of all the mornings the Rough Riders were together as a regiment, they had cause to remember none better than that of June 6. Roosevelt wrote Lodge about it:

> I had an awful morning, for the orders first came out that only four troops out of our twelve were to go, in which case I should have had to stay here with the remaining eight; but they have now sent eight and so I go. The four that are left behind feel fearfully.
>
> They send us dismounted, but we should be glad to go on all fours rather than not to go at all. It will be an outrage though if they do not send the horses after or together with the remainder of our men very soon. If not too much trouble, I wish you would see the Secretary [of War] and have him keep us in mind, and have the horses sent to us very early. It is a little bit rough to make us fight on foot with only two-thirds of our strength.

So it was a double bombshell that dropped on the Rough Rider leadership this Monday morning. Because of a lack of transports, Shafter was forced to give official notice that only eight troops

[5] By this time, it was realized the vessels on hand would be able to carry fewer than 20,000 men.
[6] Mrs. Douglas Robinson of New York City.

of seventy men each could be taken from the regiment. All horses, except those of the top officers, would have to be left behind. It was a crushing blow to men who had spent their lives on horseback, who depended upon the animal at every turn, and who were basking in vaunted fame as "rough riders." Even the Easterners, when they heard of it, protested the decision.[7]

In breaking the news to the Riders, Wood softened it as much as he could. He told them they would have to do their first two weeks of fighting on foot and that, after the initial period of the landing in Cuba, the regiment would be brought together again. He also explained that the four troops left at Tampa would have as their main duty the care of horses and mules.

A further development was the announcement of the composition of the 5th Corps, the army of invasion. It was to be made up as follows:

1st Division, Brigadier General J. F. Kent, commanding—1st Brigade, Brigadier General H. S. Hawkins; 2nd Brigade, Colonel E. W. Pearson; 3rd Brigade, Lieutenant Colonel W. S. Worth.

2nd Division, Brigadier General H. W. Lawton, commanding —1st Brigade, Colonel J. J. Van Horn; 2nd Brigade, Colonel Evan Miles; 3rd Brigade, Brigadier General A. R. Chaffee.

Cavalry Division, Major General Joseph Wheeler, commanding —1st Brigade, Brigadier General S. S. Sumner; 2nd Brigade, Brigadier General S. B. M. Young.

Independent Brigade, Brigadier General J. C. Bates, commanding.

For want of transportation, all the cavalry would be dismounted except A, C, D, and F Troops of the 2nd Regular Cavalry. The Rough Riders were placed in Wheeler's 2nd Brigade, under General Young, along with the 1st and 10th Regular Cavalry, while the 1st Brigade was made up of the 3rd, 6th, and 9th Regular Cavalry.

Both Wood and Roosevelt were delighted with their assignment. It brought back memories of a luncheon they had had with General Young at the Metropolitan Club in Washington the preceding winter. Young, then a colonel facing wartime promotion, was in command of the Yellowstone National Park. As president of the

---

[7] In his book, *The Rough Riders and Men of Action,* Roosevelt wrote of this development: "We were not used mounted at all, so that our preparations on this point came to nothing. In a way I always have regretted this."

Boone and Crockett Club, a big-game and conservation group, Roosevelt had seen a good deal of him. During the course of the meal, he and Wood told Young they hoped to see active service. Young's reply was that, if they succeeded in getting into his brigade, he would guarantee to show them some fighting. As they later learned, Young, remembering the conversation, had put in a request to have the 1st Volunteers under his command.

It was with much difficulty that selection was made of the four Rough Rider troops to be left behind. Wood announced at the start that Roosevelt and Brodie would command the two squadrons to be formed from the eight troops that were to go. Subsequent announcement of individual selections brought a reaction that shattered the Riders' reputation for toughness. Some of the most hardened of them burst into tears when they were told they must stay at Tampa.[8] Captain Luna used his pure Spanish blood as an argument that he was entitled to go. He demanded the privilege of proving that his people were precisely as loyal Americans as any others. Wood was receptive to the plea.

The troops remaining at Tampa, it was decided, would be under command of Major Hersey, the weather observer, and Major Dunn, the master of hounds. Hersey was particularly disappointed at the assignment. It was he who had brought to San Antonio the New Mexico contingent, largest in the regiment.

At 11 o'clock in the morning, the loading of commissary stores, arms, ammunition, accouterments, forage, wagon transportation, medical supplies, and animals was completed. When news of this development spread through the camps, all the Riders who could get passes hurried into Tampa to make last-minute purchases. They loaded up with tobacco, oranges, chewing gum, and many other items they suspected they would be without until their service in Cuba ended. Some went to the Tampa Bay Hotel and splurged on a fancy meal. "This was our final blowout, as it did actually prove, although we did not realize it at the time, because we had had so many false alarms," recorded Theodore Westwood Miller, one of the diners. He was a son of a wealthy farm machinery inventor who had been a founder of the Chautauqua Lectures. A boyhood friend of "Dade" Goodrich, he had attended Yale and helped found

---

[8] Roosevelt wrote: "The men who were left behind felt the most bitter heartburn. To the great bulk of them I think it will be a lifelong sorrow. I saw more than one, both among the officers and privates, burst into tears when he found he could not go."

the Kappa Psi Fraternity. The famous inventor, Thomas A. Edison, was an uncle by marriage.

Excitement reached a peak. It was generally understood by officers that the order to go on board the transports would come at any minute, so they concentrated on final details that must be attended to before they started moving.

In the midst of the hurried activity, Wood suddenly realized that the ammunition for the Colt automatic guns still had not been supplied the regiment. He hurried off a trooper to find the quartermaster. In his rounds, this fellow rode into the presence of General Adna R. Chaffee, the veteran cavalryman and Indian fighter assigned command of the 3rd Brigade of the 2nd Division. Recognizing a high officer from the stars on his uniform, the messenger blurted out:

"Say, Colonel Wood wants the cartridges for the Colt guns a heap pronto. We are a-going aboard the ship."

Chaffee was aghast.

"Don't you know enough to be a soldier?" he roared. "You should dismount, salute, and stand at attention until I notice you."

"I ain't no soldier," replied the trooper indignantly. "I'm a Rough Rider."

When those granted leave returned in the afternoon, they found orders had been issued to break camp preparatory to marching. Everything was bustle. Then came hours of waiting. The first soldiers of the 5th Corps were supposed already to be going on board the transports, but they had been delayed by circumstances under which Plant's railroad was unable to move trains on schedule.[9]

The Rough Rider troops chosen to remain behind were C, H, I, and M. At 5 o'clock in the afternoon, officers of the other units assembled to select the seventy members from each who would be permitted to go. Selections were made on a basis of the completeness of equipment. Guns were the items most in short supply. Roosevelt saved Bob Wrenn, the tennis champion, by lending him a high-powered rifle he had received as a gift from the Winchester Arms Company.

But Ted Miller of D Troop was not so fortunate. When it was found that only sixty-nine members of that unit were armed, he

---

[9] Lieutenant John D. Miley, Inspector General, reported that the first troops did not arrive at Port Tampa until 2:30 A.M. June 7.

recalled where a saddler had placed his gun. Realizing this man would have to remain with the horses, Ted hurried off and got it. But on the way back he encountered the owner, who claimed his property. Miller broke down and cried.

"I thought my goose was cooked," he wrote in his diary, "but I kept at it and hoped for something to turn up. Everybody was excited, and we heard the cheers from the different troops as they received orders."

Later that night, the men went to sleep on their arms, still waiting for orders to march. Roosevelt fumed, writing in his diary: "No plans, no staff officers, no instructions to us. An officer finds out for himself and takes his chance. We are doing as well as the regular regiments. Have very light baggage."

During the day, Sampson made history at Santiago. Early in the morning, his fleet moved in and opened fire on Morro Castle and other forts at the mouth of the harbor. For more than two hours, the shelling continued, and then the ships were ordered back to their blockade stations. The commander reported the action in a telegram to Washington: BOMBARDED FORTS AT SANTIAGO TODAY, 7:30 TO 10 A.M., JUNE 6, AND HAVE SILENCED WORKS QUICKLY WITHOUT INJURY OF ANY KIND, THOUGH STATIONARY WITHIN 2,000 YARDS. IF 10,000 MEN WERE HERE, CITY AND FLEET WOULD BE OURS WITHIN FORTY-EIGHT HOURS. EVERY CONSIDERATION DEMANDS IMMEDIATE ARMY MOVEMENT. IF DELAYED, CITY WILL BE DEFENDED MORE STRONGLY BY GUNS TAKEN FROM FLEET.

At Guantánamo, forty miles east, one hundred Marines went ashore during the day and stayed.

Most of the morning of June 7 at Tampa was taken up with cleaning camp. While the Rough Riders worked, troops comprising other units were slowly going on board the transports. Since 2:30 A.M., they had been loading, Chaffee's brigade the first to embark.

In the midst of the cleaning activities, Captain Huston of D Troop quietly approached Ted Miller and handed him a gun and cartridge belt.

"I asked no questions," Miller recorded, "but simply leaped inwardly at my good fortune. I learned afterward that a man had been asleep on guard the night before, and they had taken his gun and given it to me."

Another Rider was having luck of this sort. Ham Fish had been in the doldrums since learning that I Troop to which he belonged was one of those that must stay in Tampa. Only his soldierly qualities saved him. They were recognized by the professional eye of Allyn Capron. This officer requested that Fish be transferred to his troop and promoted to sergeant. Wood consented.

A part of the afternoon was claimed by an artist from *Scribner's Magazine,* who wanted to sketch a picture of the Rough Riders in marching order. In the midst of the posing, Roosevelt called a meeting of officers. He had received word from the quartermaster that wagons would be sent to move the regiment's heavy equipment and supplies, but he was not satisfied. He feared this means of transportation might fail to materialize, which would be a severe blow to their chances of getting to Cuba. After some discussion, he directed three officers to hire—or buy at his expense if necessary— sufficient wagons and trucks to do the job if the quartermaster vehicles failed to show up. Some of these had to be purchased, with money supplied by Roosevelt and fellow officers, but others were borrowed from the 2nd Cavalry, which was sending only a part of its force. This move proved important, for the promised Army wagons failed to arrive on time.

In the late afternoon, the men were lined up and marched to the Tampa Bay Hotel to receive their first pay. It was supposed to have been distributed on Saturday, the end of their first official month in the service, but the protests of Tampa citizens delayed the action. Remembering the reports on the disorder at Riverside Park the night Professor Beck pepped up his anvil chorus, they petitioned the Army paymaster to withhold the payroll as long as possible. Whether this or other causes lay behind the delay, the money was not paid until a few hours before two-thirds of the regiment was ready to depart. Slowly the line passed the pay window. It was noted that Willie Tiffany, the millionaire, spent a part of his thirteen dollars for two long, fat cigars.

While the Riders were being paid, exciting developments were taking place elsewhere in the hotel. An air of sadness had settled as the dreary corridors thinned of most of those who were to go and became dominated by those who were to remain behind. Even the electric lights seemed to take on the mood and to dim sympathetically. The crowd in the rotunda was smaller than it had been for weeks. To start the flurry of excitement, the Western Union telegraph operator in the hotel jumped up from his key and ran down the hallway to Shafter's suite.[10] Soon the huge general was seen lumbering behind the operator toward the telegraph office. A crowd quickly gathered.

General Miles joined Shafter, and Captain J. E. Brady of the Signal Corps took over the key. A direct line to the White House had been opened. Both President McKinley and Secretary of War Alger were at the other end.

For half an hour, behind closed doors, the keys clicked back and forth. The men at Tampa sat on three-legged stools in the dingy office, wiping perspiration and looking uncomfortable. In Washington, the officials were in more pleasant surroundings, but they were bothered by the strain and urgency of the moment and by the matter of making decisions.

First came a message from the President: INFORMATION FROM SAMPSON SAYS HE HAD PRACTICALLY REDUCED FORTIFICATIONS AND ONLY AWAITS YOUR ARRIVAL TO OCCUPY SANTIAGO. TIME IS THE ESSENCE OF THE SITUATION. EARLY DEPARTURE OF FIRST IMPORTANCE.

Next came a YOU WILL SAIL IMMEDIATELY order from Alger.

Shafter replied: I WILL SAIL TOMORROW MORNING. STEAM CANNOT BE GOTTEN UP EARLIER. THERE ARE LOADED TONIGHT ONE DIVISION OF INFANTRY (nine regiments), SIXTEEN TROOPS OF DISMOUNTED CAVALRY, FOUR LIGHT BATTERIES, TWO BATTERIES OF SIEGE ARTILLERY, AND TWO COMPANIES OF ENGINEERS, AND THE TROOPS FROM MOBILE. I WILL TRY AND GET ON THE REST OF THE CAVALRY AND ANOTHER DIVISION OF REGULAR INFANTRY BY MORNING. WILL SAIL THEN WHATEVER I HAVE ON BOARD.

At 10 P.M., the Rough Riders got their orders to move. Immediately there was a last-minute bustle. Men scurried to burn rubbish and to shovel dirt into the holes opened as sinks.

Directions were brief. The expedition would start at daybreak. If they were not on board their transport at that time, they would not go.

"We had no intention of getting left and prepared at once for the scramble that was evidently about to take place," Roosevelt related.

According to their instructions, they must be at a certain switch on the railroad at midnight. There they would be met by a train that would take them to Port Tampa. It was that simple.

[10] The Washington *Post*, in its issue of June 12, reported that Inspector General Miley was the one who alerted Shafter, but Miley, in his book, "In Cuba with Shafter," attributes the action to the telegraph operator.

Chapter 2

PORT TAMPA!

June 8 was a strange, mixed-up day for the Rough Riders. Confusion was at a maximum, lack of communication a tragedy. Grueling as were the hours from midnight to dawn, they got worse and stayed that way.

A yellow moon was shining brightly as the Riders came to a halt at the designated switch in the railway yards. Orders said for them to be there at midnight, and they were. Each man had his white blanket roll over his shoulder, his carbine, cartridge belt with 125 rounds, canteen, eating utensils, and haversack containing what rations were available. A strange crowd they were, somehow out of tune with bronco-bustin', trail riding, bullet-scarred lawmen, Indians, and college athletes. For all intents and purposes, they were soldiers, human fighting machines with their sights trained toward a foe, not of the East or of the West, but of America.

Equipment and supplies brought along in the wagons Roosevelt had hired, bought, or borrowed were trimmed to a minimum. No axes, no pickaxes, no spades. Not even the regimental reports, blanks and papers which would be needed by the sergeant major, the bookkeeper of the outfit. For that matter, not even the sergeant major. All of these, the detail factors, would have to come later. So also would the mascots—"Josephine," the lioness; "Cuba," the dog, and "Teddy," the eagle. That part of the 1st Volunteers now headed for Cuba was simply the spearhead.

Behind every order and every move lay the dominating need to hurry. Sampson had said 10,000 men could cause Santiago and Cervera's fleet to fall within forty-eight hours. Admittedly, supplies were insufficient, but the distance to Cuba was not great, and it was believed the men on duty at Tampa could make up for the shortages within a few days. As the Secretary of War saw it, it was a question of striking a sudden blow and perhaps ending the war in short order, as against delaying and prolonging the struggle indefinitely.

For a time in the bright moonlight the Riders waited patiently, looking down the line of rails for some evidence of an approaching train. As the hours passed, they became increasingly annoyed at the delay. Some stretched out on the ground and tried to sleep. Others built small bonfires and gathered around to smoke and joke and chat. Still others just lolled and smoked and rested and waited in silence. Wood and Roosevelt wandered about in search of information. Now and then they encountered a brigadier general or even a major general, but rank meant nothing. Nobody knew anything. Trains were standing about on some of the tracks and regiments, when they came to them, hurriedly got aboard. It was wasted effort. Nothing was moving. The Plant System was at a standstill.

About 3 A.M., the Riders were stirred into commotion by a sudden order to move to another switch a short distance away. There they waited and watched with renewed hope, but more hours of inaction and wondering were ahead. What they did not know and would not learn until later was the situation that had developed along the railroad. Plant's one-line spur to Port Tampa had been hopelessly deadlocked since 10 P.M., the very hour at which they received their orders to move. "I never spent such a night in my life, and felt decidedly on the bum the next morning," wrote Ted Miller.

Dawn came, and the troops began to think of food. Some went to nearby homes and aroused people from slumber. Others descended upon a store of the canteen variety, one of the shops set up hurriedly to take advantage of the deluge of spending cash provided by the Army payroll. Toward it they rushed, fearful that everything would be gone before they got there. Inside, while proprietor and clerks stood helplessly by, they raided the shelves, taking away cheese, crackers, lemonade, and a wide assortment of other items. Most of them left money on the counters, intending for it to pay for what they got, but, in the excitement of the moment, not caring too much one way or the other.

At 6 o'clock a great cheer, punctured by war whoops and Western yells, rent the morning air. Up the track on which they waited came a train of dirty coal cars. There was a mad scramble, like a pack of hounds ganging a cornered fox. The train was forced to stop. Uniformed men began to pile aboard. Both engineer and conductor stepped down and put up a vociferous protest, but Wood and Roosevelt were deaf to them. This was an emergency, they said. A war was to be fought in Cuba and these were some of the fighters who would take part in it. They told the trainmen to forget their orders. Realizing they were helpless, the railroaders shrugged and went back to their posts.

Loading operations now became more systematic. Hundreds of men toted items from the wagons to the cars. The most difficult things to be moved were the heavy guns—the two Colts and a dynamite gun that had been attached to the regiment by orders directly from Shafter the previous evening. The latter weapon, looking more like a telescope on wheels than an instrument of war, was heavy and cumbersome. It was placed under command of the one-time international playboy, Hallett Alsop Borrowe.

At last the transfer was completed, and Wood ordered the engineer to start for Port Tampa at his best possible speed. There were shouted farewells to the men left with the wagons as the train began backing southward. It looked like one of Plant's tourist excursions. Soldiers—30 officers and 580 men—were perched on the sides of the cars, on the tender of the engine, on the caboose, and jammed like sardines in the coal-dust-covered gondolas. Every foothold and handhold seemed to be in use.

Over the nine miles to Port Tampa they rocked, cheering and shouting. There they rolled down into a scene that could be described only as bedlam. Tentage, luggage, commissary supplies— the many items large and small required to put an army in the field—were stacked high on the docks. Around this great mass, thousands of men waited elbow to elbow, dressed in their campaign hats, dark uniforms, white blanket rolls, and leggings. In the background, strings of railroad cars shifted with much noise, no small part of it made by brakemen shouting and waving their arms frantically to keep the tracks cleared of loitering soldiers. Transports were loading at the wharf and others awaited their turn in the channel. Out in the bay in the distance a gunboat or two could be seen steaming lazily to and fro, flags waving, black smoke pouring from their stacks, spurts of steam from their machinery glistening in the sunshine. Roosevelt surveyed it all and came to the conclusion that here was "a good deal of higglety-pigglety business," most of it obviously caused by mismanagement.[1]

Leaving the men on the cars, he and Wood began to move about. They had expected to be met by guides, military fashion, but they soon realized they were on their own. Nobody could tell them anything, especially what transport had been assigned to take them to Cuba. At last they spotted Shafter. The ponderous general told them to find Colonel Charles Humphreys, the quartermaster. They found Humphreys' office. An assistant informed them that he did not know where the colonel was, but believed he might be asleep on one of the transports.

"This seemed odd at such a time," Roosevelt remembered, "but so many of the methods in vogue were odd that we were quite prepared to accept it as a fact."

Wood found Humphreys first. In answer to his question, the quartermaster pointed out into the canal. "There are two vessels that are going—the *Yucatan* and the *Allegheny*—you can take one of them."[2]

Wood hurried away to commandeer a small rowboat and go out and seize one of the vessels. A few minutes after he left, Roosevelt arrived and repeated Wood's question.

"You can have the *Yucatan* for your regiment," Humphreys told him. "Other troops have been assigned to it and you may find it a little crowded."

"We will take to the rigging if you will only let us go aboard," Roosevelt replied.[3]

Turning to Captain Capron at his side, he ordered him to go to the *Yucatan* and hold her in the name of the 1st Volunteers. Then he ran back to the train of coal cars after the men. While he was

[1] This expression was used by him later in testimony before the Committee to Investigate the Conduct of the War.
[2] These words were repeated by Colonel Wood before the Committee Investigating the Conduct of the War, but Humphreys could not remember the conversation. However, he did say he was confident he could not have said anything to Wood about the *Allegheny*, because the ship was fitted up with stalls and was to take only the horses and the headquarters staff of General Wheeler. See Committee Report, p. 3652.
[3] Roosevelt remained highly critical of the way the Army handled matters at Port Tampa. "As the number and capacity of the transports were known, or ought to have been known," he wrote in *The Rough Riders*, p. 58, "the task of allotting each regiment or fraction of a regiment to its proper transport, and arranging that the regiments and the transports should meet in due order on the dock, ought not to have been difficult. However, no arrangements were made in advance; and we were allowed to shove and hustle for ourselves as best we could, on much the same principles that had governed our preparations hitherto."

unloading and making arrangements for a detail to guard the baggage, a messenger came from Wood to report that the colonel was coming in on the *Yucatan* and to bring the troops on the "double."

As Roosevelt hurried the men along the wharf, he saw Wood out on the *Yucatan* waving and pointing to show him where the transport would dock. Just as he reached the designated point and took a stand, the 2nd Infantry came up on his right and the 71st New York Volunteers on his left. This caused him concern, because he had learned from Humphreys that these units were assigned to the *Yucatan* also. A quick estimate told him not half of the men in the three regiments could get on the ship, but he was determined the 1st Volunteers would be among those who did. He promptly directed the Riders nearest him to move in closely around the gangplank and to let no outsiders pass. Little trouble was anticipated from the 71st, but he realized the 2nd might be a more difficult problem, for its commanding officer was his superior in rank and doubtless knew his rights.

As he anticipated, this officer soon sent a messenger to tell him to make way, to draw his regiment off to one side and let the 2nd take possession of the gangway.

"I could see the transport coming in," Roosevelt recalled, "and I could dimly make out Wood's figure thereon. Accordingly, I played for time. I sent respectful requests through his officers to the commander of the regulars, entered into parleys, and made protestations, until the transport got near enough so that by yelling at the top of my voice I was able to get into a—highly constructive—communication with Wood. What he was saying I had no idea, but he was evidently speaking, and on my own responsibility I translated it into directions to hold the gangway, and so informed the regulars that I was under the orders of my superior and of a ranking officer—to my great regret, etc., etc.—could not give way as they desired."

Meanwhile, the 71st had had two interchanges with Roosevelt, both unsuccessful. The first was conducted by Captain Anthony J. Bleecker, commanding the leading company of the regiment.

The lieutenant colonel of the Rough Riders greeted him as he approached. "Hello, what can I do for you?"

"That's our ship."

"Well, we seem to have it," replied the smiling Roosevelt.

Later, the colonel of the 71st came up, accompanied by two photographers.

"Seventy-first Regiment, New York. We have been assigned to this ship."

"Sorry, Colonel," said Roosevelt, waving a paper, "not this ship. I have my assignment."

"I have my assignment, too," said the colonel, holding it up.

"We were here first," Roosevelt grinned, "and we expect to stay."

The colonel snapped his heels together and saluted. Abruptly turning, he marched away, leaving behind the photographers, Albert E. Smith and Jim Blackton, both so loaded down with cameras and tripods that they were in no mood to go farther in search of a ship. They looked up at Roosevelt.

"What are you young men up to?" he asked.

"We are the Vitagraph Company, Colonel Roosevelt, and we are going over to Cuba to take moving pictures of the war," Smith replied.

Appreciating chances for publicity, Roosevelt waved them aboard. "I can't take care of a regiment, but I might be able to handle you two."

He shook hands with the photographers, failing to remember Smith, who had taken pictures of him while he was New York Police Commissioner.

When the transport reached the wharf, Rough Riders hurried up the gangplank. Four companies of the 2nd Regiment also got aboard, making a total of nearly a thousand men on a vessel intended to accommodate only half that number. So did the two horses Roosevelt had purchased at San Antonio. They were led on by the faithful Marshall, the old soldier of the 9th Cavalry who had taken part in Indian campaigns and knew the ropes of the military. He had named them "Rain-in-the-Face" and "Texas."

While the Rough Riders wended their way back and forth through the crowd along the dock, sweating and toiling with the weapons and supplies they had to load on the transport, Port Tampa continued in bedlam. Soldiers were like flies. They massed in and around every building and convenience at the dock, and they were especially numerous in an area that came to be known as "Last Chance Street"—so named because it afforded the last opportunity to buy certain items before going on board ship.

The "street" looked like a country fair. Except for a two-story shack of raw, yellow boards, it was made up solely of tents. Here and there an umbrella protruded from the sand, and under it would be found a black woman frying chicken over a tiny clay stove. Under the tent flies, rigged as a sort of porch, whiskey and beer could be bought by the drink. The bartenders, dressed in white shirts without collars, usually were the proprietors. In front of each tent stood a gayly dressed girl, the come-on for customers, and behind each bartender waited one or two more. For sale was a drink, or a damsel, or both. Everybody seemed to be drinking, even the girls, although what they were actually swilling from the bottles was cold tea.

A bespectacled fellow suffering from bellyache brought on by a touch of ptomaine poisoning walked toward the yellow board shack in search of a glass of milk, an item as much out of place on "Last Chance Street" as a mint julep in the Sahara Desert. He noticed that the building had a porch, above which was the sign RESTAURANT, but inside he could see neither chair nor table. A long line of men cued out from the foot of a steep stairway at the side leading to the upper story.

"Hey, Doc, git in line!" someone yelled.

The fellow assumed he would have to await his turn for a table and guessed that the dining room must be upstairs. His belly hurt, and he felt milk was the one item he was most in need of at the moment.

Toward the rear of the line he walked. "I'm looking for the dining room," he innocently announced as he approached.

A burst of loud, raucous laughter greeted his remark. While the uproar was still in progress, he saw a door open above the stairway and a naked feminine arm wave with a beckoning motion. The man at the front of the line hastily climbed the stairs.

"I was amazed that I could have been that dumb, even as sick as I was," the fellow with the glasses wrote. "I know I was still pale from the painful contortions of my stomach, but I am certain that my blushes as I crept back past the line imitated roseate health to those twenty or thirty sophisticates waiting patiently for their turn."

In the late afternoon, the portage was completed, and Wood and Roosevelt made sure that the last of the Riders had climbed the gangplank before it was taken away. As the *Yucatan* moved out to midstream, it was so crowded the men could scarcely move about. Many of them, when bedtime came, were allowed to spread their blankets on deck. The members of D Troop, for example, were given a place on the starboard side just forward of the stern and between the cabin and rail.

The Riders on the *Yucatan* were a part of the largest military expedition that ever had left the United States. In it were 819 officers, 15,058 enlisted men, 30 civilian clerks, 272 teamsters and packers, 107 stevedores, 89 newspaper correspondents and photographers, and 11 foreign field officers, as well as 952 horses, 1336 mules with harness, 114 six-mule army wagons, 81 escort wagons, and 7 regular wagons. Only seven ambulances were included, as it was decided wagons could serve as a substitute. Artillery, in addition to what the 1st Volunteers were taking, consisted of sixteen light guns, four 7-inch howitzers, four 5-inch siege guns, one Hotchkiss revolving cannon, eight 3.6-inch field mortars, and four Gatling machine guns.

The Gatlings were taken on board the transport *Cherokee* under the direction of the second lieutenant in charge of them, John Henry Parker of the 13th Infantry. He was a West Pointer and had made a special study of the role of artillery. Each gun consisted of a cluster of ten rifle barrels, without stocks, arranged around an axle so that they revolved upon the turn of a crank. Hundreds of bullets of the Krag-Jorgensen type could be fired per minute.

Supper for the Rough Riders, their first meal in twenty-four hours, was one of shock. Trooper Ogden Wells wrote feelingly of the experience:

> Our travel rations we find are not sufficient because the meat is very bad indeed, and when a ration consists only of four or five items, which taken together just meet the requirements of a strong and healthy man, the loss of one item is a serious thing. If we had been given canned corned beef, we would have been all right, but instead of this, we have been issued horrible stuff called "canned fresh beef." There is no salt in it. At the best, it is stringy and tasteless; at the worst, it is nauseating. Besides this, there is no ice, and the water we have for drinking is brackish and not even fit to wash in.

As the headquarters ship, *Seguranca,* slipped her moorings and stood down toward the bay, a tug, whistle wide open, overtook her to deliver a telegram. Shafter and his staff already were abed, exhausted after long hours without sleep. The general was aroused and this ungrammatical message from the Secretary of War was read to him: WAIT UNTIL YOU GET FURTHER ORDERS BEFORE YOU SAIL. ANSWER QUICK.

When the import of the message from Alger broke through the general's befuddled senses, he sprang awake. Immediately a mad effort was started, by signal and messenger, to head off the transports already under way. It would go on throughout the night.

The disappointment of the men when they were awakened on June 9 was great. They had expected to be well on their way to Cuba by sunrise, but, instead, were shut up on board ship, under crowded conditions, and in a climate that was uncomfortably hot except for a few hours immediately before dawn.

Rumors as to what had caused the delay were rampant. The most logical of these seemed to be that Spanish warships had been sighted somewhere along the course that the transports were to follow. Another was that General Miles had decided the troops were not properly equipped for the voyage and that the President had agreed upon a postponement. Still another mentioned that peace proposals had been made.

The transports were recalled. As many as possible were brought into the narrow channel at Port Tampa. There they would be under the protection of field guns which had been in position for some days at the end of the pier. Those with horses on board were moved next to the dock. The gunboats, *Castine, Annapolis* and *Helena*, and the armed yacht *Hornet* were stationed at the entrance of the bay some twenty miles away.

As the morning developed, the animals were taken off and picketed a short distance up the railway. This was done mainly to protect them from the intense heat on board the transports, fourteen of them having died since the preceding morning.

Prospects of moving inside of several days seemed dim. During the morning, Shafter received a telegram from Alger asking if it were practicable to disembark the command. After conferring with other officers, the general decided that it would be better to keep the men on board the vessels and send them ashore in detachments for occasional periods of relief. There was no place in the vicinity where they could be encamped with comfort. Besides, if they were unloaded, it would take a day or two to get them back on board when the order to sail did come.

In accordance with this plan, orders were issued for the men to be given the greatest liberty on going ashore. Passes would be issued in fairly large numbers. No one was to go beyond Port Tampa, except on the most urgent matter. All were to be back on board nightly by 9 o'clock, at which time roll call was to be held.

In addition, they would be allowed to swim from the decks of the transports.

As the heat of the sun increased, there was considerable concern on board the *Yucatan* over several quarters of chemically treated beef stowed under cover on the forward deck. The stench was highly offensive and certainly of no encouragement to the men when they sat down to their rations, especially the canned roast beef, the only other meat on board ship. After reporting the smelly product, promptly referred to as "embalmed" beef, Roosevelt had it thrown into the bay.[4]

Ship routine was established during the day. Guards were mounted regularly. Drills, mainly on the manual of arms, were held twice daily, and officers' school was reopened. Inspection, the men standing by their bunks or pallets without arms, was scheduled for 7 A.M. and 5 P.M. Owing to the excessive heat, dress was optional.

By nightfall of the 9th, a correct report of the delay was received. Shafter was informed that the converted yacht *Eagle* had sighted what it took to be a Spanish armored cruiser and a torpedo boat destroyer cruising off the north coast of Cuba. Reported to Washington, this news was interpreted to mean that an enemy fleet might be within a few hours' sail of Tampa Bay, ready to sink unescorted American transports.

As another day went into the records, none was more disgusted than Richard Harding Davis, the man who considered himself a historian rather than reporter. "We are just like amateurs at war and about like the Indians Columbus discovered," he wrote.

On June 10, Roosevelt wrote his influential friend, Henry Cabot Lodge, in detail, telling him of the life aboard ship, and urging him to see that the expedition was no longer delayed. In the afternoon, the *Yucatan* was permitted to leave the channel and steam out into the bay where the men could swim. There they joined a horde of other bathers. Stanhope Sams, reporter for the New York *Times*, recorded the scene:

> At all hours, from daylight until dark, the water about the shores and close to the ships is alive with shoals of bathers. Some of the hardiest swimmers venture out a half mile to a mile,

---

[4] Upon his return from Cuba, Roosevelt learned that the beef was placed on board the *Yucatan* without expense to the government. It was done as an experiment by a packing house that thought it had discovered a new process for preserving fresh meat.

as the water is quite shallow; but most of them, fearful of sharks, remain pretty close to the ships.

The women here are frequently confronted by embarrassing situations, but they turn their faces the other way and leave the bathers undisturbed. This is not Narragansett . . . and bathing suits are neither accessible nor desired. Men plunge into the water and disport on its surface as innocent of clothing as they were when they came into the world. They are not, however, immodest; and they conceal themselves beneath the water as much as possible. Everywhere they may be seen diving from the sides of the ships; or from small boats; but they generally wait for a chance of taking their headers when no women or young girls are in sight.

Daylight of June 11 brought into view five warships lying to in the outer entrance of the bay. They had come in during the night and gave new vigor to the report that the start of the voyage had been delayed because of the appearance of Spanish war vessels.

During the morning, the *Yucatan* moved farther out into the bay, giving the appearance of being ready to sail. This possibility was strengthened during the afternoon when sailors on all of the transports were seen tightening the rigging.

Heat seemed to grow steadily worse with each successive day. In consequence, shore leave was more liberally granted. Business along "Last Chance Street" continued at a brisk pace, the girls drinking tea and the men drinking booze. Meanwhile, the upstairs door at the yellow-planked "restaurant" swung open with such regularity it was evident no one was allowed to dawdle.

About the only amusement on board ship was supplied by the band from the 2nd Regulars. These musicians had stormed up the gangplank of the *Yucatan* with the four troops from that regiment. They could play a variety of tunes, but the one most heard was "Animal Fair." This song was virtually unknown to the troops on the start, but it soon became a favorite:

> "*I went to the animal fair.*
> *The birds and the beasts were there.*
> *The big baboon by the light of the moon*
> *Was combing his auburn hair.*
> *The monkey he got drunk*
> *And sat on the elephant's trunk.*
> *The elephant sneezed and fell on his knees*
> *And what became of the monk, the monk?*"

Cries for the song came so often that the tune seemed to go on and on interminably. Whenever it was played, almost everybody on board joined in, taking part especially in the windup, stringing out the last words and making them sound like "de monk, de monk, de monk." So much volume went into the chorus that the entire transport vibrated with the rhythm. Even Captain Capron, the natural-born soldier to whom war was a serious business, gave the appearance of enjoying it. One Rider reported that it seemed to arouse Capron's "risibilities," and it was agreed he was making a great concession to allow war to be diffused with "de monk."

A heavy rain squall swept in about 8 o'clock at night, causing the vessels to strain at their cables while the wind swept through their rigging. It brought some relief from the heat, but during the midst of the downpour came something else of a far more welcome nature. It was a loud announcement by megaphone from the little tug *Captain Sam*, beating its way steadily over the rough surface of the bay: "Stand ready to sail by daylight!" Wild cheering could be heard above the roar of the storm. Flashes of lightning revealed soldiers standing in the rain and waving their hats.

During the early morning of June 12, a locomotive pushed a single Pullman car far down the pier, to a point where most of the operations out in the bay could be seen. On the car were General Miles and his staff. Soon messengers could be seen hurrying away from it. This was accepted by the soldiers as another sign that the time of departure was near. The plan to sail at daylight apparently had been changed.

At 1 o'clock in the afternoon, for the second time, came orders from Secretary Alger to move immediately. Final preparations were carried on throughout the afternoon and into the night. One of the surest indications that departure was near was the appearance of the first of the horses to be reloaded.

Another heavy rainstorm came after the men had gone to bed. It flooded the decks and soaked those trying to sleep there, but they preferred the dampness from nature to the sweaty dampness that was a constant thing down in the hold below.

General Miles's car came down along the spur early on June 13, signifying a busy day. The bustle began at sunrise, long strings of horses and mules moving toward the wharf and the gangplanks.

Shortly after 9 o'clock, the funnels of the transports began to pour forth volumes of black smoke. Along the pier could be heard the stern voices of the ship commanders giving orders. One by one, the broad gangways were pulled in, the hatchways closed, the lines cast off. Slowly the vessels, after they had taken on animals and whatever else went into the final loading, backed out into the bay to await the order of their going.

The previous afternoon, a waggish trooper among the Rough Riders had hung a sign over the side of the *Yucatan: STANDING ROOM ONLY.* This fellow was careless with his paint pot. Another wag found it and added: *AND DAMN LITTLE OF THAT.*

Port Tampa on June 14 looked like the day after a carnival. Debris littered its streets and the wharf and the canal. All the ships had gone except Shafter's *Seguranca* and the Red Cross's *State of Texas.* "Last Chance Street" had been wiped out by a flash fire, and the door in the yellow pine building had ceased to swing.

At 9 A.M., the *Seguranca* steamed away from the pier, drawing a weak but encouraging cheer from the few stragglers remaining along the waterfront. Around the middle of the day came the signal to start. The transports had been stationed in three lines of twelve ships each, headed by the *Annapolis, Helena,* and *Castina.* The *Yucatan* was number four in the second column. It was noted that the Rough Riders pulled at their anchor so energetically that the ship's crew had to play the hose on the hawser ropes to keep them from catching fire.

Immediately there was a great din of whistle blowing and cheering and disorderly music, but a little later the bands harmonized more closely. The tune that came over the waters was strictly American, the words written by Joe Hayden, a singer in the McIntyre and Heath Minstrels, and set to music by their bandmaster, Theodore Metz. It was said the author got his inspiration for the song when the troupe swung into Old Town, Louisiana.

Liltingly the tune spread from ship to ship, and soon thousands of voices were singing: "There'll be a hot time in the old town tonight." And so, with an air of minstrelsy—"where you knowed ev'rybody and dey all knowed you, and you've got a rabbit's foot to keep away de hoodoo"—America's great armada of 1898 set its course toward the West Indies.

Chapter 3

THE SLOW WAY TO CUBA

"After a wild and windy night, we woke this morning to find ourselves far out at sea with no land in sight," Ogden Wells wrote on June 15. "It is very pleasant sailing through the tropic seas toward the unknown. The men of the ship are young and strong, and we are eager to face what lies before us, eager for adventure where risk is the price of gain."

The course was southward. As the sun came up, every man seemed to be crowded above deck. It was an inspiring sight to see the long lines of ships extending for miles back over the horizon, in columns a thousand yards apart, and to realize that this vanguard carried the hopes of all America. Near the head of the middle column flew a dark blue flag with maltese cross, the mark of the headquarters ship *Seguranca*. On board her throughout the day, Shafter and his staff bent over maps spread on tables, discussing strategy and laying out plans by which they hoped to free Cuba in the shortest possible time.

Of the more than 16,000 men on the transports, only Shafter and some of the top officers knew where they were going. The privates and non-coms and even some of those of higher rank were kept in wonder, later to learn that the folks back home were fully aware of their destination. But the modes of communication of 1898 did not extend to soldiers cooped up for a week on board ship. Moreover, the routine while they sailing was not intended to allow long hours of mental cogitation.

Officers in charge of the expedition knew that idleness was no stimulator of morale, so they set a busy schedule. Inspections were held at 9 A.M. and 4 P.M. At the first of these the morning of the 15th, men were ordered to form without shoes and with their trousers rolled, ready to go through what most of them considered the undignified process of having their feet inspected. There was much griping, for some of the soldiers looked upon this as an absolute indignity—more or less a delving into their private affairs. It seemed to insinuate that they had been lax in washing their feet. But veterans of the military service took the requirement calmly. They had a secret: short-arm inspection was much harder on the dignity. And after all, they certainly were in line for one. Who among those who visited "Last Chance Street" would deny that the yellow pine door had done a lot of swinging?

Card games were taboo, and yet money changed hands. The ships' crews knew a faster way to make the soldiers shell it out. Food and water were in such scarcity and so abominable that any improvement brought premium prices. The water supplied free on board ship was so bad that Richard Harding Davis said it smelled like a frog pond or a stable yard, and was not even fit for shaving, "honest to God." It was recalled that, before leaving Tampa, the millionaire, John Jacob Astor, along on the expedition as a staff member, had offered to buy fresh water from Henry Plant at two cents a gallon if all the bad-smelling supply were emptied overboard, but no one seemed to listen. Those on the ships who could afford it drank Apolinaris water or tea, or bought from the porters water that was not repulsive to the nose. Five cents per glass was the prevailing price. If ice were added, that was a fillip that shot the figure to twenty-five cents, a fourth of what the average field hand back home earned in a day, sunrise to sunset.

Food values were bad on the start and became outrageous as the days advanced. Albert McMillan, the park commissioner's son, paid four dollars for a rice pudding. A lemon was twenty-five cents. At Tampa, pies had sold for forty cents each, but on board ship they soared to two dollars and above. The baker on the *Yucatan* was said to have made two hundred dollars the first day out.

Toward the close of the first day, when the sun sank below the horizon and night came on with its gloom, there was much inspiration for letter writing. Among those so moved was the bewhiskered, saggy-pantsed Joe Wheeler, planter, lawyer, politician, soldier, and gentleman of the first water, but not noted for his sense of humor. In the record he kept of the voyage he wrote:

> The sky in the evening is perfectly beautiful, the stars very bright, and appear much more numerous than in more northern

latitudes. At dusk we see Tortugas Light and Pass, leaving it to
our right.

From Leonard Wood, the serious thinker, came something a bit
more poetical. He wrote his wife:

Painted ships on a painted ocean. Imagine three great lines of
transports with a warship at the head of each line, steaming in
long lines, 800 yards from each other over a sea of indigo blue,
real deep blue, such as I have never seen before. Air warm and
balmy, with a gentle breeze stirring up the water. No swell or
disturbance. Simply a great peaceful marine picture. Hard it is to
realize that this is the commencement of a new policy and that
this is the first great expedition our country has ever sent overseas
and marks the commencement of a new era in our relations with
the world . . .

Roosevelt's writings revealed some detraction of stature. Although
in the upper hierarchy, he was among those who were not certain
where they were going. In a letter home he stated:

Today we are steaming southward through a sapphire sea,
wind-rippled, under an almost cloudless sky. There are some
forty-eight craft in all, in three columns, the black hulls of the
transports setting off the gray hulls of the men-of-war. Last evening we stood up on the bridge and watched the red sun sink and
the lights blaze up on the ships, for miles ahead and astern, while
the band played piece after piece, from "The Star-Spangled Banner," at which we all rose and stood uncovered, to "The Girl I
Left Behind Me." But it is a great historical expedition, and I
thrill to feel that I am part of it. If we fail, of course we share the
fate of all who fail, but if we are allowed to succeed (for we
certainly shall succeed, if allowed) we have scored the first great
triumph in what will be a world movement. All the young fellows
here dimly feel what this means; although the only articulate soul
and imagination among them belong rather curiously to ex-
sheriff, Captain "Bucky" O'Neill of Arizona.

O'Neill, as Roosevelt had noticed, was one to puzzle about. It
was somehow unbelievable to hear this hardened Western character
who could be as tough and as desperate as a stagecoach holdup
man quote Browning and Shelley and Whitman and other of the
literary greats as he leaned over the rail at sunset. When he talked,

his words were those of a tolerant and compassionate individual. He would say of the Spaniards: "They can't help being Spaniards any more than a skunk can help being a skunk. God made them that way."

One who listened with interest to O'Neill and other talkative Westerners was Wells. He wrote:

> It is interesting to listen to the Western fellows lounging in groups and telling stories of their past—stories of the mining camps and the cattle ranges, of hunting deer and bear, of war trails against the Indians, of lawless deeds of violence and the lawful violence by which they were avenged, of brawls in saloons, of shrewd deals in cattle and sheep, of successful quests for gold and silver, stories of brutal wrong and brutal appetite, melancholy love tales and memories of nameless heroes—masters of men and tamers of horses.

But perhaps the newsiest letter to come out of the Rough Riders on this particular evening was the one Bob Church, the surgeon, wrote his brother:

> We have a band concert twice a day, and it sounds funny to hear Sousa's marches and to think that I once wore a clean shirt and a dress suit and danced to their enlivening strains.

He mentioned that the 1st Volunteers no longer were referred to as Roosevelt's Rough Riders, but were now called Wood's Weary Walkers; that the Reverend Henry Brown was seasick and "invisible" during the day—"I do not think he is having a very nice time." The doctor was impressed by it all. "The men are learned by force of example to stand up and take their hats off when the band plays 'The Star-Spangled Banner,' as it does twice a day," he added. "It is rather pretty to see all the men standing reverently, bareheaded, faced to the country we love and have sworn to protect, while our own particular tune steals out across the blue water toward the soft southern sky."

The fleet was progressing at a rate of from 4 to 7 knots an hour. Originally it was estimated the trip would take about three and a half days, but, as Roosevelt mentioned in his letter, there was no doubt a much longer time would be required. The fault lay with the slower moving vessels, particularly a tank ship filled with water, as well as two decked-over barges for landing purposes. These set the rate for the entire fleet.

Toward the close of the day, the Rough Riders' ship, a 420-foot vessel that could make between 14 and 16 knots, was ordered to go to the rear of the column to see whether assistance was needed by the *City of Washington,* towing one of the barges. When the *Yucatan* fell back, the *Bancroft* sailed up with signals set. For some reason, there was delay in answering her "heave to" signal, whereupon a gun was fired and she came alongside.

Her commander was "fierce and truculent" and scolded in forthright terms. Then he asked what regiment was on board.

"The Rough Riders!" Roosevelt shouted back, and the men on the *Bancroft* cheered.

"Is Mr. Roosevelt on board?" asked the commander.

"Yes," was the reply. "I am Colonel Roosevelt!" There was sharp accent on the "colonel."

A surprised, "Oh, how are you?" was returned.

Laughter and cheers followed, while Roosevelt muttered something about having known the fellow while serving as Assistant Secretary.

Daylight June 16 revealed that the fleet had been increased during the night by several warships. It seemed to be sailing in an easterly direction now. The vessels comprising it numbered fifty-five and were spread over a 15-mile stretch of sea. The Dry Tortugas Light was passed during the dark hours and mail sent ashore.

This day would see a breakdown in the order in which the transports originally had set out. They were under civilian masters and chartered by the government, and these men, independent of the Navy's authority, refused to keep close formation. Some were lost to sight for hours, while torpedo boats and gunboats scurried about in a frantic effort to bring them back into line. One of the decked-over barges, towed by the *Concho,* was found to be missing, a hawser having snapped in the blackness of night.

As dawn developed, the sun shone brightly, baring a sky flecked with clouds of a rather threatening nature and bringing out the color of the sea. The water had an intensity of blues—ultramarine at a distance, cobalt nearer, and a lighter steely tint in the wake of the vessels where it was stirred into foam. Here and there a rank of white caps was tossed up by a breeze that had passed beyond the stage of lightness.

The busiest ship in the fleet was the hospital vessel, *Olivette.*

Back and forth she ran, her master yelling messages and orders by megaphone, giving water to some and taking sick men from some.

During the afternoon, those on board the leading ships caught sight of the Cuban coast and saw they were running parallel to it. Also seen was Salt Key, north of the Matanzas Province. Later they came abreast of Cardenas, but too far out to see or be seen.

The morning of June 17 found the transports scattered over a distance of many miles, estimated at some thirty or forty. Shafter was worried. He ordered the speed of those in front sharply reduced to give the vessels in the rear an opportunity to close up. Gradually the formation began to take on some of its original appearance.

Around 9 A.M., the coast of Cuba could be seen more clearly. An hour or so later, the leading ships were passing the Cuban lighthouse at Paradone Principe.

Late in the day, General Wheeler, estimating the land was only three or four miles away, made note in his diary:

> 5 p.m.—See very high ground in Cuba. The sea has been very blue, quite as blue as blue indigo. At night the signaling of the warships is very interesting. Bright and varied colors are displayed, by which communications are held.

Sight of the mountains seemed to cast a spell over the soldiers. The long ridge in the distance was a delicate blue and green, rising gently in flowing tiers that faded away in the amethyst blue and lavender of the higher ridges beyond. As the vessels steamed along, drills in aiming and volley firing were held on deck by squads in command of sergeants. While they drilled, the men glanced frequently at the mountains, wondering how soon they might be climbing toward their crests.

As evening fell, Roosevelt, mingling with the Rough Riders, got impressions that he later relayed to the public via magazines and books:

> Most of the men had simple souls. They would relate facts, but they said very little about what they dimly felt. Bucky O'Neill, however, the iron-nerved, iron-willed fighter from Arizona, the sheriff whose name was a byword of terror to every wrong-doer, white or red, the gambler who with unmoved face would stake and lose every dollar he had in the world—he alone, among his comrades, was a visionary, an articulate emotionalist. He was very quiet about it, never talking unless he was sure of his listener; but at night, when we leaned on the railing to

look at the Southern Cross, he was less apt to tell tales of his hard and stormy past than he was to speak of the mysteries which lie behind courage, and fear, and love, behind animal hatred, and animal lust for the pleasures that have tangible shape.

Despite skies that were a bit cloudy and showery, Spanish eyes spying across the sea on June 18 counted fourteen American ships in sight during the morning. Heliograph messages conveyed the news inland.

These ships were at a standstill, waiting for those in the rear to close up, and were carrying on wigwag communication, for typhoid fever and measles were beginning to spread among the men. The *Olivette* steamed about, picking up the sick and dodging dead horses thrown overboard after their death from heat in the holds of the vessels. Fourteen patients were lifted on stretchers to the hospital ship, among them three from the *Yucatan*—Walter S. Beebe, rancher from Prescott; Davis A. Hadden of San Antonio, and Leroy E. Tomlinson, house painter from Prescott.

At about 11 A.M., the fleet once more got under way, but its speed was held to 3 knots per hour, restraint that gave amateur strategists much to talk about. At 1 P.M., the ships came in sight of Punta Sama, near the Bay of Nipe. An hour later, it was passing Cape Lucretia, about the middle of the Province of Santiago de Cuba and almost north of the City of Santiago. "We see high hills on the Cuban coast, estimated at from 1200 to 1500 feet high," Joe Wheeler wrote. "Toward night we take direct course to the English island called Inagua Island. It is just north of what is called Windward Channel."

Ted Miller had nothing better to do early the morning of Sunday, June 19, than put out his wash. Trailing in the breeze when he finished were pants, socks, handkerchiefs, towels, and pup tent half. Then he went to church, on the after deck. He sat beside Roosevelt in the choir and heard the Reverend Henry Brown, somewhat recovered from his seasickness, preach a sermon on the subject of "Respect."

During the afternoon, the fleet rounded the harsh, gray, terraced flanks of Cape Maysi, with its long finger running out into the sea. There they picked up a new breeze, and seasickness was aggravated. General Wheeler made note that "the shore seems to be lined with high hills or mountains, say from 1000 to 1500 feet high." They could see clouds of smoke and assumed this was evidence that the

Spaniards were retreating to Santiago, estimated to be about 120 miles away.

Expectations ran high. The soldiers were informed that early next morning their objective point would be in sight. A fast scout boat was sent ahead. It would deliver to Admiral Sampson a dispatch informing him of the approach of the army and that Shafter would call upon him as soon as the transports reached the Cuban coast.

Sampson already was making plans. During the day he had had a consultation with General García, who had been brought to the flagship from a camp eighteen miles west of Santiago. The veteran Cuban leader was enthusiastic, reporting that the Spaniards were starving and freely predicting that the war would end within a few months. But his enthusiasm was of short duration. He soon became so violently seasick he had to be put to bed.

That night, as the fleet rounded the eastern end of the Island of Cuba and sailed toward Santiago, searchlights from the larger vessels poked their fingers of light along the shore. Eyes behind them stared with glasses at the heavy foliage. It was green and made ghostly by shadows, and it stimulated a creepy feeling among young American minds that sly Spaniards, dastardly foes all, cruel wreckers of beautiful Cuba, were lurking behind every bush.

At daybreak June 20, men on the transports and the convoying warships stared to starboard over fifteen miles or so of sea at the Sierra Maestra range of mountains. It seemed to rise almost from the water's edge and was wrapped in blue mist, such a beautiful panorama that it reminded the Westerners of Arizona and Montana. Without exception those who were keeping diaries or writing reports mentioned the mountains, and Joe Wheeler raised his estimate of their height to 2000 feet.

Everything was excitement and bustle. Wheeler had time only for a short entry in his diary, winding up with: "Will close this before reaching landing place, as we must pack up for disembarkation." It was the last bit of writing he would do by way of keeping a personal record of the campaign, for Joe was facing action reminiscent of his busiest days as a Confederate cavalry leader.

In the distance, the entrance to the Bay of Santiago was almost indistinguishable from the green jungle of the headlands rising on each side. Standing out faintly was the pinkish ocher of the ancient forts guarding it, with Morro Castle, the mightiest of them all, high, silent, and picturesque against the sky.

Until matters could be better organized, the fleet dropped anchor miles from land. All the vessels were there except the *Yucatan* and the ship it was escorting, the *City of Washington,* as well as the *Bancroft* and *Wasp.* These would come up at about 3 o'clock in the afternoon.

On shore, Spaniards counted twenty-one vessels, seven of them battleships. But later, from Morro Castle, it was reported that thirty-nine ships were in sight, a figure later raised to sixty-three.

Among those staring to sea when the first curl of black smoke appeared above the distant horizon was the insurgent General García and his staff, standing on a hillside and giving forth many expressions of joy. The general had fully recovered from seasickness.

At 6:30 A.M., the torpedo boat *Ericsson* was sent ahead to communicate with Sampson's fleet. From the opposite direction soon appeared a dispatch boat bringing Captain French Ensor Chadwick, Sampson's chief of staff, to escort General Shafter to a rendezvous nearer the entrance to the bay.

Sampson and Shafter came together at noon, and soon they were seated at dinner. When they had eaten, the vessel on which they conferred steamed, at Sampson's suggestion, slowly east and then west along the coast to give Shafter an opportunity to view the terrain. About 3 P.M., the two leaders got into a launch and started ashore to meet García. The Cuban leader had refused to come out to the fleet for fear of a new attack of seasickness. A number of correspondents followed in a separate boat, bringing to thirty those in the party.

As they neared land at Acerradero, about eighteen miles west of Santiago, they could see a number of Cuban officers on horseback, surrounded by soldiers on foot and by women and children. The boat with the American leaders grounded about 500 feet from the beach, in a little bay overhung with coconut palms. It was an inspiring scene. Mountains stretched back from the jungle of manigua bushes along the coast until they met the clouds in the background.

There was wild cheering from the Cubans as they rushed into the water up to their necks to pull the boat with the uniformed men in it well up on shore. The correspondents had to wade to the beach.

"Cuba libre! Vivas los Americanos!" shouted the women and children.

In the jungle behind could be seen the steep mountain trail they were to follow to the camp at Palma, about three miles inland, where García waited. Mules were brought for the American officers to ride. Much snickering occurred among the Cubans and correspondents when the huge Shafter was helped onto the back of one of these. The animal seemed to disappear from view, causing a Cuban officer to offer the comment in Spanish that "he is very small, yet he has a stout heart."

For more than a quarter of a mile the steep and winding path up the mountain side was followed, until it opened out upon a little plateau. Thin, emaciated Cuban soldiers stood on each side of the route and presented arms as the Americans passed. Half of them were black and most of the others mulatto. Only a few were white. They were poorly clad, many without shirts or shoes, but every one had his gun and a cartridge belt full of ammunition. A correspondent concluded that 75 percent of them had never worn shoes, and never would.

A mile or so farther appeared a steep hill resembling an Indian mound. On the crest of it was the camp. A large body of Cuban soldiers surrounded it, and out of this throng appeared a dozen or so officers, silver stars glistening on their wide-brimmed sombreros. Somewhere a bugle sounded a plaintive welcome.

In front of a palm-thatched hut stood García. He was tall—four inches above six feet—had an abundance of white hair, long, drooping mustaches, neat goatee, and a broad, full body. Closer up, the most noticeable feature about him was a wad of cotton protruding from an incurable hole in his forehead, dead center between his snow-white eyebrows. It had been left by a bullet he fired from beneath his chin years earlier in an effort to commit suicide while held prisoner by the Spaniards. His eyes were clear and full of light. It was said he had never been known to smile but once, and then when he fired six shots at a sleeping juntea, a small animal, without arousing it. At his elbow stood General Rabi, a full-blooded Carib Indian descendant of the aborigines of the island, a capable, dedicated, and trusted soldier.

García spoke English well. He invited the visitors into the hut, little more than a thatched roof of palm leaves that drooped over the sides to form walls. The men gathered, an odd trio, Shafter in blue blouse with double rows of buttons, Sampson in fresh white duck, García in slouch hat and linen uniform, with high military boots.

Richard Harding Davis was there, taking notes from which he would write:

It is a historical moment in the history of Cuba, if not of America, for General García, General Shafter and Admiral Sampson have met for the first time. They are grouped together under a sun so hot that it burns the eyes, on a high cliff overlooking a magnificent valley of royal palms, which meets a motionless blue sea broken only by lines of white breakers on the shore.

The three commanders are seated on boxes under the palm-leaf roof of an open hut. One of them has a blueprint map on his knees, and before they roll it up again the attack upon Santiago will be decided upon and her fate sealed.

Outside this hut are five Negro sentries, naked to the waist, and on the open space about the hut are hundreds of the Cuban army officers, well armed and well uniformed, privates of every shade of skin, with every make of weapon, and small laughing boys, armed with machetes or not armed at all.

The palm-leaf hut where the conference is taking place is open to the hot air at both ends, and on each side and standing about it or kneeling on the ground in order to obtain a better view is the strangest gathering of persons that the war has thrown together.

Colonel John Jacob Astor is crowded by a black giant with only a guard belt to cover his naked shoulders . . . There is Colonel Goetzen, the German attaché, in spotless white, and a Cuban officer, in linen blouse with bare feet, talking in signs. With them is Captain Lee, the British attaché, booted and spurred, with field glasses, helmet and immaculate khaki. Farther back are the Cuban soldiers, squatting on the ground, curious and interested, and showing their teeth and broad smiles of welcome, touching their straw hats when any one of the American officers looks their way.

During the discussion of plans, Sampson suggested that the Army storm the shore batteries and Morro Castle and the other forts on each side of the mouth of Santiago harbor, permitting the Navy to move in and take up the mines so that it could get to Cervera's fleet. But Shafter had his own ideas about the best method of attack. Before leaving Washington, he had been given some false information concerning the strength of the enemy. It was to the effect that about 20,000 Spaniards were stationed at the mouth of the harbor and at other points around Santiago, a figure that García and Rabi greatly reduced, placing it nearer 12,000. Moreover, on the way by ship the American general had studied the experience of an earlier expedition to invade Cuba—a British armada led unsuccessfully in 1741 by Lord Vernon, whose name had been given George Washington's home in Virginia. The British slowed up to build roads over which to move on Santiago and, as a result, succumbed to tropical disease and exhaustion.

Shafter decided to move inland as fast as possible, to push on despite roads and unhampered by artillery, and to wind up matters before disease could waste his army. He wanted no part of the bloody undertaking that he assumed would be involved in storming a stone fort perched on a 230-foot cliff.

As he saw it, the best chance of success lay in the very impetuosity of the attack. He proposed that Santiago be the objective, as such a plan embraced both the city and Cervera's fleet. The attack should be from the rear of the city, from the south and east, instead of by the bay. The army would move directly across land, while the Navy carried out a feint to the westward of the mouth of the harbor, shelling certain points along the coast as though landings were to be made at each. He knew the route he must follow was over rough terrain and through much tropical jungle.

García agreed with Shafter's plan and said Daiquirí, about fifteen miles east of Santiago, would be the best place at which to land.[1] It was thought only about 300 Spaniards were stationed there, and these could be driven out by a Cuban force that would be moved to that point the next day.

The meeting at the palm-thatched hut lasted about an hour. Before it ended, García placed himself and his troops under Shafter's command. The American leader, however, assured that he would exercise no authority over the Cubans, although he said he would be glad to accept their services. Realizing they long had been short of food, he gave orders for 9000 rations to be made available to them at once.

When the conference closed, the Cubans formed a hollow square. There they stood while the bugle sent forth another of its plaintive

[1] Many of the correspondents, in their early reports of the landing, identified this community as *Baiquirí.*

calls. Then the march back to the coast began, a large escort of the insurgents accompanying the Americans.

Another council of war was held on the *Seguranca* in the late afternoon. It concerned the landing, which was scheduled for the 22nd. As planned, the 2nd Division under General Lawton, accompanied by the Gatling guns, would go in first, followed by Bates's Independent Brigade and Wheeler's cavalry. Each man was to carry on his person his blanket roll, three days' field rations, canteen, and 100 rounds of ammunition.

While Shafter and his aides were working out the over-all details of attack, there was much impatience on board the ships. Wood bared his thoughts in a letter to his wife:

No one seems to know exactly what we are to do or where we are to land. You can hardly imagine the awful confusion and lack of system which meets one on every hand in this business. If the Chinese were worse, Heaven pity them. Of course, we are all right, but somehow everything seems to go in a happy-go-lucky way. I suppose they will get things fixed up in a week or two more, but if the Europeans want to intervene, nothing could give them more encouragement . . . [We are lucky] having struck a broken-down power, for we should surely have had a deuced hard time with any other.

The morning of June 21 dawned with heavy wind, rain, and a choppy sea. While some of those accustomed to the Cuban climate may have suspected it, nature was bringing on the first sample of the rainy season. Even with the best of glasses, the hazy forms of the mountains could barely be seen.

During the morning, the fleet steamed about thirty miles up the coast and lay still for the remainder of the day. Spaniards spying from Morro Castle watched the movement with interest.

By afternoon, the rain stopped and the sea fell calm. The day then proceeded normally. It was known a landing would have to come shortly for the supply of water on the transports was almost exhausted.

At sunset, the 2nd Regiment Band was finishing its usual evening chorus of "The Star-Spangled Banner" when a small boat approached the *Yucatan*, bringing a young ensign from the *Bancroft*. He climbed nimbly up the vessel's side and vaulted over the rail. Seeing soldiers and crewmen standing bareheaded and facing the colors, he, too, came to attention and waited until the music stopped. Then he made his way quickly to the bridge and drew the master aside. For a brief moment he whispered, got a nod of understanding, saluted, and hurried back over the side.

The ensign had scarcely got back to his boat before Wood and Roosevelt hurried to question the master, after which the lieutenant colonel was seen to do another of his heel-and-toe dances.

"We land tomorrow!" he shouted. "Hooray!"

Five minutes later, the little *Castine,* flying what looked like the five of clubs at her signal halyards, drew near. Officers were at the megaphones. The Rough Riders crowded to the side of their ship to hear the message.

"Be ready to land at daybreak!" yelled the commander of the little gunboat. "The *Castine* will lead the column!"

Roosevelt broke into song and went into another dance:

> *"Shout hurrah for Erin go Bragh*
> *And all the Yankee nation."*

He whirled and took Captain Capron by the arm. "Come along, you old Quaker, and let's go to supper."

In the officers' mess that evening, a strange toast was drunk. Everyone was in high spirits, fevered by the enthusiasm based on the knowledge that within a few hours they no doubt would be fighting on land. The men raised their ceremonial glasses. Together they toasted: "To the officers—may they get killed, wounded, or promoted."

After the meal, many of the Riders stared from the deck of the *Yucatan.* To some, the coast seemed to have a homelike appearance and to remind of the approaches to the Rockies. The hills now were a dull sage green, with here and there winding trails belting their scarred sides.

On the nearest point of land could be seen a settlement that strangely resembled an American mining town. Cubans on board said it was Daiquirí, a development owned by an American mining company controlled by the Carnegie Corporation of Pittsburgh. They claimed the iron ore mined there was as good as any in the world. The settlement seemed to have a railroad wharf and a few huts around the place of landing in a small cove. Back of the community rose a spur of the Sierra Cobra mountains, green as spring grass, lustrous as velvet, and rising almost to Wheeler's estimated 2000 feet. Up to the right on a lofty spur called Mount Losiltires could be made out a blockhouse with a Spanish flag at its side. Between the peaks of the range were deep defiles. The soldiers who stared knew that through these they must pass. It was said there was a Spaniard in every bush and behind every rock, waiting to give them a warm reception.

During the evening, written orders from Sampson were distributed throughout the fleet. The landing was to begin at daylight, or as soon thereafter as practicable. The Cuban General Castillo, with a thousand men, would move from the east toward Daiquirí and assist in clearing the way by flanking out the Spanish forces at that point. Ships would throw shells for miles along the coast, and feinted landings would be made at several points other than that actually chosen.

At tattoo, the men went to their bunks below or to pallets on deck. There was joking and laughter and occasionally a shout, and then someone pitched a tune: "Animal Fair." Voices swelled out into a massive chorus that reached its crescendo with "de monk, de monk, de monk." The entire ship vibrated.

part three
FIGHTIN'S THE GAME

Chapter 1

"CREEPING BUZZARDS"

It was a nervous night. After "de monk" faded away, men on guard duty stared at the many fires, some large, some small, burning here and there in the mountains back of Daiquirí and in the village itself. Those near the peak were recognized as insurgent signals to spread the word that the Americans had arrived. But the others, particularly those near the water, seemed to imply a threat. They obviously marked a path of destruction created by the Spaniards. Twice sharp explosions were heard. Was it a warning? Or did it mean retreat, an indication that a landing by the invaders would not be contested? Those awake on the transports ran appreciative fingers over their weapons. Some of these fingers were the fingers of steely-eyed veterans of the outlaw and animal trails. They had no fear of what lay ahead.

Reveille for the Rough Riders sounded in darkness at 3:30 A.M. An hour and a half later daylight revealed the transports spread out in a great semicircle. Some were five miles from shore, a background for the warships closer in, with the *Seguranca* midway between. So huge did the *St. Louis* appear as she loomed on the horizon that she could have been taken for a part of the landscape.

Inshore the entire island of Cuba seemed to be wrapped in soft mists. The air was pleasantly cool and the sea relatively calm, but a breeze was building. Dull, leaden clouds moved slowly, making way for a clear sky. Here and there fires still burned, throwing off tails of drifting smoke. As the sun came up, it touched the mountaintops with patches of green, developing a picture with the deftness of an artist.

As an indication of impending action, rations were issued each

Rider.[1] A quick breakfast, and then the men lay about waiting. Some used the time for writing. Arthur Fortunatus Cosby, a Washingtonian by birth but a New York lawyer by profession, prepared a letter to his mother. He was buoyed by the thought of landing after fifteen days cooped up on board ship. "I do not think we shall have any fighting where we are going to land, but there is always the chance," he told her. "I have often wondered how it felt to be on the eve of a battle, but it is no different from anything else. The sun is rising and we are drawing nearer shore, so goodbye."

The morning advanced while Sampson waited for the mists to rise and bare the targets chosen along a 20-mile stretch of the coast. Shafter's plan of action was now official, in writing: he intended to push the army toward Santiago as rapidly as possible, taking with him only a few wagons and pack trains.

Gradually the transports moved into a tighter circle. Troops from only eight of these were scheduled to land during the day, but they remained intact as a fleet. They were equipped with 153 small boats, enough to transport 3434 men at one time. Also on hand were the *Laura*, a steam lighter that could hold 400 men standing up, and the decked-over barges that had given so much trouble on the way down from Florida. These would be supplemented by steam launches and other craft supplied by the Navy. Even at that, according to Roosevelt, they had only a fourth of what they needed.

Teddy's Navy Department connections continued to cross his trail. Along came the converted yacht *Vixen*, commanded by his former naval aide, Lieutenant Sharp. The lieutenant gallantly offered to lead the *Yucatan* closer in toward shore. As everything was to be on a go-as-you-please basis when the signal to land was given, Roosevelt accepted. Sharp accordingly sent over his black Cuban pilot, who guided the Riders to a point at least a mile and a half nearer land. The move would enable them to be among the first to go ashore. The civilian masters of other transports, uncertain of their knowledge of the coast closer in, remained farther at sea.

At last the mists cleared sufficiently for the signal to be given to start the bombardment. All along the 20-mile stretch, guns roared, enveloping the warships in smoke and giving the soldiers their first real touch of war. The cheering was constant as the heavy shells

[1] The official ration of the war included bacon, hard bread, beans, potatoes, onions, canned tomatoes, coffee, sugar, vinegar, candles, soap, salt, and pepper, although it was seldom that all of these were issued simultaneously.

landed on the shore. Up into the air at Aguadores, Cabañas, Siboney, Juragua, Daiquirí, and other points were sent great sprays of dust and debris and broken tree limbs. For nineteen minutes the firing continued, although some of those who looked on said afterward it lasted an hour. "It was the grandest sight I ever witnessed," wrote Ogden Wells, "and I could hardly realize that the shots were fired in anger and that the warships were searching for hidden batteries." Many of the gunners off Daiquirí sent shells toward the blockhouse on Mount Losiltires, but not one hit its mark. The Spanish flag had disappeared during the night.

When the guns fell silent, there was much staring at the landing place at Daiquirí. Fires still burned, but there were no signs of life. The Spaniards had fled before 9 A.M. As the silence extended along the hillsides, Cuban insurgents appeared in scattered groups on the far ridges, frantically gesticulating in an effort to let the Americans know the enemy had departed.

While the men were piling into the boats, an acrid exchange took place on the promenade deck of the *Seguranca*. Richard Harding Davis, the beau sabreur of the correspondents, approached General Shafter, who was busily observing the activities across the water.

"General," he said, "I see the order for disembarkation directs that none but fighting men be allowed in the boats of the first landing party. This will keep back reporters."

Shafter admitted that was true. He explained it was not meant to indicate any unfriendliness toward reporters, that it was done to make sure there would be sufficient fighters in the first boats to be able to return the fire of any Spaniards who might happen to remain at Daiquirí.

Davis persisted. He looked upon himself as an international journalist, one deserving the utmost respect. "I am not an ordinary reporter," he said. "I am a descriptive writer."

The Shafter temper, recognized for its short fuse, exploded. "I don't give a damn what you are! I'll treat you all alike!"

Davis went back to his cabin to sulk. In the future, certain reports on the operations in Cuba would give less space to the commanding general. Some pencils would be notoriously sharp when they wrote about this bulky individual.

At the signal for the landing to start, the fleet became a madhouse of activity. Troops fought to get their horse-collar blanket rolls and haversacks in order. The transports swung out their davits.

Little steam launches of the Navy, with saucy one-pounder guns perched in their bows and American ensigns at their sterns, ran about like water bugs, pulling strings of boats, each packed with sixteen soldiers. Somewhere out among the fleet, a band struck up "A Hot Time in the Old Town." Others joined in and the soldiers sang, their voices spreading out across the sea with more volume than harmony.

As they approached shore, the men in the boats could see that Daiquirí was a squalid little village in a narrow cut through low hills stretching back to the high mountains beyond. On its outskirts was open ground that offered space for re-forming the troops and establishing camps, corrals, and supply dumps.

Among the first boats to go in was that carrying the two black 10th Cavalry troopers who would be crushed against the pilings and for whom Bucky O'Neill would dive in vain. Ahead up through the village rushed Lawton's regulars. They came upon sacks of coconuts left by the Spaniards, and some of the men stopped. Coconut would be a change of diet. Insurgents demonstrated how to crack the shells with machetes. One private asked for two coconuts and held out some coins, but the Cuban addressed shook his head—two coconuts, yes, but money, no.

The hospitality proffered by this coconut-cracker was the exception rather than the rule. Already the Cuban image was fading. Most of those who came down from the hills seemed on the bum for anything they could get from the Americans, even though their "*vivas*" were loud and long. "They were a motley-looking crowd, big, black fellows with shiny bodies, most of them only half-clad and some nearly naked," recorded Wells, "but they gave us a friendly greeting and disposed of all the hardtack we gave them in a manner most mysterious." While they were destitute of clothing, they gave no evidence of physical hardship. In a letter to his parents, Corporal James M. Dean of Santa Fe expressed thoughts already beginning to build in the minds of many of his comrades:

> "The American army cannot depend on them for assistance . . . Altogether I have made up my mind that they are poor warriors. We never think of Cuba in our progress: it is for revenge on a people for cowardly blowing up our boys in Havana harbor."

Scattered here and there around the village were debris and deserted property—empty wine and whiskey bottles, a broken saddle, a few boxes of dried peas. General Castillo had set up head-quarters in a cottage on the slope, and men on horseback were gathered around it. In its yard lay an overturned bathtub. A Cuban officer explained it had belonged to an American mining official. The Spaniards shunned it, he said, remarking that they used only powder—one layer after another.

In what had been the roundhouse stood a Baldwin locomotive, so gray with ashes it looked like a ghost. Two others were in the remains of the machine shops. All were damaged, but not beyond repair. Other items included a large lathe made in Hamilton, Ohio, and numerous mechanics' tools of American manufacture. Thousands of exploded cartridges littered the ground.

The noise and confusion on shore increased. Bugles were blown, men hurried off to find their comrades, and sergeants scurried about rounding up stragglers. Meanwhile, more boatloads came.

A British correspondent landed with a boatload of the 1st Volunteers. He watched them as they ran through the village. Women and children were coming in from their hideouts by this time, and someone among them whispered into a Rough Rider's ear. He put his nose into the air and hurried away, followed by companions. Soon they were back, with a dozen or so scrawny horses, most of them almost as small as ponies. At sight of them, a bare-legged, ragged Cuban rushed up in great excitement, his hands waving wildly above his head.

"*Americano no caballero!*" he screamed. "*Cuban caballero!*"

The Rough Riders shoved him away. "Get out!" they shouted.

He disappeared, but later he returned. He had been to see General Castillo: Castillo had sent a messenger to communicate with Shafter, and Shafter passed along the word: horses found in the village were to be given up to the Cubans.

The Britisher was disgusted, for his hopes had been raised at sight of the animals, the only thing he so far had seen that represented transportation. "There is nothing for it but to walk," he wrote his newspaper, "and how anyone is going to walk more than five miles a day in this climate and over these hills I dare not try to think."

About the village was much evidence that the Spaniards had left in a hurry, possibly hastened by suspicion that there would be a bombardment. Before leaving, they had cut the pipeline bringing water to a huge tank from springs six miles back in the mountains, but this was quickly repaired. The Americans found the supply excellent. The tank became a concentration point, for the sun was hot and the soldiers were thirsty for good water.

Spanish occupation of the village, it was learned, had begun about three months earlier. Mining company employees and Cuban residents were forced to flee and their homes were commandeered. Despite all the litter in the community, it could be seen there had been preparation for resistance. Clearly outlined were earthworks, trenches, rifle pits, breastworks, all carefully laid out. Up in one of the houses was found a letter left by the officer in charge of the post. In it he assured the commanding general that he was abundantly able to resist any attack on Daiquirí, either by land or sea.

In rapid succession, boats pushed into the inlet. Out on the *Seguranca*, Shafter finally gave word for the correspondents to land. Davis, still in his cabin sulking, missed the boat, but someone thought of him before it had gone far. As he was looked upon as sort of the dean of the journalists corps, they put back for him. He was angry enough at Shafter, but he got angrier when he reached shore and learned that his colleague, Burr McIntosh of the New York *Journal*, newspaper reporter as well as prominent actor, had got there ahead of him. Burr tried to stow away in one of the longboats, but his six feet and 250 pounds gave him away. Back on the transport, he shed his clothes, wrapped them around his camera and handed them, along with a folded greenback, to a sergeant just about to enter a landing craft. Then he dived into the water, grabbed a towline trailing a passing boat, and was the first journalist to step on land at Daiquirí.

By midafternoon, the wind had strengthened and a high surf was crashing along the coral reefs, making it more of a problem for the men to climb from the boats to the wharf. Guns, bugles, knapsacks, and other items fell from their grasps into the water as they went through the difficult process. But the Army, like the mailman, was inviolable. To its aid came two expert swimmers who had landed with the first boatload of Rough Riders, Charles E. Knoblauck, member of the New York Stock Exchange, and Alfred M. Judson, New York broker. Knoblauck was particularly well known. Wealthy before he was out of his twenties, he had gained a wide reputation as an all-around athlete. Better than six feet tall and weighing 165 pounds, he was a member of the New York Athletic Club's famous water polo team and of the club's crew that had won the national championship twice in a row. He was a boxer, wrestler, professional horseman, and back at home, tied up until his return, was his fancy yacht, the *Bonnie Kate*. For hours these two men remained at the dock and dived to retrieve items which fell overboard.

Late in the afternoon, Joe Wheeler came ashore and directed Leonard Wood's attention to the vacant flagstaff standing beside the blockhouse on the hill. At the colonel's direction, three Rough Riders set out up the mountainside. They were Chief Surgeon Henry Lamotte, a retired Navy surgeon and a man especially adept with a rope; Color Bearer Albert P. Wright, cowboy and mining engineer from Yuma, one of the tallest men in the regiment, and Clay Platt, chief trumpeter. With them they carried the hand-made flag presented by the Women's Relief Corps at Phoenix. A few minutes later, when the banner swung out in the breeze as the first American emblem raised in the 5th Corps invasion, it was quickly spotted. Thousand of voices, scores of steam whistles, and dozens of brass bands joined in a great outburst of noise that made no secret of the fact that the men from the United States were landing.

The Rough Riders who went up to the blockhouse took a careful look at it. One of many built throughout Cuba by the Spaniards, it was twelve feet square, with a pyramid roof. Walls were banked with gravel on the outside to a height of about four feet above the floor, where an aperture for firing extended all around the building. Upper walls were of double plank, filled in loosely with small stones. In one corner was a pile of green rushes spread for a bed and in another a five-gallon can of rice flour.

As the afternoon advanced, attention was turned to the horses and mules. Finally, it was decided to force them into the water and let them swim ashore. Accordingly, hundreds of animals were driven into the sea. Some swam directly toward land, but others, becoming confused, headed in the opposite direction, and a few were drowned. Suddenly a bugler reacted to the emergency: he raised his instrument and sent out over the waves the notes of the call "right wheel." Cavalry horses snorting with terror caught the sound, came around to the right, and swam toward shore, showing the way to other animals not sensitive to the notes of the bugle.

Roosevelt went back to the *Yucatan* to supervise the unloading of his two horses. A band was placed around the belly of "Rain-in-the-Face" and was attached to a spar for hoisting. As the animal was swung over the side, a huge breaker smashed against it and plunged it into the sea, where it drowned. Snorting like a bull and stamping back and forth, Roosevelt "split the air with one blasphemy after another," reported photographer Albert E. Smith, the Vitagraph Company representative. With misery in their eyes, crewmen looked at the second horse, "Texas," and became overly cautious. They hoisted it with great deliberation and exchanged opinions after each pull of the hoist. Even when the lieutenant colonel roared, "Stop that goddamned animal torture!", they did not hurry, and the animal was lowered safely into the water and swam to land.

The landing proceeded rapidly. Besides the horses and mules, 6000 men—nearly all of Lawton's division, all of Bates's brigade, and one brigade of Wheeler's cavalry—were brought ashore. Baggage and supplies remained on the ships and would have to come later.

The dynamite and Colt automatic guns were landed, but Parker and his Gatlings ran into unexpected trouble. His command was sharing the *Cherokee* with the 12th and 17th Infantry, and was standing by ready to come ashore. But immediately after the last infantryman stepped into a boat, the transport's captain turned her about and headed to sea. Parker was frantic. It was only after much heated argument that he succeeded in having the vessel return to the fleet, close enough for him to megaphone to Shafter what had happened. It is recorded that no megaphone was needed to relay the general's reply that the machine guns had better be brought in early in the morning.

On reaching shore, the troops pushed inland. Strong detachments under Lawton's direction were posted for guard duty at strategic points around the village. All necessary steps were taken to insure that the landing would be permanent.

About 4 P.M., Lawton was notified that the bombardment had driven the Spanish out of Siboney, the next village on the route to Santiago, some ten or twelve miles away. He was ordered to occupy the place, entrench, and guard the railroad near the point where it crossed the main road to Santiago. Landing facilities were lacking there, he was told, but boats could go in to the beach. A pier would have to be built.

Immediately Lawton started the 1st and 2nd Brigades along the trail. It was called a wagon road, although practicable only for two-wheel carts. On each side was scrubby undergrowth—clumps of bushes, cane interspersed with cactus, Spanish bayonet, rough brambles with long, curved thorns, all made inpenetrable by trailing vines. Someone said it was ideal country for guerrilla warfare, and someone else said he pitied the guerrillas who might be subjected to it.

Progress of Lawton's brigades was slow. He tried to hurry the march, but this became impossible after darkness settled. Finally he ordered a halt for the night. Men lay down wherever they could find enough clear space to stretch their bodies. The line extended for more than two miles, its head resting at a point called Remajayaho. This was definite evidence that the Cubans had no scruples about giving a scattering of huts the dignity of a name.

In the meantime, Wheeler, the old Confederate who liked to keep his cavalry on the move, had not been idle. After suggesting the flag-raising to Wood, he went forward on a scouting trip with members of his staff some three and a half miles. It was late at night when he returned.

The Rough Riders went into camp on a dusty, brush-covered flat a few hundred yards inland. On one side lay a dense growth of jungle, on the other a shallow, fetid pool fringed with palm trees. A moon in its quarter lightened the sky.

Most of the men stretched their tent halves on the ground and spread blankets over them. Others erected tents, while a few of the more energetic, aided by Cubans, threw up palm-thatched huts. Some of the palm leaves they used were ten feet long.

Now supplied with good water from the mine company tank, the Riders made the most of their rations. The meal they prepared consisted mostly of hardtack and beans. Native food was at a minimum. Besides coconuts, which had been left simply because both the Cubans and Spaniards had become tired of them, they found a few chilis, but mangoes and limes were not to be had.

Darkness brought out the crimson flare of the burning roundhouse and shops, now a bed of coals, adding to the ghostliness of the locomotives. Off in the distance, insurgents gathered around their campfires and sang native songs—weird, half-savage melodies, accompanied by the booming of improvised drums. From the ships at sea searchlights gleamed, sending their prying beams along the mountainsides, illuminating cleared areas, but foiled whenever they struck hidden pockets of jungle.

Orders called for the Riders to sleep on their rolls, with guns in easy reach. It was cool and damp, a sharp change from the hot hours of the day. But the men had no trouble going to sleep. The ground was to them much softer than the deck of the transports or the hard bunks below. Before reclining, Roosevelt made entry in his diary that matched a record for brevity: "June 22—landed." The only thing he had brought ashore except the clothing on his back was a light mackintosh and toothbrush.

While the men slept, pale light from the moon lay revealingly over the brush-covered flat. Only history would note that this one spot on God's green earth was honored this night to have as its guests America's oddest and most famous military outfit of the moment. Citified youths of New York and Boston lay beside the sunburned cowboys of Tucson and San Antonio.

As the night wore along, a guard walked post on the side next to the jungle. He was naturally a bit nervous, for this was his first experience as a soldier on foreign soil. The searchlights out at sea had stopped their prying. The only break in the semidarkness was from the tiny picket fires of debris and dried foliage burning around the sleeping assembly.

To the guard's attention suddenly came a rustling, clacking sound. It arose from the surrounding jungle. He imagined it the noise of guerrillas or bushwhackers stealing up on the camp. After all, the invaders covered a wide area, and some had marched off toward Siboney.

He crouched in the shadows and waited. Then his eyes caught a moving object near one of the fires. It was the strangest creature he had ever seen, a thing that sidled along like a spider surrounded by numerous legs. Two huge pincers extended off at an odd angle, and between them were two small eyes mounted like round berries on the ends of short pedicels. Directly below them was a mouth that appeared to be formed by two horny, beaklike mandibles.

The creature was moving toward the rows of sleepers. A creepy feeling swept the guard as he raised his gun and fired at the tiny eyes. His aim was good. The thing seemed to sink in the middle, its many legs twisting and entwining madly around its central body in a maze of uncoordinated confusion. Finally it lay still, only the extremities of its appendages trembling nervously.

Armed Riders swarmed around the guard. With the barrel of his carbine, he pushed the creature nearer one of the fires. In the brighter light he could see it was colored in diversified shades of red, scarlet, light yellow, orange, and black.

Among those drawn by the excitement was Captain Thomas P. Ledwidge, the Illinois filibuster who had created so much attention when the Riders were mustering at Santa Fe. He stared momentarily, snorted in disgust, and muttered audibly as he turned back to his blankets: "Land crabs—creeping buzzards!"

Chapter 2

SIBONEY

The day before is like the moment one drifts into the nether world of an anesthetic. It is not a standout recollection; at best, it is recalled as a cog in a development leading to another development, the way one step succeeds another in a march toward a goal. Rough Riders on June 23 did things they would never forget. It would go down in history—not as a hallowed occasion like Christmas or the Fourth of July, but as the eve of *the* day when the 1st Volunteer Cavalry gave evidence it was not along just for the glory.

Lawton's infantry moved early, going into Siboney at daybreak. The village was found almost intact. So precipitately had the Spaniards abandoned the place that they had had little opportunity for destruction. Residents reported that General Arsenio Linares, commander of all Spanish troops in the province, had hurried away by train as late as 4 A.M. Among appreciable items left were several locomotives, one hundred cars of coal, a sawmill, and a large warehouse. Also abandoned were twenty-five or thirty barrels of whiskey and wine, contraband quickly placed under heavy guard.

Advance troops in the march on the village included some two hundred Cubans from Castillo's forces and fifty picked American soldiers. The latter were under command of Lieutenant Colonel Arthur Lockwood Wagner, a rather individualistic officer who had been sent to Cuba specifically to set up a Bureau of Military Information. Because of the speed with which the military campaign was being conducted, however, it was something he would never get around to doing. To be useful in the meantime until he managed to get his indiscriminate ducks in a row, he was serving as a voluntary aide on Lawton's staff.

Even before daybreak, the advance sent back word that Siboney had been abandoned. Meanwhile, the men hurried on through the village on the trail of the Spaniards. Finally they caught up with them four miles farther along, on high ground suitable for camping purposes, a rather strategic military position. The fight that followed was a scattered and somewhat disorderly affair in which Cubans were wounded, none seriously, Lawton reported.

Siboney lay in a gap between hills, its settlement of houses extending down to an easy-shelving, shaded beach protected from the prevailing southeast swell by a headland. Through the gulch in which it was situated, a sluggish creek ran down and emptied into a stagnant pond separated from the ocean by only a few yards of sandy beach. Skirting it was a slimy swamp, an ideal breeding spot for the fever-generating anopheles mosquito. Two roads wound westwardly from the village toward Santiago, four creeks and a dozen or so miles away. One of these routes was a wagon trail to the right that followed a valley, while the other was little more than a path. It went up over a ridge to the north of town and then gradually bore around until it converged with the other, four miles farther on. The valley along which lay the main route gradually widened as it extended back from the sea. It was marked by several steep ascents or terraces, referred to by the Cubans as *altares*. The last of these, just before reaching the city, was known as San Juan. It consisted of a series of ridges, the final one descending into a sort of lowland, on the far side of which sat Santiago. Such was the terrain over which the Americans must advance.

At 9:20 A.M., Lawton prepared a dispatch notifying Shafter that he had occupied Siboney. He gave no indication of pushing farther. This met with Shafter's plans, for the commanding general wanted to unload the ships, reorganize the army, and rest the animals before beginning the push toward Santiago. Just the day prior, after the landing had begun, he prepared a message addressed to the "senior officer at the front." It called for two regiments to be pushed on to Siboney, there to occupy a point where the railroad crossed the main road to Santiago. If no opposition was met, the troops were to go into camp, entrench, and remain in that locality. This was an important message, for it was meant to govern the initial movements on shore. But it was delayed in delivery and did not figure in the action that immediately followed.

Next morning, Wheeler, who was the senior officer at the front, got other instructions telling him to send Wood's regiment ahead for the purpose of patrolling the road from the railroad crossing to Siboney. As one who liked to look before he leaped, the little bewhiskered general rode away at once, arriving at Siboney before noon. Cubans there informed him that fighting was going on a few miles to the westward. He prepared a report to that effect for Shafter and then rode off in the direction of the skirmishing.

The Rough Riders, still at Daiquirí, spent the morning perfecting the comfort and beauty of their camp. They were acting under the belief that they were to occupy it for some time. Its location seemed ideal. A few hundred yards to the west flowed a clear, swift-running little stream that gave them an opportunity to take the first bath they had had since leaving Florida. They went about their chores with military precision, and also made further efforts to get their baggage ashore.

While they worked at various tasks or bathed in the nearby creek, groups of Cubans and regulars could be seen moving to and fro. The Cubans were particularly interesting, especially their dress. Stephen Crane wrote of them: "They looked like a collection of real tropic savages at whom some philanthropist had flung a bundle of rags; some of the rags had stuck here and there." One old fellow, black as night, came along wearing only an artillery coat he had stolen the night before. Although sweat was coursing down his naked body and dripping at his feet, he kept the overcoat tightly buttoned, its bright red cape thrown back in a flash of color that contrasted sharply with his dark skin. Whenever a campfire was lighted, Cubans appeared like genies, to stand around in the hope of getting a handout of food. As one newsman put it: "The Cuban insurgents regard every American as a kind of charitable institution and expect him to disgorge on every occasion."

Ogden Wells, the night before, had been impressed with the difference between the Cuban women and those back home. At the first native hut he visited, he found three olive-skinned girls dressed only in short skirts. "Thinking I had intruded as they were about to retire," he confided in his diary, "I beat a hasty retreat, but this morning I find that there are few of the women that are more than half dressed, a cotton skirt reaching to the knees constituting the only garment of the majority."

At 1 P.M., Wood received orders from Wheeler to be ready to

move at a moment's notice. Within an hour, the camp the Riders
were trying to beautify was a shambles. Everything was bustle.
Shoulder packs were arranged and haversacks rejammed with rations and personal items. Wood was the martyr. He had brought
ashore an extra horse, a pretty little Kentucky thoroughbred mare.
When faced with the necessity, he ordered a pack-saddle thrown
across her back, distorting the fine lines of a show animal, and
had it loaded with the regimental headquarters kit. There were
tears in his eyes as he watched it done.

Soon the orders came to move. The column got under way.
A little Cuban boy who knew the way and could speak English
rode at the front on a tiny native stallion. Next came Wood,
accompanied by Edward Marshall, correspondent of the New York
Journal, by staff representatives of both Generals Wheeler and
Young, and by Color Bearer Wright, holding aloft the flag flown
the day before from Mount Losiltires. Wright was a standout in
any body of men. He had the appearance of a typical cowboy
of fiction. His face had been tanned by a life on the Plains,
and it was broken by a quiet smile that blended with pleasant
light blue eyes. A native of Fairfax, Virginia, his thirty-nine years
had been spent largely in the West.

The first troop in the line was L, led by Capron, senior captain. At the rear, leading his horse, came Roosevelt and the hospital
corps. All efforts to get the lieutenant colonel to mount failed.
"I don't want to ride while my men are walking," he repeated
steadfastly. This attitude strengthened the bond that had been
building between him and the Riders since their first days together
at San Antonio.

The heat was terrific. "I shall never forget the terrible march
to Siboney," recorded Marshall. Ogden Wells remembered it, too.
He wrote in his diary:

> Our march was like a pipe organ, having many stops. We
> were in full marching order; that means each man carries a
> carbine, a hundred rounds of ammunition, canteen, poncho, half
> a shelter tent, the army blanket, rations and other necessary
> articles we were obliged to have. As we struggled up the hill-
> sides and tramped down the slopes, the packs shifted and
> slipped and bore down on our aching shoulders. As the sun
> beat down on us, the packs and bundles slid about as though
> they were alive and gained in weight from pounds to tons.
> In the woods the packs caught on overhanging underbrush and

sent us stumbling and falling. In the open places, the sun was like a furnace and the packs were like lead. At last we could stand it no longer and we began to throw away our blankets; after the blankets went cans of meat, then our coats and underclothes, until some only had their guns and ammunition left, for these were essentials.

Wood moved fast, wanting to make sure the 1st Volunteers had a part in any movement Wheeler might order. The march began in column of fours, but soon narrowed to twos, and finally to single file. A man without a pack had to carry an ax or a pick or shovel. Before they had moved a mile, their clothing was wringing wet. The route led much of the way over a winding mountain road, through sand and mud and thicket, through little creeks which the natives called rivers. An occasional abandoned sugar estate was passed. Often along the roadside could be seen remains of coconuts. These had been hacked open with machetes by the Cubans to get the swallow or two of sweetened liquid inside.

At times the route went up over steep hills, and there was much stopping and starting. Comment along the line reminded that they were earning their nickname of "Wood's Weary Walkers." It was surprising how little straggling there was among men so unaccustomed to walking. Small squads of regulars who were unable to push on with Lawton were frequently encountered.

The country through which they passed smelled like a fragrant overheated conservatory. Here and there were picturesque splashes of tropical colors from oleanders and other flowers. Often it was necessary for the men to walk in water. This caused them to recall jokingly all the medical advice they had received about wet feet, night winds, and perspiration-soaked bodies. Also about the need to boil water before drinking it.

At one point, Wood called a longer halt than usual. He had seen what he thought was Spaniards on a mountain about 1500 yards to the left. The regiment was closed up, deployed in an old field, and ordered to lie down facing the mountain. After half an hour, laughter suddenly rang through the jungle. The "enemy" had been found to be nothing more than leaves of tropical trees, the white under sides of which, when moved by the wind, giving the appearance of white-clad figures in motion.

While the Riders marched, Wheeler, about nightfall, came back to Siboney from his reconnaissance. He had ridden out three or

four miles, to the scene of the fighting, and had seen the Cuban
wounded, as well as one dead Spaniard. Shortly before his return, the head of Wood's column passed through the village and
set up camp in a coconut grove a little beyond. Lawton's infantry
was in three locations, one battalion occupying the heights, another
lying along the railroad track, and a third scattered here and
there about the settlement. For fear of vermin, the men were told
they could not sleep in homes or vacant buildings.

In short order, the Riders lit fires and got busy cooking supper.
Barely had they started when a tropical storm broke. It was a
deluge that put out the campfires and turned the ground into
ooze. "We thought the whole ocean was being dumped on us
and that such a rain in old Noah's time would have made his
flood in one-fifth of forty days," wrote the correspondent of the
Oklahoma State Capital. One trooper recalled with appreciation
the old adage that nothing takes the spirit out of a soldier quicker
than wetting the seat of his pants.

When the downpour slackened, the routine of making camp
continued. Fires were rekindled, and men stood around in groups,
drying their clothes and laughing and talking. There were many
rumors about what their next action would be. Now that they
were on the way to Santiago, no one had any idea that they
would remain still for any length of time, especially the cavalry.
Joe Wheeler had been on the move all his life. Some wag dropped
the fidgety thought that the reason Joe's pants were so baggy
was that they were full of ants. Anyway, the wiry little fighter
must uphold his reputation. Roosevelt sized him up as a regular
gamecock anxious to get first blood and to move the cavalry
division to the front as fast as possible.

Most everyone seemed to be anxious to find out what was ahead.
Thomas Winthrow Hall, adjutant of the regiment, met a classmate
who had been one of the fifty picked American soldiers with the advance. This fellow said the Spaniards were in force on the second
ridge back from the coast, in a position from which the Cubans
had never been able to drive them or to pass during the entire
three years of the current war.

As the evening advanced, campfires grew brighter and seemed
to draw the men closer together, to bring out personalities, and
to stimulate a camaraderie that was far more evident than that
manifested when they were marching amid the discomforts of the
trail. It was around the campfires, the lively nests of flickering

flames or the beds of coals ready for the cooks' pans, that the
odd friendships formed among the volunteers from the East and
those from the West were most noticeable. Strangest among them
was that between Woodbury Kane, the aristocratic, polo-playing
officer of K Troop, and little Billy McGinty, the toughened, bow-
legged cowboy who rode for the love of riding, grace bedamned.

Another combination was Ham Fish, the wealthy New York
playboy, and Ed Culver, half-breed Cherokee brought up on the
cattle ranges of Indian Territory. During the rain, the two stood
together under a tree, both getting badly soaked. "Old boy," said
Fish, "this is soldiering."

A little later, when the rain had stopped, Roosevelt and Capron
strolled over to the fire where Culver was busy making coffee
and cooking meat while Fish watched.

"They was complimenting us about the march and talking about
the Spaniards," Culver later told a reporter. "They was fine men,
them two, Colonel Roosevelt and Captain Capron, and the boys
all liked them."

It was while at the campfire that Roosevelt had an opportunity
to study those about him. "As we stood around the flickering
blaze that night," the leader later recalled, "I caught myself admiring the splendid bodily vigor of Capron and Fish—the captain
and the sergeant. Their frames seemed of steel, to withstand
all fatigue; they were flushed with health; in their eyes shone
high resolve and fiery desire. Two finer types of the fighting man,
two better representatives of the American soldier, there were
not in the whole army."

After the visitors had gone, Fish turned to Culver. "Old boy, are
your father and mother living?"

Culver replied that his parents were living out in Indian Territory, and so were a sister and three brothers, "leastways if the
brothers haven't enlisted since I left."

"I suppose the people at home are thinking about us now,"
commented Fish, in solemn mood. He did a lot of talking before
going to bed. Some of the Riders recalled hearing him say, "It
would be just my luck to be put out of the way in the first scrap
and not see any of the war."

Fatigue was a great boon to the soldiers that night. Throughout
its hours there were disturbances which otherwise might have
prevented sleep. Fires burned as men cooked supper or breakfast.
Others cavorted along the beach in the nude, enjoying the water

1. The future leader of the Rough Riders clothed in buckskin hunting suit during his days on a ranch in North Dakota.

2. Captain Charles L. Cooper, United States Army (No. 3), pictured as he swore in the New Mexico Rough Rider volunteers, including Major H. B. Hersey (No. 1) and Dr. J. A. Massie (No. 4). The Governor, M. A. Otero (No. 2), stands with them.

3. The New Mexico contingent is pictured in front of the Fire Department (No. 1) at Santa Fe on its way to the railroad depot on May 6, 1898. No. 5 at the right is Captain Maximiliano Luna. The flag bearer (No. 2) is Sergeant Fred Wesley, and to his left are Sergeant R. A. Prentice (No. 3) and Captain W. E. Griffin (No. 4).

4. Colonel Theodore Roosevelt
in uniform.

5. Captain William O. O'Neill.

6. Captain Allyn K. Capron.

7. Rough Rider Captain James H. McClintock of Arizona.

8. Rough Rider David L. Hughes of Tucson, Arizona.

9. The diminutive General Joe Wheeler, whose effective cavalry tactics spanned two wars.

10. The Exposition Hall at San Antonio in which the Rough Riders first were quartered.

11. Left to right, Roosevelt, Wood, and Brodie, the three top officers of the regiment, seated beside their tents at San Antonio.

12. Officers' mess at San Antonio, with Wood and Roosevelt seated at the far end of the table.

13. A gathering at San Antonio. Left to right, Major George Dunn, Major Alexander Brodie, General Joe Wheeler, Chaplain Henry A. Brown, Colonel Wood, and Colonel Roosevelt.

14. Teddy Roosevelt seated in his tent at San Antonio.

15. Officers of the 1st Volunteer Cavalry at San Antonio, with Josephine, the lion, lying in front of them.

1. Col. Wood	11. Lt. Patterson	21. Lt. Goodrich	31. Capt. McGinnis
2. Lt. Col. Roosevelt	12. Capt. Alexander	22. Lt. Winchey	32. Lt. Devereaux
3. Maj. Brodie	13. Lt. Nichols	23. Lt. Wilcox	33. Capt. Llewellyn
4. Maj. Hersey	14. Capt. Huston	24. Lt. Greenway	34. Lt. Kane
5. Maj. Dunn	15. Capt. Luna	25. Capt. O'Neill	35. Lt. Green
6. Lt. Hall	16. Capt. Bruce	26. Lt. Frantz	36. Surgeon Church
7. Lt. Schweitzer	17. Lt. Weakley	27. Lt. Ballard	37. Lt. Day
8. Lt. Carr	18. Capt. Muller	28. Lt. Kelly	38. Lt. Haskell
9. Lt. Sayre	19. Lt. Griffin	29. Capt. Capron	39. Lt. Leahey
10. Capt. McClintock	20. Capt. Curry	30. Lt. Keyes	40. Lt. Rynning

and the warm climate, or waded into the ocean up to their necks
to help bring ashore the supplies now being unloaded in the
convenience afforded by the coast at Siboney. Searchlights on the
ships kept the hillsides and the water's edge aglow, and there was
noise aplenty.

Since Wheeler's return to Siboney, he had been the central
figure in numerous conferences. Somehow or other, Colonel Wagner
of the Bureau of Military Information took these to be mysterious.
He learned that, in addition to individual conversations, Wheeler
had gathered with Young and Wood at General Castillo's house
in the village. He also heard of the reconnaissance Wheeler had
made in the afternoon. So suspicious did he become that he informed Lawton he believed preparations were under way for an
attack on the Spaniards by a portion of the Cavalry Division.

After dark, Lawton talked with Wheeler himself, but there was
no mention of an immediate offensive. However, he heeded Wagner's warning and tried to get in touch with Shafter. But the
Seguranca was still standing several miles offshore, and a high
sea running since nightfall made any attempt to reach it by small
boat dangerous and impracticable.

Out on the *Seguranca* during the afternoon, Shafter directed
preparation of the following order, which was considerably delayed
in reaching division commanders:

> The commanding general begs to say it is impossible to ad-
> vance on Santiago until movements to supply troops can be
> arranged. Take up strong positions where you can get water
> and make yourself secure from surprise or attack. Lawton's di-
> vision will be in front; Kent's near Siboney; Wheeler's near
> Daiquirí; and Bates's command where it will be in support of
> Lawton.

Although he had not seen this order, some parts of it would
not have been to Wheeler's liking. According to the placement
of troops, the cavalry would be in the rear at Daiquirí and,
since it was traveling on foot and at the same pace as the infantry, would be the last to get into action. But already the
arrangement had been upset: Lawton was at the front and so
was a part of the cavalry, the latter on the side of Siboney
nearest Santiago, where it could easily outflank the infantry.

Young, leading the 2nd Brigade, to which the Rough Riders
were attached, reached Siboney about 7:30 P.M. and found

Wheeler. When he inquired about camping ground, the ex-Confederate said the Spaniards occupied the best site.

"General Wheeler," Young said, "if you have no objections, I will move out in the morning and see what is there. The ground here is not fit for camping. I would like to move out there and get that camping ground for ourselves."

Wheeler told him he had no objections and took him to see Castillo. Young used a little tallow candle to sketch a description of the country as he understood it, and the Cuban leader said it was pretty nearly right, making a few alterations here and there. However, Castillo added it was his opinion that the Spaniards would retreat into Santiago and, if they did not, they would be reinforced.

Young then asked the Cuban how many men he had and was told there were five hundred that could be depended upon. These Castillo agreed to send with Young, but said he could not go himself because he had to stay at Siboney to meet General García.[1] But after all, he added, there should be no difficulty so far as directions were concerned. If they marched along the trail until they came to the body of a dead Spaniard, the one Wheeler had seen during his reconnaissance, the enemy would not be far away.

When Wood came out of the final conference late that night and made his way into the Rider camp, he noticed Capron standing in the reflection from a fire and went up and told him what the plans were. Their conversation was brief. In closing, the colonel assured the captain that his troop again would be in the lead when they started moving in the morning.[2]

Capron spoke in the tone of a veteran as Wood moved away: "Well, tomorrow at this time the long sleep will be on many of us." June 24 would be his twenty-seventh birthday.

Wood went from troop to troop, talking briefly to each captain and making sure all was in readiness. At the headquarters tent, he stretched out beneath a poncho with his clothes on. Roosevelt had gone to bed earlier—after making another brief entry in his diary: "June 23—Marched." But he was still awake. He listened to the plans as Wood related them in a low voice:

---

[1] The nature of this meeting between the American officers and the Cuban general was revealed by Young in testimony before the Commission to Investigate the Conduct of the War.

[2] "He wanted it and I wanted him to have it," Wood afterward wrote. "I had known him from a boy, seen him win promotion from the ranks, and knew that in his hands the advance was as safe as in the hands of any man living."

Wheeler had decided to make a reconnaissance in force, going in front of Lawton's infantry. They would start at sunrise. Young would take four troops of the 1st Cavalry and four of the 10th —423 men—and follow the longer but more easily traveled wagon trail that led through the valley, while the 500-odd Riders would take the shorter but more difficult path over the hill to the left, never more than a mile and a half distant from the other. This they would follow until it came together with the valley route where it went over a spur of the mountain chain before turning downhill toward Santiago. At this juncture, the enemy was expected to be met. When contact was made, the regulars under Young would make a feint in front, while the volunteers under Wood would strike them in the flank.

Quiet settled over the Rough Rider camp as the hours went into the early morning and the noise down on the beach continued. It was unknown to that part of the regiment at Siboney that typhoid fever during the afternoon had taken the life of a B Trooper, Leroy E. Tomlinson, the house painter from Prescott, who had been taken aboard the hospital ship *Olivette* on the way down from Florida. He would be buried at Daiquirí.

The New York *Herald* that day told the people back home: "The advance troops of General Shafter's army are now skirmishing to the westward of Daiquirí, and it is expected that the entire American force will be in front of Santiago by Sunday." To this bit of news the New York *Press* added: "The Cubans expect the first stand of the enemy to be made at Sevilla, and they have proved good prophets in the past."

Before going to sleep, Trooper Wells made dutiful entry in his diary as he stared down toward the beach. "The scene is a most weird and remarkable one," he wrote. "An army is being landed on an enemy's coast in the dead of night. On either side lies black, overhanging ridges; in the lowlands between are white tents and burning fires, and from the ocean comes the blazing, dashing eyes of the searchlights, shaming the white moonlight."

Chapter 3

LAS GUÁSIMAS

The swing was westward toward Santiago. It would be by way of the San Juan ridges, the strategical key to the city's defenses. But closer at hand and of more importance at the moment was Las Guásimas, on the second of the land rises. It was a deserted village named for a tree prevalent in the neighborhood, a tree with low, wide-spreading branches, bearer of nuts used for hog feed. Once a fairly busy community, it had deteriorated into a Godforsaken spot more specifically identified as the junction of the wagon trail and the footpath along which Young's troops and the Rough Riders were to move. But desolate or not, the spotlight of history was on it now, for at that point were supposed to be waiting the Spaniards the insurgents had encountered the day before.

At Siboney, in the pre-dawn of June 24, the air about the cavalry camps was one of smugness and triumph. Most everyone —at least on the cavalry side of town—knew that foxy old Joe Wheeler was going to pull a fast one on the infantry. Those old enough to remember recognized the logic of the situation: "Fightin' Joe" was unable to resist the ants in his pants and was aching to go. After all, foot soldiers had never scouted in advance of his cavalry in that earlier war to which he belonged. Joe was a marvel. Past three score and still pushing his horsemen, now reduced to footmen! He was doing so this time side by side with the Yankees instead of against them.

Men were shaken out of their blankets at 3 A.M. Hastily they bolted down at least a smattering of hardtack and bacon. Ahead was what they had every reason to believe would be a day of excitement. Most of them had slept in wet clothes and were actually shivering when aroused, so it was not difficult to get them on their feet. One of the most impatient to take the trail was Telden W. (Buck) Dawson of Indian Territory, chief herder in the regiment's pack train. His physical makeup was extraordinary. Only five and half feet tall, he was of ruddy complexion, with black hair and brown eyes, flexing the muscles of a brickmaker, but a master with animals. He would be free to fight until such time as the bulk of the mules arrived from Tampa. Then he would have to go back to herding.

Somehow or other, activities connected with this early morning start toward the enemy appeared to be a bit awkward. Everyone was willing and eager, but there was general confusion of organization and assembly. Nearly three hours seemed a long time to be just getting ready, and yet that was what it took. Perhaps this was because things were new to most of the men, especially the volunteers, for they had had virtually no training in the field. Officers with military experience were patient, expecting the troopers to do better when they had had more practice.

It was a quarter to 6 o'clock before Young's column, with two Hotchkiss mountain guns, started moving out along the valley road. By then, it was evident the day would be hot. Not a cloud could be seen.

The road Young's men would travel had been there half a century. At one period in its history, it had been in such excellent condition it was given the name of Camino Real (Royal Road). But political turmoil had not been to its advantage, and now it was suitable only for the passage of horses and cattle and two-wheel carts. Farther along, where the ground leveled off, however, it got better and was more convenient for troop movement.

The valley up which it ran as it came out of Siboney was marshy, spotted with stagnant pools and lagoons, and lined with sparse clumps of coconut trees and royal palms. Heading up into the mountains of the Cobre range, its atmosphere seemed hot and close, marked by a foul, rank odor of decaying vegetation suggestive of various forms of fever. About two miles farther along, the trail turned to the left and ran up over a series of densely wooded ridges or foothills leading to the crest of the watershed beyond Sevilla, a village a short distance beyond Las Guásimas.

Fifteen minutes after Young moved away, the Rough Riders set out in column of fours. With the exception of two blue-clad aides from the staffs of Wheeler and Young, every man was dressed in the drab, brownish fatigue uniform, soon to be soaking wet with perspiration. They went along the winding path to the left, up the steep hillside, their feet leaving numerous tracks in the soil still damp from the rain the night before.[1]

Before they passed out of sight of Siboney, they were forced to narrow down to single file. Frequently as they struggled along they looked back at the village, at the little scattering of huts and at the confusion out in the water along the beach. They were excited, so much so that they paid little attention to the leg soreness caused by the march the day before. Not a cowboy or college athlete in the lot would willingly have surrendered his place, even for dozens of horses or worldwide fame. Somewhat pityingly but gloatingly they thought of the infantry under Lawton they were leaving behind, and they jollied and snickered to themselves with the lightheartedness of schoolboys. Some of them had heard Wood say they would smell powder before the day ended. But that seemed to bother them not at all. They trudged on, a valiant crew, some with the fresh, uncertain look of youth, others with the suntanned, steely jawed countenances attuned to the danger-laden paths of the wilderness.

Wood had carefully arranged the line of march. Two Cubans familiar with the countryside walked 250 yards in advance, followed by a point of five men, one of them Ham Fish, and some yards farther back by a support of twenty. Next came L Troop under Capron, all its members strung out Indian file. A few yards farther back moved Wood and his aides.

With the colonel also were two correspondents, Edward Marshall and Richard Harding Davis. Marshall was conspicuous in a white coat. Davis, acting his role, was in full regalia, including felt hat with white puggree, high, white composition collar, blue coat, trousers tucked into field boots, and field glasses slung over his shoulder, a handsome fellow favoring one leg because of an attack of sciatica. Someone later would comment that the gods had favored these two journalists. Here they were accompanying the Rough Riders, an outfit that amounted to a society page,

---

[1] In a letter written to a friend two days later, Richard Harding Davis told of still another trail, one not mentioned by the Cubans, that would have taken them more directly to the rear of the Spanish position. Had they followed this route, he said, "General Young would have caught them [the Spaniards] where they expected him, and we would have caught them where they were not looking for us."

a financial column, a sports section, and a Wild West show, all
rolled into one.

The men who made up the little group around the colonel
were the only ones mounted, on horse or mule. Stepping along a
few yards back was Roosevelt, at the head of the 1st Squadron,
"Texas" at his side. Brodie and the 2nd Squadron were next.

At the top of the rise, which they reached in twenty minutes,
they came upon a detachment of the 22nd Infantry, stationed
there on guard duty since dark the night before. Greetings were
exchanged, and there was a bit of banter, as well as cheering
words and a touch of exciting news: the Spaniards were definitely
at Las Guásimas, for they had been heard during the night
felling trees and strengthening their fortifications.

The path led through dense underbrush, like a footway walled
in barbed wire. The countryside was undulating, with little fields
girdled and squeezed in by thick growths of vines and bushes
and low trees. To the right, in the direction of the valley up
which Young's men were marching, the land dropped off somewhat
sharply. Land crabs scuttled out of sight as the column came
along, and overhead swarms of flies and gnats and beetles
menaced in a manner that kept the troopers slapping and cursing
as they walked along.

The march was rout step and jovial. Little about it indicated that
it would lead into battle. The tropics inspired Roosevelt. As he
and Davis advanced, they conversed in light mood. Trees and
birds, the latter of special interest to Teddy because of his boyhood yearning to become a naturalist, were pointed out to him
and were keenly observed. The cooing of a brush cuckoo caught
and held his attention, and later he learned that the call of this
bird at that very moment was being imitated by the Spaniards
to give signal that the Americans were approaching. Occasionally
they came to glades or rounded hill-shoulders and could look
off and see splendid royal palms, with now and then a tree covered
with a mass of brilliant scarlet flowers that looked like a flat-
topped acacia. But most of the time the trail was bordered by
dense, tangled jungle so thick that it was almost impossible for
a man to force his way through it. This made it impracticable
to put out flankers. Roosevelt commented that it looked like good
deer country. It had been, Davis informed him, before it was
desolated by the Spaniards.

Wood urged the column on at a rapid pace, fearing arrival at

Las Guásimas too late to make an effective flanking attack. Before
they had traveled half of the four miles they would have to go
to reach their destination, the strain of walking at such a fast
clip began to tell upon the men. Blanket rolls and knapsacks
and occasionally a trooper were left behind along the trail.

Once when they halted for a brief rest, they could see through
the jungle growth off to the right a deserted structure that apparently had been a fine hacienda. It was falling apart now, and
a palm tree that had grown up through the floor was lifting
its roof. While they stared, trying to picture the life that once
had been a part of it, Roosevelt happened to drop his eyes and
spy two shovels lying in the grass. He picked them up and fastened them to his saddle.

Over in the valley, Young had moved with steady progress. At
7:30 o'clock, his point, well in advance, discovered the Spaniards.
They lay along a ridge separated by a deep ravine from the hill
path to the left along which the Rough Riders would come. Some
were in pits, some stretched out in the heavy jungle, and some
off along the remains of what had once been a large Cuban
ranch and distillery. There were stone breastworks flanked by
a succession of the peculiar Spanish blockhouses on that part
of the ridge pointing in an obtuse angle toward the spot where
the two trails came together.

The American column drew up along a small creek crossing
the road at that point. An open glade of tall guinea grass extended
for some distance in front. Officers and men acted with precision.
Canteens were ordered filled from the stream. The Hotchkiss guns
were placed in position out of sight in the jungle some 900 yards
back, and squadrons were deployed. Young, astride a mule, watched
the movement with satisfaction, making no effort to hurry it.
Because of the rougher path over which the Riders were moving,
he knew it would take them longer to arrive, so he delayed action
to give them a better chance to get into position. A Cuban
guide was hurried off to find Wood and notify him of the situation.

While Young waited, Wheeler rode up and was informed of the
plan of battle. After listening carefully, he gave his approval and
told the younger officer he had a free hand to fight as he chose.
The New York *World* would comment: "It is felt to be characteristic
of the dash and impetuosity of Wheeler that he should be leading

the advance, and it is taken as answering some of the comments made upon the age of some of the volunteer leaders."

Wood had been urging his column along for more than an hour. The air was already hot and moist. Occasionally he stopped to rest, but never for long. All at once, the advance halted uncertainly, as if awaiting directions: the two Cubans serving as guides had come upon the body of the dead Spaniard. It lay face up, its dull eyes staring at the sky. Clothes were dusty, the face unshaven, the black hair closely cropped. Holes in badly worn shoes bared the bottoms of the victim's feet. A bullet wound in the head and a machete stroke across the neck told of the insurgents' violence.

The entire column came to a halt. According to Castillo's advice the night before, the enemy would not be far away.

As Wood swung out of the saddle, he saw Capron hurrying back along the trail and went to meet him. They talked briefly. Returning, the colonel passed word down the line for the men to fill their magazines and stop talking—the latter a precaution intended primarily to silence the ebullient Roosevelt. Some acted without spirit, among them reporter Davis, for he, like the others, thought it was a false alarm, that the Spaniards had retreated into Santiago.

Where they had halted, the path became narrower and proceeded sharply downward. On the left was a five-strand barbed-wire fence, shutting off fields of high grass broken here and there by growths of tangled trees and chaparral, while on the other side was a thick mass of jungle. As they waited, the men dropped down on the ground to rest, some chewing blades of grass, some fanning themselves with their hats. Davis began taking photographs of the members of L Troop, several of whom asked for and were promised copies. Overhead a number of buzzards circled slowly in the sky, the boundaries of their orbit drawing an imaginary line around the spot beside the trail where lay the dead Spaniard.

Over it all—the trail and the jungle and the long line of sweating men—there was tenseness that contrasted sharply with the light mood in which they had started out from Siboney. A correspondent wrote: "A cicada suddenly struck up its sharp whirring note in one of the trees, and I saw a man who was half kneeling start at the sound as though a hand had been laid on his shoulder."

As if not certain about some particular point, Wood went again to confer with Capron. When he returned a second time, Roosevelt approached and saluted.

"Colonel," he said, "Dr. Lamotte reports that the pace is too fast for the men and that over fifty have fallen out from exhaustion."

Wood whirled on him: "I have no time to bother with sick men now!"

"I merely repeated what the surgeon reported to me," Roosevelt said quietly.

Wood's tone changed: "Well, I have no time for them now. We are in sight of the enemy."

Apparently not in the least embarrassed by the manner in which Wood had flared at him, Roosevelt turned and walked slowly through the masses of men lying about in the grass. He stopped, took off his glasses, and cleaned them with the corner of a bandanna handkerchief. The men looking on marveled at his calmness, for he appeared as cool as if seated at his desk in the Navy Department. Then he spied Marshall, the correspondent, and moved toward him to talk about a luncheon he had had at the Astor House in New York with William Randolph Hearst, publisher of the *Journal*. As he talked, he stood near the barbed-wire fence, the strands of which had been cut and were lying on the ground. Suddenly he reached down and picked up one of them.

"My God!" he exclaimed, holding the wire close to his eyes. "This wire has been cut today."

Marshall got up and looked at it.

"What makes you think so?"

"The end of it is bright. There was enough dew during the night for it to be slightly rusty had it not been cut lately."

At that moment, Surgeon Lamotte, who at his own request had been placed in charge of what was available as a pack train, blundered up on a mule. He was coaxing the animal along in an exasperated voice, his purpose to warn the leaders of the alarming number of men falling aside from exhaustion. Roosevelt jumped at him, cautioning him to be quiet, in the process making more noise than the medico.

Just as Roosevelt moved to silence Lamotte, two guns sounded off to the right, down in the valley. They caused a startling break in the silence that up to then had enveloped Las Guásimas. These, the first shots of the war fired in battle by the 5th Corps, came from Young's one-pounders. Whether so intended or not, they were the signal for the start of action. An answering volley came immediately from the front, from the Spaniards in the bushes along the trenches on the hill. It was an explosion of noise that reverberated through the jungle with a volumn similar to that of a large cannon. Instantly the Riders crouched or lay flat in the grass, staring ahead, trying to see the enemy. It was 8:15 A.M.

Start of the battle could be credited to the inquisitiveness of old Joe. During the time they waited for the Rough Riders to come up, Young's men occasionally spotted through the dense foliage at their front the heads of Spaniards or Cubans, which they could not tell. Wheeler, as curious as any, at last suggested that shots be fired from the Hotchkiss guns to see what happened. The resounding volley they touched off was the answer.[2]

Immediately the Americans realized that the Spaniards were firing Mauser rifles and using smokeless powder that left no tell-tale trails to show where the bullets were coming from. Not a trace of smoke could be seen. Ever afterward the men who were the targets would remember the sound of that firing and of the bullets as they clipped the bushes and grass in their vicinity. Some described the noise as like the humming of telephone wires, while others remembered it as a sharp and sickening *"whit-whit,"* or an incessant *"z-z-z-z-eu-u-u."* The report of the Spanish rifle, compared to the heavier roar of the Krag-Jorgensen, was more of a short pop. Not until the damage done by the bullets was seen did the noise it made particularly impress or terrify those at whom they were aimed. Tests revealed that the Mauser bullets sank nine inches deeper into yellow pitch pine than did those of the Krag.

On both sides, the firing became heavy, Wheeler remarking that he could recall no hotter action during the Civil War. Sharp above the general uproar sounded the two machine guns employed by the Spanish soldiers on the hill. The Rough Riders' two rapid-firing Colts had not arrived from Siboney, a mule having stampeded and run away with some of their vital parts. The dynamite gun, moving toward the front under the mother-hen direction of Borrowe, also had run into difficulties. It had been landed at Dai-

[2] Wheeler wrote: "I was afraid there was some doubt of their being Spaniards and I examined their line with my glasses for about twenty-five minutes before giving the orders to fire . . . The fire was very different from what I had seen before. Thirty-three years ago we fought at short range. Here we commenced at 700 or 800 yards . . ."

quirí on the 22nd, had been hauled across the mountains toward Siboney on the 23rd, and then had been stopped by the commander of a Massachusetts regiment who felt that troops should be given the right of way over such an infernal machine. After sitting up all night, a part of the time in the rain, Borrowe and his fellow crewmen finally on the morning of the 24th were permitted to proceed. Wheeler was particularly disappointed that this gun was not on hand for the fight at Las Guásimas.

When the firing started, Wood was talking. He finished what he was saying and then began to give orders. Those who watched The sobriquet of "Icebox" would be added to his record before him this day saw why he had been awarded the Medal of Honor. the action ended.[3]

Already Wood's plan of battle was mapped out in his mind. He would extend his right wing until it connected with Young and, at the same time, send his left wing around to flank the enemy, the strategy talked over the night before. Accordingly, Roosevelt was directed to deploy three troops to the right of the trail and Brodie to move out with his men on the left. Up front, Capron had spread L Troop with the promptness of an experienced Indian fighter, stationing its members about ten yards apart. All had been told not to shoot unless they saw something at which to shoot.

Orders went down the line. A quick footfall at the point where the man had been startled by the cicada, and Adjutant Tom Hall strode past. He stopped briefly to speak to Captain O'Neill. The latter at once hurried forward, returning in a few moments and giving the command: "Column right, march!" The troop swung off behind another that was moving in that direction. Within three minutes, Roosevelt had G Troop under the giant Llewellyn and one platoon of K Troop under Kane in position along the firing line. To move through the almost impenetrable growth was an undertaking. Men cut their way with knives and sabers. Occasionally they met wire entanglements and became more deeply involved. Briefly, Llewellyn and Roosevelt huddled in the grass, talking over strategy and making sure they understood what was to be done.

Young's troopers were putting up a brisk fight off on the right,

[3] Of this battle, Jess Langdon wrote the author: "At no time during combat did I see Teddy Roosevelt or Wood in a prone position. Both of these officers stood up at all times to observe the deployment of troops and the enemy through binoculars."

making desperate effort to keep the enemy occupied until Wood could strike the flank. The trees and jungle and even the air around the Riders seemed filled with the rustling sound of the Mauser bullets. The Spaniards were familiar with the location of the trail along which Wood was advancing, but their aim was high. Roosevelt concluded they were not very good shots.

Up in the advance of the Riders, the point spread out. The two Cuban guides had disappeared at the first shot, and now Tom Isbell, Cherokee from Indian Territory, was in front. Capron had moved up and was walking next, in the center of the trail. On the left flank was Ed Culver, the half-breed Cherokee, and, on the right, cowboy Bud Parnell of Indian Territory. Spaced out behind were J. W. Shelton of Texas, Tom Meagher, twenty-year-old Irish student, also from the Territory, and W. J. Breen, the New York policeman.

Isbell saw a Spaniard through the brush and killed him. It was like setting off guns rigged as a trap, for a fusillade of bullets poured down upon him. He was wounded seven times—thrice in the neck, twice in the left hand, once in the right hip, and once in the head. The head wound was what induced him to go to the rear.

Private Culver dropped behind a rock near the trail. Ham Fish crawled up beside him. Some foreboding talk had taken place between them at breakfast. They had only two items of food —hardtack and canned tomatoes. While Culver was frying the hardtack to give it a little taste, some of the members of Fish's squad asked for more tomatoes.

"How many tomatoes do we have?" Fish asked.

"Several cans," Culver told him.

"Open some more," directed the sergeant. "We're all liable to be killed today, so we may as well eat as much as we can while we're still alive."

As they later headed out of the village, Fish had an extra pair of shoes tied around his neck, a pair he said had cost him seven dollars. When perspiration began flowing farther on, he suddenly jerked them free and threw them into the bushes.

"They may come in handy," cautioned Culver.

"No, I don't think I'll need them any more," Fish said. The half-breed thought he noticed a touch of sadness in his companion's tone.

When Fish took position beside Culver, he asked: "Got a good place?"

"Yeh," grunted the Indian. He was lying head onto a slight bank, his body stretched across the trail.

Fish fired four or five shots and then gasped: "I'm shot! I'm badly wounded!"

"So am I!" said Culver.

"That bullet hit both of us," Fish mumbled. It had gone in his left side, emerged on the right, and struck Culver just above the heart.

Fish raised up on one elbow. "Give me your canteen."

Culver handed it to him and fainted from the exertion. When he came to seconds later, Fish was smiling faintly. "You all right?" he said to the Indian.

"Sergeant, are you hit hard?" asked the half-breed.

There was no answer. Fish sank to the ground, the smile gone from his face. Culver reached over and took off his hat. The sergeant was dead.

Stunned, Culver stared for seconds. Then he got up, crouching low, a hand to his chest, and crept to the road, blood spreading rapidly across the front of his uniform.

Private Schuyler Whitney of L Troop, twenty-nine-year-old stonemason from Indian Territory, was shot while loading his gun. The bullet struck the magazine of the rifle, and parts of it ricocheted into his scalp, ear, and neck. He was soaking in blood as he crept rearward, looking much worse hurt than he actually was, for he would be back in action in a matter of days.

The heavy volley firing from the fortifications continued. As the bullets came nearer and nearer, some of the Riders began cursing.

"Don't curse—shoot!" shouted Wood.

Wood's line advanced slowly. It was an inspiration to watch these raw soldiers in their first hostile action. They pushed steadily forward, no matter how hot the fire from the enemy. A section of the line would rise, run forward, drop, and fire. The reports from their guns seemed to be a signal for another section to do the same thing. It was dogged and relentless, this pattern of fighting. There were determined to advance, no matter what lay in their path.

Here and there men could be seen on their knees, bandaging their own wounds or those of comrades. Now for the first time they were getting an opportunity to realize the value of the little first-aid packets issued them by the government—two gauze compresses, a triangular bandage, a handkerchief sling, two safety pins, and a bottle of aromatic spirits of ammonia, all encased in rubber sheeting.

O'Neill's troop was far to the right, trying to make connections with Young, but having extreme difficulty because of the jungle. With it was the remainder of K Troop, fighting under Micah J. Jenkins of Young's Island, South Carolina, a West Point graduate and son of a Confederate general killed in the Battle of the Wilderness. A veteran of ten years' service with the 4th Cavalry, this young man was an enigma. Around camp, he was gentle, soft-spoken, and courteous. But in battle he was a demon. Roosevelt said danger acted like wine on him.

Off on the left, the troopers under Brodie charged across an open glade. On the far side, they captured an old distillery, from behind which the Spaniards had been firing, and drove them back up on the ridge where the main fortifications extended. Cowboys and athletes fought side by side in silence. They kept their heads down and crouched or lay flat and fired, or rose and pushed forward with that grim intentness that marked the entire line. It was easy to pick out the veterans who had served in Indian campaigns under Custer or Crook or Miles; also Cassi, the trumpeter, who had fought with the Chasseurs d'Afrique; or Charley McGarr of Prescott, who had had a stretch of twenty-eight years in the Army. Somehow or other there seemed to be a deliberate coolness about these men, demonstrating clearly that experience had driven away their fear of battle. Rarely did a yell sound above the shooting. Grass was so tall a man lying in it could not be seen by anyone on the same level.

Marshall of the *Journal*, standing in white coat, looked on at close range. He had been thrown from a horse before leaving Tampa and his elbow sprained, so it was necessary for him to place his notebook against a tree in order to write. Looking along the battle line, he could tell where the Riders were by the indentations they made in the grass. He saw Richard Harding Davis off to the right, shooting with a rifle taken from a wounded man. Correspondents were supposed to be non-combatants, to take no part in battle action, but Davis for the moment seemed to be lost in what he was doing. Marshall realized he had smokeless powder cartridges in his own revolver. They had been given him by Sir Bryan Leighton of the British Army at Tampa. He took out the gun and began firing—"cheerfully," he later wrote.

The part of the line under Roosevelt pushed forward until it came out on a shoulder jutting over the ravine that separated them from the ridge on which lay the Spaniards. Beyond that ridge the regulars under Young were pushing their attack. Llewellyn, Kane, John Greenway, Yale football and baseball star, and Roosevelt stared through the jungle, trying to see some evidence of the whereabouts of the enemy so their fire could be delivered with more effect, but the smokeless powder baffled them. Suddenly a voice spoke from behind them.

"There they are, Colonel! Look over there! I can see their hats near that glade."

They turned to see Davis staring through glasses and pointing across the ravine.[4] Following his directions, Roosevelt spied the hats and called them to the attention of the three or four best marksmen lying near. They raised their carbines and fired. At first there was no indication of results, but as the shots from the Riders continued, the Spaniards suddenly sprang up out of the undergrowth and ran to another spot.

Roosevelt brought more men up to that point and directed them to quick-fire. The Spaniards retreated farther to the left and disappeared from sight. At that moment, another body of the enemy came into view along the ravine, following the retreat of those who had just been driven from cover. No one could tell whether they were Cubans or Spaniards and, as it was supposed a large number of Cubans were with Young, no fire was directed at them.

Over in the valley, Captain William D. Beach, chief engineer of the Cavalry Division, stood near Wheeler. Finally he said: "General, we have nine big regiments of infantry only a few miles back. Let me send to General Lawton for one of them and close this action up."

---

[4] Dispensing with modesty, Davis included an account of this incident in his report of the battle forwarded to the New York *Herald*, writing: "At the conclusion of the fight, Colonel Roosevelt expressed his thanks to Richard Harding Davis, the *Herald*'s correspondent, for his services rendered to the troops during the engagement.

"While the bullets flew over the heads of the American skirmishers in the thickets, who were unable to see the enemy, Mr. Davis discovered some Spanish soldiers on a hilltop close by, and called Lieutenant Colonel Roosevelt's attention to them. At the latter's orders, they were dispersed by fire. Mr. Davis followed the skirmishers into the bush and was with Lieutenant Colonel Roosevelt during the heaviest firing."

The old general hesitated, studying the fighting going on within his view, but finally nodded and said, "All right."

Beach called a mounted orderly, hurriedly wrote out the following message, and directed that it be delivered to General Lawton:

> June 24, 8:30 a.m.
>
> General Wheeler directs me to say that he is engaged with a bigger force of the enemy than was anticipated and directs that any forces you may have be sent forward on the Sevilla road as soon as possible.
>
> W. D. BEACH,
> Captain, 3rd Cavalry.

As the battle raged, Davis made his way back to the trail to see what was happening along the center of the line. When he reached it, he found it looked like a retreating army had fled along it. The grass was splattered with blood and dotted about were blanket rolls, haversacks, and canteens. He hurried down it toward the front, loose stones rattling under his feet. Suddenly a hospital steward, marked by an arm band, appeared out of the jungle and called to him.

"Lieutenant Thomas is badly wounded in here, and we can't move him! We want to carry him out of the sun to some place where there is shade and a breeze."

The correspondent turned back and followed the steward. A few yards into the jungle they came upon the judge's son, a large, powerfully built man. He had been shot through the leg just below the hip. The wound was bound with tourniquets made of handkerchiefs and sticks.

Davis caught up a corner of the blanket on which the wounded trooper lay.

"You're taking me to the front, aren't you?" cried Thomas. "You said you would. They've killed my captain! Do you understand? The goddamned Mexicans. They've killed my captain!"

He soon fainted, and the men lowered him to the ground and poured water over his face. Davis left them kneeling over him and made his way back to the trail. Fifty feet farther along, he passed Thomas's captain, Allyn Capron, lying with his head on the knee of Surgeon Church. Capron had been wounded while firing madly near the body of Ham Fish, having killed two Spaniards just before he was shot himself. "Don't mind me, boys, go on and fight," he said as other Riders gathered around him. The bullet had entered his left shoulder as he lay prone and had passed down through his stomach.

Rounding a turn in the trail, Davis came upon a trooper lying behind a rock. He was young, with ruddy complexion and black hair. A bullet had struck him between the eyes, but his chest was still heaving with short, hoarse noises. The correspondent lifted his head and tried to give him some water, but it would not pass through his clenched teeth. In the pocket of his blouse, Davis found a New Testament. The name scribbled inside in pencil was Telden Dawson.[5]

A hundred yards farther on, the correspondent came upon the body of a huge sergeant lying across the trail. He recognized it as that of Ham Fish. Stopping, he felt in the dead man's pocket and took out a fine, expensive watch. On the back of it were engraved the words: "God gives." Davis realized he was at the spot where the point first had encountered the enemy.

The shooting from the ridge where the machine guns were located became hotter as volley after volley was delivered by the Spaniards. Roosevelt, pushing his men forward, took cover behind a palm tree. Just as he stuck his head out—"very fortunately," he later observed—to look around it, a bullet passed through the tree, filling his left eye and ear with bark and splinters.

Only a few yards away, Henry J. Haefner of G Troop went down, mortally wounded by a bullet through the hips. He fell without uttering a sound, and the two men closest to him dragged him behind a tree. There he pulled himself up to a sitting position and asked for his carbine and canteen, which Teddy handed him. He then resumed firing. The line pushed on, for orders had been issued for no man to drop out of action to help the wounded. There his body would be found after the battle ended.

A little later, Roosevelt realized he had lost touch with the part of his wing under O'Neill and Jenkins. He singled out three men— Lieutenant Greenway, the Yale athlete; Marcus Russell, New York millionaire; and George Roland, New Mexican cowpuncher—and directed them to go off to the right and see if they could establish contact.

Soon troops began appearing across the ravine, not far from where had been seen the men who could not be identified as either

---

[5] In writing of this incident, Davis misread or mistakenly remembered Dawson's first name as "Fielder."

Cubans or Spaniards. Roosevelt suspected they were some of the missing part of his own wing and, for fear they did not recognize him and those around him, directed Joseph Jenkins Lee of K Troop, a New York clubman and socialite, to climb a tree and wave a guidon. This was done, under great danger, and brought an answering signal.

As he now knew his far right was in position, Roosevelt decided to leave O'Neill and Jenkins to maintain contact with the regulars while he himself led Llewellyn's troop back to the trail to join the rest of the regiment, which he suspected was in the thick of the fight. In his own case, he was not sure just what he should do. He was still uncertain as to the location of the main body of the enemy and exactly what lines the battle was following, but he knew he would not be wrong in going forward. He hoped to find Wood and get more specific directions.

Just before he moved off, Greenway and Roland returned. Saluting, they reported that they had made contact with the troops on the far right as ordered, but that they had run into unexpected opposition, with the result that Russell had been shot down and killed. The gory detail of the New Yorker's death came later in a report Harmon Wynkoop of E Troop dutifully forwarded to his home-town newspaper, the Santa Fe *New Mexican*. In telling of the Spanish bullets, which some of the Americans thought were explosive, he wrote: "One of them struck Russell in the head and exploded inside. The result was awful, blowing a very large hole in his head. The cowardly devils!"

Greenway and Roland resumed their positions on the firing line. As Roland knelt and pushed into the grass, Roosevelt noticed bloodstains on the side of his uniform and, approaching, inquired as to the cause. The cowpuncher shrugged him off, saying the wound was slight. But the lieutenant colonel insisted on examining it more closely and found the bullet had gone in through the lower ribs, breaking one of them. He directed the trooper to go to the hospital in the rear. Roland got up, grumbling, and moved away.

A few minutes later, Roosevelt noticed Roland again in the line, down on his belly in the grass, rapidly loading and firing. If Teddy had had hackles, they would have stood straight out. In a voice that carried above the din of battle, he ordered Roland to the rear—to stay!

Then Roosevelt started back to the trail with G Troop, moving ahead of it. He had no trouble finding his way. Later, he passed the body of Fish and stopped momentarily to study it.

When he reached the front, Roosevelt found the men spread out in a thin line, advancing over fairly open ground, each man taking advantage of what cover he could find, while Wood strode about leading his horse. The colonel seemed taller than ever, browned to a burn, with even his sandy mustache grizzled by the sun. All who saw him marveled that he was not hit by a bullet. Brodie was only a few yards away, standing as much in the open as the colonel.

But none was reported to be more conspicuous for bravery than Surgeon Church, a tall, powerful man. Sleeves rolled up and his arms crimson with blood, he seemed to move all over the battlefield, sometimes carrying off the fallen on his back or in his arms. Spying a wounded man in the line of fire, he hurried to his side, dressed the wound and, walking unceremoniously back, soon returned with two troopers and a litter.

Roosevelt had left his horse back on the trail when the shooting started. He wished he had left his sword, for it kept getting between his legs.

Suddenly a number of Spaniards burst out of a clump of bushes some distance ahead and ran in panic toward the rear. Riders turned their guns on them and opened a hot fire.

Wood screamed: "Don't shoot at retreating men!"

A few minutes after Roosevelt arrived, Brodie was struck, the bullet shattering one arm and whirling him around. The veteran Indian fighter refused at first to go to the rear, but, growing faint, at last consented and stumbled away, the blood dripping freely from his sleeve.

With Brodie disabled, Wood directed Roosevelt to take charge of the left wing and bring it forward. The lieutenant colonel jumped at the chance. Captains commanding troops in that part of the line were Luna, Muller, and Huston, all good officers. He led them forward, through the high grass of a fairly open forest. A hail of bullets seemed to be sweeping over them as they advanced. They saw a number of Spaniards, far in front, apparently retreating, and aimed their fire at them, watching some of them fall. Wood was not close enough to see what they were doing.

Kennett Harris, correspondent of the Chicago *Record*, was an eyewitness to this part of the fight. His eyes fell on Captain Luna.

"The face of the brave little descendant of the Mexican conquistadores," he remembered, "was positively beaming. Lieutenant Colonel Roosevelt, who was near him, shouted some remark that I could not hear, and they both laughed. I was rather disgusted with their levity. I could not imagine anything funny enough to make me laugh."

Moving from one point to another, reporter Marshall came upon a trooper seated alone in the bushes and thought he had found a coward. But the man had an excuse. He held up a foot, encased in one of the army issue shoes that got stiff and fell apart when wet. It had no sole, and he explained he was unable to get about because of the thorns. The correspondent disappeared in the direction from which he had come and soon returned with a shoe. He had taken it off the foot of the dead Trooper Russell.

Shortly afterward, Marshall was struck by a bullet that penetrated near the spine. He fell in the tall grass, where he lay until three soldiers came upon him and carried him to the shade on half a shelter tent. A little later, Wood approached and gave him a merciful sip from a small flask of Scotch whiskey.

When Marshall went down, Adjutant Tom Hall got only a glimpse of a falling body, in a spot where only a short time before he remembered seeing Wood standing. In great confusion, he leaped to what seemed a logical conclusion: the colonel had been killed. This caused him to panic. Madly he dashed away, toward Siboney, shouting incoherently in a loud voice.[6]

As Roosevelt, leading the left wing, studied the enemy layout in front, he became convinced that much of the fire aimed at them was coming from some red-tiled buildings, remains of the old ranch. He took a rifle from a wounded man and began firing. At that moment he spied three empty cartridges near the body of a dead Spaniard, grabbed them up and dropped them into his pocket, intending them for his children.

It was hot and some of the Riders were becoming exhausted. As they plunged deeper into the undergrowth, Roosevelt realized he again had lost touch with the main body under Wood. He called a halt, directing that the fire be aimed at the red-tiled buildings, still some 500 yards off. Then he heard cheering on the right

---

[6] Hall was a West Point graduate and had served until 1889 in the Cavalry. Since then, he had devoted his time to writing. The manuscript of a novel was completed just before he joined the Rough Riders. At San Antonio, when he had the duties of quartermaster before he was made adjutant, he was disliked by other members of the regiment, who accused him of paying too much attention to irritating non-essentials. They predicted he would run away the first time he faced hostile action.

and supposed this meant Wood was leading a charge, so he sprang up and ordered the left wing to storm the buildings. A volley came from the Spaniards, most of it passing over the heads of the Americans, and then the firing ceased altogether. The Rough Riders rushed on ahead and stormed breathlessly into the structures, finding only heaps of empty cartridges and two enemy dead, shot through the head.

Roosevelt was uncertain exactly what had caused the firing to stop and decided to wait for developments. Just at that moment, one of the Riders who had become exhausted farther back and fallen out of line came up and announced that Wood was dead. The information he was relaying had come from the panicked Hall.

During the fighting, Roosevelt had been particularly impressed with the coolness and courage of Sergeants William E. Dame of F Troop, a forty-year-old, blue-eyed miner from New Mexico, and John A. McIlhenny of E Troop, New Orleans planter, manufacturer, big-game hunter and book-lover, with an island all his own. In consequence, Teddy now ordered them to go with small pickets to keep watch in front and on the wing. Other men were sent to fill canteens and the remainder were spread out in a long line in a disused sunken road. The wounded and those suffering from heat exhaustion were taken into the buildings.

When everything had been arranged to his satisfaction, Roosevelt started in the direction of the main body. Along the way, he was surprised and pleased to meet Wood, who told him the fight was over, that the Spaniards had fled. The final break came when the right wing under O'Neill and Jenkins pushed forward and dislodged the Spaniards from the ridge across the ravine and were joined there by the regulars from the other side.

Wood advanced his men to the last position occupied by the Spanish and there stopped. Later, well after the shooting had ended, a number of Cubans came up and made a short reconnaissance beyond that point, reporting on their return that the enemy had fled into Santiago. Along the trail they found much blood and a great quantity of abandoned equipment.

Meanwhile, over on the valley side, Young's men were still laughing over an incident that occurred just as the battle was ending. Seeing the Spaniards retreating, "Fightin' Joe" sprang forward and shouted, "Come on, boys, we got the damn' Yankees on the run!" Even he, when told what he had said, joined in the laughter.

Engineer Beach looked at his watch as the firing died out. It had been an hour and five minutes since the first shot was fired.

Shortly after the fighting was over, three troops from the 9th U. S. Cavalry, the experienced black Indian campaigners, arrived on the left of the line. Wood put them on outpost duty about 800 yards beyond the Riders. Reporter Harris described these men:

> The chagrin of the brawny colored troopers when they found that the engagement was over was almost pathetic. They had come up over the trail on the double-quick, their dark faces aglow with eager excitement and their broad chests heaving with the exertion of the run. The last time I had seen them was some six years ago. Then they were pounding along the pine-fringed old Custer road in the Black Hills, against a flurry of snow that powdered their blue uniforms until it was a matter of some conjecture where their gray horses ended and they began.

After watching the 9th Cavalry form outposts, Harris moved to the hospital which had been placed on the brow of a hill when the fight started. There he watched Dr. Church dress the shattered leg of a man who ground his teeth and cursed in a constant stream. Finally he broke off and apologized to the surgeon for his language, but Church laughingly assured him that he could curse as much as he wanted so long as he did not set the grass afire.

Dr. Lamotte was bending over a man stripped to the waist and lying in the shade of a tree, his head pillowed on a folded coat. Harris looked more closely at the wounded man and recognized Captain Capron. He knelt and took hold of one of the stricken man's hands. It was cold and nerveless. He looked at Lamotte.

"He is dying fast," the surgeon whispered.

Nearby, leaning against a rock, was Major Brodie. His arm had been bandaged and hung in a sling. While puffing away on a corncob pipe and sending forth little puffs of smoke, he was restless and impatient and complained frequently because he had not been able to get back into the fight.

Reporter Stephen Crane had come to the battle scene with Young's column. When the shooting ended, he crossed over to where the Riders had been fighting. Along the way he met a soldier who recognized him and announced that "there's a correspondent up there all shot to hell."

Crane asked him to go back and show him the wounded man.

The soldier complied and guided him through the jungle to the point where Marshall lay.

"Hello, Crane," Marshall muttered as the other reporter bent over him.

"Hello, Marshall. In hard luck, old man?"

"Yes, I'm done for."

"Nonsense! You'll be all right, old boy. What can I do for you?"

"Well, you might file my dispatches. I don't mean file 'em ahead of your own, old man—but just file 'em if you find it handy."

Crane was convinced Marshall was doomed. "No man could be so sublime in detail concerning the trade of journalism and not die," he later commented. So he knelt and began taking notes while his fellow newsman talked between convulsions of pain.

In the afternoon, when Crane walked back to Siboney to file the dispatches, he learned of the mischief Adjutant Hall's panic had created. Officers of the regular units were denouncing Wood and Roosevelt for their rashness in taking the Rough Riders into battle so precipitately. Hall had told them the volunteers were ambushed and most of them slain. He said Wood had been mortally wounded and that he had knelt beside the colonel and taken down his dying message to his wife. This was enough confirmation for the reporters who heard him, and they began filing their dispatches.

Still later, Marshall was brought into the village on a stretcher. As he was borne in, he lay smoking a cigarette and singing "On the Banks of the Wabash Far Away."

Back at Las Guásimas, Wood ordered the Riders to go into camp. Soon fires were burning, and over them were hung or set kettles and pans of beans, an item of food found in bags near the body of a dead Spanish mule. While some men cooked, others were sent to search the jungle for additional dead and wounded, and still others were put to work digging a long, wide trench on the side of the trail.

Among the bodies brought in was one from A Troop. The vultures already had found it. As Roosevelt and O'Neill stared at it, the latter turned and asked: "Colonel, isn't it Whitman who said of the vultures that 'they pluck the eyes of princes and tear the flesh of kings'?" Teddy replied that he could not for the moment place the quotation, but later, upon reflection, concluded that the reference was to the words of the prophet Ezekiel: "Speak unto every feathered fowl . . . ye shall eat the flesh of the mighty and drink the blood of the princes of the earth."

16. A part of the regiment is photographed as it rides along a Texas road. Roosevelt, in light uniform, is shown at the right front.

17. Teddy, seated on horseback between two of his men at the San Jose Mission, one of the terminals of their frequent rides at San Antonio.

18. Roosevelt and Major Dunn confer with reporters Stephen Bonsall (left) and Richard Harding Davis during the training period at San Antonio.

19. Roosevelt and some of the Rough Riders gather around their mascots—"Teddy," the eagle, "Cuba," the dog, and "Josephine," the mountain lion.

20. The 1st Volunteer Cavalry, with Wood (left) and Roosevelt in front, pose for a photographer near the end of the San Antonio training period.

21. Rough Riders gathered behind the two Colt automatic rifles presented by some of the members of the regiment while they were in camp at San Antonio.

22. Lieutenant John C. Greenway, one of the most popular men in the regiment.

23. Rough Rider William Pollock, son of a Pawnee Indian chief.

24. A buggy approaches the gateway of the Tampa Bay Hotel, Henry Plant's monstrosity of Moorish architecture to which the Rough Riders went for periods of relaxation.

25. Soldiers and citizens loitering on the porch of the Tampa Bay Hotel during the period the Rough Riders were waiting at Tampa for orders to embark.

26. Transports gathered in Tampa Bay to transport 5th Corps troops for the invasion of Cuba.

27. The scene at Port Tampa as the Rough Riders boarded the *Yucatan* for the trip to Cuba.

28. General William R. Shafter, commander of the 5th Corps in the Cuban campaign.

29. General Calixto Garcia, the bullet scar in his forehead plainly visible, stands with some of his officers beside the thatched hut in which he conferred with the Americans.

30. A boatload of Rough Riders starts away from the *Yucatan* toward the landing at Daiquirí while another behind it prepares to load.

31. The dock at Daiquirí where the two members of the 10th Cavalry were crushed to death during the landing.

The period following battle is one of the most fleeting in man's experience. At such time, the mind seems to be in a state of insouciance, as if stunned by the nervous strain and tension which grip like paralysis while the action is in progress. Behavior for the moment is strange and not always polite or proper, and exultant relief at having escaped death or maiming temporarily sidetracks grief over losses. The requiem is completely forgotten in a spirit of rejoicing over still being alive. But this characteristic of human nature apparently was not understood by photographer Burr McIntosh as he stood with his camera in the camp of the Rough Riders.

The dead lay in a row under canvas. There were eight. Besides Capron, Fish, Dawson, Haefner, and Russell, they included Louis (Doc) Doherty, carpenter and telephone operator, who had joined at Santa Fe and who had thrice fallen out with sunstroke before he was killed, a violently sick man; Edward Liggett, teamster from Jerome, Arizona, and William T. Irvine of Albuquerque.

McIntosh lifted the covering over the face of Ham Fish and took a picture of the body. Then he heard laughter, and the sound seemed at the moment to imply so much disrespect that he made a photograph of the group of men, standing only fifteen feet away, from which it had come.

"The photographs were taken with a heart filled with resentful bitterness," McIntosh confided.

Late in the day, a message came to Wheeler. It read:

> The Commanding General directs me to say he is glad to hear such good news, that you are occupying the enemy's ground. A battery will be sent to you as soon as it can be unloaded; horses are all off. Will also send you some saddle-horses from artillery. The mounted cavalry will be dispatched as fast as possible. Rations will be in Juragua-city tonight, and we will have pack-trains out for you during night—one for each division.

Less than a third of Shafter's army was at Las Guásimas by the night of the 24th—only a fragment of the cavalry division and a part of Lawton's division. Bates's Independent Brigade was at Siboney, all of Sumner's 1st Brigade at Daiquirí; Kent's division was at Siboney, or still on the transports; the artillery had not passed beyond Siboney, and the only mounted American troops in

Cuba still had not been sent to the front. García's men had arrived at Siboney, but were still on the ships.

Young busily prepared a report of the battle. In it he stated: "Both Colonel Wood and Lieutenant Colonel Roosevelt disdained to take advantage of shelter or cover from the enemy's fire while any of their men remained exposed to it—an error of judgment, but happily on the heroic side."

Night came on, with a clear sky, a quarter-moon, and an enveloping host of stars. Troop movements as the Americans drew their forces together would go on unbroken. Beside the trail, the artist, Frederic Remington, decided to make camp. "At night," he wrote, "I lay beside the road outside of Siboney and cooked my supper by a soldier fire, and lay down under a mango tree on my rubber, with my haversack for a pillow. I could hear the shuffling of the marching troops, and see by the light of the fire near the road the white blanket rolls glint past its flame—tired, sweaty men, mysterious, and silent, too, but for the clank of the tin cups and the monotonous shuffle of feet."

The Rough Riders went to bed early. They had had their first day of fighting and were proud of it. In the reports back home, they would be given a lion's share of the credit for the victory, and the regulars who fought under Young would be only casually mentioned. The New York *World* had this comment:

> When the historian writes of the Spanish-American War, the 1st United States Volunteer Cavalry will furnish a fruitful and conspicuous topic for his pen. No regiment in the world's wars has been quite the equal of it in address or composition. Diverse to the borderlands of the ridiculous, with its mixture of society darlings and Western bad men, it presents a splendid homogeneity in the chief requisites of the soldier—courage to the limit, a knowledge of weapons and horses, a daredevil hunger for danger and, above all, a mighty notion that the genuine American can lick anything on the face of the earth.

In Santiago that night, the Spanish soldiers were still talking about the men they had met on the battlefield that day, men who fired and advanced instead of firing and falling back, the standard procedure under Spanish and Cuban military rules. "They tried to catch us with their hands," was said over and over.[7]

---

[7] Shafter wrote Miles: "Reports from Spanish sources from Santiago say we were beaten, but persisted in fighting, and they were obliged to fall back."

Chapter 4

THE RAINS COME

Dawn of June 25 opened on enveloping mists and cool air, a sort of repetition of the preceding morning, but the rising sun soon changed things into a tropical oven. The night had not been restful. All movement from the coast, some of it frantic and to a degree desperate and disorganized, was in the direction of the more perfect camping ground that Wheeler's cavalry had taken away from the Spaniards. There the Americans would concentrate, amassing their forces and getting ready for the big push on Santiago.

In the jungle near where the trails met, a detail of guards moved about slowly. They walked near an oblong, canvas-covered mound. Occasionally they stopped to throw more wood on fires spaced only a few feet apart and forming a divider between the curious heap and the thick undergrowth beyond.

Hour after hour throughout the night these men had taken turns of duty. As they paced, they kept their eyes on the wall of jungle. Out of its recesses now and then poked the hideous fore claws of land crabs. The mailed creatures were a relentless threat. And added to this ground-level menace as the sun rose would be the danger from the raptorial birds soaring tirelessly overhead.

The guards used sticks, gun butts, and even their feet to ward off the crabs. Some—"as big as rabbits," in the estimate of Teddy Roosevelt—lay crushed and battered. Over near a fire and only a few feet from the mound were the remains of a huge fellow that seemed determined to reach its goal. The trooper nearest the resolute invader checked it by using his carbine as a club. To fire a gun would seem disrespectful to the battle victims whose bodies lay beneath the canvas. It also would bring howls of protest from comrades asleep in the low pup tents scattered through the guinea grass nearby. Though quickly put out of action, the crab's long fore claws still stuck out ominously, like a drawn saber in the death-stiffened grasp of a warrior saint. Even after nearly an hour, some of its many legs continued to quiver nervously.

Since dusk the night before, a ghostly rustling had sounded at times from the jungle. It was such a noise as guerrillas or bush-whackers would make in stealing upon a camp. Guards were kept tense and alert. They realized the crabs alone might not be respon-sible for these flesh-crawling sounds. True, the Spaniards had been seen to flee precipitately, but a beaten enemy is known sometimes to be re-nerved by separation from the battle line, and back they might stealthily come. With this in mind, the men on duty listened attentively to the noises. Quite often they were repeated. As if urged on by leaders, the crabs, sensing the presence of the dead, continually scurried through the underbrush, their horny, beak-like mandibles aimed at the circles of fires, bodies tilted sidewise, and awkward claws thrown upward and outward like vicious ra-piers.

By aid of blazing bonfires, the digging of the long trench at the crest of the trail a few yards away had gone on throughout the night. At dawn, the ditch was beginning to take definite shape and was approaching the boundaries marked out for it. Hours of work still remained to be done before it would be completed, but this was no cause for concern. The surviving comrades of the dead Rough Riders under the canvas wanted them to have the best burial that could be provided in the Godforsaken jungle of Las Guásimas.

At 5 A.M., reveille sounded through the hastily arranged camp. Men immediately began to squirm out of their blankets in the hip-high tents. Colonel Wood was too dedicated a soldier to allow battles or burials to interfere with Army routine.

Breakfast was a haphazard affair. Most of the Riders' food had been stolen by the Cubans while the battle was in progress and things were still too disorganized for KP details to go on duty. Over individual campfires men prepared what few rations they had— rancid bacon, hardtack, and coffee without sugar. As soon as they had eaten, squads of them were detailed to go through the jungle in search of additional dead and wounded. They also were told to recover packs and personal items which might have been dropped during the fighting.

Other men, meanwhile, prepared to take the wounded back to Siboney, where they might get better treatment than Lamotte and Church could provide with the limited medical supplies brought from Las Guásimas. Crude litters were improvised from tree branches. Of the thirty-four wounded Riders—nearly twice as many as suffered by the other two regiments combined—all who could not walk were carried laboriously along the trail to the coast. There at Siboney they were left in a temporary hospital hurriedly set up in the railroad shed abandoned by the fleeing Spaniards.[1] They were laid in rows along the floor and identification tags were pinned to their clothing. So crowded did the building become that attendants were unable to move among them without difficulty. By coincidence, in the distance off the coast during the morning appeared the Red Cross ship *State of Texas*. She had on board 1400 tons of food and medical supplies.

Around 11 A.M., the searchers came back from the jungle. They had found a few packs, but reported all the dead they had seen were Spanish. Buzzards and land crabs had got to them first.

Shortly after their return, a bugler sounded the call for burial service. The bodies, wrapped in blankets, were moved from beneath the canvas and placed at the side of the grave, in a shady dell not far from the battlefield. Only seven were there. Through respect for the father, of the same name, on duty in Cuba as a captain of artillery and considered one of the best in the business, Capron's had been taken to Siboney for interment.

The men filed to the graveside. Color Sergeant Wright led the line with the flag at half mast, bullet holes plainly visible in its folds. The Riders maintained military step as best they could, but, somehow or other, there was much about the entire affair that resembled a crowd coming together for a burial at a country churchyard. All of them seemed to move with reluctance. It was a

---

[1] Compared with the eight killed and thirty-four wounded of the 1st Volunteers, the 1st and 10th Regulars fighting under Young lost eight killed and eighteen wounded, making a total of sixty-eight casualties out of 964 men engaged.

Commenting on the part played by the Rough Riders, the New York *Times* said in an editorial: "It is really an amazing showing. Of course it will not do to reckon upon a repetition of that which has no precedent. Though not disciplined soldiers, there were picked men, and their performance shows that in extreme cases men of high individual courage, intelligence, and self-reliance, led by men like themselves, may be as efficient a fighting force as an equal number of men who have been drilled to respond to orders with the precision of a machine."

sad occasion. In battle they may have laughed and joked, but now they stood silent and choking.

A quartet had been organized. It opened the service by singing "Rock of Ages." Other singers joined in, creating a chorus not distinguished for its agreeable sound. Then Chaplain Brown, attired in a gray suit and overalls, stepped forward and halted at the head of the grave. Slowly he began reading the solemn burial service of the Episcopal Church. A hush lay over the jungle as he intoned the words. All was quiet and still around him, but aloft in the skies vultures circled ominously, warning that nature had a way of disposing of the dead if man did not.

When the chaplain had finished, the bodies were placed one beside another in the bottom of the trench. As they were lowered upon a thick lining of guinea grass and palm leaves, their feet to the east, the chaplain called out the name of each. He did so without identifying them as herder, rancher, cowboy, carpenter, or wealthy gentleman. When all were in place, they were covered over with a layer of huge palm leaves.

Notation was made of the location of each body. First on the right was Ham Fish. Of all who died in the war, none would be more widely mourned. It seemed a violation of the laws of society to be burying this husky playboy-athlete, only a few months past twenty-five. Throughout his short life he had loved animals and people. After leaving college, where he was an outstanding athlete, he had roughed it for a while as a railroad brakeman in Utah, but returned home after injuring a finger while coupling cars. When he heard of the Rough Riders, he quickly joined. Members of his family had been warriors before him. In politics, his namesake grandfather, while serving as President Grant's Secretary of State in 1874, drove the entering wedge for Cuba's freedom. Young Ham's big moment as a volunteer came when Capron was successful in obtaining his transfer and promotion, enabling him to write home: "I am going into the fight with my stripes." Although he had only three weeks in which to prove himself, Roosevelt described him as "one of the best non-commissioned officers we had." His spirit would live on with the Riders.

"Let us pray," the chaplain said at the close of the service. Those of the Episcopal faith took off their hats and knelt. Soon all were kneeling.

The quartet started another song, "Nearer, My God, to Thee." Again the giant chorus swelled through the jungle.

At the conclusion of the singing, there was a moment of silence, unplanned, deep, affecting. It ended when Bugler Cassi, at a signal from the chaplain, started the sad, silvery notes of taps, the call that winds up the soldier's day.

The final note on the bugle marked the close of funeral proceedings. Shovelers moved into position and began filling the graves. Slowly the throng dispersed, ending the saddest moment so far experienced by America's crack volunteer outfit. Men walked dispiritedly back toward camp, the echo in their ears that of dirt falling on palm leaves.

Among those who moved away from the grave was reporter Davis. In describing the burial place in his dispatch for the day, he tried to provide some degree of consolation for the bereaved families back home: "No man could ask to lie in a more lovely place . . . The sun smiles upon it; fresh, cool breezes sweep across unceasingly, moving great trees and royal palms so that they bend over above it."

Back in camp, the Riders tried to shake off their sadness. Some rested, some cleaned guns, some talked over the battle. Fortunately, more of their baggage arrived from the coast by mule, in it Roosevelt's bundle. He promptly wrote Corinne that for the first time in four days he was able to shed clothes that were constantly drenched with rain, dew, or perspiration.

While the Riders busied about camp or loitered with the pastime of their choice at the moment, regular units of artillery, cavalry, and infantry passed, moving toward the front. Invariably they cheered at sight of the volunteers, but the cheers were not appreciably received. "We continually think of the dead and count our victory dearly won," wrote Wells.

The battle seemed to be on the mind of everybody. One subject that was commonly discussed and left unsettled was the size of the Spanish force encountered. Estimates ranged from 1200 to 4000, with most of the Riders setting the figure at 2000.[2] Another was the reaction of General Lawton to Wheeler's hasty action in pushing on to meet the enemy.

Later reports stated that Lawton was outraged and maintained

[2] Wood, who served as Military Governor of Santiago after the surrender and had ample opportunity to talk with knowledgeable Spanish authorities, placed the enemy numbers in the Las Guásimas fight at 2850. In an exchange of correspondence, he accused Roosevelt, who accepted the 2000 figure reported by the Spanish General Toral, of "greatly underestimating" the strength of the Spaniards.

Wheeler had ignored orders by not stopping at Siboney. This charge was made ridiculous by the fact that Wheeler, the "senior officer at the front," to whom the order was addressed, did not receive it until after the battle had been fought. It was also said that Lawton had stamped into Wheeler's headquarters and shaken an admonitory finger under the little general's nose.[3]

Perhaps the unkindest thing reported to have been said was that the action at Las Guásimas was unnecessary. Opponents of Wheeler's action maintained it had uselessly sacrificed lives, that the Spaniards had already decided upon withdrawal, and that this unscheduled battle seriously embarrassed the plan for the main American advance. If such a claim were made, it was ignored. Only laudatory messages came from Wheeler's superiors.

Whatever the charges, kind or unkind, the cavalry unquestionably had driven the enemy back behind the ridges of San Juan, forcing it onto the third and last plateau between the coast and the city. This action made available to the Americans a fairly open and well-watered area in which to rest and prepare for the final assault.[4]

Wood and Roosevelt also came in for criticism in view of the erroneous reports filed from Siboney on the strength of information

[3] Lieutenant C. D. Brooks, first aide-de-camp to the Inspector General, kept a diary of his experiences in the war and, under date of June 25, wrote: "I was told by one who said he was present that General Lawton had harsh words with General Wheeler over the event yesterday. It seems that Lawton's division was primarily given the advance on Las Guásimas, Wheeler's division passed Lawton at 5 A.M. yesterday, and engaged the enemy. Lawton is said to have told Wheeler that this was no political campaign, but a military campaign; that he [Lawton] had been given command of the advance and he proposed to keep it, even if he had to post a guard to keep other troops in the rear."

In Wheeler's defense, Roosevelt wrote: "General Wheeler was in command ashore; he was told to get in touch with the enemy and, being a man with the 'fighting edge,' this meant that he was certain to fight. No general who was worth his salt would have failed to fight under such conditions; the only question would be as to how the fight was to be made. War means fighting; and the soldier's cardinal sin is timidity."

[4] Some military authorities point out that the Las Guásimas fight was strategic in that, if the Spaniards had held there, they could have blocked the American forces on the miasmic coastal strip until yellow fever dissipated their ranks. They cited that Wheeler struck quickly, before the enemy could reinforce the position. Moreover, his offensive action boosted the morale of the invading army and set the pace for the remainder of the campaign.

Wheeler explained his action in this manner: "There was an impression that we ought to get ashore and go right to the enemy. I took that view myself. We came there for business, and it was necessary to move upon the enemy with rapidity. We all knew the country was a yellow-fever country. We knew this malaria fever often affected even the natives, and it seemed that promptness of action was more essential than anything else. I went ashore and kept going on to the front."

brought by Adjutant Hall. This gave rise to suggestions back in the United States that the two officers should be court-martialed for taking their men into a trap, but these quickly died out when the true account was made public. Even crack reporter Davis was guilty of using the term "ambush" in an early story, later retracting it and admitting he was in error.

When he got an opportunity after the funeral, Wood sat down to write letters. One of these went to his wife, a newsy bit of correspondence that wound up with an anonymous reference to Adjutant Hall:

> I hope you did not get the report that I was killed that went through the back command. Poor Marshall was shot through the back alongside me, and . . . (one of my officers) looked around after a volley and, as I had gone, mistook Marshall for me and marched back to the sea for reinforcements and gave out this report.[5]

Cuban refugees from Santiago began to arrive in the vicinity of the Riders' camp during the afternoon. They came, bedraggled and starved, with numerous questions. They could not understand what was happening. *La Espana,* one of three newspapers published in the city, had appeared that morning with an article that told of the fighting at Las Guásimas and stated that the Americans had been repulsed with heavy losses. This seemed puzzling to the refugees, for they had watched the Spaniards fall back with their dead and wounded, and here were the Americans pushing after them.

Lieutenant Parker and his Gatlings, a much more important part of the invasion than was recognized at the moment, were

[5] Owing to the calm wisdom of Leonard Wood, the shameful action of Adjutant Hall was kept comparatively quiet. The resentment against him was so strong among the other Riders, however, that they sent Captain Llewellyn, the gruff old veteran, to inform the commander of their feelings. Wood is reported to have replied: "Captain Llewellyn, if you submit such a complaint, I shall have to call a court-martial. But I hope you will not submit it. We have just been through a sharp engagement. The men have done magnificently. Eight or nine of them have died. If we bring that man before a court-martial, the bravery of five hundred will be forgotten and the cowardice of one alone will be remembered. The stigma of his act will fall to some extent on every man in the regiment. Besides, I want to remind you that Frederick the Great ran away in his first fight." To which Llewellyn is said to have replied: "Quite true, sir, but this son of a bitch will run away in every fight."

Records in the Adjutant General's Office show that Hall resigned from the 1st Volunteers as of August 1, 1898.

moved in the direction of the front during the day. Pack trains were beginning to be fitted out, ready to haul supplies, and Bates's Independent Brigade was encamped at Siboney with orders to work on the road leading to Sevilla and to do all that could be done to make it passable for wagons and artillery.

On June 26, the Red Cross ship *State of Texas* drifted in closer to Siboney. With glasses, Clara Barton studied the sandy strip that served as a landing place and back of it two steep bluffs rising to a height of perhaps 250 feet. The scene was so inspiring she recorded it:

> We were awakened at daybreak to see the soldiers filing up over the hill in marching order, forming in lines by ones and twos, winding up, in and out among the hills, higher and higher, like a giant anaconda. As we watched them through a glass, they became a moving line trailing on toward the clouds, till lost in the mist, and we can only think as we look at them on how many or on which is set the mark of death.

Her reference was to the movement stemming out of Siboney toward the area around Sevilla where the bulk of the American Army was camped. Shafter reported to Sampson during the day that the last of the men would be on shore by night, but that it probably would be Tuesday before they reached the advance guard. He indicated the attack on Santiago would be delayed until more forage and rations could be landed and moved to the front.

Among those who continued to push forward from Siboney were Lieutenant Parker and his Gatling gun crew. Under their direction, the guns were dragged by mules over the rough trail at as rapid a pace as the mud and slime would permit. Parker hoped to reach the front and get in some practice before the next battle opened.

Other activity at Siboney concerned the pack trains. It was found these would be unable to transport to the front all the supplies needed by an army as big as Shafter's, so orders were issued for sixty six-mule wagons to be given priority in the unloading. Orders also specified that the first three landed should be assigned to the Chief Surgeon, so that medicine chests could be carried forward. But once ashore, the next problem would be that of getting them over the only available route to Sevilla.

The Rough Riders also were on the move. Ogden Wells made note:

This being Sunday, of course we had to move. It seems as if Sunday is a favorite day for breaking camp. At 8 this morning, we broke camp and marched two miles under a blazing sun to a new camping place with sweeter odors, for we have learned from experience that a battlefield is not the best camping ground imaginable. We are now camped in a marshy, open spot, close to a beautiful stream of water.

This move by the Riders was a part of a general advance. Wheeler reported that there was not sufficient ground between Las Guásimas and Sevilla for the American forces to camp and was directed by Shafter to move nearer Santiago, but not to encounter the enemy.

The road westward from Sevilla wound through jungle and growth of small wood in an intervening valley. It was flanked on the right, toward the north, by the village of Caney.[6] Past this point it debouched on open ground leading to the outer defenses, about a mile from Santiago itself, called collectively San Juan Hill, although the name properly applied only to the highest of the chain of elevations, that on which stood a large blockhouse. To the right of the road was a less imposing rise, on the crest of which could be seen large kettles of the type used in making sugar. This promptly was dubbed Kettle Hill by the Americans. Shafter understood that a garrison of about 12,000 Spaniards, half the number in the entire province, was posted on these hills.

As battle plans were developed, two points stood out importantly. Shafter decided to knock out Caney first, dispersing 520 Spaniards stationed there under General Vara del Rey. With that out of the way, the drive would be against San Juan Hill. If the Americans were successful in charging past the latter embattlements, he felt sure he could make the Spaniards surrender, or drive them toward the guns of the fleet waiting off the harbor to the south of the city. But the reduction of Caney was considered essential to the protection of the advance and this must come first.

The Riders' camp was near El Pozo Hill, once the site of a sugar factory. It was a high elevation some four miles south of Caney and the same distance from Santiago, at the foot of which were the remains of an old hacienda much damaged in the guerrilla warfare that had been going on in Cuba for years. Off on a ridge to the right were the nearest of the Spanish outposts.

---

[6] Many reports from Cuba referred to this community as El Caney, but most Cuban maps identify it only as Caney.

By climbing El Pozo Hill, the Riders could see over the crest of the San Juan ridges and beyond to the red-tiled roofs of buildings in Santiago. Every hill and mountain north and east of the city seemed to be occupied by blockhouses, while on the east side trenches gashed each knoll and bit of high ground. Thirty-four of these were counted. Spies who came in from that direction reported that inside the entrenchments were four parallel lines of rifle pits, shoulder deep, and each fronted by marked ranges and several rows of barbed wire.

During the afternoon, there was new cause to believe the rainy season had begun. Rain poured so hard for a time that the shelter tents offered scant protection. Trails were turned into torrents and the camp ground into a quagmire. As soon as the storm ended, the sun came out, and soon the air was steaming hot.

These rains, which occurred nearly every afternoon, were additional incentive to the soldiers to discard their heavy uniforms and accouterments. A horse-collar blanket roll, bulging haversack, full canteen, beltful of ammunition, and a carbine were awkward enough to handle when dry and disgustingly aggravating when wet. The line of march from Daiquirí to Siboney and beyond to Sevilla was strewn with paraphernalia. The New York *Sun* correspondent reported:

> It is likely that the men will fight in the coming battle nearly as naked as nature made them. Many of the regulars are already walking about clad in only a cartridge belt or a rifle and a chew of tobacco. The officers overlook these eccentricities, knowing that their men will go farther and fight better if left unhampered by burdensome regulations.

Into the camp that afternoon came Cowboy Roland, the trooper Roosevelt twice had ordered away from the firing line after he had been wounded at Las Guásimas. At the hospital in Siboney, the doctors examined him and announced that his injury was so serious he would have to be sent back to the States for treatment. Making no comment, the patient waited until dark and then slipped out through a window. This time Roosevelt let him stay.

Wheeler continued to keep on the move, although he followed instructions not to engage the enemy. These had come almost simultaneously with a telegram from Secretary of War Alger informing the little general that he was conveying President McKinley's thanks TO YOU AND YOUR ARMY FOR THE GALLANT ACTION at Las Guásimas.

Though forbidden to bring on another engagement, Wheeler did not interpret his new orders as preventing his reconnoitering. With members of his staff, he moved over a wide area, studying enemy lines, estimating the strength of the Spaniards at certain points, including Caney, and forming in his mind a plan of action. When Shafter called a conference at Siboney that night, he was prepared.

Other leaders at the meeting included Kent, Lawton, and the two Cuban generals, García and Castillo. During their discussion, Wheeler described the Spanish defenses to Shafter and urged that he be permitted to attack with a large force of artillery. He maintained that fire from a number of guns upon the forces at Caney would soon make their position untenable. He felt that a division of infantry or dismounted cavalry placed between that point and Santiago could catch the Spaniards as they attempted to retreat. Shafter admitted the feasibility of such a plan, but that was as far as it got in the initial discussion. Little artillery was available.

Food was becoming a problem for some of the American units. A few had gone without rations for an entire day, while others were on half-rations. Pack trains were loaded down with bacon, hardtack and coffee, with a promise that such things as potatoes, onions, and canned tomatoes would come later. The Riders were among those badly in need of supplies. For dinner this Sunday night they managed to get hold of a quantity of beans and, as Roosevelt wrote Corinne, "Oh, what a feast we had!"

Long, yellow pits visible near the crest of San Juan Hill the morning of the 27th left no doubt that the Spaniards were preparing to fight. Many men were digging, their straw sombreros bobbing up and down in the ditches like popcorn in a popper. Other such entrenchments were taking shape at Caney to the right, and along the streets of the village there was much movement of troops. It was evident that steady progress was being made despite muddy conditions brought on by another tropical rain during the night.

Blame for lack of action on the part of the invaders lay with Shafter. But he seemed justified in what he was doing. Knowing that the American Army could not delay, he was just about to call for an advance when he received a message from Washington informing him reinforcements were on the way. He decided to wait, assuming they would arrive soon.

Shafter bared his plans to Wheeler in a message telling the little general that he would see him in the afternoon. At that time, he added, he would like to know whether a division could be moved to the right so as to come out at Caney, a point he identified as one from which he did not believe they would be expected to come. His engineer officer already had informed him that there was a road leading off to the left in the direction of the San Juan River, a stream the Americans would have to cross.

After receiving Shafter's message, Wheeler rode out toward Caney. He went as far as half a mile beyond the picket lines. This he did in the hope of getting a good view of the terrain. Finding he could not do so because of the luxurious tropical growth, he dismounted and climbed a tree, from which he was able to look over a large part of the area.

General Young and his staff also went out to look around, moving as far as they could toward the front and making sketches as they went. Upon returning, he went to talk with Wheeler. From what he had seen, he reported, he was confident he could take Caney if he were supplied with just two pieces of artillery. Wheeler replied that he had been cautioned by Shafter that there was to be no advance until orders to that effect came from him. Young was disappointed, even though he was not feeling well and was aware that his temperature was rising.

General Chaffee was still another who did reconnaissance work. He was more concerned than either of the other two officers over what he saw. It was obvious the enemy must be attacked on San Juan Hill. In order to do so, the American troops would have to march along two trails through a wooded area that led into open ground extending up to the Spanish position. Here lay the threat. He could see that there would be a great loss of men unless concealed trails were cut parallel with the entire front of the wooded area, with innumerable little trails leading out of it, thus enabling troops to debouche in large numbers.

"Of course the enemy knows where those two trails leave the woods and have their guns trained on them," he pointed out upon his return. "If our men leave the cover and reach the plain from those trails, they will be piled up so high they will block the road."

Throughout the day, American troops continued to move toward the front. This now lay beyond the first crossing of the Rio Guamo, a stream fed by springs up in the mountains. During the afternoon, García's troops came up and went a half mile past the Rough Riders. Also moved up were the Gatlings. No high ground on

which to place these guns could be found nearby, but reconnaissance revealed there were points farther ahead from which an
effective fire could be directed on the Spanish positions.

Despite the rain during the night, sickness still had not become
a serious problem, although an epidemic of measles that had
started on the ships was spreading. Drinking water was obtained
from the Rio Guamo. The stream was carefully guarded against
pollution. No bathing in it was permitted.

Food continued to be a serious problem. Pack trains were organized and were making trips—one day from Siboney, two from
Daiquirí—but a day's supply was the most they could move on
each trip. Ammunition had to be hauled by mule. Under these
circumstances, it was realized an attack might not be wise until
after the road had been opened to wagon trains.

As he had notified Wheeler, Shafter rode to the camps at the
front during the afternoon. He spent some time at Wheeler's headquarters, returning to Siboney that night. As one correspondent
reported, he "came ponderously ashore" to inspect his forces, adding that the troops made irreverent bets as to how many men it
took to get their corpulent commanding general into the saddle.

At Siboney during the day, Captain Capron of the 4th Artillery,
en route to the front with his battery of four guns, stopped to visit
the grave of his son. He found it on a hill a hundred yards or so
back from the beach, a crude wooden cross marking it but not
identifying its occupant. After nightfall, a detachment from the
4th visited the spot in company with a newspaper artist. Aided
by a lantern, they wrote the following inscription on the cross:
CAPTAIN ALLYN CAPRON, 1ST VOLUNTEER CAVALRY, FELL JUNE 24,
1898.

The New York *Evening Post* correspondent at Siboney was an
observant individual. On the 28th he sent off a dispatch to his
newspaper that included two rather innocent sentences: SOME
ROUGH RIDERS CAME THIS MORNING TO SWIM IN THE OCEAN. THE
TROOPERS WERE LEARNING HOW TO ENDURE THE SUN, AND ARE FULL
OF ENERGY. But, as news-minded as he was, this reporter got only a
part of the story.

The detail of Rough Riders was in Siboney under the personal
supervision of Colonel Wood. The day was extremely hot, so he
allowed them to take a swim. Then he led them to a point along
the beach and there spoke to them in a voice so modulated as not
to carry beyond their ears: "You men form in a line on both sides

of those picks and shovels and, when I give you the order to march, see that none of them stay behind."

Roosevelt was in the village with another detail of men for an entirely different purpose. He wanted food. A moderate supply was obtained, but only after resorting to cajolery, eloquence, and even threats.

Back at camp, some of the food was promptly cooked. The lieutenant colonel was among those who sat down to partake of it, thereby becoming the principal figure in a mystery that had all the appearances of an ill-timed practical joke. On the trip to Siboney, he had worn his saber, assuming it would serve as a persuasive tool in the official campaign for supplies. This he placed upon the ground beside him when he sat down to eat. On arising, he reached for it, but found only the scabbard. Excitement swelled almost to the red-faced stage of apoplexy before the missing weapon was found back in the bushes—and near it the land crab that had been fascinated by the blue tassel on its hilt.

By this day, the fourth since the front had been established following the initial battle, the area between the coast and the camps on the Rio Guamo began to look like war. On the way back, the Rough Riders got a firsthand view of it. So did a newspaper reporter riding through the country on a mule. He was so touched that sympathy poured from his pen when he wrote his next dispatch:

> Cavalrymen, dismounted for the first time in years, and infantrymen from cool Michigan and Massachussetts, toil hour after hour along these so-called roads and paths through the jungles of cacti, poisoned vines and high grass that cuts like a razor, in a bursting sunlight that makes the skylines with the distant hills shimmer and waver before the eyes, or from the stagnant pools strange, gray mists float upward, and vultures with outstretched wings look greedily down from above.

Vegetation torn down and trampled by the troops was converted into a high state of fermentation by the rain and sun. In consequence, the sour breath of a giant seemed to sweep over the land, bringing curious stenches from the earth and from hidden places in the jungles.

Overhead the sun was like a great yellow furnace, torturing everything living and turning everything dead into a thousand mysterious forms of terror. It was so hot the soldiers dreaded to light campfires, both because of the heat thus generated and because of the struggle they had to go through to find suitable wood.

Along the sides of the road, thousands of gigantic land crabs, spotted with yellow and red and other colors, their whitish claws clicking ominously, wriggled and twisted in and out of view. They were a ghastly sight to young soldiers fresh from New York and Boston and Tucson and Albuquerque. Ragged Cubans slipped noiselessly through the undergrowth, or sprawled in the shade of gossamer trees. These fellows watched with disinterest the steady trodding of their American defenders and managed successfully to turn their backs on the road crews struggling with picks and shovels in inches of sticky mud.

During the day, Shafter again visited the front. One Rider who saw him wrote that "he looks like he could carry the mule he was riding better than the mule could carry him." The general revealed to some of the officers with whom he conferred that he had been informed a force of more than 8000 Spanish regulars from Manzanillo was on its way to reinforce Santiago.

Another who traveled the route from Siboney on the 28th was Clara Barton. The aged woman walked the entire distance—eight miles—with some of her Red Cross staff. She went as far as the Rough Rider camp, which had been moved to a point beyond that of García's Cubans. From there she watched the Spaniards at work on their fortifications.

Rain poured in the early afternoon. Many of the soldiers wrote about it, picturing it as dissolving everything into one huge muddy stew of braying mules and cursing drivers, clamorous colonels and half-starved men.

The New York *Sun* correspondent felt pity for the soldiers, writing:

> No man who has not gone over this trail, no man who was not in the terrible downpour of rain that drenched the American army to the skin this afternoon, can understand the suffering of our troops and the heroism with which they bear it.

He depicted the rain as coming straight down, not slantwise. He said it extinguished campfires, sent rivers of mud and red water swirling along the narrow road, and dashed over rocks where the trail sloped downward. Lieutenant Parker was equally emphatic: "Not such rains as the people of the United States are familiar with, but Cuban rains. It was like standing under a barrel full of water and having the bottom knocked out."

Oddly enough, the storm was followed by a mysterious trans-
formation of the tropics. The whole army shivered in unusual cold,
and those who had quinine swallowed a dose. Officers hurried here
and there, urging the men to strip and dry their clothes at campfires. Reported one newsman:

> Presently thousands of men were standing about naked while
> the sun drew up thick vapors from the earth and vicious tropical
> flies stung their white skin. The American army is a noble body
> of men when it is stripped.

A touching scene had taken place at Las Guásimas while the
storm was in progress. During the downpour, groups of soldiers
stood unsheltered around the graves of the Rough Riders. Cataracts
of water poured from their hat brims. A newspaper correspondent
present at the time observed that a monument might be erected
to the men lying in the grave, "but there can never be a nobler
tribute than this."

Appearance of Shafter and his headquarters staff at Wheeler's
camp at Sevilla the morning of the 29th indicated that the time
for battle was drawing nearer. He had left the *Seguranca* at 8
o'clock and mounted a large bay horse. Standing by to watch
him struggle into the saddle was a large group of soldiers and
Cubans.

It took him three hours to get over the trail, a hot and trying
experience. Along the way he saw ample evidence that the transportation problem had not been licked. Streams were swollen and
in places impassable. Wagons, now supplementing the work of the
pack trains, were bogged down in mud, some so hopelessly that
they had been there overnight. Men and animals struggled futilely
to get them free.

Arriving at Sevilla, Shafter went immediately into conference
with Wheeler and García. The subject of discussion was the report
that the Spaniards were preparing to reinforce Santiago. He had
since learned that the troops to be sent to the relief of the city
would be under command of General Pando. García wanted to
move at once to head them off, but Shafter felt differently about the
matter. He knew the food and water supplies of the Spaniards were
short. "Let them get into Santiago, and then we will know where
we have got them," he said.[7]

---

[7] In a subsequent interview published in the New York *Tribune*, General O. O.
Howard said: "In regard to the Cubans allowing the Spanish reinforcements to enter

After the conference, Shafter rode to El Pozo. From there for the first time he stared at the entrenchments on San Juan Hill and beyond at those around Santiago. His mind was made up. Although most of the promised reinforcements had not arrived, he knew he could wait no longer, that he must act quickly. Even as he stared, an exchange of fire between pickets on the front lines could be heard in the distance. Moreover, the rains presaged trouble. His communications problems might become insuperable. On top of that, the sickness of a tropical country would soon begin to spread among his men. On the way back to Sevilla, he began to feel tremors of fever himself. Wheeler had a similar complaint, and Young, with a temperature at 106, already was down. Shafter knew that malaria was beginning to strike in the pup tents around his new headquarters and in the scattered clearings along the road.

The general's presence gave rise to rumors that a battle would be fought on the morrow. Staff officers scoffed. They said it would be impossible to get the army in shape so quickly. But it was evident that action would be started soon by either one side or the other. Deserters were coming in from Santiago with reports that Admiral Cervera was preparing to make a dash out of the harbor.

General Chaffee in the meantime opened the road to Caney. "We had to get out the brush and use picks and shovels and everything of that kind," he reported. "The road was simply a mule track, and a difficult mule track at that. I also cleared a position for the artillery. This position was about 2400 yards from the town and southeast of it."

Shafter sent off a message to the War Department that he still had not unloaded his siege guns. He said that he would do so as soon as he could, but that he did not intend to take them to the front unless forced to do so. He reported also that the four light batteries under Capron were at the front and that they were heavy enough to overcome everything the Spaniards had.

In another development, a hospital—known as that of the 1st

Santiago from Manzanillo, I would say that I met Shafter on board the *Vixen*, and from my conversation with him I inferred that he intended to allow the Spaniards to enter the city, so as to have them where he could punish them more."

Outlook magazine republished the interview and added this editorial comment: "It is hoped that General Howard misunderstood General Shafter, because such strategy as that indicated would suggest the tactics of the pugnacious John Phoenix, who, in a fight in the editorial room, put his nose into the mouth of his adversary in order to hold the latter more securely."

Division—was established in a field about three miles east of Santiago. It was situated in the valley through which ran the Siboney-Santiago road, beside a brook running down from a range of mountains about two miles away.

During the day, Richard Harding Davis wrote a long letter to his father from Rough Rider headquarters:

> We expect to move up to Santiago the day after tomorrow, and it's about time, for the trail will not be passable much longer. It rains every day at 3 o'clock for an hour, and such a rain you never guessed. It is three inches high for an hour. Then we all go out naked and dig trenches to get it out of the way. It is very rough living.
>
> I have to confess that I never knew how well off I was until I got to smoking Durham tobacco and I've only half a bag left. The enlisted men are smoking dried horse droppings, grass, roots, and tea. Some of them can't sleep, they are now so nervous for want of it, but today a lot came up and all will be well for them . . .
>
> This is the best crowd to be with—they are so well educated and so interesting. The Regular Army men are very dull and narrow and would bore one to death. We have Wood, Roosevelt, Lee, the British attaché, Whitney, and a Doctor Church, a friend of mine from Princeton, who is quite the most cheerful soul and the funniest I ever met. He carried four men from the firing line the other day back half a mile to the hospital tent. He spends most of his time coming around headquarters in an undershirt of mine and a gold bracelet fighting tarantulas. I woke up the other morning with one seven inches long and as hairy as your head reposing on my pillow . . .

Senator Henry Cabot Lodge, back in the United States, also did a bit of writing on this date. One of his letters was addressed to Theodore Roosevelt and closed with the following paragraph:

> The newspapers are nominating you for Governor of New York and I have not the least doubt that you can go to Congress if you want to, which I think you would like by and by, and if you keep on as you have been doing and succeed in living through the war, you can hope for much better things than a seat in Congress.

Chapter 5

CONFERENCE FOR BATTLE

Photographer Burr McIntosh, who sometimes could be an understanding sort of fellow, said Richard Harding Davis possessed a very powerful pair of field glasses that were in no way neutral. It was through them, Burr explained, that Davis looked at the people around him. Shafter, for example, was seen through the big end, so that the poor general, though huge of body, appeared as a minute, misshapen individual of no great importance. Roosevelt on the other hand was of imposing stature, for he was seen through the smaller end and thus was magnified in proportions natural to binoculars when properly employed.

On June 30, in reporting developments, Davis brought Shafter into customary focus. Still fresh in his mind was the treatment he had received at the commanding general's hands on the transport while preparing to land at Daiquirí. According to this reporter's account, the bulky officer lay flat abed, exhausted by the trip he had made the day before to El Pozo Hill and, consequently, was unable to join his army. But reports not based on biased glasses showed him up and very much about, busy with plans for battle.

Actually, the general, early on the morning of the 30th, rode again to El Pozo with members of his staff. There he stared along the crest of the San Juan ridges and off to the right toward Caney. The terrain in the basin-like triangle before him was a tropical jungle. Over it lay acres of meadow separated by tangled underbrush, magnificent palms, mango and lime trees. But across the San Juan River and leading up to the ridges beyond, it was open and free of cumbersome foliage. This would mean the men who waded the river and charged up to the Spanish lines would have no handicap underfoot except the tall grass, and yet at the same time they would have no protection from the enemy bullets.

Also out on reconnaissance early this morning, somewhere in the direction of Caney, was Lawton and along with him a party of staff officers. It was their purpose to try to figure out in advance problems which might arise in the assault on the tiny, picturesque village, once a thriving community. It was understood the attack would be the kickoff in the forthcoming battle.

After scanning the countryside for some time, Shafter came down the hill and rode along the road to Santiago until he was stopped by Cuban pickets. They told him the enemy's advance lines were not 200 yards away. The general did not persist on going farther. No matter what fault was to be found with the Cubans, they had to be admired for their ability to picket the Spaniards, watching every footpath and knoll with the patience of a cat waiting for mice. Reluctantly, he turned back, making it to his headquarters by noon. Shortly afterward he sent for the division and brigade commanders.

About the same time, in came Lawton's party from Caney. They reported the Spaniards were occupying six blockhouses and a stone fort, as well as a stone church loopholed for rifle fire. Trenches, barbed-wire entanglements, and sharpshooters' nests in trees surrounded the entire area. Of all the fortifications, the fort seemed the most formidable. A 35-by-45-foot structure, with walls three feet thick, it occupied a commanding position on a prominent knoll about seventy-five feet high and 800 yards southeast of the church. But opinion was unanimous that the assault would be over in two hours at the most. Cuban refugees confirmed that only about 600 Spanish regulars and seventy guerrillas were stationed there under command of Del Rey.

It was easy to reason what would happen. If 964 men had driven 2000 or more Spaniards from the ridge at Las Guásimas in little more than an hour, well, surely about 7000 yelling Americans could drive through Caney on equally as fast a schedule. Even "Fightin' Joe" had talked of the speed with which he would conduct such an assault. At the moment, however, he was being dosed with quinine and purgatives. A good patient he turned out to be, all on the promise that he would be back in action sooner if he took his medicine. With General Young it was a different story: he was sicker and by nightfall would be out of his head.

Shafter carefully went over his plans for the benefit of the offiers whose duty it would be to carry them out. He sketched the battlefield as a huge triangle. The base was the Santiago road, with El Pozo at the right angle, San Juan Hill at the left angle, and Caney at the apex. The movement against Caney was to begin as soon as the light of day permitted. After the village had been taken, Lawton's forces were to swing toward Santiago and join in a combined assault, coming in on the city from the north while Kent's division and the cavalry struck from the east. This was set for 10 A.M. A total of 15,367 men would be involved on the American side at the various points of attack.

While Lawton was assaulting Caney, the other two divisions, with the cavalry in the lead and guided by an observation balloon soaring above the woods and jungle, would prepare to emerge from the thick growth and deploy at the foot of the San Juan ridges, the cavalry to take the right and Kent's infantry the left. This meant funneling about 8000 men through the two trails opening out of the jungle, for Chaffee's suggestion of cutting other trails to permit quicker deployment and to avoid the guns trained on the existing openings had not been followed.

Off along the coast far to the left, Michigan and Massachusetts troops just arrived by ship would attack the railroad bridge at the little port of Aguadores, supported by several vessels of Sampson's fleet. This was designed to confuse the enemy, leaving him in doubt as to whether the main assault was coming from the direction of Morro Castle and Santiago harbor, or from San Juan and Caney, closer by.

Four light field batteries had been moved inland from the coast. One of these, Capron's, would go with Lawton. Another, under Captain Grimes, would be mounted on El Pozo Hill to batter the San Juan trenches, and the other two, along with Bates's Independent Brigade, would be held in reserve. Except for the shelling at Aguadores, Shafter made no call upon Sampson's guns, having a poor opinion of naval bombardment. He also was averse to sharing the glory of the campaign with a rival branch of the service.

Shafter's plans were as bold as those of a distinguished Confederate general at the Battle of Chancellorsville in one of the most crucial periods of the Civil War. Around Fredericksburg, Virginia, in 1863, Robert E. Lee violated the old truism that in unity there is strength and divided his forces into three parts, a stark breach of military tactics. But his daring was rewarded, for he was successful in blocking Hooker's army. Now four veterans of the same war—

Shafter, Lawton, Kent, and Sumner—were agreed upon a similar plan of action against the Spaniards.

As the conference ended, Lawton moved over to talk with Adjutant General E. J. McClernand, a West Pointer serving as Shafter's right arm. Lawton said emphatically within the hearing of others: "McClernand, do not order the other divisions to attack until I get up. Give me time to reduce Caney." With that, he turned and left the meeting.

Soon after the conference broke up, Wood was informed of the realignment of command made necessary by the sickness among the officers. General Sumner was to take charge of the cavalry division in Wheeler's place, turning his brigade over to Colonel Henry Carroll, while Wood was to be in command of Young's 2nd Brigade. This meant that Roosevelt at last would be at the head of the Rough Riders. The changes were made in the excitement of the moment, without formality.

Since early morning, things had been buzzing along the trail from the coast. Everything seemed to be moving to the front, including García's Cubans, who came along in a sort of jog. Mule train after mule train loaded with supplies and ammunition passed the camp of the Riders. "It looks as if a heavy battle is expected," Wells noted. "The men are all eager for the struggle and will not need much urging. The rations are still short and are beginning to get tiresome. Coffee and hardtack three times a day is not much to look forward to."

Monotonous or not, enough rations for three days were distributed early in the afternoon. Then Roosevelt gave the men orders to break camp and prepare to march. Already the muddy trail was choked with moving columns. One item that caused a jam wherever it happened to be was the observation balloon. Many of the soldiers had never seen such a thing before and stared at it in awe-stricken fascination. It floated along just above the trees, attached by cable to a huge reel on an army field wagon carrying the gas-generating equipment. Men exchanged bits of information about the gigantic war machine. They said it took 17,000 cubic feet of oxygen to inflate it, that it could lift 400 or more pounds, that it made possible observation over a 40-mile-square area. Someone remembered that it had arrived from France on the steamship *Teutonic* in May, accompanied by its manufacturer, Maurice Mallet, billed as the greatest astronaut and balloon expert in the world.

The 1st Volunteers, when given the command, drew up in

32. Scenes at Daiquirí as the Americans poured ashore and started their march toward Siboney and the battle action around Santiago.

33. Mount Losiltires, the hill at Daiquirí on which the Rough Riders placed the first American flag planted during the invasion.

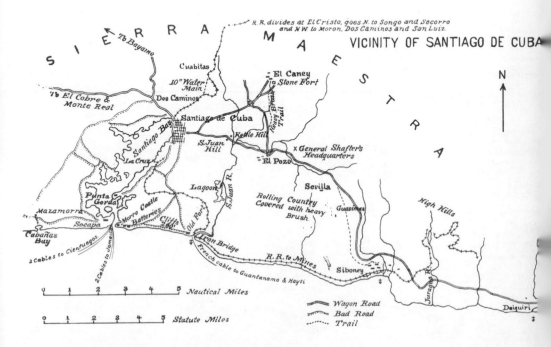

34. A map of the area around Santiago invaded by the Americans.

35. This artist's sketch from *Harper's Weekly* of July 9, 1898, depicts the Rough Riders in their fight at Las Guásimas.

36. Rough Riders moving through the tall grass at Las Guásimas.

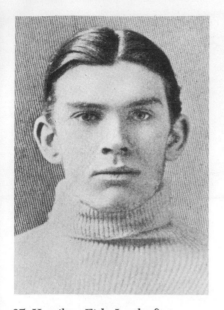

37. Hamilton Fish, Jr., the first
Rough Rider casualty in action.

39. Lieutenant James Church, the
regimental surgeon who carried
wounded men from the battlefield
on his back.

38. Lieutenant Colonel Brodie,
wounded in the battle of
Las Guásimas.

40. The graves of the Rough Riders killed in the battle of Las Guásimas.

41. A Rough Rider stares down at the grave of Captain Allyn Capron on the hillside near Siboney.

42. The wharf at Siboney finally completed by the Americans.

43. Capron's battery as it trains its guns upon the little village of Caney.

44. The village of Caney, taken by the Americans on July 1, 1898.

45. The stone fort at Caney from which the Spaniards put up their chief resistance on July 1.

46. Capron's battery firing upon the town of Caney the morning of July 1.

47. The stone fort at Caney after the American guns had damaged it and its Spanish defenders had surrendered.

48. The countryside around El Pozo where Grimes's battery was posted.

column beside the road in rear of the 1st Regular Cavalry. The entire outfit was there, including the Colt automatics and the dynamite gun, with enough mules to insure dragging them to the front. It was to be a slow process, this matter of moving men and guns the two or three miles to the firing line. For hours they waited while regiment after regiment passed, interspersed with Cubans and mule trains. Among the first to go were Lawton's brigades, moving so precipitately that provisions and ammunition had to be hurried up to them during the night.

In front moved the balloon, not an innovation from the standpoint of military use, for the Union Army had employed aerial surveillance early in the Civil War. But it was something new to Stephen Crane, the distinguished young author. He stared at it for long periods at a time and was moved to write: "The military balloon, a fat, wavering, yellow thing, was leading the advance like some new conception of war-god. Its bloated mass shone above the trees, and served incidentally to indicate to the men at the rear that comrades were in advance."

At last, around 4 P.M., Roosevelt got his orders to move. It was with the enthusiasm of a young officer in his twenties, instead of a man nearing forty, that he rode out in front of the regiment as its new commander. He was dressed in a dark blue shirt, with improvised shoulder straps of yellow matching the "U.S.V." in yellow cloth sewed to his collar. A blue bandanna handkerchief was tied around his neck and another hung loosely from the rear brim of his hat. The silver leaves on his shoulders marking his rank resembled spoons more than they did leaves. The uniform he wore was sloppy, looking like he had slept in it every night he had been in Cuba. But this was nothing new. The man who had been an official of the top echelon in Washington and New York, a man of wealth who knew good clothes and could wear them, was a soldier of action, in the ranks for service—no longer to be referred to as the "eyeglassed dude." Not a Westerner in his outfit made such disdainful reference to him now.

The Riders were ordered to move behind the 1st and 10th Cavalry, with Kent's infantry following. Many stops occurred, even from the beginning. The heat was intense, made worse by the close jungle walls through which they passed and the mud of the partially improved road over which they had to march. Whenever a halt came, Teddy saw that the men sat or lay down, loosening their packs the better to rest. Now and then they passed open spaces where regiments were camped. Sometimes a regiment, losing its proper place, forced its way into the column, confusing the order, but never completely upsetting the slow movement toward the front. Occasionally the path led through streams.

"It was as though fifteen regiments were encamped along the sidewalks of Fifth Avenue and were all ordered at the same moment to move into it and march downtown," Davis wrote for the benefit of his readers back home. "If Fifth Avenue were ten feet wide, one can imagine the confusion."

Then came the rain. Men slogged along in mud and water, wet and uncomfortable, little rivulets pouring from their hat brims. They stared repeatedly at the huge balloon, still visible above the trees. Both black soldiers and white soldiers were scattered along the line. As far as the eye could see, there was action. The road was bristling with carbines and guidons, the mounted figures of officers, swearing teamsters cracking their whips in sweaty and rain-soaked ill humor, mule trains following doggedly behind the bell mares. The squish of boots in muck, the click of cups swinging against bayonet scabbards were dominant noises. Many of the men, knowing what the muck would do to government-issue shoes, had taken them off and swung them around their necks. They splashed along with leggings off, trousers rolled, and feet bare.

Stephen Crane watched some of the infantry file past and wrote: "The pitiful thing about this advance was to see in the hands of the boys those terrible old rifles that smoke like brush fires and give the regimental lines away to the enemy as plainly as an illuminated sign."

At one point, Roosevelt led his command across a wide meadow that brought them out upon a narrow road walled by almost impenetrable jungle. Along the way they passed a camp of hundreds of Cubans preparing for the evening meal. At sight of the Americans, the natives grinned amiably, pointing westward toward Santiago and making ferocious gestures with their black forefingers across their throats. "God help Santiago if those fellows get in," remarked a trooper as he eyed them with disfavor.

The rain was almost like a squall, hitting with driving force at first and then slowly dying away. After it had ended, the balloon lifted higher into the sky. Soldiers cheered at the soaring antics of the huge bag of oiled pongee silk. The two men from the Signal Corps occupying its basket, one of them Colonel G. McC. Derby, the officer in charge of its operations, could be seen busily focusing their powerful telescopes and pointing them in the direction of the Spanish lines.

As darkness neared, the balloon was hauled down. It had reached an estimated height of 2500 feet. Once down, Colonel Derby and his companion shook free of their astronautical paraphernalia and headed back along the road toward Shafter's headquarters. Soldiers who saw them go wondered what they would be able to report.

The long lines of soldiers continued to push forward into the growing, misty gloom. After dark, the moon came out, brightening their spirits, and here and there a song was raised as compatible voices blended in feeble attempts to break the strain and monotony. Sometimes the words of a parody stirred cheers: "There'll Be a Hot Time in Santiago Tomorrow."

A group of correspondents moved to the front and pitched camp about a mile from where they were told the battle at Caney would open. In the darkness they heard Capron's guns go past toward the village. By midnight, they were informed, most of Lawton's division was far enough up to move quickly into position at dawn. Sleep was impossible so near all the turmoil and excitement that was going on, but they tried their best to relax, taking turns in keeping a lookout to be sure they missed no important action.

In the darkness the Riders turned to the left and began to climb El Pozo Hill. They found Wood there ahead of them, busily inspecting the terrain and selecting a place for his brigade to rest. It was no time for Army routine. Men simply threw down their packs, spread their ponchos and their blankets, and dropped their tired bodies. The noise and banter of the trail had stopped. They were cautioned that they were to have no fires, strike no matches, and must speak in whispers. A heavy picket line was thrown out along the hillside.

One important bit of business had been delayed until it could be attended to under cover of night. Now a special detail was assigned to work on it. Under Lieutenant Parker's direction, the Gatling guns were moved to a previously selected elevation and there set up for action, ready to break loose with their sharp, monotonous death rattle at daybreak. Jess Langdon was one of the strong young bucks who threw their strength behind the guns.

Off toward Caney, Capron's battery of four pieces was put in position, just 2000 yards from the village. Up on El Pozo, Grimes's battery was waiting.

On hand watching as an experienced observer was reporter Davis. He was faithful to his newspaper and disregardful of Shafter. Before going to bed, he got off a dispatch:

> The attack on Santiago is to begin in a few hours—at 4 o'clock tomorrow morning. From this ridge we can see the lights of the city street lamps, shining across a sea of mist two miles wide and two miles long, which looks in the moonlight like a great lake in the basin of the hills.
>
> Three columns of United States soldiers are to descend tomorrow morning into this basin and attack the city, eating up on the way the little villages of Caney and San Juan.
>
> They have been pouring down, since early this evening, the narrow trail that leads from Siboney to Santiago. They came in two single lines over footpaths on either side of a trail a foot deep with water and mud.
>
> The line seemed interminable. Thousands of men, slipping and stumbling in wet grass and mud, passed slowly, and as there seemed to be no end of them, someone said they were the same men marching in a circle around a hill to impress the Spanish outposts.
>
> The hours passed and still the men moved forward in unbroken lines. The moon rose, and still they pass, great stalwart giants in brown, and young volunteers in brown, and cavalry mounted and unmounted, white and colored, and pack trains of mules following the leader's bell . . .
>
> Now near midnight, General Sumner and his staff are making maps in pencil, by the light of a candle. The troops are still passing in the moonlight, and the lamps of Santiago have been put out. . . .

Roosevelt's men lay as still as logs, the tired, muddy, rain-soaked body of an Easterner blending into the shadows of the moonlit hillside with the same natural ease as the man from the bronco-bustin' West. As one of those so gathered observed, "there was just a little something in the air which made saying 'good night' a gentle farce." Mauser bullets would find many of them on the morrow.

SAN JUAN HILL

The mythical god of war Mars, eyes fierce and loins girded for battle, must have aroused Theodore Roosevelt the morning of July 1. For the Rough Rider it was to be a day of days—one he had long dreamed of and one that would take him into the halls of greatness. At last, after years of make-believe, he would lead his vaunted cowboys and trappers and lawmen and college athletes in an impetuous charge against a foe of the United States. And as he rode, an invisible guardian angel would gallop by his side, for the Grim Reaper was along, too, and running wild.

Reveille was at 4 A.M. For some, it seemed to come only a brief moment or two after they had stopped marching and dropped down upon their ponchos in the muddy darkness. For others, there had been no break at all: throughout the night they had pushed doggedly and steadily onward toward the front.

The stars were still shining when the men gobbled down their breakfast. For most of them, it was a rather meager affair of hardtack and water, but for Roosevelt it was a bit more elaborate. The night before he had been too busy with command details to worry about rations for himself and had marched away without them. He would have gone to bed on an empty stomach had not Wood's aides, Captain A. L. Mills and Lieutenant W. E. Shipp, both tall, handsomely built men, presented him with a sandwich. This he promptly divided with his orderly, William H. Saunders, a Harvard boy from Salem, Massachusetts. During the night, Marshall had caught up with him, bringing among other things coffee, sugar, and a quantity of beans, and now the tables were turned and Teddy was able to repay hospitality.

As the dawn crept in, bringing a hot July day, attention centered on the series of broken, grass-covered ridges about Caney. Stephen Crane depicted them as "at the base of a high, willow-green, crinkled mountain." Atop one of them Captain Allyn Capron's battery waited, about an easy shot from the village. It was known the opening blast would come from this point, and correspondents were gathered nearby, mumbling in excited, expectant voices. There had been much talk about the way the captain would seek to avenge the death of his namesake son. To his support, moving with all the stealth possible in so large a force, were gathering Lawton's army of 7000 men. Some had been on the march since 4 A.M.

The village, with its red-tiled roofs and scattered white walls, was plainly visible from the elevation on which sat the battery. The entire community seemed still asleep. No sign of life was apparent in any quarter, even around the blockhouses. Nothing was in evidence to reveal that every row of bushes, every leafy tree, every bit of earth large enough to hide a man, had its armed contingent. Prominent were the twin towers of the church, an historic old building in which it was said Cortez had prayed before going to conquer Mexico. At the moment, its beauty was marred by irregular loopholes cut in its walls. Through these openings men with rifles peered as the dawn brightened, while others stared from the towers above. Off in the outskirts waited the greatest threat— the stone and brick fort, built for just such an emergency.

As the Americans watched, the first sign of life, an ominous sign, came to their attention. Briskly up the flagpole atop the fort climbed the flag of Spain, waving defiantly like a flame-colored tongue in the swelling light.

Capron and his lieutenants puttered around the guns, examining fuses and ascertaining distances with their little brass range finders. They were impatient to begin. Caissons were some yards to the rear, while the horses had been tethered even farther back in the bushes.

The observers stood behind the caissons, speaking in quiet voices which seemed not even remotely connected with war. Among them were the reporters, who had broken camp at 4:45 A.M. and hurried forward along with a number of Cuban camp followers. James Creelman of William Randolph Hearst's staff stood off to the side, wrapped in thought. Somehow or other, through his mind ran the strange idea that before the day was ended that banner would be in his possession. John Fox, Jr., one day to be famous for his *Trail of the Lonesome Pine*, was there, too, thinking that nobody was as solemn as the occasion demanded, for soon one of those guns was going to fire. "It was not going to be a salute, nor a sunset gun, nor a Christmas or Fourth of July explosion," he wrote. "It would be loaded with a shell and was to be aimed at living men, and was meant to kill somebody."

Couriers moved about in various directions, tirelessly dedicated to their cause. Shortly before 6:30 A.M., one of them came up to Capron. He saluted and spoke tersely. The captain whirled and yelled: "Cannoneers, take your places!" Then, after a brief pause: "Fire!"

Fox, who had originally intended to join the Rough Riders before taking advantage of an opportunity to go to Cuba as a correspondent, reported:

> The man with the lanyard gave a quick jerk. There was a cap explosion at the butt of the gun, a bulging white cloud from the muzzle, the trailer bounded from its shallow trench and the wheels whirled back twice on the rebound, and the shell was hissing through the air . . . You could hear that awful hiss so plainly that you seemed to be following the shell with your naked eye; you could hear it above the reverberating roar of the gun up and down the coast mountain; hear it until six seconds later a puff of smoke answered beyond the Spanish column where the shell burst. Then in eight seconds—for the shell traveled much faster than sound—the muffled report of its bursting struck our ears, and all that was left of the first shot that started the battle was the thick sunlit smoke of the gun sweeping off through the brush, and the little mist-cloud of the shell rising slowly upward beyond the Spanish column, which seemed not to know that any harm was possible and near.

Realizing the shot was too high, the artillerymen made adjustments. Then all four of the pieces blasted forth in a united blast. Off where their shells struck, fountains of earth spouted into the air, and pinwheels of mortar dust, brick, and stone whirled off the fort. The correspondents and Cubans cheered, and Capron looked on with appreciation. He could see they had found the range.[1]

---

[1] This was Capron's last battle. On September 18, 1898, shortly after his return from Cuba, he died of fever at the home of his mother at Fort Myer, Virginia, across the Potomac River from Washington. Among the flowers on his grave was a wreath from President McKinley.

And then gradually from the grass and bushes surrounding the village came the sound of rifle fire. "It began as corn begins to pop, irregularly and with pauses," wrote one reporter. "Then it gathered volume and rippled and rolled and spread till it awoke a great echo somewhere in a little gully of the hills."

Straw hats moved without order along the Spanish trenches, bobbing up and down as men straightened to fire, or slunk down out of sight after pulling the trigger. The explosion of guns and the hiss of bullets could be heard, and yet the landscape in the village failed to take on the look of a battleground. This was attributable to the use of smokeless powder.

By then the morning had fully developed. The sun topped the San Cobre Mountains, spreading its warmth and bringing out the beauty of the palm trees towering over the lower growth. Through them crawled Americans in outmoded uniforms bent on killing Spaniards "to set old Cuba free." Sometimes they stood out in the cathedral light of some cleared space in the forest, or lay spread over the grass, in and out among the clumps of bushes. They moved in waving lines, running hither and thither, firing and reloading and firing. Through the aisles of foliage could be seen the floating smoke from their rifles. Sometimes it went up in little balls, white or bluish signals inviting death. Stanhope Sams was so impressed by the scene he gave it prominent space in his war dispatch for the day:

> I have never seen a more beautiful, a more magnificent spectacle. The sun seemed a huge ball of fire, ablaze on the topmost peak. It had not yet assumed that white glare it has at a higher station in the heavens, but seemed a fire kindled on some vast altar height. Its first beams fell in radiance on the doomed village of Caney, and flooded the brick fort until the ugly little fortification glowed like a jewel.

Capron's guns continued to bark. A shot tore a hole in the wall of the fort. So did another. Still another knocked down the flag, bringing more cheers from the correspondents and Cubans. Others broke the earth on all sides, leaving flaring scars in the greensward. But the Spaniards held their ground, firing steadily. Meanwhile, nearer drew the American soldiers, squirming on their bellies through the bushes and tall grass.

A British reporter, John Black Atkins, was late arriving. He picked his way along the road, staring ahead cautiously. At first he could see nothing and was conscious only of the growing sound of gunfire. But soon he met wounded men being helped or carried to the rear. Then he came upon a dead man, another, and another. "The sounds turned from confused rattling like the clapping of hands heard at a distance into sharp, crisp, metallic poppings, each with a meaning and a distinctness of its own," he recorded. "Still I could see nothing. But at last a thinning of the wood; small trees gave place to large trees; I passed through a mango grove, and there again was the village." He saw Chaffee's brigade and recognized it by its commander. He watched the general sitting astride his horse, hat on the back of his head, uniform soaking with sweat, his index finger poking the air as he excitedly gave orders and indicated directions.

Chaffee sent his men off to the right, along intricate ravines and valleys, through masses of tangled undergrowth. Next in line, in the center, was Ludlow's brigade, ordered to strike the Spanish in front and press toward their right flank. Coming also toward this flank, nearest to Santiago, was a brigade under Colonel Miles. This last unit had been held in reserve at the start, for it was thought the village would fall so rapidly its three regiments would not be needed.

The sound of battle carried clearly the three or four miles to El Pozo Hill, where Grimes's battery was as impatient to begin action as Capron's had been. This artillery took position during the early morning. Ogden Wells, on hand when it got there, told of what happened:

> A short consultation was held, and then it was determined to plant the guns on the crest of the hill and open fire. It was a fine sight to see the great horses straining under the lash as they whirled the guns up the hill and into position, the men using whips, spurs and oaths freely, and all at once, and the officers running alongside waving their arms violently, shouting words of instruction and encouragement.

From where they stood around the guns, the artillerists could see across the distance to the ridges of San Juan, sparsely dotted with trees. Ringing the great sweep were mountains that made an amphitheater of the battle area. A pond could be seen in the meadow, just across San Juan River, a stream only about ten yards wide and from a foot to waist deep. Here and there were summer villas, most of them owned by wealthy families of Santiago. They had roofs of red tile, resembling Javanese homes. But all of them, to meet the present emergency, had been converted to war purposes, with loopholes and barricades. Up along the crest of the hills were yellow streaks marking the rifle pits of the Spaniards. Aimed at these, fully 2500 yards away, were Grimes's guns.

McClernand was there on Pozo Hill, too, watch in hand, with responsibilities great. At 3 o'clock that morning, one hour before reveille, he had been summoned to Shafter's tent. The huge commanding general lay prostrate in bed, incapacitated, he explained, by gout and his exertions the day before. He wanted the Adjutant General to take his place at the front, to establish battle headquarters on El Pozo, and to direct action from that point. Lieutenant John D. Miley, his aide-de-camp, would assist.

And now McClernand was waiting on developments at Caney. General Sumner, commanding the ill Wheeler's cavalry, and General Kent, in command of the infantry, were at his elbow, standing by for orders to start moving. Sumner became impatient. "Well, when are we going to begin this thing?" he demanded. In reply, McClernand reminded him of Lawton's parting words at the previous day's conference: the other divisions were not to be ordered to attack until he had been given time to capture Caney.

But by 8 o'clock McClernand was convinced Lawton was materially delayed, that Caney was not the easy prize they had anticipated. The longer the fighting to the right went on, the more the Adjutant General worried. It was his fear the Spaniards might send troops from San Juan and defeat Lawton before the divisions waiting behind El Pozo Hill could cross the San Juan River and go into action.

At last McClernand decided to wait no longer. He gave his orders. Sumner was to move across the river and deploy to the right, with his left resting on the Santiago road. Immediately on his heels would come the infantry under Kent, to deploy to the left, with its right next to the road. After reaching position, they were to await further orders.

As Sumner and Kent moved away from headquarters, McClernand sent word to Grimes to open fire. It was a sight to watch the artillery captain in action, for he had about him the bespectacled air of a professor and would have seemed more in character approaching a blackboard with chalk in hand. But his role on this day was that of a soldier. He gave signal to the number one gun. As its charge belched forth in a cloud of white smoke, photographer Burr McIntosh, camera set at fifty feet, squeezed the bulb, taking a picture that would go into the annals of American history. The other guns joined in, and, correspondingly, there was evidence of panic at certain points along the Spanish lines. Surprisingly, the Spaniards did not immediately reply.

Wood, waiting beside Roosevelt, remarked that he wished the brigade under his command could be moved elsewhere. Scarcely had he spoken when a peculiar, whistling sound was heard and a shell burst in air above them. The Spaniards had sighted their guns against the great cloud of white smoke that poured from Grimes's guns and were firing at dead range.

Wood and Roosevelt sprang to their feet and leaped on their horses. Just as they did, a second shot exploded overhead, showering shrapnel. One piece struck Roosevelt on the wrist, barely breaking the skin, but it quickly raised a bump as big as a hickory nut. He whipped out a handkerchief and tied it in such a manner as to stem the blood, commenting, "The Spaniards will have to do better than that."

Four other Riders were wounded by this shell, one of them Mason Mitchell, a man whose name was a byword around the Lambs' Club and theatrical circles of New York. He was a prominent, middle-aged actor with such a fine physique that he once had demonstrated gymnasium equipment in a Broadway window. Described as "a gentleman in every way," his life had been adventurous. He was a personal friend of Robert Louis Stevenson, the author, and possessed a medal presented him by Queen Victoria for his services as chief of scouts in the Riel Rebellion in Canada. His wound, a shrapnel strike in the shoulder as he started to rise from the ground, was not fatal, but it would end his participation in the war.

Other havoc was dealt out by the Spaniards. "There was music in the air and death all around," Rough Rider Frank Wilson wrote home.

Off to the left stood a group of Cubans. A shell struck among them, killing and wounding a number, and they scattered wildly. For the Rough Riders it also was an inelegant moment. Roosevelt directed them to the underbrush on the back side of El Pozo and later had much trouble getting them together again. Before Wood could get his lead horse over the brow of the hill, it was shot through the lungs.

For fifteen or twenty minutes, the firing continued and then gradually died away. When it ended, Wood, hearing from Sumner, formed his brigade, with the Rough Riders in front, and ordered it to follow the 1st Brigade to the ford across San Juan River.[2] Packs were cast aside under care of a special detail.

Among the Riders who got in line was Ted Miller. As he waited for the march to begin, he made the last entry in his diary:

> I went up the hill in advance, and got a glimpse of an outpost; small village occupied by Spaniards. Bombarding began about twenty minutes after six, and was centered on a small village in our rear. About an hour later, after constant bombardment, a skirmish took place. Must stop. Now in line. Goodbye; will send this. Please excuse mistakes, for I have written in a hurry.

In column of fours, the Riders formed. Slowly along the jungle trail they moved, stepping rapidly when the crowded conditions would permit, but generally advancing at a torturous pace and stopping frequently. Later the path along which they trod became so narrow they had to move in single file. Dead horses and punctured canteens lay along the way.

At one point they passed a strange group of men. Minds assembled therein were bridging the gap from the present state of war to a future when there would be peace. As each individual broke away from the cluster, he did so shudderingly. Through the legs of a man who lay upon the ground in their midst had passed a piece of shrapnel. It had left headless an appendage assigned by nature to two major functions. The victim was the orderly of Major Philip Reade, Inspector General.

At the field hospital set up the day before, wounded men began streaming in from the direction of Caney before 9 o'clock. They struggled along a road that reporter Crane said "should have a tragic name like the sunken road at Waterloo." Some walked unaided, with an arm or shoulder that had been hastily bandaged. Others hobbled or clung to comrades, their slit trousers exposing bloody wrappings. Some were shot horribly about the head or face and had to be led. The badly wounded, the insensible, and the dying lay on stretchers borne by soldiers or hospital attendants. Many sat along the road, unable to continue. All, regardless of their

---

[2] Colonel McClernand testified before the Committee to Investigate the Conduct of the War that, moving on foot, he personally gave Roosevelt orders to move, "which seemed to please him."

condition and including those with Red Cross bands on their arms, were in danger of becoming targets of the sharpshooters in the trees. To these assassins the brassards of mercy men meant nothing.

After a while, the firing from the Spanish trenches indicated to the Rough Riders that the head of the 1st Brigade had reached the ford and was crossing. Later, as the 1st Volunteers neared the ford, Roosevelt was instructed to move across, march half a mile or so to the right, and halt until he received further orders. He hurried his men along, spurred by the sight of the balloon approaching the river. He presumed correctly that it would be a special target for enemy fire. Just as the Riders were climbing the bank on the far side, after wading through water up to their knees, a barrage of fire sounded from San Juan ridge. Henry Haywood, the big New York policeman and ex-Cuban ship pilot, was struck in the stomach by a bullet. Men near him thought it sounded like someone jamming a fist into a pillow. Yards behind, the balloon partly collapsed, in a confusion of death and destruction among the members of the 1st and 10th Regular Cavalry and the infantry nearest the site. The time was 11:15.

Of this balloon it would be said in official War Department reports that "it was a relief to know that it was crushed to earth never to rise again." Some reports said it brought death or wounds to over 400 men in an area no larger than a city block, in a path not as wide as a city sidewalk. Stephen Crane watched it fall and was moved by the sight. He pictured the moment:

> The balloon was dying, dying a gigantic and public death before the eyes of two armies. It quivered, sank, faded into the trees amid the flurry of a battle that was suddenly and tremendously like a storm. The American battery thundered behind the men with a shock that seemed likely to tear the backs of their heads off. The Spanish shrapnel fled on a line to their left, swirling and swishing in supernatural velocity. The noise of the rifle bullets broke in their faces like the noise of so many lamp-chimneys or sped overhead in swift cruel spitting. And at the front the battle sound, as if it were simply music, was beginning to swell and swell until the volleys rolled like surf.

But while it had caused a heavy toll, the balloon brought one helpful result. From its basket before it sank into the jungle, Colonel Derby spied a trail to the left, a short distance back, that led to a ford lower downstream. Some of the congestion could be relieved by directing the left wing to follow this route until it got into position.

As the balloon fell to earth, Derby leaped from the basket and ran to tell General Kent about his discovery. Waiting near the entrance to the alternate route were three battalions of the 71st New York Infantry. Among them were quite a few elites, but more than three hundred of the members had never fired a gun. The first battalion swung into the trail. At that moment a barrage of shrapnel descended upon it, just as General Chaffee had warned would be the case. For a few minutes there was a melee as the New Yorkers fell to the ground in terror or doubled back upon the trail. Only by forming a human barrier with members of his staff and himself was Kent able to stop the fleeing militiamen. A *Herald* correspondent wrote defensively in words remarkable for their understatement:

> It is true that one battalion showed nervousness. It was the first time it had been under fire, and it showed an inclination to get out of the range of shrapnel without waiting for orders, and began to retire. This confusion was only momentary, and the battalion quickly regained presence of mind and marched forward into the thick of the fight.

But the behavior of this one battalion tainted the reputation of the entire regiment. Members of other units heaped ridicule as they marched past the prostrate New Yorkers to go into battle. Afterward there would be an investigation of the affair.

At 11:25 A.M., Grimes's guns opened again. They were fired for the purpose of drawing some of the artillery shells away from the marching columns.

Though Grimes's battery was doing its duty, it was not enough in the eyes of the British correspondent, John Black Atkins. He wrote: "But this hill—the look of it was enough to stagger any man. Was this to be taken practically without the aid of artillery? Artillery should have battered, and battered, and battered the position, and then the infantry might have swept up on the run. But this had not been done. The infantry stood before the thing alone."

In the intense heat, Roosevelt led his Volunteers through the high grass to the open area at the foot of San Juan ridge. He kept on until he came to the Santiago road, at that point a sort of sunken lane. There he called a halt and told the men to find cover. Captain Mills was with him. The other aide, Captain Shipp, was lying back on the trail, dead from a Spanish bullet.

The firing from the Spaniards was growing steadily hotter. The point where the Americans waited would in the next hour or so earn a place in history as another "bloody angle." Directly in front, from left to right, were the 9th, 6th, and 3rd. But the lines of all the regiments already were overlapping in places, for the cactus and Spanish bayonet were so bad that the men could not move through them and were forced to detour.

Bullets from the Mauser rifles seemed to drive in sheets through the trees and tall jungle grass. In most instances, they made a small hole that quickly healed. But occasionally they seemed to explode in air as the brass coating on them came loose. It was then they had a jagged edge that left a ghastly wound.

The road along which the Riders lay was bordered by wire fences. It led up toward and between the hills at their front, Kettle Hill on the right, closer to them, and San Juan Hill, on the left. Roosevelt rode his horse along the lane, an ecstatic figure. He was buoyed by excitement and by his natural bent to be doing something at all times. Many of the men lay close under the side of the road. Others slipped into the San Juan River and crouched behind its banks. Still others squirmed into the incomplete security of patches of tall grass. Those who survived would never forget the intense heat.

With telling effect, volleys of firing came from the ridge. Horace Devereaux, the expert pistol shot and end rush from Princeton, was dangerously wounded while lying with his troop on the edge of the river. A bullet whizzed through the fingers of Lieutenant Sherrard Coleman of Troop E, causing him to think for a moment his hand had been shot away. He was a thirty-three-year-old Virginian, native of Louisa County, who had helped build the Chesapeake & Ohio Railroad from Richmond to Newport News before coming West to Santa Fe, where he was employed as a special agent of the Justice Department. Ernest Haskell, a West Point cadet gaining battle experience during his vacation from the Academy, was shot in the stomach. Roosevelt saw him fall and rushed to his side. "It's all right, Colonel, I'm going to get well," the youth assured him. "Don't bother about me." Roosevelt, who treated all of his men as if they were his sons or brothers, held him momentarily by the hand, mistakenly positive that the wound was mortal.

As Roosevelt straightened, he noticed his orderly, Saunders, had been felled by the heat and was lying in the grass nearby. He went to his side and examined him. Seeing the gravity of his condition, he summoned another soldier only a few feet away to serve in his place. This fellow rushed up, snapped to attention, and saluted. He was told to go back and ask whatever general he encountered if the 1st Volunteers could advance, as they were being badly shot up. The man saluted again. But before he could move away, he was struck in the throat by a bullet and fell, dying, across Roosevelt.[3]

Farther along the line, Bucky O'Neill, mustachioed and every inch a Westerner, strolled up and down in front of his men. He was calmly smoking his customary cigarette and did nothing—not so much as stoop his shoulders—to avoid enemy bullets.[4] Cries for him to lie down came from several points. Many tales had come out of the West of the bravery of this colorful character, and here was an example. One of his sergeants screamed above the others: "Captain, a bullet is sure to hit you!" Bucky took the cigarette from his mouth, blew out a cloud of smoke, and smilingly shouted back, "Sergeant, the Spanish bullet isn't made that will kill me!" He turned for a moment to discuss with Captain Robert Sewall, General Young's adjutant, the direction from which the enemy fire was coming. As he faced the ridge again, a bullet struck him in the mouth and emerged at the back of his head. The poetry-loving mayor passed into the beyond before he hit the ground.

Fire from Spanish sharpshooters now became especially annoying. It sounded along the edge of the jungle across the river, seemingly coming from every tree with leafy coverage. Some of the Riders attempted to return it, but the smokeless powder used by the Spaniards failed to provide a target.

It was now approaching 1 P.M. Roosevelt began to act with frenzy. He was not the officer to stand by inactive when he thought action was advisable. For close to two hours they had been waiting while other regiments moved into position. More messengers were sent back in the hope of getting permission to advance. From O'Neill's troop, temporarily confused by the death of its leader, appeared a huge Arizona miner, Henry Bardshar. Without waiting for orders, he attached himself to Roosevelt as his orderly, and it was only circumstances that kept this fellow, too, from being sent in search of a general.

Just as Bardshar approached, up rushed Captain Mills, one of

---

[3] Roosevelt did not recognize and could not identify this Rider in later references to the incident, an odd development in view of the fact that he prided himself on knowing by name every man in the regiment.

[4] "He had a theory," Roosevelt wrote, "that an officer ought never to take cover—a theory which was, of course, wrong, though in a volunteer organization the officers should certainly expose themselves very fully, simply for its effect on the men."

those Roosevelt had sent to the rear. He reported that he had found Sumner and that the general ordered the 1st Volunteers to move forward and support the regulars in the assault on the hills in front. "The red-roofed house yonder is your objective," added Mills.

"The instant I received the order," Roosevelt related, "I sprang on my horse and then my 'crowded hour' began."[5]

Quickly he formed his column in troops, some on each side of the road and each extended in open skirmishing order. It was a flashback to the hot, dusty days in training camp at San Antonio. Micah Jenkins, his eyes dancing with excitement, was leading the first squadron. Roosevelt took position at the rear of the regiment, as customary, but he was not to stay there long. He had in mind going into action on foot as at Las Guásimas, but the heat was so oppressive he knew he would be unable to move about much and, besides, he could see and be seen better on horseback.

Back and forth he galloped, calling to the troopers to go forward and shouting brief instructions to the officers. They ran in spurts, a section going forward a few yards and then dropping to the ground to fire. Instantly another section advanced, repeating the movement.

Suddenly Roosevelt noticed he was urging the rearmost line forward at such a pace that it was crowding the one directly in front. He rode through both of them and on to the head of the regiment. There he came upon the rear platoons of the 9th Cavalry, the unit of black Indian fighters. They were prone in the grass, with their white officers standing and shouting to them encouragingly.

Roosevelt spoke to a captain. He shouted that the Rough Riders were ordered to support the regulars in the attack on the hills and that in his opinion they could be taken only by rushing them.

The captain replied that he had been told to keep his men lying where they were, that he could not charge without further orders.

[5] In February 1913, only four months after a would-be assassin wounded Roosevelt at Milwaukee, he was the guest of honor at a dinner given by twenty-two of the Rough Riders at the Plaza Hotel in New York. In telling of the attempt on his life, he said: "For an instant it flashed on my mind I must behave as the brave boys of my regiment would expect me to behave. If I had been shot down in Cuba, I would have had to keep up to the limit. That's what the boys would have expected of their colonel—to keep on leading them to the end. Well, that's the way I felt out there, and that's the way I tried to act."

"Where is your colonel?" shouted Roosevelt.

The captain shrugged.

"Then I am the ranking officer here," Roosevelt said, "and I give you the order to charge."

The captain hesitated.

Roosevelt's horse was prancing. Behind him were his sturdy Rough Riders, waiting for the signal to push on, waiting to battle on foot and not in the stormy, whooping, Indian-fashion charge by horse that they had envisioned at San Antonio.

Roosevelt shouted, "Then let my men through!"

Forward into the lines of the 9th he rode.[6]

The Riders followed. Next on the left was the 1st Regular Cavalry and, farther over, some on one side of the road and some on the other, were members of the 3rd, 6th, and 10th Cavalry. As they watched the 1st Volunteers go forward, they, too, caught the spirit of the moment and joined in the charge.[7] Cheering sounded,

[6] The captain Roosevelt addressed was Henry Anson Barber of Cambridge, Missouri. Throughout the campaign, this officer wrote notes on a small pad kept in his pocket, tearing out the pages and mailing them to his wife at the first opportunity. Awaiting him upon his return home was this entry concerning the incident at the foot of Kettle Hill:

"The tension on the men was great. Suddenly a line of men appeared coming from our right. They were advancing through the long grass, deployed as skirmishers, and were under fire. At their head, or rather in front of them and leading them, rode Colonel Roosevelt. He was very conspicuous, mounted as he was . . . I heard someone calling to them not to fire into us, and seeing Colonel Carroll, reported to him, and was told to go out and meet them, and caution them as to our position, we being between them and the enemy. I did so, speaking to Colonel Roosevelt. I also told him we were under orders not to advance, and asked him if he had received any orders. He replied that he was going to charge the Spanish trenches . . . And so we started. Colonel Roosevelt, of the Rough Riders, started the whole movement to the left, which was the first advance of the assault."

[7] Hardened by years of service, the black soldiers of the 9th and 10th Cavalry made new reputations in Cuba. Harmon Wynkoop, the Rough Rider reporting the war for the Santa Fe New Mexican, wrote the newspaper: "Every word that has been said in regard to the bravery and efficiency of the Negro soldier can be fairly appreciated by every man, at least, who is in Cuba, and more so by the Rough Riders, who were in the battles of Las Guásimas and San Juan with them, than by any other regiment. We saw them make their great, fearless charges, and we cheered them, too . . . Too much cannot be said of the Negro soldier, and words can never be found to express the praise due them."

A similar opinion was expressed by Trooper Alexander H. Wallace, who wrote his sister: "We have not a Rough Rider in the regiment who will not take off his hat to the 10th Cavalry—the colored regiment—as fighters. They do not know fear. Excellent shots, greatly ambitious in the extreme."

One of the Rough Riders, Frank Knox, got separated from the regiment in the charge at San Juan and fought for a time with a troop of the 10th Cavalry. He later stated in a letter home: "In justice to the colored race, I must say that I never saw braver men anywhere. Some of those who rushed up the hill will live in my memory forever."

was taken up on the left, and in the distance rolled on and on, American soldiers joining together in a mighty charge, as they had done down through the years of history—except in the 1860s. A Pawnee Indian, William J. Pollock, master penman, artist, musician, and son of Chief Big Eagle, let out a warwhoop that men within hearing remembered ever afterward and talked about.

Staring from El Pozo Hill, an eyewitness described what he saw:

> Suddenly a thin file of men appeared against the bright green of a meadow, just to the right of the valley road and near the edge of the woods in front of San Juan. Everyone was intensely astonished, for it hardly seemed possible that our men could have advanced so far under so murderous a hail of bullets and shrapnel. But there was no mistaking the dark blue shirts of the American soldiers . . . Before we had done wondering, the same file had gone through the last belt of wood, had crossed the river, whose bed was marked by a thicker line of heavy trees, and was going up the hill to the right toward a small red building, apparently a hacienda full of Spanish soldiers.
>
> It was a glorious, almost incredible sight . . . It was magnificent. Probably it is against all the rules of modern warfare to attack so strong a position without the aid of strong artillery. This attack was covered by only one battery of light artillery . . .
>
> Soon we could see dark figures stealing out from the trees in the center and left. Kent's men executed a simultaneous movement with wonderful precision, so that a quarter of an hour after the Rough Riders first broke cover, the whole green meadow bottom between the woods and the ridge was live with our soldiers darting on through the grass, crouching as they went along, to avoid as much of the fire as possible.

An exuberant observer among the press corps yelled: "By God, there go our boys up the hill!"

Wrote Stephen Crane:

> There is many a good American who would give an arm to get the thrill of patriotic insanity that coursed through us when we heard that yell. Yes, they were going up the hill, up the hill. It was the best moment of anybody's life. An officer said to me afterward: "If we had been in that position and the enemy had come at us, we would have piled them up so high the last man could not have climbed over."

Crane was particularly observant of the foreign attachés standing nearby. "It is very gallant, but very foolish," he heard one of them say. Another agreed: "Why, they can't take it, you know. Never in the world. It is slaughter, absolute slaughter." The reporter noticed that the Japanese representative shrugged his shoulders and said nothing.

Nearer the advancing men, sitting his horse off to one side in the shade of a tree, watched the ill Wheeler. He was accompanied by his son, serving as his aide, and by two orderlies. The sound of the firing had been too much for him, and he had disobeyed his doctor and left his bed to go to the front. The first part of the trip was made by wagon, but when he saw wounded men lying along the roadside, he insisted on mounting a horse and releasing the vehicle for their use. A reporter was among those who observed him, "looking frail and white and ill," and thought he had the distrait air of a man who had been eating Cuban mullet. Another reporter interpreted his behavior differently, writing that he was the only man he saw "who did not dodge or duck during all the terrible firing of shot and shell." Running through the ex-Confederate's mind must have been thoughts of Shiloh and Stones River and Knoxville and Atlanta. He may even have imagined that the soldiers whose progress he was watching were garbed in gray.

A young officer in the 10th Cavalry, facing a bright military future, described the action as the Americans went up San Juan Hill: "White regiments, black regiments, Regulars and Rough Riders, representing the young manhood of the North and South, fought shoulder to shoulder, unmindful of race or color, unmindful of whether commanded by ex-Confederate or not, and mindful only of their common duty as Americans." He was John J. Pershing, one day to lead khaki-clad doughboys to victory on the battlefields of France.

Richard Harding Davis was impressed by the smallness of the charging force. It gave him the impression that someone had made a terrible mistake. "One's instinct was to call to them to come back," he wrote, adding:

> The thing that impressed one the most was that they were so few . . . You felt that someone had blundered and that those few men were blindly following out some madman's mad order. It was not heroic then; it seemed merely terribly pathetic. The pity of it, the folly of such a sacrifice was what held you.

They had no glittering bayonets, they were not massed in fighting array. There were a few men in advance, bunched together and creeping up a steep, sunny hill, the tops of which roared and flashed with flame. The men held their guns pressed across their breasts and stepped heavily as they climbed. Behind these first few, spreading out like a fan, were single lines of men, slipping and scrambling in the smooth grass, moving forward with difficulty as though they were wading waist-high through water, moving slowly, carefully, with strenuous effort. It was much more wonderful than any swinging charge could have been. They walked to greet death at every step, many of them, as they advanced, sinking suddenly or pitching forward and disappearing in the high grass, but the others waded on stubbornly, forming a thin blue line that kept creeping higher and higher up the hill. It was as inevitable as the rising tide. It was a miracle of self-sacrifice, a triumph of bulldog courage, which one watched with breathless wonder.

Roosevelt, remembering his awkward experience at Las Guásimas, was riding without saber. In the saddle, he seemed taller in body. His hat was forced down over his head at a jaunty angle, almost completely hiding his sideburnless haircut. With eyes snapping, he constantly shouted, baring his overly prominent teeth and waving his arms scythe fashion as a signal for his men to follow.[8]

The black troopers of the 9th tore down the fence at one point. Roosevelt rode through, remembering in detail his movements:

By that time we were all in the spirit of the thing and greatly excited by the charge, the men cheering and running forward between shots, while the delighted faces of the foremost officers . . . as they ran at the head of their troops will always stay in my mind. As soon as I was in the lane, I galloped forward a few

[8] A frequent comment made of Roosevelt by his men in later years was: "At San Juan, he didn't say, 'Go on'; he said, 'Come on!'"

Roosevelt seemed to be much more in stride in this battle. He later wrote: "I had not enjoyed the Guásimas fight at all, because I had been uncertain as to what I ought to do. But the San Juan fight was entirely different."

His actions on this date led one of his men to write: "If the colonel was looking out for a prospective governorship, it must have been in Hades, for no one courted death more."

Richard Harding Davis reported: "No one who saw Roosevelt take that ride expected him to finish it alive. As the only mounted man, he was the most conspicuous object in the range of the rifles, and only 200 yards ahead. It looked like foolhardiness, but, as a matter of fact, he set the pace with his horse and inspired the men to follow."

yards until I saw that the men were well started, and then galloped back to help Goodrich, who was in command of his troop, get his men across the road so as to attack the hill from that side. Captain Mills had already thrown three of the other troops of the regiment across the road for the same purpose.

Wheeling around, I then again galloped toward the hill, passing the shouting, cheering, firing men, and went up the lane, splashing through a small stream . . . Being on horseback, I was, of course, able to get ahead of my men on foot, excepting my orderly, Henry Bardshar, who had run ahead very fast in order to get better shots at the Spaniards . . .[9]

As Roosevelt rode, the blue polka dot handkerchief on the back of his hat flapped behind him like a shirttail in the wind.[10] A part way up the hill, he encountered another barbed-wire fence. Jumping off his horse, he turned the animal loose, never expecting to see it again. It had been scraped by a couple of bullets, one of which had nicked the rider's elbow.

As Roosevelt now hurried on by foot, Bardshar, in front of him, stopped to shoot. Two Spaniards fell, and the leader remembered that they were the only two of the enemy he saw fall to aimed shots by any of his men. Among the Americans who went down at this point was Captain Mills, shot through the head by a bullet that destroyed the sight of one eye permanently and temporarily impaired that of the other.

Now and then, above the steady roar of battle, sounded a noise like a giant rapping on a door. It was the Colt automatics, firing with the compliments of the Rough Riders.

Past the ranch buildings, to the top of the hill, the Americans

[9] One of the Western members who witnessed the charge got this impression: "It's a sight to see him in a fight. You'd think his hide was double-chilled steel and three thicknesses, and that he known it watching him running around waving his gun to bring the boys up and taking a crack at the Spaniards now and then, just to show us how. I don't never trust no man with gold-rimmed glasses and a beaming smile no more. When I seen him at San Antonio, I figured he was raised a pet and wouldn't kick if you tickled his heels with a toothpick. I wouldn't undertake to harness him with a pitchfork."

[10] Jess Langdon says that Roosevelt's eyeglasses were shot off during the charge and that, without breaking the stride of his horse, he fumbled in a pocket for the extra pair he always carried. He recalls that the bullet came from the rear and hit the outside left rim of the heavy, steel-rimmed spectacles that the colonel always wore when engaged in strenuous activity of any kind. He also deduces that Roosevelt made no mention of the incident for two possible reasons: (a) politics—the 71st New York fired on the Rough Riders by mistake, thinking from the type of their uniforms that they were Spaniards, and (b), if he had attributed the shooting to the enemy, he would have been accused of facing to the rear.

pushed. The Spaniards retreated across a wide valley to the next line of hills, where they opened fire with rifles and one or two pieces of artillery. The crest of the first ridge was soon swarming with men, both Riders and the black troopers of the regular cavalry, and afterward there would be debate over who got there first.[11]

Off to the left they could see the infantry charging up toward the blockhouses on San Juan Hill. At the front was the white-haired, white-bearded Hawkins, tall and erect in battle, waving his hat and yelling, "Come on!" Men ran a few yards and then fell to the ground, forming a dark battle line that gleamed on a sunstruck field. Flags fluttered above them, red, white, and blue in a kaleidoscope of green. The hot, dangerous flashes of the rifles were visible, pouring out clouds of smoke that drifted slowly and insolently across the fields. The crescendo was deafening, haunting, shocking man with the guilt of what man could and would do to his fellow man. In the distance, figures seemed to be lying behind a long gray wall: it was smoke that gradually drifted away, baring more flags, all pushing to the front.

Inspired by the sight, Roosevelt hurried about, shouting directions and pointing toward the enemy trenches around the blockhouses. Finally he managed to bring some order to the confused throng, and it opened a heavy fire.

All at once above the roar of the carbines could be heard a drumming noise, sharp and ecstatic. "The Spanish machine guns!" cried some of the men. Roosevelt noticed the sound came from the flat ground to the left. He suddenly recognized what he heard and yelled with more than customary Rooseveltian exultation: "It's the Gatlings, men, our Gatlings!" Cheering spread all along the line of cavalrymen.

For eight and a half minutes the Gatlings kept up their fire. They caused a definite break in the fighting, for signs of wavering were noticeable along the Spanish lines. Parker ordered them silenced only because he was afraid of hitting some of the advancing Americans.

Thinking his men would follow, Roosevelt now decided to lead another charge. He made his way through some barbed-wire entanglements and started running. Only a few noticed his action. One of these was young Oliver Norton, who lay in line beside his

---

[11] In his report to Wood, Roosevelt wrote: "The guidons of Troops E and G were first planted on the summit, though the first men up were some A and B troopers who were there with me."

brother, Edward G., corporal of B Troop and soon to be made a
sergeant. Both were University of Michigan boys. Oliver leaped to
his feet. "For God's sake follow the colonel!" he shouted. Just as
he uttered the words, a bullet passed through his head, killing him
in the manner Bucky O'Neill had died.[12]

For a hundred yards or more, Roosevelt ran before turning and
seeing that only five troopers were with him. Bullets were ripping
the grass around them. One man, Henry Clay Green, a twenty-eight-
year-old North Carolina mining engineer who had moved to the
West, fell mortally wounded. Another, Winslow Clark, Harvard boy
from Milton, Massachusetts, drew the attention of a sharpshooter
and was shot successively in the leg and through the left lung.

Realizing there was no use in going on with the three men
left and fearing the enemy would think a retreat was under way
if they all ran back together, Roosevelt told the others to wait while
he brought up more troopers. He dashed away, running like a youth,
and went over the crest of the hill. He was angry at his Rough
Riders for not following him.

The Roosevelt teeth were much in evidence when he returned
to where the others waited. He shouted and pointed. The men
nearest him understood.

"We didn't hear you!" they cried. "We didn't see you go. Lead on.
We'll follow."

Roosevelt wanted other regiments in support. He saw General
Sumner farther down the hill and ran to him, asking if he might
make the charge. Sumner told him to proceed with it, that he
would see that the men followed.

A general rush started as Roosevelt ran over the crest of the hill
and again across the valley. Lieutenant Goodrich found himself beside his old college chum, Ted Miller, who seemed to be enjoying
himself immensely. They charged, stopped to rest, then charged
again, their eyes on a rise of ground ahead that would give them

---

[12] The father of these two boys, E. G. Norton of Eustis, Florida, when he heard of
Oliver's death, sent to Santiago another son, Gould G., to join the Rough Riders.
With him the boy brought a letter of introduction from his parent addressed to
Captain J. H. McClintock of B Troop. It stated: "This is my third son. I send him to
you to take the place of my son, Oliver, who was killed. It is religion with the
Nortons to serve their country."

The following year, the then Secretary of War, Elihu Root, asked Roosevelt to
recommend members of his regiment whom he considered good officer material. The
colonel replied: "E. G. Norton of Eustis, Florida, would be a first-class man for a
commission. He was a sergeant under me and did his duty in every way. His brother
was killed by my side at the top of Kettle Hill."

49. An officer stares with glasses into the distance from a point near a hacienda on El Pozo Hill.

50. The dynamite gun taken to Cuba by the Rough Riders.

51. The trail from El Pozo Hill along which the Rough Riders moved.

52. Rough Riders fording a stream en route to Kettle Hill.

53. Rough Riders moving to the front prior to the charge up Kettle Hill.

54. The balloon floating above the jungle at San Juan just before Spanish bullets brought it to the ground.

55. The fighting along El Pozo as depicted by artist William Glackens.

56. One of the huge sugar kettles that gave the hill up which the Rough Riders charged its name.

57. Some of the black troops who fought beside the Rough Riders and earned their esteem as fighters.

58. Wounded Rough Riders going to the rear meet a companion headed toward the fighting.

59. An ammunition train moves past the Rough Riders on its way to the front.

60. Entrance to Santiago Harbor, showing Morro Castle on the promontory in the distance. The wreckage of the *Merrimac* rises above the water nearest the camera, while the ship aground nearer shore is the Spanish vessel *Reina Mercedes*, sunk by the American fleet when she attempted to escape.

61. Wheeler's cavalry camp at the foot of San Juan Hill.

62. Scene along a part of the line held by the Rough Riders, showing the tents and huts in which they tried to avoid the frequent rains.

63. Roosevelt, surrounded by Rough Riders, pictured on a hill overlooking Santiago.

protection. Just as they neared it, a volley came from the Spaniards. Five men dropped, Miller among them. Only thirty bullets of the 110 issued him the day before were still in his belt. Goodrich ran on, unaware of what had happened.

Sharpshooter Henry Love of Danville, Kentucky, lying near, shouted: "Miller, I'll come to you in a minute!"

Miller shouted back: "That's all right, Love! Don't bother about me!"

Harrison J. Holt, Harvard boy, reached him first. Miller knew he was badly hurt, knew his body was paralyzed below the shoulders.

"I'm going, Harry," he whispered to Holt. "But it's in a good cause, isn't it?"

Holt examined him. A bullet had entered the left shoulder and passed out through the right shoulder, injuring the spinal cord along the way.

Goodrich, up ahead, noticed that Miller was down and rushed back.

"It's hard to breathe," the wounded trooper told him, "but I feel little pain."

Goodrich directed Love and Holt to remain there, found a hospital attendant and ordered him to aid Miller, after which he hurried on to catch up with the charging Roosevelt. The Spaniards were beginning to fall back before this new surge from the Americans. Their flight was hurried by the sound of Parker's Gatlings, pushing toward the front, bent on being a part of the final action. Whenever they were heard, cheering burst forth above the sound of battle along the line of charging men. It echoed like a wave rolling in to shore.

Henry Bardshar, who had got separated from the colonel, was now beside him again. When they were within ten yards of the trenches, two Spaniards leaped up and fired. As they turned to run, Roosevelt blasted away with his revolver, missing the first, but killing the second.[13]

There was more confusion than ever as this second line of trenches was overrun. White and black Americans, regulars and volunteers, were intermingled, waiting for leadership. Roosevelt got a mixed lot of them together and pushed on after the enemy. The

[13] Later, in recommending Roosevelt for a Congressional Medal of Honor for his bravery in the battle of San Juan, Leonard Wood wrote: "During the assault, Colonel Roosevelt was the first to reach the trenches in his part of the line and killed one of the enemy with his own hand." The gun used by Roosevelt had been salvaged from the sunken *Maine* and given him by an admirer.

Spaniards were driven through a line of palm trees and over more hills, these without trenches. On reaching the crest of the last of them, the Americans found themselves overlooking Santiago, with the enemy backed up to the city's last line of fortifications, 700 yards away. There at the front, ready for action, were Parker's Gatlings.

"Our flag was within a thousand yards of the walls of Santiago," prematurely wrote Davis. "We had first seen our men cross the meadow on this side of the river at 12:30, and by 1:30, an hour later, Santiago was ours."

While Roosevelt and those around him were staring at the city, one of Sumner's aides came up with orders to halt and not to advance farther, but to hold the chain of hills at all hazards.[14] Similar instructions were received by Wood.

Half an hour or so after the San Juan ridges were in the possession of the Americans, the firing at Caney started anew. Moved to a new position nearer the village, the artillery opened from a point where it could aim a more direct fire at the blockhouses. Now the battle became more heated than at any time during the day. The entire forces of Chaffee, Ludlow, Miles, and Bates were thrown into action, and they closed in with deadly effect. General del Rey, the Spanish commander was dead, and so were two of his sons. The slaughter became terrific. At 4 o'clock in the afternoon, hours after it was thought the village would fall, the Spaniards sur-

[14] The man who delivered this message was Robert L. Howze of Texas, later a general and commandant of cadets at the United States Military Academy. The following December he wrote Roosevelt from West Point: "I saw you lead the line up the first hill—you were certainly the first officer to reach the top . . . In this your life was placed in extreme jeopardy, as you may recall, and as it proved by the number of dead left in that vicinity . . . After the line started on the advance from the first hill, I did not see you until after our line was halted, under a most galling fire, at the extreme front, where you afterward entrenched. I spoke to you there and gave instructions from General Sumner . . . You . . . scolded me for having my horse so high up on the ridge; at the same time you were exposing yourself most conspicuously while adjusting the line, for the example was necessary, as was proved when several colored soldiers . . . started at a run to the rear to assist a wounded colored soldier, and you drew your revolver and put short and effective stop to such apparent stampede—it quieted them. The position was hot, and now I marvel at your escaping there . . ."

In the 1920s, after the death of Roosevelt, a drive was started to erect a monument at Santiago. In a statement published in the New York *Times* on July 20, 1923, John C. Greenway, chairman of the fund-raising committee, explained that it was to commemorate "the day Colonel Roosevelt himself regarded as the greatest day of his life," adding: "Shortly after the battle he stated that he would rather have led the charge up San Juan than to have served three times in the United States Senate. He frequently remarked in later years that the battle of San Juan made him President."

rendered. It was estimated only about forty of the 520 engaged in the fight managed to escape in the direction of Santiago.

An eyewitness described the windup:

> Always our infantry advanced, drawing nearer and closing up on the village till at last they formed under the mangrove trees at the foot of the hill on which the stone fort stood. With a rush they swept up the slope and the stone fort was ours . . . You should have heard the yell that went up from the knoll on which the battery stood. Gunners, drivers, Cubans, correspondents swung their hats and gave a mighty cheer . . .
>
> From the blockhouses and isolated trenches from which the Spaniards could not safely retreat, flags of truce were waved. Guns and side arms were being taken away from such Spaniards as had outlived the pitiless fire, and their dead were being dumped without ceremony into the trenches after Spanish fashion.[15]

At the dressing station at San Juan ford, Captain Newgarden and his assistants were having a busy time administering to the wounded. Their supply of bandages long ago had been exhausted, and now they were tearing up shirts, underclothing, handkerchiefs, and other items as substitutes. As they worked over the ever increasing line of men, buzzards circled slowly overhead, gliding silently in a tireless motion significant of peace and serenity rather than a conclave of scavengers attracted by the dead strewn over a battlefield. Adding a similar touch, land crabs occasionally ran out onto the edge of the sandy stretch, stopped momentarily as if taking in the situation, and then scurried sidewise back into the security of the jungle.

Bullets flying through the air, clipping twigs and leaves from trees in their flight, reminded the medicos of giant mosquitoes. These dutiful workers bent with their labor, giving attention to a multitude of chores. During the battle, they had watched lines of men moving in opposite directions, those from San Juan the casualties and those meeting and passing them the reinforcements hurrying to the front. Sometimes these soldiers moving up were

---

[15] Jess Langdon walked along the trenches after the battle had ended. "I was ashamed of myself to be killing them because most of them were kids," he said in later years. "Many of them seemed like little boys with men's shoes on—manila rope-soled, canvas shoes—and some of them had three or four bullet holes in their heads. They looked like children."

struck by bullets or shrapnel while they waded the river, and the medical men had to drop what they were doing and rush out into the water to rescue the victims before they drowned.

Newgarden moved about more than the others. He reassured the wounded they were in less danger if they remained quiet. Those who were conscious lay with their eyes focused on the trees along the river bank, for from there were coming the deadly bullets of the sharpshooters. These enemies, most of them disguised in green uniforms which blended with the foliage, were reported to be life-term prisoners released from the Spanish jails under a promise of amnesty if they survived their deadly work. They shot at anything in sight—even the defenseless wounded lying on stretchers and the surgeons busy with their administrations.[16]

At one period during the battle, a dramatic incident took place within sight of the wounded lying under the protection of the river bank. Nearby was the dynamite gun that Hallett Alsop Borrowe and his crew had deserted after it jammed on the first discharge. Some of the crew waited around, among them Basil Ricketts, Princeton man, son of a general, like Borrowe a member of the social set. As shells struck around them, he and others madly dug a trench in which to bury the cases of dynamite stacked near the gun. Just as they lifted the boxes into the pit, Ricketts fell with a sharpshooter's bullet in the groin. "Cover them up!" he cried. "Don't mind me!" As one of his comrades lifted him and started through the river to a place of safety, he looked back and screamed: "Put logs and rocks on top!"

Over along the ridge facing Santiago, Roosevelt flattened his men out about fifty yards from the crest of the hill. A dozen or more of them had been wounded, but refused to go to the rear.

Before night came on, two officers of the 3rd Cavalry approached Roosevelt. They had heard a rumor, they said. There was talk of retiring from the position the Americans had fought so hard to take during the day. What they wanted to do was to protest such action in the strongest manner. Roosevelt said he had heard no

---

[16] Major General John C. Breckinridge, Inspector General and an ex-Confederate, told the Committe Investigating the Conduct of the War: "Some men threw ponchos, etc., over their heads for protection. Riding along the Sevilla-Santiago road, I counted eighteen dead soldiers along a path not 850 yards long and was piteously appealed to by many of our wounded to remove them to the undergrowth or elsewhere, where they would be concealed from the view of the sharpshooters."

such rumor, but he assured them he was in accord with their opposition to such a move.

Soon after dark, General Wheeler appeared. During the afternoon, he had resumed command of the cavalry division, and now, in characteristic fashion, was with the men nearest the enemy. "A very few words with Wheeler reassured us about retiring," Roosevelt recorded. "He had been through too much heavy fighting in the Civil War to regard the present fight as very serious, and he told us not to be under any apprehension, for he had sent word that there was no need whatever of retiring, and was sure we would stay where we were until the chance came to advance.[17]

Wheeler set up his headquarters in a cut between two hills. Immediately he gave indication he was there to stay, ordering ammunition brought to the front and the work of digging trenches pushed as rapidly as possible. At 5:40 P.M., he wrote Shafter that he thought it important to fortify the ridge, suggesting that the Engineers lay out the lines and the generals supervise the work. By getting these defensive preparations well forward during the night, he advised, it could be continued the following day, affording the men comparative security.

Later in the evening, Wheeler sent another message to Shafter:

> I examined the line in front of Wood's brigade, and gave the men shovels and picks and insisted on their going right to work. I also sent word to General Kent to come and get entrenching tools, and saw General Hawkins in person and told him the same thing. They all promised to do their best, but say the earth is rocky . . . A number of officers have appealed to us to have the

[17] In his autobiography, Roosevelt gave this account of the appearance of Wheeler: "Late in the evening [afternoon] after the fight, General Wheeler visited us at the front, and he told me to keep myself in readiness, as at any moment it might be decided to fall back. I answered: 'Well, General, I really don't know whether we would obey an order to fall back. We can take that city by a rush, and if we have to move out of here at all I should be inclined to make the rush in the right direction.' The old general, after a moment's pause, expressed his hearty agreement, and said that he would see that there was no falling back. He was a gamecock if ever there was one, but he was in very bad physical shape on the day of the fight. If there had been any one in high command to supervise and press the attack that afternoon, we would have gone right into Santiago."

Rough Riders within hearing distance remembered other words from Roosevelt: "It is a disgrace for the American Army to retreat at any time, especially three days prior to the anniversary of the signing of our Declaration of Independence. Is it compulsory to obey oral orders? If not, I will remain to die by the American flag, if I die alone."

line withdrawn and take up a strong position farther back, and I expect they will appeal to you. I have positively discountenanced this, as it would cost us much prestige.

The lines are now very thin, as so many men have gone to the rear with wounded and so many are exhausted; but I hope these men can be got up tonight, and with our line entrenched and Lawton on our right, we ought to hold tomorrow, but I fear it will be a severe day. If we can get through tomorrow all right, we can make our breastworks very strong the next night. You can hardly realize the exhausted condition of the troops.

During the day, Shafter sent two messages to Washington. At 9:34 A.M., he wired: ACTION NOW GOING ON, BUT FIRING ONLY LIGHT AND DESULTORY.

After the firing had ceased, he reported: HAD A VERY HEAVY ENGAGEMENT TODAY, WHICH LASTED FROM 8 A.M. UNTIL SUNDOWN. WE HAVE CARRIED THEIR OUTER WORKS AND ARE NOW IN POSSESSION OF THEM. THERE IS NOW ABOUT THREE-FOURTHS OF A MILE OF OPEN COUNTRY BETWEEN MY LINES AND CITY. BY MORNING TROOPS WILL BE ENTRENCHED AND CONSIDERABLE AUGMENTATION OF FORCES WILL BE THERE . . .

As Roosevelt set the men to digging trenches, he made a quick check of the casualties. He had gone into action with about four hundred men. Eighty-six of these had been killed or wounded, and half a dozen were missing. Forty had been prostrated by heat. Six even then were lugging the paralyzed Miller toward the field hospital in the rear. Of the eight troops, two were now commanded by captains, three by first lieutenants, two by second lieutenants, and one by a sergeant.

At Siboney, William Randolph Hearst, the newspaper magnate accused of helping bring on the war, sat down to prepare personally the report of battle for his New York *Journal* and San Francisco *Examiner*. He did so because his reporter, James Creelman, the eyewitness who had watched the Spanish flag rise at Caney during the morning and had imagined that it would be in his possession by nightfall, was now lying in the hospital seriously wounded. Hearst had been at the front, too, and was still tingling from the sights he had seen, including the collapse of the balloon and the can of pressed beef on his pack mule that had been pierced by a piece of shrapnel. His thoughts poured on paper:

Tonight as I write, ambulance trains are bringing wounded soldiers from the fierce battle around the little village of Caney.

Siboney, the base of the army, is a hospital and nothing more. There is no saying when the slaughter will cease. Tents are crowded with wounded, and hard-working surgeons are busy with medical work. There is an odor of antiseptics, and ambulances clatter through one narrow street.

Under the fierce firing of far heavier artillery than it was supposed the Spanish had, the American infantry and dismounted cavalry have done their work and done it nobly.

As Roosevelt directed the men in digging trenches—with bayonets and meat cans and tools left by the Spanish—he was approached with a proposition by Trooper Warren Crockett, the slim, spare Internal Revenue officer from Georgia. He had never been much good at using a shovel, he explained, but he had found some coffee and, if the colonel approved, he would serve the other men with this refreshing liquid while they did the digging. It was agreed, and a routine that went on into the night was started.

For ten minutes at a stretch a man dug, then stepped aside to allow someone else to take his place. While they worked, they could hear people hurrying through the streets of Santiago, and they wondered whether the city was being abandoned.

Around midnight the digging was halted. After hours and hours of marching and fighting and shoveling—many without food—the men dropped down to sleep wherever they could. The packs they had left back at El Pozo had met an unkindly fate. The guard detail assigned to watch them was diverted during the excitement of battle to transport wounded to the rear and, as they moved away, hungry Cubans swarmed in to take what they could find. The blankets in particular were needed by the Riders. A few had been left behind by the Spaniards, and under one of these Roosevelt stretched out with Bardshar and Goodrich. The night was cool and the dew heavy.

Before lying down, the leader scribbled in his diary: "Rose at four. Big battle. Commanded regiment. At extreme front of firing line."

At Washington, D.C., a War Department bulletin announced during the day that the American Army was engaged in battle, but further messages were slow arriving. Reporters hustled about, some mentally conjuring dire fate for the men who had gone on the expedition. Finally, they cornered Adjutant General Henry Corbin. What about Shafter?

"He's fighting, not writing!" snapped Corbin.

Chapter 7

IN THE TRENCHES

Ogden Wells, starting another tour of guard duty, lay in the small pit called a Cossack post and munched on hardtack and raw bacon. The food, his first in nearly twenty-four hours, had been given him by Tom Moran, acting corporal, when he came around inspecting outposts shortly after 3 A.M. Tom was a thirty-seven-year-old professional soldier, native of Leeds, England, and had behind him many years of military service.

"Be alert," he whispered as he left Wells. "If the Spaniards attack, it will be before long, for the night is always darkest just before dawn."

Even though ravenously hungry, Wells at times stopped chewing to listen. Once or twice he thought he heard a crackling in the sparse jungle in front, but it was not loud enough for him to be positive. He realized he might have been tricked by his mind, for through it were running the opening lines of a poem handed down from the Civil War:

> *"All quiet along the Potomac tonight, they say,*
> *Except that now and then a stray picket*
> *Is shot, as he walks on his beat to and fro,*
> *By a rifleman hid in the thicket."*

In a larger pit fifteen yards behind Wells waited his relief, another D Trooper, Walter Cook, twenty-six-year-old cattleman from Enid, Oklahoma Territory. They had both taken part in the trench digging before midnight and then had started the hourly tours of duty out in the little pit in front, an excavation scarcely big enough to admit more than one man at a time. Farther back, along the trench line, every fourth man had to stay awake while the other three slept beside their rifles.

Wells thought he heard another rustle. He raised his carbine and rested it on the edge of the hole. The trigger was cocked, but there his actions stopped, for the darkness was so intense he could not see to sight the weapon. Thought of a Spaniard creeping toward the American lines brought goose pimples to his skin.

When Cook came on duty at 4 A.M., it was a shade lighter. Wells promptly whispered his suspicion that a foe was near. Then, after patting the cattleman encouragingly, he squeezed out of the hole and ran chicken fashion back toward the relief post. Barely had he crawled into it when Cook's gun roared, and a dog, yelping in fright and pain, dashed madly through the brush toward Santiago, trailed by heavier, more bulky running.

Now all along the line firing sounded from both sides and continued for fifteen or twenty minutes. It was a harmless exchange. The night still was so dark shots had to be fired without aiming.

Some distance back of the relief post, Bardshar's huge form stirred under the lone blanket he was sharing with Roosevelt and Goodrich. He awoke in a tremble, his sweaty body shaking in the chilly night air.

Next to him Roosevelt stirred. "What are you doing?"

Bardshar answered between chattering teeth: "I am going to the front—as soon as I quit shaking."

"So—am—I," chattered Roosevelt, nudging Goodrich.

The future President recorded their actions:

> It was about 4 o'clock in the morning, at which time men's courage is said to be at the lowest ebb, but the cavalry division was certainly free from any weakness in that direction. At the alarm everybody jumped to his feet and the stiff, shivering, haggard men, their eyes only half open, all clutched their rifles and ran forward to the trench on the crest of the hill.

But not Wells. He lay low in the hole, taking no part in the activity and enjoying his period off duty. Finally he dozed, slugged by fatigue, and seemed to be in another world when Moran shook him and muttered it was 5 o'clock.

Gray streaks of dawn were spreading across the sky. Wells ran once more, zigzag pattern, across the fifteen yards to the little hole in front. There he squeezed in beside Cook.

"What happened?"

"I thought I saw two heads and fired low," Cook replied. "Guess I hit a dog."

Without further comment, the cattleman crawled out of the pit. As he did so, sharpshooters opened from trees nearer the Spanish lines, but their shots went wild.

Moran in the meantime had crawled farther back toward the command post. With daylight setting in, it would no longer be necessary to maintain an advance guard, and he wanted permission to withdraw. Captain Huston granted it.

As Wheeler had predicted in his letter to Shafter, July 2 was indeed a day of trial. One cheering development, however, had occurred shortly after midnight. Bates's brigade appeared from the direction of Caney and was placed in position along the left of the line. Its arrival brought to an end a heroic episode of endurance. With the exception of a brief period of rest on the night of June 30, this unit had been marching and fighting continuously for nearly thirty hours.

The start of the day was a setback for the Americans. During the night, more artillery arrived from Siboney, three batteries of which were moved to the ridge. When the light increased, they fired at the Spanish lines some 600 yards away, fuses cut to zero. This brought a heavy fire in return, for the Spaniards could easily spot the telltale volumes of smoke pouring from the guns. The pieces were hastily withdrawn.

Despite such misfortunes, there were occasional instances of cheering. One of these occurred when a new noise sounded on the firing line and was recognized. It came from the dynamite gun, which Borrowe and his crew, with the aid of Parker, had succeeded in repairing and bringing to the front.

Early in the morning, a handsome young officer in the uniform of a Rough Rider approached Lieutenant Parker and saluted. "Colonel Roosevelt directs me to report to you with my two guns," he said. It was Sergeant Willie Tiffany, the socialite and New York's best dressed.

"Where are the guns?" Parker asked.

Tiffany pointed to the rear, where a corporal and six troopers waited beside the Colt automatics.

"How much ammunition do you have?" Parker inquired.

Tiffany indicated four boxes.

"Not much for guns that shoot 500 bullets a minute," said

Parker. "But that's all right. My men have captured quite a supply of Mauser shells. We'll use those."

Tiffany saluted and started away.

"Wait a minute," said Parker, in afterthought. "How did you get those here?"

"On our backs," replied Tiffany, smiling triumphantly.

Firing was almost continuous as the day developed. The sun burned down on the trenches and brought vapor from the damp uniforms of the men, wet from sweat and from wading San Juan River and other streams. It was obvious the temperature would climb to above 100 degrees.

Roosevelt set up his headquarters tent under a little tree just over the ridge. A few minutes after he moved in, a shell burst above the spot, scattering shrapnel in all directions and wounding and killing five Rough Riders. One of the wounded was Stanley Hollister, the champion half-miler from Harvard. He was struck in the left thigh.

Behind the lines, the trail leading to the front was so tragic in appearance that it would often be recalled unhappily by those who saw it. Caspar Whitney of *Harper's* magazine traveled it during this second day of battle and described it as follows:

> It will be many days ere the scenes on that El Pozo road, in the gray dawn of July 2, are effaced from my memory. Dead men lying beside the road, ghastly in their unstudied positions; men dying, men wounded, passing back to the division hospital, some being carried, some limping, some sitting by the roadside, all strangely silent, bandaged and bloody. Beyond the second crossing, the road was strewn with parts of clothes, blanket rolls, pieces of bacon, empty cans, cartridges; at the forks the marks of bullets everywhere—the trees shot through and through.

During the middle of the day, nearly twelve hours behind Bates's brigade, Lawton's men arrived and were placed on the right of the cavalry. Other reinforcements had come up—the 34th Michigan, stationed in rear of Kent, and the 9th Massachusetts, thrown in line on the left of Bates. García and his force of Cubans were there, too, and were sent off to keep reinforcements from getting into the city through the gap between Lawton's right and Santiago Bay.

Buoyed by the arrival of Lawton, the veteran Wheeler took steps to bolster morale. He directed officers to reassure the men that they were in twice as strong position and twice as strong numeri-

cally as they had been the day before. His mind definitely was
made up against withdrawal. Ammunition had been coming forward in fairly ample supply, but food, except for unsweetened
coffee, was still a scarce item.

While the attention of the Americans was centered on the lines
around Santiago, it occasionally was diverted by the constant
threat from the sharpshooters. Sams of the New York *Times* came
upon the bodies of four soldiers lying with their faces covered near
an unfinished grave. "The diggers of the grave had fled from
inquisitive Mauser bullets, and the four were keeping their last
vigil on the hillside," he reported.

The sharpshooters finally became so annoying that Roosevelt organized a detail of picked marksmen to hunt them out. His choices
were from the experienced woodsmen and mountain men among
the Riders. One of these was Trooper James C. Goodwin, a thirty-
four-year-old rancher from Arizona, man of medium height, calm
and deliberate, expert with rifle, pistol, and sling. Another was
Proffitt, the North Carolina mountaineer. They killed eleven without receiving so much as a scratch themselves. Some of the victims
of their bullets were clothed in tunics of palm leaves and canvas
jackets quilted with sand.

Along with the excitement of battle, the Rough Riders had to
reckon with the mystery of what happened to Chief Surgeon
Lamotte. The medic was found lying on the ground, out cold.
When he came to, it was discovered he was suffering from con-
cussion, as confirmed by a swelling on the top of his head. But the
bump gave no answer as to whether it had been raised by a falling
coconut or by a piece of spent shrapnel. He was sent to the hospital for observation.

Since Thursday, there had been no rain. But now, in midafternoon, the customary torrential downpour returned, soaking the
men and the trenches and the countryside. It was a heavy downfall. To some it was a discomfort, but the wounded who had been
lying in the broiling sun, waiting for medical attention or without
proper covering after they had been treated, found it welcome.

Through the mud and slush of late afternoon, Adjutant General
McClernand made his way toward battle headquarters on El Pozo
Hill. A staff officer met him and stopped to report: "I just ordered
a pack train loaded with ammunition and going to the front by
your order to halt and unload at El Pozo House."

"Why?" asked McClernand in astonishment.

"Because we are going to fall back tonight."

McClernand hurried toward El Pozo. There he found the pack train and ordered the ammuntion reloaded and taken to the front. Then he went on toward Shafter's headquarters, moving with the determination that makes the eyes narrow and shoulders square.

At his headquarters during the day, Shafter had been receiving disturbing reports. He was told the Spaniards had placed siege and field guns to enfilade the American lines, that batteries on El Pozo Hill would be unable to dislodge these guns. He heard stories of the sharpshooters infesting the jungle on both sides of the road to the front, and of the shower of bullets falling at least a mile behind the lines. And he was reminded that two more days of rain might make the road from Siboney impassable.

In the late afternoon, Shafter sent for his aide-de-camp, Lieutenant Miley, and told him to summon the division commanders to a meeting at 7 P.M. Miley hurried couriers in various directions.

At the appointed hour they gathered—Wheeler, Kent, Lawton, and Bates. The meeting was held in the open at El Pozo, with guards stationed to keep at a distance everyone except those summoned. Shafter was still ailing and lay stretched on a door taken from its hinges at the El Pozo farmhouse.

Richard Harding Davis was there watching, but not from a close point. He recorded that the general's aides were some distance away, and farther back were the members of Shafter's cavalry escort, leaning on their saddles "and wondering, as we all did, as to what the conference might bring forth."

In opening the meeting, Shafter said: "I have called you here to have an expression of your opinion on the state of affairs at the front. I have been told by a great many this afternoon that we cannot hold the position, and that it is absolutely necessary for us to retreat in order to save ourselves from being enfiladed by the Spanish lines and cut off from our supplies, as an attack by the Spanish with a few fresh troops would result in our utter defeat."

Lawton, the junior officer, present, was allowed to speak first. He did so at length, followed in order of seniority by the others.

When the bearded Wheeler took up the subject, there was an air of tragedy, and yet somehow of comedy, in his manner. He seemed so incongruous, so out of tone with the younger officers around him. His clothes hung sloppily over his withered frame, accentuating the boyishness of his frail figure, and he looked one part and spoke another. A touch of the fate that is beyond the

warrior's control was added to his words by the random shots
sounding along the firing line in the distance. It seemed that he
was speaking from the past, from those battle trails of the South
where the words "Wheeler's Cavalry" had caused invading Yankees
to look over their shoulders and dig in their spurs.

"I am not surprised that our brave men in their exhausted condition are apprehensive," he said. "They know that we have only
some 3000 men on the ridge, facing a force of some 7000. They
know that appeals of the strongest character have been made for
the army to withdraw for fear an attack will drive them in rout
from their position. But we met the enemy at Las Guásimas, attacked and defeated him, and here again we have successfully
charged and taken his breastworks, driving him from a very strong
position. These facts will convince the Spaniards that we will continue our attack upon their next line; and with that expectation it is
unreasonable and not to be expected that they will return and
attack us in the strong position we now hold."[1]

After nearly two hours of discussion, Shafter asked for a vote.
Bates, Lawton, and Wheeler were against withdrawal, Kent for,
explaining that his opinion was based on that of his brigade commanders. Without further ado, Shafter reminded that the decision
was his. For the next twenty-four hours, he said, the troops would
remain in their present position, after which he would call another
conference.

The night was extremely dark as the generals left the meeting
and went to their respective posts. In the mountain passes off to the
right, fires shot up in the dense blackness, adding to the eeriness
of the situation and leading to the assumption that the Spaniards
were either burning their blockhouses or sending signals to Santiago.

Suddenly down in the jungle between the lines, Spanish fire cut
into an American picket post, seriously wounding Warren Crockett,
the Internal Revenue officer from Georgia who had served coffee
to the trench diggers. Evidently both sides were on the alert, for a
tremendous outburst of firing swept all along the line. Roosevelt
ran up to the trenches and stared over toward the enemy.

"At night it was far easier to place the Spanish lines than by day,
because the flame-spurts shone in the darkness," he reported. "I
could soon tell that there were bodies of Spanish pickets or skir-

[1] Roosevelt said later of Wheeler: "He was second in command; and to him more
than to any other man was due the prompt abandonment of the proposal to fall back."

mishers in the jungle-covered valley, between their lines and ours, but that the bulk of the fire came from the trenches and showed not the slightest symptom of advancing."

The late evening outburst occurred just as Shafter reached his headquarters. For an hour it continued and then died away, allowing the Americans to go back to extending trenches and perfecting breastworks. Most of the effort was concentrated on opening approaches to the trenches so that the men could enter them without being exposed.

As the troopers went about their duties, making as little noise as possible, the clouds that had caused the blackness of night fell away, baring a climbing moon. It was bright and shone down to make tree shadows in the open countryside, but its glow was blunted on the shapeless mass of jungle. Crickets began to chirp in the heavy growth, hidden toads made their signals, and now and then a nocturnal bird sent out a sound that resembled the shaking of a billiard ball in a wooden box. As one eyewitness wrote, "the teeming life of the tropical wilderness, frightened into silence for a time by the uproar of battle, took courage from the stillness of night, and manifested its presence by chirps, croaks, and queer, unfamiliar cries in all parts of the encircling jungle."

Except for the trench-digging, most of the activity that went on through the dark hours was centered at the division hospital back in the jungle. After the short tropical twilight ended, candles were lighted around the operating tables, and surgeons, some naked to the waist, kept on with their work, having gone hours without rest. They talked in half-audible voices as they gave directions to assistants or discussed among themselves the nature of injuries. Off in the darkness stretched the line of wounded men—hundreds of them —waiting to be treated. Some were conscious, some unconscious, but all were silent, except for an occasional moan or cry of pain. Also there was the line of dead, one of them the big New York policeman, Henry Haywood, who had succumbed to his stomach wound. Now and then a cry of "litter squad here!" was raised, and another patient so badly wounded he could not be taken back to the hospital at Siboney was carried off into the tall grass and laid on the wet ground, there to lie unattended throughout the night. One of these was Winslow Clark, the Harvard boy wounded while charging with Roosevelt.

The Medical Department was swamped, and something must be done. In the afternoon, a telephone line had been completed between Shafter's headquarters and Siboney. One of the first messages to go over it was to Clara Barton of the Red Cross. Her assistant, George Kennan, was calling. He had been to the front and had seen. Blankets, clothing, malted milk, beef extract, and tents were badly needed, he said. The aged lady of mercy, working in her second war, promised two four-mule wagonloads of supplies as quickly as they could be assembled. Even as she talked, men were wading up to their necks through the surf at Siboney, where the dock had not yet been completed, and were bringing in medicine and food from a ship that had been moved as closely to shore as possible.

In the wee hours of the morning of July 3, two worried officials in Washington, President McKinley and Secretary of War Alger, gave up and went to bed. Since early evening, they had sat waiting for some report of the progress at the battlefront. Not a word had come all day, and the air was filled with disturbing rumors. Press dispatches told of the illness of Shafter, and of Wheeler, next in command, and that yellow fever had appeared among the troops. It was embarrassing that the War Department must depend on the press for its war news. A few hours later, the Washington *Evening Star*—in a highly unusual development for Sunday—published an extra on the war.

Shafter in the meantime was having his troubles. Doubt, despondency, and other personal problems were mounting. To begin with, he was sixty-three years old—and fat enough to be bothered by the heat. Moreover, he had malarial fever, an ailment almost always accompanied by mental depression. And on this day his gout was considerably annoying.

So there were factors other than developments along the San Juan ridges influencing him when he sent to Washington, hours after McKinley and Alger had gone to bed, the following message:

WE HAVE TOWN WELL INVESTED ON THE NORTH AND EAST, BUT WITH A VERY THIN LINE. UPON APPROACHING IT WE FIND IT OF SUCH A CHARACTER AND THE DEFENSE SO STRONG IT WILL BE IM- POSSIBLE TO CARRY IT BY STORM WITH MY PRESENT FORCE, AND I AM SERIOUSLY CONSIDERING WITHDRAWING ABOUT FIVE MILES AND TAKING UP A NEW POSITION ON THE HIGH GROUND BETWEEN THE SAN JUAN RIVER AND SIBONEY, WITH OUR LEFT AT SARDINERO, SO AS TO GET OUR SUPPLIES, TO A LARGE EXTENT, BY MEANS OF THE RAILROAD, WHICH WE CAN USE, HAVING ENGINES AND CARS AT SIBONEY . . .

This was written before 7 o'clock in the morning. It would cause the Secretary of War to make note: "Sunday, July 3, was the darkest day of the war." To Shafter he cabled in reply that he desired San Juan heights to be held if possible, though he would leave the matter to the general's judgment.

Firing along the front as the day developed was desultory, so dispirited that McClernand had a moment to think, and in that moment he recalled the strategy sessions on board ship on the way down. At one of these Shafter had said that he would place the army around Santiago and demand surrender, after which he would proceed as developments dictated.

McClernand walked into Shafter's tent. The general was lying on a cot, obviously ill.

"General, let us make a demand on them to surrender," McClernand suggested.

Shafter stared at him for what seemed a full minute, long enough for the Adjutant General to feel uncomfortable and expect to be rebuked.

"Well, try it," Shafter finally replied.

At 8:30 A.M., McClernand sat down under the tent fly that served as his office and addressed the following note to the commanding general of the Spanish forces:

I shall be obliged, unless you surrender, to shell Santiago de Cuba. Please inform the citizens of foreign countries and all women and children that they should leave before 10 o'clock tomorrow morning.

Had the contents of this message been announced to the troops out in the trenches, there would have been loud cheering, for the strain was beginning to have its effect. Reporter Davis wrote:

The situation in the rifle pits on the morning of the 3rd was really most critical. One smelt disaster in the air. The alarmists were out in strong force and were in the majority. The enlisted men had been without a night's sleep since 4 o'clock of June 30. For the greater part of that time they had been under a constant fire. They had not been fed. To avoid the enemy's fire, they were forced to move about on their hands and knees. Their clothing was as wet as constant perspiration and dew and rain and the fording of the streams could make it. Through sitting bent double in the trenches, their limbs and backs were stiff and cramped, and they were weakened by a fierce tropical sun.

From his pen on this date also came a more personal message home:

"We never get enough to eat . . . My clothes smell so that I can't use them for a pillow."

Roosevelt, like Shafter, suffered from a bit of uncertainty on the morning of the 3rd. When he had time, he wrote a few pungent lines to his friend, Senator Lodge:

Tell the President for Heaven's sake to send us every regiment and above all every battery possible. We have won so far at a heavy cost, but the Spaniards fight very hard and charging these entrenchments against modern rifles is terrible. We are within measurable distance of a terrible military disaster; we *must* have help—thousands of men, batteries, and food and ammunition. The other volunteers are at a hideous disadvantage owing to their not having smokeless powder. Our General is poor; he is too un-wieldy to get to the front. I commanded my regiment, I think I may say, with honor. We lost a quarter of our men. For three days I have been at the extreme front of the firing line; how I have escaped I know not; I have not blanket or coat; I have not taken off my shoes even; I sleep in the drenching rain, and drink putrid water . . .

Stephen Bonsal of the New York *Herald*, a reporter accused of being a heavy intellectual whose dispatches knew more than it was humanly possible to know, approached the Rough Rider trenches from the direction of the pond at the foot of San Juan Hill. Long before he reached them, he could hear Roosevelt's voice above all other noises. When the newsman drew closer, he saw the colonel moving about, patting men on the back, asking about the condition of the wounded and the ailing, and generally spreading cheer, as though he were the master of a jubilee.

"To the weary camp-follower," Bonsal wrote, "a glimpse of Roosevelt's men and a few minutes spent in his camp had the bracing effect of a brandy and soda as nearly as any substitute for this blessing in the black tropics possibly can have. I often thought, as I rode away from this happy regiment, which under such extraordinary circumstances and by such unusual methods had become the remarkable fighting machine it proved to be, that it must have been much in this way that the trappers and the backwoodsmen of the Mississippi Valley worshipped 'Old Hickory,' and so the Texas Rangers adored 'Rough and Ready' Taylor."[2]

A few miles away in Santiago Bay, where the American fleet was watching Cervera's embattled ships, the morning had dawned with slackened wind and a fairly calm sea. There was a haze at first, but this later cleared and the sun shone brightly. Shortly before 8:30 A.M., the flagship *New York* hoisted the signal: DISREGARD MOVEMENTS OF COMMANDER-IN-CHIEF. Then, a few minutes later, accompanied by the armed yacht *Hist* and the converted lighthouse tender *Suwanee,* she started at easy speed toward Siboney, conveying Admiral Sampson, togged in leggings and spurs for a horseback ride to Sevilla, where he was to confer with Shafter. Just the day before, the general had asked that the Navy force the entrance to the bay, and the admiral in reply reminded him of the mines, adding that the bay could be entered only after the forts had been captured by the Army.

Behind the *New York* as she steamed away, the blockade was somewhat broken, four other ships having gone off during the night to recoal at Guantánamo. Still on duty in a semicircle around the entrance were the *Indiana, Oregon, Iowa, Texas, Brooklyn,* the armed yacht *Gloucester,* and the converted yacht *Vixen.*

At 9 o'clock, Sunday morning routine on board the ships went on as usual. Since it was the first Sabbath of the month, inspection was followed by the reading of the Articles of War, and then by a muster of the crew and by divine service.

At 9:35 o'clock, the navigator on the forward bridge of Commodore Schley's ship shouted: "After bridge, there! Report to the commodore and the captain that the enemy's ships are coming out!" The call to general quarters was immediately sounded and the deck cleared as the crew rushed to battle stations.

The Spaniards had decided to make a desperate run for it, feeling that if the Americans captured the squadron Spain's cause was lost, for the fleet could not be recovered. At the front of the

---

2 Bonsal gave this advice for future wars: "In my judgment, the reason why the Rough Riders won the admiration of the Regulars while the other Volunteers only enjoyed their sympathy was not because the Rough Riders were superior in courage to the men of the other volunteer regiments, but simply because they were led and not merely sent into battle . . . If we ever fight another war with volunteers, the experience of this most serviceable regiment will bear careful examination. Another thing it is well to bear in mind, upon the firing line of this regiment the frontiersmen never got ahead of the men from the Avenue."

line of ships moved the *Infanta Maria Teresa*. Next came the *Vizcaya, Cristobal Colon,* and the *Oquendo*. They advanced rapidly until they came to the narrow entrance, 1100 yards in length and at one point only seventy-six yards wide. At this narrow point, they had to make a turn at moderate speed to avoid the rocky shore and then to squeeze past the scuttled *Merrimac*. Minutes seemed like hours as the American gunners waited for the signal to fire. A little later, two more ships, the *Pluton* and *Furor* emerged.

As the Americans opened on the Spanish ships, the soldiers along San Juan Ridge heard the firing, but to them it seemed more like the sound of demolition. It was their conclusion that the Spaniards were blowing up the ships in the harbor and were transferring their guns and crews to the defense of the city.

Stimulated by the noise, the firing from the ridge grew hotter—"like the roll of machine guns, punctuated by the heavy boom of the Spanish batteries," wrote the Washington *Post* reporter. The correspondent of the New York *Herald* came upon the Rough Riders and found them especially busy. "Sharpshooters and cowboys were firing at Spanish guerrillas in the trees as impressively as though they were contesting for badges in the rifle range," he reported. He watched James C. Goodwin, expert with sling and rifle, bring down six. "The other men were lying on their backs watching him," he added.

Shortly before noon, as a flag of truce moved between the lines from the American side, the firing died out, except for an occasional blast from an unobserved sharpshooter in the trees. Soon a delegation appeared from the Spanish trenches. Even as the two groups met out in the open, there was occasional sniping from the tree tops.

Time passed slowly after the surrender demand was delivered. It would go to General José Toral, for General Linares had been wounded on July 1 and was no longer in command.

At 2:30 P.M., McClernand wrote Wheeler:

> The Commanding General directs me to ask if any reply had been received to our message sent under flag of truce, and for the situation generally. A good many of our men can be seen straying away from the trenches where they would be at a disadvantage if the enemy should attack suddenly.

While Shafter and his staff waited for a reply to the surrender demand, good news came from the direction of Santiago Bay. It was to the effect that the Spanish fleet had steamed out that morning and that every ship had been sunk or driven ashore.

Up front, Wheeler impatiently watched the Spanish lines for the appearance of a delegation bringing the reply. He also glanced occasionally at the sky. Dark clouds had begun to form and to move nearer. Soon the skies opened in a massive downpour. "It began to rain this afternoon as it had never rained since our arrival in Cuba," wrote a correspondent. Claps of thunder were so loud horses screamed in terror. Yards behind the firing line, men stripped to the skin, tucked their clothes under ponchos and tents, and went about the merry game of leapfrog, enjoying the first bath they had had in days.

As the rain died out in the late afternoon, a flag of truce appeared from the Spanish side. Wheeler sent a party to meet it. The message delivered was hurried back to Shafter. It read:

> I have the honor to reply to your communication of today, written at 8:30 A.M. and received at 1 P.M., demanding the surrender of this city; on the contrary case announcing to me that you will bombard this city and that I advise the foreign women and children that they must leave the city before 10 o'clock tomorrow morning. It is my duty to say to you that this city will not surrender and that I will inform the foreign consuls and inhabitants of the contents of your message.

A short while later, the British, Portuguese, Chinese, and Norwegian consuls came into the American lines and asked that the noncombatants be permitted to occupy the town of Caney. They also asked that the bombardment be delayed until 10 o'clock on the morning of the 5th, as about 20,000 persons wished to flee the city. While they conferred, someone whispered to Shafter that, despite Toral's reply, the Spaniards were seriously considering surrender. He consented to both requests.

Late in the day, Shafter wrote Sampson that the Spanish force from Manzanillo the Cubans had talked of blocking had managed to get into Santiago. He placed the number at 5000.[3] "Now if you will force your way into the harbor," he added, "the town will surrender without any further sacrifice of life. My present position has cost me 1000 men and I do not wish to lose any more. With my

---

[3] This force was commanded by Colonel Federico Escario and totaled 3600 men. It had left Manzanillo on June 22, taking eleven days to travel 160 miles over difficult mountain trails.

forces on one side and yours on the other, and they have a great terror of the Navy, for they know they cannot hurt you, we shall have them."

The two army wagons that rolled out of Siboney were, metaphorically speaking, loaded to the gills. Their cargo consisted of what might be termed "best hospital material"—meal, flour, condensed milk, malted milk, tea, coffee, sugar, dried fruits, canned fruits, canned meats, and many other items, among them a bolt of cotton cloth. In the vehicle rode Clara Barton and her top Red Cross aides, Dr. and Mrs. Gardner, Dr. Hubbell, and Mr. McDowell, the last named a veteran of four years and twenty-six battles of the Civil War.

The road over which they traveled was a rank foe to progress. It was wet and muddy and clayey, and the wagon wheels sank to the hubs. But the sturdy horses kept pulling them onward and, after a trip of four hours, they reached the 1st Division Hospital, now a station of great importance.

The scene that greeted the Red Cross delegation was in the language of Clara "indescribable." The area was covered with long, tangled grass, skirted by trees, brush, and shrubbery, and was flat and not conducive to drainage. In the center were the larger hospital tents, and scattered around were a few of the little pup tents, which to Clara seemed "not much larger than would have been made of an ordinary tablecloth thrown over a short rail."

Soldiers with muddy uniforms had been stripped of their clothing when placed on the operating table, and some of them now lay out in the open entirely nude. As the aged Clara and Mrs. Gardner passed, they drew their hats over their eyes and turned their faces away as much as possible—"for the delicacy of the poor fellows who lay there with no shelter either from the elements or the eyes of the passers-by."

They went toward a spot in the background where smoke rose from a low fire. There they found a pitiful excuse of an oven that made Clara prouder than ever of the experienced McDowell. It consisted of half a dozen bricks laid about a yard apart, with pieces of wagon tire iron across them, so near the ground that the wet wood could not get enough air to burn. At hand were two kettles, one filled with soup and the other with coffee, and a small frying pan with some of the abominable canned beef in it.

The Red Cross workers, without waiting for the approval of the head surgeon, Major (Doctor) M. W. Wood, took matters into their own hands. McDowell hastily formed a large fireplace out of bricks and tire iron, and soon kettles were boiling. Included on the emergency menu were corn meal gruel, hot malted milk, beef extract, coffee, and a beverage called "Red Cross cider." The "cider" was a concoction made by stewing dried apples or prunes in a large quantity of water and adding lemon or lime juice. It had a tang that was especially appealing to the famished soldiers. Out from the wagons came the bolt of cloth, and strips six or seven feet long were cut and distributed to cover the nakedness of the men lying in the grass. On through the night the work continued.

The aged Clara was in her glory. "I had not thought ever to make gruel again over a campfire," she wrote. "I cannot say how far it carried me back in the lapse of time, or really where or who I felt that I was." She hustled about like a woman of thirty, while the fires burned, the gruel steamed, and buckets of food and drink were divided among the eight hundred men lying in the hospital.

At one point, a huge man in the uniform of a Rough Rider came into the camp from the direction of the trenches. He was Captain Llewellyn of G Troop, the versatile New Mexico miner and cattleman. Though beginning to feel the effects of fever, the visit did not concern himself. He was looking for a member of his troop, Winslow Clark, the Harvard boy who had fallen while following Roosevelt. Finally he found him, lying beside a tent. There he had lain without attention since his removal from the operating table. Llewellyn called Miss Barton's attention to Clark. She assured he would get the best.

Clara's appearance at the 1st Division Hospital immediately improved its curative capabilities. But other smaller hospitals nearer the front were less fortunate. One of these was a camp set aside for fever victims, now increasing in population at an alarming rate. Many of the men had surrendered to the illness only after the truce. Another was a little field unit set up by Surgeon Church under the shoulder of a hill in the rear of the Rough Riders. In this lay many of the eighty-six casualties out of the four-hundred-odd Riders who had gone into battle on Friday.

Church was working under grave handicaps. He was sick with fever himself, and had little medicine and virtually no apparatus with which to work. But he, like Roosevelt, was opposed to sending men back to the larger hospitals in the rear, where he feared lack of attendants would rob them of a chance to recover. Men lay

64. Wounded soldiers recuperating in the field hospital set up in the jungle. An attendant, with arm band, waits in background while one of them drinks from a cup.

65. Tents and shacks of the Rough Riders thrown up behind their lines during the siege of Santiago.

66. A closeup of Roosevelt wearing the battered hat and uniform, with bandanna, in which he was seen during the Cuban campaign.

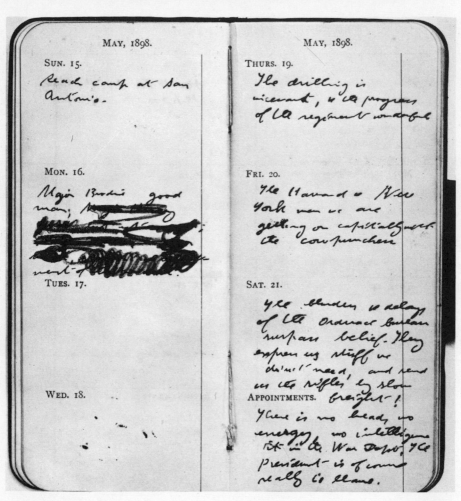

67. A page from the diary kept by Roosevelt, now on display at the Widener Library at Harvard University.

68. Rough Riders cheering at the rear of the trenches dug on the heights overlooking Santiago.

69. Trenches of the Rough Riders at Santiago, with Lieutenant Tiffany's Colt guns under the flag at the left. The flag at the right is that of the 10th Cavalry, one of the black units fighting near the Rough Riders.

70. More of the trenches occupied by the Rough Riders.

71. The Surrender Tree, shown at a more peaceful period.

72. The Palace at Santiago shown with the United States flag atop it following the surrender.

73. Americans fire the town of Siboney in an effort to stop the spread of the dreaded yellow fever.

74. Rough Riders grinding coffee with their pistol butts.

75. Colonel Roosevelt seated astride his horse at Camp Wikoff after his return from Cuba.

76. A Rough Rider astride a wild horse attracts an interested audience at Camp Wikoff, New York, following the return from Cuba.

77. Sergeant Albert Wright, one of the tallest men in the regiment, holding the battle-torn flag presented by the Women's Relief Corps of Prescott, Ariz.

about on blankets and ponchos, if they had them; if not, they lay in the mud. Their only nourishment was hardtack and bacon, a diet scarcely suited to fever patients. Food, rather than medicine, was the crying need among the wounded, and Roosevelt promised to do something about it.

Ahead in the trenches, James Harvey McClintock, a veteran Western newspaperman, who with Brodie and McNeill had been most active in raising the Arizona contingent, nudged back to write a letter to Governor McCord.[4] It reviewed the developments of the last three days, including the death of Bucky O'Neill, and concluded: "The Rough Riders have won a name. The Swedish attaché voiced it when he watched the battle line and said, 'They are devils.'"

At 2 A.M., July 4, Secretary Alger left the War Department in Washington and walked toward his home. Along the way, he heard newsboys crying: "Full account of the destruction of the Spanish fleet!" In his pocket he carried the last message from Shafter, received at 1:15 A.M. It consisted of a single sentence: "I shall hold my present position."

During the night the Rough Riders had worked diligently on a bombproof they were digging in a hillside. "I was never so tired in all my life as I am this morning," recorded Wells.

Shortly before dawn, a special detail of twenty Riders stole away into the jungle, taking part in another move by Roosevelt to stop the sniping from the trees. Each had a canteen of water and a little food. They were to spend the day between the lines, moving about with great stealth and picking off the sharpshooters, who had been heard during the night calling to one another, using the cry of the cuckoo as a signal.

Riding the morning mists was a fearful stench of death. As the sun topped the horizon, it shone down on bodies swelled beyond recognition, further bloating them and adding to the strain of the burial crews trying to get them in the ground.

Shafter was still down with gout. For that reason, he sent Lieutenant Miley to confer with another delegation of foreign government representatives. They were assured ample time would be given for them to leave the city, once it was decided necessary for them to do so. Already long lines of old men, women, and

---

[4] McClintock later served as Governor of New Mexico, having been appointed by Roosevelt after the latter became President.

children were pouring out of it, moving in the direction of Caney and taking what few possessions they could carry on their backs.

Inside Santiago, windows and doors were closed. Not a single store was open. Horses were running about hungrily grazing on the grass growing along the sidewalks. Dogs remained at the entrances of the houses their masters had abandoned, patiently expecting a handout. During the night, lamps had not been lit and the streets were as dark as wolves' dens, making it difficult for people to move about, but offering a golden opportunity to the house-breakers waiting to prey on a stricken population.

At the 1st Division Hospital, what few wagons and ambulances could be rounded up stood by to be loaded with the wounded men able to be transported over the rough, pitiless road to Siboney. Stretcher after stretcher was taken out of the camp. Seventeen men had died during the night.

F. H. Nichols, correspondent of the New York *World,* watched as the men were transferred to the waiting vehicles. What he saw caused him to send a dispatch to his newspaper that was highly critical and more in the nature of an editorial than a news report:

> The lack of transportation for the wounded is the one great stain on the conduct of the American attack on Santiago. Why ambulances that should have been at the front are now in the holds of transports, why there is no field hospital within two miles of the front, are questions that men have asked as they died out under the cactus in the blazing sun—died because there was no one to care for their wounds.
>
> Someone has blundered and blundered badly. Over rough, corduroy roads heavy army supply wagons are now jolting, filled with groaning soldiers on their way to hospitals far in the rear . . .

At noon on this important day in American history, flags waved along the lines and in the camps and, wherever a band could be got together, it struck up patriotic music. There was general rejoicing and a feeling of confidence.

In the spirit of the moment, Shafter, strengthened by his first nourishment in four days, sent across another demand for surrender—"to save needless effusion of blood and the distress of many people." It got in reply: "The same reason that I explained to you yesterday I have to give again today; that this place will not be surrendered . . ."

Shafter was now fully determined to hold his position. His lines almost completely surrounded the city.

But the general was not performing his duties in such a manner as to bring him glory. Roosevelt, finding time to write from the trenches, informed Lodge: "Not since the campaign of Crassus against the Parthians has there been so criminally incompetent a general as Shafter . . ."

In his diary on this day, Teddy wrote of the situation more tersely: "Truce. Mismanagement horrible. No head to army."

On the very day that Roosevelt was writing Lodge, the senator prepared a letter to the colonel:

> Great news this morning and I cannot resist sending a line to tell you how rejoiced we are. You again brilliantly distinguished yourself at San Juan on Friday. You are one of the popular persons of the war and deserve to be. Pray God you come out all right. We have been living with our hearts in our mouths. . . ."

Other praise for Roosevelt and his Rough Riders came this day from the gifted pen of reporter Davis. In a dispatch to the New York *Herald*, he stated:

> This regiment when it was first organized was criticised and ridiculed. It was compared to the regiments of Bowery boys and volunteer firemen who ran away at Bull Run. But the difference lay in the fact that the personnel of this regiment is somewhat higher than that of the men who robbed drunken sailors and administered knockout drops to the countrymen who go sightseeing on the Bowery.
>
> The Rough Riders, as they are now universally called, have been in the two hardest fights of the war and in the front of each. They have lost in killed and wounded half their number, and between the Western man and the Eastern man there is nothing to be said of either except of praise.
>
> The grit of the cowpunchers has never been doubted, but whenever we have wished to illustrate the fact that the swell will fight, we have had to refer to the English Guardsmen and Dandies of Alman Balaklava. Now we can refer instead to the courage of the young men of the universities and of the Knickerbocker Club when they forced the pass at Guásimas and charged up the hill of San Juan. It is a more uptodate example, and the men are Americans.

Another letter came from the trenches. It was written by Captain McClintock to the widow of Bucky O'Neill. It told of the burial of her husband, of the last rites conducted by Chaplain Brown, "his old friend and yours," and it added: "The grave is in a beautiful mountain valley. At the head is a tree, on which has been deeply carved the name and date. Around him are a numerous company of our brave fellows in their last sleep."[5]

The New York *Sun* reported on this date that, of the 568 Rough Riders who had landed in Cuba, "only 339 are fit for service, the rest having been killed or wounded."

When darkness settled on this day, the Riders concentrated on getting the Gatlings, the Colts, and the dynamite gun set up in the trenches. The wheels were removed and each piece was placed by hand in advantageous position, where they could blaze away whenever an enemy head was seen.[6]

Many of the Riders watched with particular interest as the dynamite gun was placed, for there overseeing the job was Hallett Alsop Borrowe. Somehow after the gun had jammed back at the ford near Captain Newgarden's hospital, a rumor got started that Borrowe had been killed. But here he was, along with his younger brother, Beekman, both popular members of the regiment, working like a beaver and exuding confidence. A reporter wrote of the dynamite gun: "It is predicted that its charges, consisting of twenty pounds of gun cotton and gelatine, will work havoc in the Spanish trenches when it opens fire."

Just as the work of relocating the guns was completed, the rain came, with thunder and lightning. Clara Barton remembered that it was "one of the most fearful storms which I have ever seen." Men in the trenches lay in inches of water.

Near midnight, guns blazed again in Santiago harbor. Searchlights in Sampson's fleet had spotted a vessel it was thought was

[5] When they learned Bucky O'Neill had been killed, the black residents of Phoenix, Arizona, in appreciation of his attempt to save the two black soldiers drowned at Daiquirí, held a mass meeting and adopted a resolution lamenting his death. In acknowledging it, his widow wrote: "He was a friend of everybody, regardless of race or color."

The *Arizona Republican*, in reporting O'Neill's death, commented: "One of Arizona's modern heroes, his name will live and be spoken with reverence as long as Arizona shall live."

An equestrian statue of O'Neill, executed by Solom Borglum, brother of the celebrated sculptor, Gutzon Borglum, stands today in the Court House Square at Prescott.
[6] Roosevelt, who in his book on the Rough Riders gave Parker more credit than any one man for the success of the Santiago campaign, finally placed the Colts and dynamite gun under the lieutenant's command, giving him a battery of seven guns.

trying to escape. It was the *Reina Mercedes*, an old ship with defective machinery, the guns of which had been taken into the city. The Spaniards hoped to scuttle her and further block the channel, fearing the mines were inadequate. The Americans promptly helped with the sinking, but sent her to the bottom in a place of their choice.

Sound of gunfire in the harbor during the night caused new panic among the residents of Santiago. They imagined the invading fleet was forcing its way into the city and that the threatened bombardment would follow. As a result, dawn of July 5 found a general exodus under way. The road to Caney was jammed with refugees—young women with babies in their arms, women with no food supplies but a bottle of wine, old men with bundles on their shoulders, a boy rolling a bedridden old woman in a wheelbarrow, four women carrying an older one on a litter borne on their shoulders, some wearing large crucifixes, some telling their beads.

In the trenches, Roosevelt and his Rough Riders moved about like muskrats. The rains had turned ditches, dugouts, and bombproofs into sticky, clayey mire. Clothes were covered with a muck which they could not wash off. Bathing or washing in the nearest streams, half a mile away, was forbidden, because from there came the drinking water. Shoes were falling to pieces, campaign hats were in tatters, and some officers had their shoulder straps pinned to their shirts. A New York *Evening Post* reporter wrote his newspaper that, if the soldiers should be taken back and marched down Broadway or Fifth Avenue as they were presently clothed, "their appearance would tell a much more expressive story of the hardships of this war than anyone could write."

But clothing was not the major concern. Foremost now was the question of how long the Spaniards could hold out. There was much discussion of the wisdom of rushing the enemy lines, for the Americans were confident they could be carried, although the resulting loss of life might make such a move too costly. On the other hand, the increasing number of fever victims, in most cases tropical malaria, created a problem that could not be taken lightly.

Referred to by some as "head exhaustion," the fever came on victims with a severe onset, often with great delirium, and with temperatures from 104 to 106 degrees. It was known more than a hundred cases already existed. The huge Llewellyn was down with it, and vigorous use of quinine appeared to bring him no relief.

His ravings became so violent that Roosevelt finally ordered him taken to the hospital at Siboney.

Clara Barton was among those concerned about the fever outbreak. As she watched the increasing number of patients brought into the 1st Division Hospital, she determined that the best thing for her to do would be to return to the Red Cross ship at Siboney and try to keep it free of congestion. In the late morning she and her aides climbed into their army wagon and started back to the coast. In less than twenty minutes, rain began falling and for two hours "fell as from buckets," while they huddled under a piece of tarpaulin. Clara recalled that the water was from a foot and a half to two feet deep in the road as they passed along.

But when she arrived at Siboney, the sun was shining brightly. The town was a mass of people, most of them milling about in considerable confusion. Clara later wrote: "My medical knowledge was not sufficient to allow me to judge if everybody there had the yellow fever, but general observation would go far toward convincing a very ordinary mind that everybody had gone crazy."

Shortly after Clara arrived, a mule train bringing scores of wounded and sick appeared and moved slowly toward the beach. Red Cross and Army nurses, already exhausted from long hours on duty, took on the responsibility of getting them on board ship, finding their greatest handicap a shortage of litters. Medical authorities were gravely concerned. Matters might get better at Siboney as more ships arrived with personnel and supplies, but what about Caney, devastated by battle and now being overrun with refugees?

Noon passed without the promised bombardment. Rain may have been one factor that held it off, but others were the refugees still pouring out of the city and the consent of the Spaniards to receive the wounded prisoners held by the Americans. Miley had agreed to meet with the consuls between the lines again, but none showed up. At a conference at Shafter's headquarters during the afternoon, it was decided that the Army and Navy would make a joint attack on the city at noon July 9.

Back at the 1st Division Hospital after the rain ended, Red Cross activities continued under the direction of Dr. Gardner. He worked from a tent marked by the Red Cross flag and in and around which were stacked boxes and bags of stores. From large kettles swung over open fires nearby, nurses ladled gruel and rice and carried it to the patients, now at last covered by tents. Onto this scene strode a man in a muddy uniform, a bandanna hanging from the back of his hat to protect his neck from the sun—and mosquitoes.

"I have some sick men with my regiment who do not wish to go to the hospital and who are unable to eat the army rations," he said as he approached Gardner, speaking in a voice accustomed to command. "Can you sell me some of the things you are issuing here?"

"Not for a million dollars, Colonel Roosevelt," Gardner replied, having instantly recognized the unkempt figure.

"But, Doctor, you have the things I need for my men. I think a great deal of my men. If you will not sell them, how can I get them?"

"I suppose you might ask for them, Colonel."

"Then I do ask for them."

"All right. Make out a list of things you need and send for them."

"Give me some of them now. I'll take them myself."

Gardner filled a sack with rolled oats, condensed milk, malted milk, rice, dried fruit, and other items.

Roosevelt shouldered it easily. "I am proud of my men," he said as he walked off into the jungle, the bag partially hiding the bandanna on his hat.[7]

As night settled on this day filled with more than the usual run of worries, Robert Hector Munro Ferguson, the Scotsman friend of the Roosevelt family, wrote a letter to Corinne about her brother. He said Theodore "moved about in the midst of shrapnel explosions like Shadrach, Meschach & Sons in the midst of the fiery furnace," that he preferred to stand up or walk about "snuffing the fragrant air of combat." He added: "I really believe firmly now that they cannot kill him." Despite the mud and slime, Ferguson grew lyrical and wrote as he brought the letter to a close in words out of harmony with the scenes around him:

> The "bob whites" whistle all around these plantations, and transport one straight back to Sagamore Hill on a summer's day. The mountains here are glorious; the valleys, a dream of drooping palms, and dark, cool, shaded mangroves clustered;

[7] In his book, *The Life of Clara Barton,* published by the Macmillan Company in 1915, Percy H. Epler relates this incident as though it had occurred to Miss Barton. However, it was first recounted by Dr. Gardner in a letter dated from Bedford, Indiana, September 16, 1898, and published in the New York *Tribune* of September 23, 1898.

soft bamboo waves near the creeks and smiling ridges, once all under cultivation.

Odgen Wells, the dutiful diarist, also found a moment to write:

The men are completely worn out; very few of them have had over ten hours' sleep out of the last 120 hours. We pushed our entrenchments forward last night, and that kept us busy until dawn when we had to go into the entrenchments again. A man is lucky to be on outpost duty now, for if he is not, he has to work all night on the entrenchments. Our tents came up this afternoon, but the Cubans have stolen all the rations, so we have received only empty haversacks. The Cubans can eat even if they cannot fight.

BEHIND THE GUNS WERE AMERICANS

A definite air of confidence pervaded the American lines by the 6th and spread so generally that all talk of withdrawal ended. The push was toward the front. Such an attitude among the Rough Riders no doubt got some of its steam from Roosevelt. The colonel bragged about them so much that their morale could only go upward. He even told them: "If you knock the bottom out of this thing, I'll take all of you to the Paris Exposition in 1900 at my expense."

This confidence extended to members of the press. A New York *Sun* reporter stared from a point along the trenches occupied by the 1st Volunteers and then wrote his newspaper:

> The view is magnificent. The ridge overlooks the city, quaint and beautiful in all its rampant hostility, as it lies throbbing in the sun, its red and yellow walls of stone and brick standing out in bold artistic contrast to the green mountains behind it. The red and yellow Spanish flag is flying from many buildings. A blood red Maltese cross on the field of white flutters before the hospital far down in front, where but a few hundred yards from our lines stretch the yellow mounds of Spanish rifle pits . . . No infantry in the world can take these ridges now, for instead of Spaniards behind the guns there are Americans.

The same tone underlined the words of Lieutenant Joshua D. Carter of Troop A, thirty-six-year-old bachelor clerk from Duluth, Minnesota. While on guard duty and sitting in full view of the Spaniards on the bank of a trench occupied by forty-eight Rough Riders, he wrote the following to a brother at Prescott:

We have been at it over five days. Captain O'Neill fell bravely the first day, July 1, about 10 A.M. He wouldn't have fallen if he had not been too "nervy." We had a heavy flank fire on our troop, and begged him to take a little cover until we changed our position, and he wouldn't do it. He never knew what struck him, never even moaned.

. . . We have taken magnificent ground, better in some respects than the Spanish are still holding. If they don't surrender, we will surely make it warm for them. They tried a little charge on us the other day, and it was very similar to shooting fish . . . I can see the Dons standing over there in the trenches. We expect to fix them as soon as they take down their white flag.

Rains came again in the afternoon, in the midst of an exchange of prisoners. From the American lines appeared Lieutenant Miley, followed by a covered wagon in which were three blindfolded Spanish lieutenants. Miley moved 400 yards down a road and turned into a field, where the bandages were removed from the prisoners' eyes, and all sat down under a tree to await the delegation that could be seen advancing from Santiago under a white flag.

Men along the trenches on both sides watched as the two parties met and conversed. When the American delegation turned back toward the lines, the soldiers recognized Richmond P. Hobson, the hero of the *Merrimac,* riding on a horse in front. Immediate cheering began all along the lines, and regimental bands, hastily assembled, struck up patriotic tunes.

In the late afternoon, another white flag was seen coming from Santiago. With it was a Toral messenger who asked to be taken to Shafter. Ordinarily, he would have been blindfolded before he was permitted to move through the lines, but the Americans now were too confident to bother about such a precaution. Instead, they gave him a guided tour. Some of the heavy guns were pointed out to him. So were the trenches, and the bombproofs, and the muddy, sun-tanned men waiting impatiently for the shooting to be renewed. He seemed to be much impressed with what he saw.

At Shafter's headquarters, the messenger delivered his communication with considerable ceremony. He reported that Toral would surrender the city if permitted to take his army to the mountains.

Shafter insisted on unconditional surrender. In that case, said the intermediary, Toral had two requests: he would like the truce extended until he could communicate with his government at Madrid, and he desired cable operators to send messages—only those pertaining to the surrender demands—over the lines from Santiago to Kingston, Jamaica. These formerly were sent, he explained, by British subjects who had fled. Shafter consented to both, extending the truce until 4 o'clock the afternoon of Saturday, the 9th.

Roosevelt made no entry in his diary on this date. But while his pen remained idle, that of his friend Lodge did not. In Washington, the senator addressed a long letter to Teddy, telling him: "You have won yourself a high place already as one of the popular heroes of the war . . . I hear talk all the time about your being run for Governor and Congressman, and at this moment you could have pretty much anything you wanted."

The bell of a locomotive clanged along the hillside at Siboney. Its ringing notes echoed down the ragged, dirty tassel of squalid Cuban huts fringing the sea line, where every billow was sweetened by refreshing trade winds that murmured low among the rocks. It could have been a peaceful scene, but it was not. Off from shore, swinging on their anchors, stood the warships that little more than two weeks prior had stopped at Daiquirí and unloaded thousands of American soldiers. Busy little steam launches, as focused on what they were doing as water spiders playing games, plied between ship and shore.

Up in the village, contradicting the industry implied by the engine bell, refugees from Caney, El Pozo, San Juan and Santiago milled in a confused mass—"pensioners on our bounty," wrote an American newspaperman. Many of them were blacks from ruined coffee and sugar estates who had been living in the woods like animals. They were allowed to mix indiscriminately, as no sanitary regulations were in effect. The environs of the village soon were so defiled that, in a tropical climate without quicklime, only a fetid plague spot could result.

One area was an exception. This was where long rows of white tents, orderly and finically spaced, signified the abodes of the military. Nearby, as disarranged as the others were arranged, stood those of the war correspondents who found life at Siboney more suitable than that nearer the front.

Siboney had been converted primarily into a hospital base. Around the buildings and tents in which lay the wounded and sick, the confusion was less and organization far better. The major items lacking were medicine and food, but before the day was out there was cause for rejoicing. Only a few hours away was the hospital ship *Relief*, fresh from New York, loaded with enough supplies to equip a 750-bed hospital for six months—more than 700 tons.

The *Relief* was a welcome sight. While guns along the San Juan ridges were for the moment quiet, there were other developments that would multiply demands on the Medical Department. A few miles back from the coast, in the trenches and around Caney and El Pozo and other points where soldiers were waiting and refugees were gathering, cases of diarrhea and "low fever" were increasing at a rapid pace. Forty ambulances now were in use, an encouraging sign. Yet they could handle only a part of the load. While the 1st Division Hospital had been cleared of most of its patients, in readiness for another battle, the lines of prostrate patients in the fever camp were growing like shadows in a late afternoon sun.

The fever was referred to in medical circles as "calenture," but such a word meant little to the soldiers. A large dose of sulfate of magnesia, followed by quinine and calomel, if available, was the customary prescription. With proper care, a patient could be expected to be over the worst danger in four days to a week, but usually suffered a week or two longer from languor and frustration.

Several of the Rough Riders were stricken, the worst case that of Captain Llewellyn. But all cases were worries to Teddy Roosevelt, constantly moving about, looking after "my boys" and asking after them in a voice not at all regulated to the bedside of the sick.

Things were looking up in the section of trenches in which the 1st Volunteers lay. The night before, a new Gatling gun and several mortars had arrived, and these were masked on the regiment's right, next to the 1st Regular Cavalry. Protective measures, most of them centered on the dugouts and ditches, were constantly in progress. Rations were still short—coffee and bacon and an occasional can of beef. This day, for the first time in two weeks, mail overtook the Riders, a cheering development.

Along the trenches in the morning sun, Lieutenant Joshua Carter took occasion to write another letter to his brother in Prescott:

> We had a quiet night last night, but it is not according to program. We were notified that hostilities would resume at 5 P.M. yesterday, but I guess it was a bluff, because up to this moment, 8:30 A.M., there has not been another shot fired, and flags of truce are constantly passing to and fro, "making medicine" our boys call it. While this has been going on, unarmed details of Spanish can be seen in the rain between our trenches building fires over dead bodies that are past burial . . .
>
> Shrapnel is bad business; it caught Harry White and Stanley Hollister of our troop; also O'Brien. Hollister is a Harvard boy, one of the most lovely men I ever knew. His wound was ugly, but not fatal. The same bomb threw dirt in my face and wounded Frantz in the little fingernail.[1] None of these wounded men should be in any danger of dying . . .

Shafter on this date reported to War Secretary Alger that the general health of the command was good and the men were in fine spirits. Adding that they were making themselves more secure every hour, he said he had five days' subsistence on hand, that wounds were not too serious, with few amputations, and that he was feeling much better.

The general was overly optimistic and apparently unaware that some of his lieutenants were castigating him in writing. Leonard Wood, for example, on this date wrote in a diary he was keeping:

> Quiet. No effort being made to get up artillery, or to do anything which seems to me ought to be done. A most awful state of affairs . . . Only partial rations and not enough artillery to do anything with, all of which is simply criminally negligent, as the artillery captains have begged to be allowed to unload it.

Roosevelt expressed his disapproval of the way Shafter was handling the army in one of his "jeremiads" to Cabot Lodge. He mentioned that he and Wood felt they were entitled to pro-

[1] Frank Frantz, first lieutenant of A Troop. He had left a job as clerk in a hardware store at Enid, Oklahoma, to join the Riders. After the war, Roosevelt appointed him the last territorial Governor of Oklahoma.

motions and that General Wheeler had told him he intended to recommend him for the Medal of Honor, adding:

> It is criminal to keep Shafter in command. He is utterly inefficient; and now he is panic struck. Wheeler is an old dear; but he is very little more fit than Shafter to command. Our part of the battle fought itself under the brigade and regimental commanders . . . The mismanagement has been beyond belief . . . We are half starved; and our men are sickening daily. The lack of transportation, food and artillery has brought us to the very verge of disaster; but above all the lack of any leadership, of any system or any executive capacity.

A member of the 2nd Massachusetts Volunteers sat that night on the brow of a hill overlooking Santiago and wrote a letter. All along the line regimental bands were playing "The Star-Spangled Banner." But this soldier's attention was not with the music-makers. Instead, he was thinking of the Rough Riders:

> Roosevelt's men are well named; they know no fear; one man after emptying his own cartridge belt tore the belts from two dead comrades and, rushing alone, for the troops had been ordered to halt, after the Spaniards, emptied both belts.

A detail of sixty men, including some from other regiments, worked in bright moonlight to dig a long, zigzag trench to a knoll well in front of the Rough Riders' lines. On the knoll, under Roosevelt's supervision and in defiance of the truce, they dug a deep, semicircular ditch and arranged bags filled with dirt along the edges, so as to provide loopholes. Greenway and Goodrich were especially active in this line of duty. Shortly before daylight of July 8, the earthwork was completed and was promptly named Fort Roosevelt. Out in this advance fortification would be stationed a detail of sharpshooters, one of them Jess Langdon. They would be under the command of Lieutenant Tiffany.

Throughout the night, as on most nights, Roosevelt at some irregular hour visited every part of the line. Each man who came into his path got attention from him—a pat on the back, a cheering burst of laughter, and in almost every instance was called by name. Rank seemed to make no difference.

The sun had not been up long before the Riders were treated to a sight they had not seen since entering the trenches. It was

Shafter. He came along in a buggy, with gouted foot wrapped in a gunny sack. His huge form tilted the vehicle sickeningly to one side, forcing its wheels far down into the almost bottomless mud. He went as far along the front as he could, devoting much of the day to his first inspection in person since before the start of battle. Upon returning to headquarters, he reported to Washington that the lines were impregnable. The truce would expire at noon the next day, at which time he expected the firing to be resumed, but he added that he planned to make no assault or advance until the Navy came into the bay.

Early that morning, Toral had repeated by letter his suggestion that he be permitted to march his army, with all baggage, arms, and munitions, to the mountains. Shafter delayed further reply until he heard from Washington.

No rain fell during the day, and the occasion was used to move more food to the front. The Rough Riders got a full ration of bread and meat, two-thirds of a ration of coffee, and half a ration of sugar and tomatoes. Beans were distributed a hatful to a troop.

Roosevelt in the meantime had improvised a pack train out of some broken-down mules and horses, some of them wounded by bullets or shrapnel, and sent it back to Siboney after supplies. These he paid for out of his own pocket or with money given him by Woodbury Kane and others of the wealthier members of the regiment. He found that Chaplain Brown and Trooper Knoblauck were especially adept at acquiring food once they reached the village.[2]

At Siboney during the early afternoon, death came to Ted Miller, the diarist. He was buried on a hillside behind the hospital by a detail from the 33rd Michigan Volunteers. A board with his name on it was placed by the grave, and later it was further marked by a bottle with name and address in it.[3]

Around the time of the Miller burial, Rough Riders in the trenches, unaware of what was taking place at Siboney, joined in a round of cheers. The elation was caused by news that Wood had been promoted to a brigadier generalship and Roosevelt to a full colonelcy.

A ragged, half-starved Spanish soldier, calling out plaintively and holding his arms above his head, came into the Rough Rider

[2] Roosevelt later testified during the investigation of the conduct of the war: "Our chaplain was a rustler for food. If there was any food around, he could get it."
[3] A gateway at Yale University was erected as a memorial to Theodore W. Miller.

lines soon after sunrise July 9. He was taken prisoner and promptly given a bit of hardtack, bacon, and coffee. Soon some of the Spanish-speaking Westerners got him in conversation. He talked freely. From him came information about the location of the big guns in the city. He also told what he knew of the numbers of Spaniards still able to fight, adding that most of them would desert were they not afraid the Americans would shoot them down.

About 9 o'clock in the morning a white flag appeared from Santiago. It was carried by a messenger from Toral who repeated his offer to surrender if permitted to march his men into the mountains. In his diary, Ogden Wells expressed the sentiment that seemed dominant along the American lines: "We hope his terms will not be accepted, for we have got him where we can go right in and brand him, as one of the cowboys said."

During the day, two batteries of light guns arrived from Siboney, after horses and soldiers had struggled with them over the road that not even corduroying made passable. Still on shipboard were the heavy siege guns, each weighing 8000 pounds, each requiring twenty-four horses.

As the hours passed, the Rough Riders became more inured to the strain of trench life, but at the same time increasingly concerned over the sickness that was spreading among them. The spirit with which the regiment was serving was indicated in a letter Lieutenant Sherrard Coleman, the Louisa County, Virginia, boy, wrote friends in Santa Fe:

> I took off my shoes last night for the first time in a week, and this morning washed my face for the first time in seven days. Well, I would better not mention my clothes . . . There is considerable sickness in our regiment, mostly from the heat. The boys are simply exhausted, having to work all night and lie in the sun all day in the trenches. We have to build our own fortifications, but we are getting along all right. A man does not, as a rule, remain sick more than a day before he comes back to the ranks.
>
> I've lost nearly everything I had. I have no coat, and have on a pair of ragged trousers. I have lost my cap, too. Someone stole it and my saber. I got only a scratch in the fight. A bullet brushed my wrist and made a small bruise. I have had a number of close calls.

Among the sick was Jess Langdon. Fever had come upon the youth soon after the battle, but he refused to leave the front. Roosevelt watched him with particular attention. The leader estimated 25 percent of the men were unable to carry a pail of water the 800 or more yards from the nearest stream to the trenches. Men went thirsty rather than go through the agony of bringing canteens of water up the hill. Some of them staggered into any kind of shade, lay prostrate, and gasped.

Out of Washington during the early afternoon, Adjutant General Corbin sent Shafter a message that spelled the course the American Army was to follow:

> Your telegram setting forth terms on which the enemy will evacuate Santiago has been submitted to the President by the Secretary of War, who instructs me to say that you will accept nothing but unconditional surrender, and should take extra precautions to prevent the enemy's escape.

Upon receiving the message, Shafter sent Toral another ultimatum: he must surrender unconditionally; an answer would be expected by 3 P.M. on the 10th; if unfavorable, active operations would be resumed an hour later.

But Shafter was not conveying the sentiment of himself and most of his lieutenants. At 9 o'clock that night, he sent this long telegram to Washington:

I FORWARDED GENERAL TORAL'S PROPOSITION TO EVACUATE THE TOWN THIS MORNING WITHOUT CONSULTING ANYONE. SINCE THEN I HAVE SEEN GENERAL OFFICERS COMMANDING THE DIVISIONS, WHO AGREE WITH ME THAT IT SHOULD BE ACCEPTED. FIRST, IT RELEASES AT ONCE THE HARBOR; SECOND, IT PERMITS THE RETURN OF THOUSANDS OF WOMEN, CHILDREN, AND OLD MEN, WHO HAVE LEFT THE TOWN FEARING BOMBARDMENT AND WHO ARE NOW SUFFERING WHERE THEY ARE, THOUGH I AM DOING MY BEST TO SUPPLY THEM WITH FOOD; THIRD, IT SAVES THE GREAT DESTRUCTION OF PROPERTY WHICH A BOMBARDMENT WOULD ENTAIL, MOST OF WHICH BELONGS TO CUBANS AND FOREIGN RESIDENTS; FOURTH, IT AT ONCE RELIEVES THE COMMAND, WHILE IT IS IN GOOD HEALTH, FOR OPERATIONS ELSEWHERE. THERE ARE NOW THREE CASES OF YELLOW FEVER AT SIBONEY, IN MICHIGAN REGIMENT; AND IF IT GETS STARTED, NO ONE KNOWS WHERE IT WILL STOP. WE LOSE BY THIS SIMPLY SOME PRISONERS WE DO NOT WANT AND THE ARMS THEY CARRY. I BELIEVE MANY OF THEM WILL DESERT AND RETURN TO OUR LINES. I WAS TOLD BY A SEN-

TINEL, WHO DESERTED LAST NIGHT, THAT 200 MEN WANT TO COME, BUT WERE AFRAID OUR MEN WOULD FIRE UPON THEM.

Shafter's telegram gave only a partial picture of the fever situation. A count at noon revealed 400 patients lying on the ground under the trees in the special hospital camp set up for fever victims. These were cases of malaria, but Army surgeons had definitely identified the three soldiers in the Michigan regiment as suffering from the dreaded yellow jack, and three other cases of it had been found among Cubans living in abandoned Spanish houses on the coast near Siboney.

As for the refugees, the British consul made this note:

The people are starving. The Red Cross Society cannot get provisions up in time for want of means of transportation, nor can the Army . . . In some houses you will find fifty in a small room, and among them one dying of fever, another with diarrhea, and perhaps a woman in the throes of childbirth, and all that with not a chair to sit on or a utensil of any kind, and all in want of food. You cannot buy anything for money, though I know one man lucky enough to buy five biscuits of about two ounces each for a five-dollar piece.

Not all the refugees were gathered at Caney. Some, described as "Spanish courtesans, well dressed and good-looking," were affiliating with the American soldiers, accepting even hardtack in payment for favors. It was reported that apprehension existed among the officers, who feared that "the dalliance of Mars and Venus will be followed by treatment of Mercury."

In the limited circles of the White House and War Department at Washington, Shafter's long telegram was hastily studied. Other than the yellow fever threat, the information from the front was nothing short of satisfactory, and the American Army and Navy seemed still in a position to make unconditional surrender the best way out for the enemy. At 11:15 P.M., Corbin dictated a telegram to Shafter repeating that Toral's proposal was not approved and adding that the American force should take Santiago when it was strong enough to do so. He reminded that reinforcements were on the way and commented that "nothing is lost by holding the position you now have."

Reinforced by the telegram from Corbin, Shafter soon after sunrise July 10 repeated his demand for unconditional surrender.

Toral was informed that, unless a favorable reply was received by 3 P.M., hostilities would be resumed an hour later. Notice of the action was given each division commander in writing by Adjutant General McClernand, with the advice that a shot from the battery serving with Lawton's command would be the signal to commence firing.

While waiting, Roosevelt wrote Lodge:

We on the firing line are crazy just at present because General Shafter is tacking and veering as to whether or not he will close with the Spaniards' request to allow them to walk out unmolested. It will be a great misfortune to accept less than unconditional surrender. Thanks to General Shafter's incompetency and timidity we were, on the night of July 1st, in grave danger. By hard fighting and hard work, without any aid from him, we have steadily bettered our position, until we have the upper hand completely; the reinforcements of artillery which we sorely needed have come (in spite of outrageous delay here, at headquarters, in hurrying it after it reached the landing); we can surely get the whole Spanish army now, at the cost of probably not more than a couple of days' fighting, chiefly bombardment.

While Roosevelt wrote, the Rough Riders lay about, waiting, impatient to get into action again. It was their feeling, as many of them indicated, that they should complete the job they had started and get on with the war, in Porto Rico or elsewhere, before more of them met death by bullets or were stricken by fever. This attitude was strengthened by news from Siboney of the death of Ted Miller.

More artillery, including the 4th and 5th Batteries, arrived off Siboney, but some of this would not be unloaded. Shafter's chief aim at the moment was to close the gap still existing between the bay and Lawton's division on the right of the line. Two newly arrived National Guard units, the 1st Illinois and 5th District of Columbia, were hurried toward the front for this purpose. The commanding general wired Washington that the lines were very strong and that the encirclement would be completed on the morrow. He added that he had been riding all day and was feeling much better.

After 3 o'clock, no reply having been received from Toral, the white truce flags along the American lines were removed. Men began filing back into the trenches, ready to end the days of idleness. They could hear the Spaniards talking, and their movements were closely watched. And from the mountains in the background sounded the faint rumblings of a thunderstorm.

Shortly before 4 o'clock, a sharp clap of thunder seemed to be a signal to the Spaniards, for they immediately began firing, anticipating the Americans. All along the line the roar of guns increased in volume. Sharply on the hour, Sampson's fleet opened from the bay, sending shells over a mountain top to strike the city. The artillery along the San Juan ridges, including Grimes's battery, went into action, too, adding to the din. The Gatlings and the Colt automatics and the dynamite gun were all employed.

The storm soon broke, in a sky-rattling mixture of thunder and lightning and rain. On the ground, men were locked in activity known for its noise, while the gods of the heavens struck above in such a fierce accompaniment as to belittle the action down below. Some of the battlers from the States said it was by far the worst storm to sweep the area since they had arrived in Cuba.

As the firing continued, much attention and even outbursts of triumphant laughter were stimulated by the teamwork of the crews handling the dynamite gun and the Gatlings. The former, firing a charge of four and a half pounds of explosive gelatin equal in force to nine pounds of number one dynamite, was pointed in the same manner as a mortar. It threw a shell toward a designated point and, in the resulting confusion, brought on by the earth-shaking explosion, the Spaniards invariably exposed themselves, providing targets for the Gatlings and for the sharpshooters thrown forward into Fort Roosevelt. A battery of two three-inch guns, directly in front of the Rough Riders and near a brick hospital, was completely wiped out in this manner.

Some time after 6 o'clock, the firing slackened and the Rough Riders began to prepare for the night. Small fires were built in sheltered places, and cans and coffeepots were brought into use. High up on the ridge, Trooper Amaziah B. Morrison, Baptist preacher and family man from Las Vegas, sat back under the protection of a traverse to attend to his brew. He had calculated the danger zone and found that, by getting close to the traverse and sitting erect, he could prepare his food in comparative safety.

This man would go down in the annals of the regiment as a

dedicated soldier and a good one. He had joined on May 5. At that time, the Santa Fe *New Mexican* reported that he "has expectations of accompanying the regiment as chaplain." This brought a prompt reply from the minister:

> I noticed in your issue of yesterday an editorial with reference to my enlistment in the Volunteers, in which it is stated that I had "expectations" of accompanying the regiment as chaplain. I wish to say, for fear some may be misled by the statement, that I did not enlist as a place hunter; but with a desire, if I know my own heart, to do the best for the honor of Old Glory, the good of my fellow men, and the glory of my God, in any capacity; and believing all of the officers to be in every way worthy of the confidence and obedience of every trooper, myself as well as any other one of the regiment, I am at their service. To be sure, if they may be pleased to appoint me to that position, I certainly would appreciate it beyond my power of expression, but that is entirely in their hands.

As Preacher Morrison, one-time resident of Coffeeleo, Tennessee, went about his culinary routine, he came to the attention of others, Roosevelt among them. Teddy wrote: "I watched him solemnly pounding the coffee with the butt end of his revolver, and then boiling the water and frying his bacon, just as if he had been in the lee of the roundup wagon somewhere out on the plains."

Around 9 o'clock, up on the hillside at another point below the firing line, four Rough Riders stretched on blankets in a little eight-by-eight-foot shack covered with banana and palm leaves. It was the headquarters of Woodbury Kane, who on this evening shared it with Captains Jenkins and Luna and a newcomer, Benjamin Harney, sculptor of considerable reputation and grandson of the veteran General William Selby Harney, hero of the 1855 battle of Ash Hollow in which Little Thunder's band of Sioux Indians was almost exterminated in retaliation for the Grattan massacre on the California Trail. He had come to Cuba determined to join the Rough Riders, had walked the distance from Siboney, and had stopped along the way beside the grave of the Las Guásimas victims.

At Shafter's headquarters, Harney stayed long enough to eat lunch; then he pushed on toward the front, arriving on the left of the line just before battle action was resumed. Following the trenches and keeping his head down out of the way of Spanish bullets, he reported to Roosevelt about 6 o'clock, finding him lying in a tent scarcely large enough to permit him to stand erect.

Roosevelt seemed a picture of health, his teeth dazzlingly white against sunburned skin. With the eye of a sculptor, Harney noted the leader's canvas breeches and blue-flannel shirt, as well as the army hat with the polka-dot bandanna fastened at the back. After congratulating the newcomer on his energy in searching out the Rough Riders, the colonel turned him over to Kane, who appeared to Harney quite fierce with his long mustaches.

And now the sculptor was huddled for the night. He was a welcome addition, having brought a bundle of newspapers and also a can of baked beans to be added to the fare of hardtack, bacon, and coffee. This night would not be quiet. The newcomer was just dozing off when Jenkins jumped up with curses and threw the entire shack into confusion. A tarantula had fallen from the leaves onto his forehead. Before dawn, a new rainstorm broke, bringing a downpour heavier than that of the previous afternoon. In the midst of it, firing sounded out along the lines, and soon Lieutenant Ferguson, Roosevelt's wealthy Scotch friend, put his head in and announced that the Spaniards had driven the pickets back. Kane, responsive to his duty, got up stiffly from his blanket and walked off into the night.

A heavy mist shutting in mountains and valleys delayed the shooting as daylight of July 11 crept in along the San Juan ridges. Rough Riders stirred, awaiting the time when they could resume warfare. They knew the day would be different, for new orders had been issued regarding conservation of ammunition. Shafter realized the heavy rains were flooding streams and making roads impassable, a threat to the matter of bringing up new supplies, so he gave instructions for the men to aim at definite objects before firing.

Sculptor Harney watched with interest as the Riders came out of their soggy tents and shacks and struggled about in water up to their knees. He saw them stretching their clothes on bushes to dry, and he shuddered when his attention was directed to one point along the trenches. There a guard had knelt on what he thought was a mound, only to find at dawn that he had been kneeling on the grave of a Spaniard, whose elbow and head were plainly exposed. Harney wrote a friend: "I will have great subjects to sculpt, if yellow fever, which I fear more than bullets, spares me."

As 6 A.M. neared, the fog lifted enough for the Spanish lines to be seen, and the American guns opened. It was not the boom-boom of the afternoon prior, punctured by the sporadic crack of rifles and the occasional heavy blast of the dynamite gun. Shafter's new orders brought on an atmosphere of target practice as the men became more deliberate with their aim. But the return fire was desultory, as if the Spaniards had lost heart. The Gatlings were kept silent.

Off in the distance at 8:25 A.M., a heavy shot from one of the battleships gave notice the Navy was cooperating. An hour or so later, a vigorous bombardment sounded from the coast. Three ships, the *Brooklyn, Indiana,* and *New York,* lobbed shells over the hills, guided by the wigwagging of a signalman on the crest of one of them. This action was not completely to Shafter's liking: he still wanted the ships to push into the harbor and had made his wishes known to Washington.

Throughout the morning the shooting continued. Noon passed. Shortly before 1 P.M., Shafter gave orders to cease fire. As the guns grew silent in response, they finally but informally brought down the curtain on open warfare in the Santiago campaign.

Truce flags again were raised, and soon a messenger went off from the American lines to deliver a message to Toral. Shafter had received notice from Washington that, if the Spaniards surrendered unconditionally, they would be returned to Spain at the expense of the United States Government.

The message from Washington was simultaneous with the arrival at the War Department of the first of the wounded men to return directly from the war front. Among them was Sergeant Walter S. Cash of the Rough Riders, a handsome, athletic member of K Troop, talkative but modest. He had been wounded in the forearm.

When the veteran appeared at the War Department, Secretary Alger abruptly ended a conference with the sixty-nine-year-old Senator William Boyd Allison of Iowa and came to greet him. Alger seemed especially interested in Cash, having just received the following telegram from Major Hersey, commander of the Riders left at Tampa, a message slightly out of tune with command developments since the Americans had reached Cuba: FIRST UNITED STATES VOLUNTEER CAVALRY, WOOD'S ROUGH RIDERS, 560 PICKED MEN, FULLY ARMED AND EQUIPPED, DRILLED, DISCIPLINED AND ACCLIMATED, ALL READY, WITH HORSES AND PACK TRAINS, TO GO ON BOARD MOHAWK AND MISSISSIPPI, WHICH HAVE JUST ARRIVED.

After leaving Alger, Cash talked freely with a reporter from the local *Evening Star*. He spoke of the fighting, the roads, the weather, and then got on the subject of Roosevelt. He said the colonel, in the Battle of San Juan, stayed at the front, cheering his men on, that he could not see the Spaniards, "but kept his revolver popping at points where he believed them to be."

While Cash was giving Washington a firsthand account of the situation at the front, his buddies back in Cuba were preparing to move out of the trenches to a new site. Roosevelt had been ordered to take his regiment a mile or so to the right and guard the road from Caney.

Three vessels bringing reinforcements and food supplies, meanwhile, dropped anchor at Siboney. On one of them was General Miles, sent down from Washington because of the disturbing reports of Shafter's illness. Upon hearing of the outbreak of yellow fever, he immediately ordered every building in the village not used as a hospital to be burned.

The new supply of food included potatoes, tomatoes, and onions, along with the usual issue of bacon, hard bread, coffee, and sugar, but the problem was getting it to the points at which it was so badly needed. The rains had completely cut off Caney, where the refugees had congregated, and there the situation was tragic. The suffering horde was urged to go to Firmeza, in the neighborhood of Cuban mines, to which food could be brought by rail, but most of them were too weak to walk the ten miles to that point.

The last straggling shot had been fired before the Riders moved into their new position on the Caney road. Their camp site was free of the deep mud of the trenches, but it also was without the bombproofs and huts they had prepared to give them protection from bullets and rain. After slogging through wet terrain to the new location, they went busily to work, erecting what few tents they had and throwing up the palm-leaf shelters the Cubans had taught them to construct. While they labored, the 1st Illinois Infantry marched past. "They presented a fine sight, 1300 strong, and all with bright new uniforms and clean flags," Ogden Wells recorded. In contrast, the 1st Volunteers were a pitiful sight. With rare exception, they could be described as muddy, unkempt, and unshaven, their shoes and clothes, as Roosevelt noted, literally dropping to pieces.

In the late afternoon, the American lines around Santiago were

78. Tom Darnell, the red-headed, blue-eyed cowboy who was one of the best riders in the regiment, exhibits his skill while in camp after returning from Cuba.

79. President McKinley doffs his hat as he rides to address the returned soldiers quartered at Camp Wikoff near New York City.

80. Teddy, as he made his farewell remarks to the regiment and thanked the men for their parting gift, the "Bronco Buster," Frederic Remington's masterpiece, on the table beside him.

81. Roosevelt bidding farewell to his men as they prepare to leave the detention camp on Montauk Point. On the table behind him is the Remington statue they had just presented him.

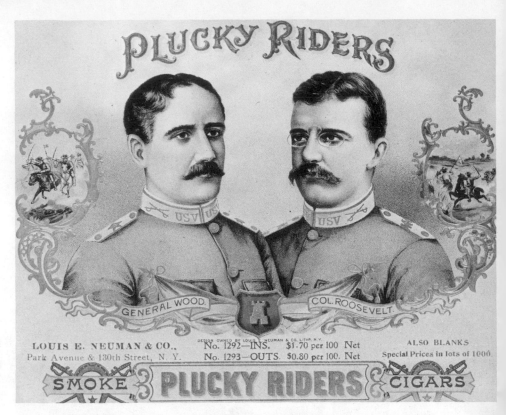

82. The Rough Riders became a popular advertising medium even before they returned from Cuba. A New York tobaconnist adopted this cigar band depicting Wood and Roosevelt, with galloping cavalrymen in the background.

83. Two of several of the songs about the Rough Riders that became popular shortly after the war ended.

Roosevelt's Roughriders and Cowboys
Reunion at Las Vegas, New Mexico
August 1, 2, 3, 1952

Back row, Tuttle, Prentice, Folk, Loughmiller, Wilkens, McGuire, Hamner, Lisk, Roberts, Crimmins, Wetmore, Brown, Langdon.
Front Row, Murray, Culver, Shaw, Gibson, Brumley, Yost, Denny, Brito, McGinty, Love, Hall, and Wyncoop.

84. Of this group, gathered at Las Vegas for the 1952 reunion, only Hamner, Langdon, and Brito are still alive.

85. Left to right, Rough Riders McGinty, Shanafelt, Tuttle, Hopping and Langdon post during the 1952 reunion of their regiment.

86. Those at the 1963 reunion—left to right, Charles O. Hopping, Jesse D. Langdon and Frank C. Brito. Of this trio, only Langdon and Brito survive.

87. Jesse D. Langdon, pictured on the lawn of his home at Red Hook, N.Y., in the fall of 1968. "Take it from the side. It makes me look like an Indian."

Las Vegas, New Mexico
Home of the

ROUGH RIDERS

First Reunion held here in 1899 at which time the National Association of Roosevelt Rough Riders was formed. It was attended by Theodore Roosevelt, then Governor of New York with more than 600 of his comrades.

From this gathering grew the Cowboy Reunion held at Las Vegas in August of each year. In 1952 it was voted to hold all subsequent Reunions here "To the Last Man."

88. This marker at Las Vegas records the decision of the Rough Riders to meet there annually "to the last man." Since 1966, Jesse D. Langdon of New York and California has been that "last man."

extended to close the remaining gap. Arrival of reinforcements had enabled Lawton to shift a brigade to the far right to rest on the bay, thus completing the investment of the city.

With battle action at a standstill, all but those on guard duty dropped down for sleep early in the evening. A stillness settled along the American lines, broken occasionally by a scream in the night from some poor soul who imagined a tarantula had crawled into his blanket. These hairy spiders had never ceased to be a major fear to the invaders, some of the men looking upon the pest as worse than land crabs. Reputation and imagination were the combination that sent a man into convulsions, causing him to leap up and shout and go into tantrums. No one cared or stopped to realize that society had found the repulsive arachnids were not particularly poisonous to man.

Roosevelt went to bed in his tent with perfect peace of mind. Woodbury Kane again was in charge of the guard, and he knew "Woody" would be out along the lines at all hours of night taking care of things. For the first time in two weeks, the colonel completely divested himself of clothing.

Some time between 10 and 11 o'clock, familiar rumblings from the distant heavens stole into the silence, getting louder. In a matter of minutes after the first peal was heard, the storm broke. If the Americans had been comparing in intensity one downpour with another, they could not fail to rank this one first, for it caused the night to go into campaign histories as "the night it rained." Streaks of lightning ripped across the sky and ran like great trains of fire along the mountaintops. Then came deafening cracks of thunder that made the ground tremble, "as if creation were tumbling into chaos," wrote one soldier. Rain fell in torrents.

Early in the deluge, down went Roosevelt's tent. He crawled from under the soaking canvas into the driving downpour and groped blindly for his clothes in the liquid mud. "And so I basely made my way to the kitchen tent, where good Holderman, the Cherokee, wrapped me in dry blankets, and put me to sleep on a table which he had just procured from an abandoned Spanish house," Teddy reported.[4]

[4] Bert Holderman, Indian farmer from Artopa, Kansas, served throughout the camp as headquarters cook. Once, while at San Antonio, he yelled in the direction of Wood and Roosevelt's tents, when those two officers were slow in coming to dinner, "If you fellows don't come soon, everything'll get cold." Appreciating the cook's concern, Wood observed that, militarily speaking, this was not according to the manual of instructions.

Chapter 9

THE SURRENDER

Little food came to the front during July 12, causing offers for
hardtack to go to a dollar for a single piece. As Roosevelt had
prepared for just such an emergency, the Rough Riders were
scarcely affected. But not so fortunate were their new neighbors,
the more presentable members of the 1st Illinois. Their plight
came to Teddy's attention. In generous gesture, he sent over some
beans and coffee for the officers and two cases of hardtack for
the men. Then he rode toward headquarters, "half fording, half
swimming the streams." Late in the evening he came back with
half a mule train of provisions for the Illinois troops.

Awaiting him was a telegram from headquarters relayed by
Wheeler. It asked for two squads of twelve men each from the
Rough Riders to handle two pack trains standing idle because of
the sickness of their drivers. Though an admirer of Wheeler, Roosevelt gave a rather abrupt reply:

> All right. Will send the twenty-four men, but this most seri-
> ously depletes my already thin line; I have but 340 officers and
> men fit for duty all told; I should have some relief for the men
> in the trenches against possible attack.

While in this mood it was fortunate for Roosevelt that mail
forwarded to Cuba from the United States could not be delivered
in a matter of hours, for Lodge on this date wrote him a letter
that might have been interpreted as a bit snippy but for their
strong mutual friendship. It read in part:

> . . . We know that you will take every possible opportunity
> to get killed if you can, but now that you are colonel of the
> regiment, we venture to suggest that your first business is to

look after it and not run ahead of it in every charge that is made.

Despite the rain, a truce flag moved early in the morning. It came from Toral, accompanied by a request for further delay until he could hear from Madrid. He appealed to Shafter's chivalry as a soldier. It was his contention that he should be permitted to leave the city and terminate the war under conditions honorable to Spanish arms.

But Shafter remained steadfast, even though conditions around him gave no cause for optimism. His headquarters was a swamp and the trenches were full of water. Everything seemed wet, even the sick. As ordered by Miles, Siboney—fifty buildings or so, including the post office and telephone station—was burned over the protest of the affected Cubans, who were driven to caves in the overhanging cliffs along the shore. Simultaneously, complaints of a different nature came from García's men. They objected to being moved farther to the right and giving up to the Americans the trenches they had dug. The only development of the day that might tend to cheer Shafter was completion of the wharf at Siboney.

Rain fell throughout the day. At 1 P.M., a heavy downpour occurred. Before it slackened, General Miles arrived at Shafter's headquarters for a conference. The two leaders were not together long before a messenger was sent toward the Spanish lines to request a meeting with Toral at 9 A.M. the following day.

Wigwagging from land, to Sampson's ships off Santiago harbor, began at 7:55 A.M., July 13. The message conveyed was from Shafter: "General Miles and I are going to have a conference with General Toral this morning about the surrender of the place. Please have no firing until due notice."

On this day, General Kent was in the saddle by 8 A.M. It was hot and muggy, with more rain on the way. He rode toward the 1st Division Hospital, having to cover a distance of not quite two and a half miles. En route, he moved through water that was only stirrup deep. But on the return, it was a different story. The water had risen so fast it was necessary for him to swim his horse across two of the fords. At one of them he got the seat of his pants wet. The drenching was of minor concern to him, however; he was far more disturbed by sight of the flood submerging graves of soldiers killed at the Battle of San Juan. Some of these had been dug on the banks and in the low ground skirting the Aguadores River, the stream from which Americans were getting their drinking and cooking water. He even spotted the body of a horse buried twelve days past and now floating in an eddy near the shore. Sight of it caused him to recall that most of the officers had some facilities for boiling water, but, with rare exception, the men did not.

At 9 A.M., a delegation moved out from the American lines to meet General Toral. In it were Generals Shafter, Miles, Wheeler, and García, as well as Lieutenant Miley. Toral came out with two staff members and an interpreter. The two groups met under a large ceiba, a massive tropical tree of the silk-cotton family. Clothing worn by the men was in sharp contrast. Miles had on a plain blue uniform, while the other American officers wore white linen. Much gold lace set off the dress of the Spaniards.

On the start, the conversation was largely between Shafter and Toral, but finally Miles got in a word. He told Toral that he had left Washington just six days past and thus knew better than Shafter the mood of the United States Government. He said it was determined either to destroy or capture Santiago, that sufficient forces were on hand to accomplish either objective, but that 50,000 more men could be brought to the front if needed. He added that the offer of the United States to convey the Spanish army back home was liberal, especially since the Spaniards were on an island without succor and without transportation.

Toral replied that Spanish law would not permit him to surrender as long as he had ammunition and food; furthermore, that he must maintain the honor of the Spanish arms. In his account of the meeting, Miles wrote: "My reply was that he had accomplished that; that he must now surrender or take the consequences and that I would give him until daylight next morning to decide. He appealed for a longer time, saying it was impossible for him to communicate with his superiors, and upon his request I granted him until 12 o'clock noon."[1] The conference lasted an hour and a half. Upon adjourning, it was agreed to meet again for the final answer at 11 o'clock next morning.

[1] In his book, The Spanish-American War (New York, Harper & Brothers, 1901), Secretary Alger tells of the conference and adds in a footnote: "Miles wanted to break off the truce at sundown that day. Shafter wisely decided not to do this. On the other hand, he extended the truce from 5 A.M. July 14 to noon of that day. His good judgment on this occasion undoubtedly saved much bloodshed."

Back at his headquarters, Shafter telegraphed a report of the conference to Washington. In it he made no mention of Miles, saying that he himself expected an unconditional surrender and that, if it did not come by the time the truce expired, he would open on the Spaniards with every gun he had.

But along with the good news, Shafter passed on some bad. His telegram ended with the following announcement:

THERE IS A GOOD DEAL OF NERVOUSNESS THROUGHOUT THE ARMY ON ACCOUNT OF YELLOW FEVER, WHICH IS AMONG US CERTAINLY. TWENTY-NINE NEW CASES YESTERDAY AND PROBABLY 150 ALL TOLD. WHATEVER HAPPENS, ONE OR TWO IMMUNE REGIMENTS SHOULD BE SENT HERE TO ACT AS HOSPITAL GUARDS AND GARRISON THE TOWN.

With the truce in effect, much of each Rough Rider's time was spent in getting and preparing something to eat. The daily issue included two spoonfuls of roasted coffee, which had to be pulverized with the butt of a hunting knife or other pestle, usually in a tin cup or can. "The operation is tiresome, requires patience, and ends up in the destruction of the tin cups," one of them reported. In addition to coffee, every seven men received one and a half pounds of sugar, fourteen ounces of hard bread, and one two-pound can of tomatoes. All cans, when emptied, were carefully preserved for the purpose of boiling water.

Although the rain continued to keep everything in a sea of mud, policing routine was carried out daily and so effectively that there was no odor about the camp. Sinks on San Juan Hill were covered over and new ones dug in the bottom lands 300 or more yards away. Tents were moved daily to give the ground a chance to dry and, whenever a storm was not in progress, blankets were aired on nearby bushes.

By this time, officials in Washington were thoroughly alarmed over the fever threat, but they had little in the way of prevention to offer. Adjutant General Corbin wired Shafter that, as soon as the surrender was accomplished, the entire 5th Army Corps should be put in camp on ground above the fever belt. Later, if it was found advisable to bring the troops away, it would be done, he advised. All further shipment of troops from the United States was halted.

But anyway, the matter of urgency was the surrender, and that got first attention. Before the hour agreed upon for the final conference on July 14, Toral sent word that he had received instructions to proceed with terms of capitulation, with the understanding that they were to be approved at Madrid before they would be final. Accordingly, as agreed, the two groups came together again under the ceiba tree, and commissioners to arrange the surrender were named. Shafter chose Generals Wheeler and Lawton and Lieutenant Miley.

As the meeting ended, the American officers moved away with the understanding that a surrender was in effect. A cablegram reporting capitulation was sent to Washington at 12:55 P.M. Shortly afterward, the news reached the troops and caused sporadic cheering, but this soon ended on orders from Shafter, who contended that the enemy had fought bravely and should not be humiliated.

At 2:23 P.M., Miles signaled Sampson: THE ENEMY HAS SURRENDERED. WILL BE DOWN TO SEE YOU SOON. Sampson promptly cabled the Navy Department: SANTIAGO HAS SURRENDERED. Directions were issued for the trenches to be evacuated, leaving only a small guard on duty. These were complied with immediately, for the heat was stifling and more rain began falling.

But all was not as rosy as it seemed. When the commissioners came together under the ceiba tree at 2:30 P.M., it was found matters were far from being as final as Americans were trying to make them. Throughout the afternoon the meeting ran, with the Spaniards obviously using delaying tactics. At 6 P.M., a halt was called for Toral's representatives to go into Santiago for further instructions.

During their absence, a tent was erected and candles were placed in it, ready for a night session. When the Spaniards returned, the discussion centered on the evacuation of all fortifications and the removal of obstructions from the mouth of the harbor. No agreement could be reached. Finally, Toral's men suggested that the meeting be adjourned until the next day, but Wheeler, Lawton, and Miley persisted in the hope that negotiations could be completed that night.

Faced with an impasse, it was finally agreed that Toral should be brought to the meeting. He arrived at 9:40 P.M. and immediately explained that he was helpless to surrender until he heard from Madrid, that the government might not even permit his army to be returned to Spain unless he obtained proper approval. He also insisted that he had not conceded surrender to Shafter during the midday conference, that he had been misinterpreted if that was the conclusion of the Americans.

After this turn of affairs, Wheeler and company realized further delay would be necessary. It was obvious to them that Toral was sincere, so at half an hour after midnight they agreed to adjourn until 9:30 o'clock in the morning.

At the appointed hour on the 15th, the commissioners went back into session. Soldiers on both sides of the battlefront stared toward the tent as the day moved along and wondered what was transpiring. Thoughts ranged far and wide. Ogden Wells wrote in his diary:

> The report of the surrender was confirmed this morning. Twelve thousand troops under Linares and 8,000 in Holquin under General Pando are to lay down their arms and to be shipped to Spain at the expense of the United States. It is further reported that our troops are under yellow fever quarantine for five days, and that if no fever breaks out by the end of the quarantine period, we are to go to Porto Rico with General Wheeler. We are to boil all our drinking water and are not allowed to leave camp or talk with any Cubans.

The spread of fever was most noticeable at the special hospital camp set up out of sight of the valley in which negotiations were taking place. It was cut off from communication with the remainder of the army except for the train of wagons, marked by a sinister yellow flag, that moved back and forth several times a day to bring in more patients and supplies. Many of the inmates lay in the mud, without cots or shelter, and most of them were without blankets.

From Santiago harbor, Admiral Sampson wigwagged to shore at 10:37 A.M.: WHAT ARE THE TERMS OF SURRENDER, AND WHEN IS IT PROPOSED TO OCCUPY THE CITY AND HARBOR? Shafter replied: HITCH IN NEGOTIATIONS; WE MAY HAVE TO FIGHT IT OUT YET.

During the afternoon, reports of a favorable nature began to filter from the tent under the ceiba tree. Then came the word: the protocol of the surrender had been agreed upon and signed. Wild shouting sounded from the American camps, not all of it in elation over the capitulation, for there was other reason to rejoice. The men were enjoying a day without rain and meals made more palatable by a minimum supply of onions and potatoes, the first they had tasted in weeks.

But Shafter was not yet sure that everything was over but the shouting. Late that night he cabled Washington that the delay in reaching a surrender agreement was caused by the Spanish commissioners' insistence on awaiting approval from Madrid. I THINK THEY FEAR DEATH WHEN THEY GET HOME, he added. WE MAY HAVE TO FIGHT THEM YET.

Rough Rider Wells made an unprecedented entry in his diary in recording the happenings on July 16. "This is a red letter day in my army experience," he wrote, "for we had oatmeal for breakfast this morning. To say it tasted fine would be expressing it mildly; it seemed as if I couldn't eat enough."

He failed to make note of the source of the oatmeal, but Roosevelt reported it had come from regular issue. He also managed to obtain a supply of cornmeal and rice from the Red Cross. The leader's buoyance continued to dominate, with his major interest the welfare of his men. So concerned was he with their health that he belatedly started them digging a well, seeking a source of water that would be far purer than that hauled from the corpse-lined Aguadores.

That very morning in the New York *Times* note was made that Roosevelt's name was coming forward prominently in the state campaign to select a governor, that since the American successes in Cuba politicians of all classes had been discussing him as a probable candidate on the Republican ticket. Already campaign buttons with his name on them, the first in the field, were having wide circulation.

For the second day in a row, no rain fell along the trenches. Many of the men took advantage of their hours away from duty to climb trees and examine the seats and foot-rests placed there for the convenience of Spanish sharpshooters. Two of them, who had unwisely taken pot-shots at Rough Riders advancing on water detail, were slain several hours after the truce went into effect. Those not killed or wounded in their lofty nests apparently had climbed down under cover of darkness and returned to their lines.

Early in the morning, Shafter received a message from Toral announcing that the government at Madrid had authorized him to capitulate and asking the American leader to designate an hour and place where his representatives should appear to edit the articles of surrender. Shafter suggested 4 P.M. in the tent under the ceiba tree.

Reveille sounded in the Rough Rider camp on July 17 for the first time since the charge up Kettle Hill. It opened a day of massive significance. Five months and two days had passed since the sinking of the *Maine*. Battle action was in the past, and the goal was at hand.

At an early hour, refugees from Caney began passing, for word had quickly spread that Santiago was to be surrendered. As the women and children and old men moved along the road beside which the Riders were camped, the pity of the volunteers was aroused. They offered what food they had, and many gave assistance, supporting the weak and toting children or bundles as far as they were permitted to go from camp.

Shortly after sunrise, six Spanish officers rode up to the American picket line on the Sevilla road. They were wearing Panama hats set off by rosettes, suits of cotton trimmed in narrow stripes of blue and white, and black leather boots. One of them carried the silver-encased sword of General Toral. This was delivered to Shafter.

At 9:30 A.M., mounted officers began to assemble near Shafter's headquarters. Rapidly they came until there were ninety-two. A bugle sounded, and a troop of cavalry on bay horses formed in the trail below. A few minutes later, Shafter came out of his tent. A white English pith helmet was perched on the back of his head. He stepped gingerly, his gouty foot encased in a shoe.

The general was assisted to the back of a huge bay horse, an animal that stolidly bore the weight thus suddenly thrust upon it. With Wheeler at his side, Shafter rode off toward the Sevilla road, followed by division and brigade commanders, staff officers, and Spanish envoys. After a short ride, he came to a halt on a gentle slope between the two lines of trenches. The cavalry was spread in formation on the left, facing toward the commander, with his staff and the generals and their staffs all formed into a dozen lines.

The cavalcade had hardly come to a standstill before Toral, a fine-looking, soldierly type with grizzled mustache, appeared at the head of one hundred infantrymen. He reined in opposite Shafter. His escort, with buglers in front, marched past and down the line of American cavalrymen at quick-step, bugles blasting in salute. At the end of the line, the Spaniards countermarched, and American buglers joined in in an odd medley of notes, continuing to blow until the column halted. Then Shafter rode forward a few paces and was met by Toral. With the aid of an interpreter, a few words of greeting were exchanged.

It was a solemn occasion. Soldiers in the surrender party stood stiffly at attention or sat their horses like men of stone. In the background were thousands of fighters, Americans and Spaniards, eyewitnesses to the formalities that would bring the war to a close. They looked on informally, with no pretense at military formation, in a scattering of faces that extended back out of sight over the ridges.

Suddenly Lieutenant Miley, who had halted his mount only a few yards behind Shafter, whirled the animal and galloped away. He soon could be heard shouting: "Bring the sword!" An orderly appeared with it, the belt and slings twisted around the hilt, and Miley quickly carried it to Shafter. With all the dignity he could assume, America's bulging commanding general extended the token to Toral, and also passed to him the sword and spurs of General del Rey, killed at Caney and buried there by his foes.

After accepting the items, Toral made a few brief remarks in Spanish. When he finished speaking, the bugle salutes were repeated. At command, the cavalry executed left front into line, forming in single rank and facing the dismounted Spanish infantry. Battlers who had fought so bitterly on San Juan Hill were again face to face, this time only a few yards apart. A military order rang out, and the lines dissolved.

Much handshaking followed as the generals on each side were presented to one another. After a few minutes of mingling, another bugle sounded, and the two commanding generals rode side by side toward Santiago. García had been personally invited by Shafter to go with him into the city, but the Cuban leader refused on the complaint that the Spaniards were still in authority there. Along the way they passed carcasses of dead horses, bridles still hanging to the vulture-picked skeletons of some. The stench was strong on the air.

Back along the trenches as the cavalcade moved away, Rough Riders and other Americans, many of them obviously ill, watched until it disappeared. Thirty percent of the 1st Volunteers were sick and disabled, it was estimated, but every one who could manage to do so had come out to watch the proceedings.

At 11:45 A.M., at a time when 22,789 Spanish soldiers were stacking arms, bugles sounded again along the American trenches. Quickly units were formed at attention. Over in the city, sharply on the dot of noon, the flag of the United States was run up over the Governor's Palace. It could have been a moment of complete victory for Shafter, but it was not. Some of the glory was taken away by an incident involving Sylvester Scovel, a New York *World* reporter described as "a disreputable-looking American,

with a black coat and a battered black derby hat." When the
newsman was ordered down from the Palace roof, to which he
had climbed without permission, he rushed toward the obese
general and struck at him. Soldiers quickly grabbed the obstreper-
ous correspondent and dragged him away.

It was an embarrassing moment for Shafter, occurring at the
peak of a dramatic occasion and distorting formalities as a spoiled
child does crying out in church. But the general was equal to the
occasion. The old Indian fighter who had spent most of his life as a
soldier quickly recovered and restored order.

As the American flag moved slowly upward above the Palace
roof, a military band crashed out the national anthem. Off toward
the trenches, signaled by the music more than the ascending banner, Capron's battery fired a salute of twenty-one guns. Then
other bands struck up "The Star-Spangled Banner." Wild cheering
sounded from all points. Something like 20,000 men took part.
Trooper Garfield Hughes of the Rough Riders called for three
cheers for Roosevelt, and the colonel, in response, proposed three
cheers for the Army.

Looking on with eager interest was Ogden Wells. His thoughts
were summarized in his diary:

> At last, after seventeen days of fighting and waiting, the city
> is ours, but at what a fearful cost. As I glance down the line
> and see the many vacant places, I think of the comrades who
> are not present to exult in the reward of their bravery, and
> my happiness gives way to sorrow. But Santiago now is an
> American city, and our Santiago campaign with its hardships
> and fighting is over.

Wells was a bit inaccurate in describing the campaign as closed.
Still remaining was the matter of occupying the captured island,
of transporting the defeated army back to Spain, and of returning
to the United States the troops no longer needed in Cuba. Late in
the afternoon, the Rough Riders broke camp and moved to another
part of the entrenchments three miles to the right.

Around the same time, the Red Cross ship *State of Texas* came in
past Morro Castle, accompanied by the war vessels *Vixen* and
Spitfire. On the morrow, there would be food for the inmates of
Santiago and for the starving refugees—mercy food from an organization accustomed to handling emergencies.

part four

THE ROUNDUP

Chapter 1

FLIGHT FROM YELLOW JACK

It was a pitiful column of men that started walking toward Caney from the San Juan battle site at noon July 18. Nothing about them justified the nickname of Rough Riders, so far as the human eye could see. The only animals they could have mounted were the battle-torn, half-starved wrecks pulling a single wagon, a vehicle the regiment had kept in strict violation of orders.

Directed by Shafter, the entire 2nd Brigade of the Cavalry Division began breaking camp at 9 A.M. Three regiments—the 1st and 10th Regulars and the 1st Volunteers—were involved. By the time they started marching, the hot sun of midday was beating down. A slow pace was set, but men weakened by poor food, constant exposure to heat and rain, grinding labor in the trenches, fever, and dysentery fell out by the score. At least fifty of the Riders suffered from heat prostration.

On the march to the new camp site, none was more energetic than huge Captain Llewellyn, now apparently recovered from his sickness. He led his troop and even carried a pick and shovel for one of his men who complained of not feeling well. Later, he doubled back with a mule and brought in a trooper who had fallen out from the heat.

The trail followed by the Riders led to Caney and then turned southward a mile or so farther on into a little secluded valley five miles from Santiago and only two miles from the bay. Near the site assigned them were a mountain stream of clear water and a high hill topped by a blockhouse. It was the best camping ground they had had since reaching Cuba. From the hill they could get a good view of Santiago. Visible were its tiled roofs and dark and gloomy adobe and rock houses, its dark and ill-smelling alleys, "so rocky a jump cart can hardly jostle along." Also from there they could get a view of the harbor, by this time alive with activity.

It seemed only a skeleton of the Rough Rider force that pitched the new camp. Roosevelt placed the total at three hundred, half the number with which he had landed. This depletion also applied to individual units. F Troop, for example, had reached Cuba with a membership of seventy, but on this date only thirty-eight reported for duty.

The night ahead was one of discomfort, with scanty shelter and scanty food. But there was hope for improvement. Roosevelt had sent a detail of six officers and men into Santiago for a supply of food and clothing, telling them to obtain it "even if we have to pay for it out of our own pockets."

That night he wrote in his diary: "Shifted camp to foothills. Half of my regiment dead or disabled by wounds or sickness."

July 19 was the quietest day the Riders had had since reaching Cuba. Guard duty was light and the men were given every chance to rest. The only requirements were that they fall in for morning roll call and that they draw their rations of flour, coffee, and bacon. The rest of the time they could employ as they liked.

Roosevelt spent a part of the day writing letters. One of these went to Lodge. In a sense, it seemed an answer to that the senator had written him on the 12th taunting him about his rashness in rushing ahead during charges, but it could not have been, for that particular missive was not received until later. He maintained that he was justified in coming to Cuba. "Somehow or other I always knew that if I did not go I never would forgive myself," he explained, "and I really have been of use."

Surgeon Bob Church, who had so recklessly toted wounded men off the battlefield, learned by experience that Roosevelt could at times be stern and shed his fatherly attitude. While they sat at lunch on July 20, the colonel mentioned that he had seen certain charges the doctor had preferred against a trooper and had dismissed them.

"Then hereafter," said Church, blood rushing to his face, "I will not bother to prefer any charges."

Roosevelt looked at him with glittering blue eyes that were to Church unwholesomely large.

"You will prefer charges when you think it proper," the colonel announced coldly. "If you do not, I will take such measures as may be necessary."

The surgeon left the table in sulky silence and retired to a hammock under a mango tree at the rear of the regimental hospital tent. About an hour later, Roosevelt sent for him. A hospital steward answered the call and reported that Church had a temperature of 104 and a very bad chill.

"In a few minutes," the surgeon afterward related, "I heard Roosevelt's voice asking where I was. The next thing I knew the colonel had both arms around my shoulders and was saying, 'My dear boy, I am so sorry. I might have known at lunch you were sick. Please forgive me, will you?'"

Roosevelt's fractiousness at the table may have been attributable in part to his worry over Captain Llewellyn. The huge officer's exertion on the march had brought on a relapse. So sick did he become, going completely out of his senses, that he was removed on this day by ambulance to the transport *San Marcus* at Santiago. Many of the Riders who watched as he was hauled away were confident they would never see him again. Actually, he would have a narrow escape from death. Neither a doctor nor a pound of ice was on the ship that carried him back to Florida, and of no encouragement was its stop en route to bury the dead at sea.

Another development at this time was the appointment of Leonard Wood as Military Governor of Santiago. The selection would cause some jealousy among the regular officers, but this later disappeared in the face of able performance. Captain Luna, the descendant of Spanish conquistadores, went along with him temporarily as interpreter.

A heavy rain set in at 5 P.M. It closed down on an invasion force that had won a victory, but was having its troubles. On top of the worries over fever and lack of food and transportation, Shafter received a long, angry letter from García announcing that he had tendered his resignation and was withdrawing his army to the interior. His peeve was over the way the surrender had been handled and over orders forbidding the Cuban soldiers to enter Santiago for fear of massacres and revenge against the Spaniards.

"Allow me, sir, to protest against even the shadow of such an idea," wrote García. "We are not savages ignoring the rules of civilized warfare. We are a poor, ragged army, as ragged and as poor as was the army of your forefathers in their noble war for independence. But, as did the heroes of Saratoga and Yorktown, we respect too deeply our cause to disgrace it with barbarism and cowardice."

Shafter sent a patient reply to the Cuban, reminding him that he had declined an invitation to go into Santiago to witness the surrender. He added: "This war, as you know, is between the United States and Spain, and it is out of the question for me to take any action in regard to your forces with the surrender, which was made solely to the American Army . . . Full credit has been given to you and your valiant men in my report to my government, and I wish to acknowledge to you the great and valuable assistance you rendered during the campaign."[1]

The most important developments July 21 were down in the harbor. A ship appeared with a cargo of refrigerated beef, and there the *State of Texas* finished unloading and headed back to the United States for more supplies.

Additional tents began to reach the Army, some carried on the backs of troopers. At the Rough Rider camp, Teddy Roosevelt, now bearing the responsibility of the 2nd Brigade command vacated by Wood, continued to make his rounds. He repeatedly expressed concern over the increasing sickness among his men. It pained him to see those with high fever trying to eat hardtack and bacon at a time when they should have been fed a light diet.

July 22 was particularly remembered by the Rough Riders because it brought them the first fresh beef they had had since June 6. With it came almost a full issue of potatoes and onions. Also included was a supply of canned roast beef, but this was laid aside untouched.

Shafter reported to Washington that sickness continued to increase. Some regiments had as many as two hundred down from one cause or another, but only eighteen deaths had been reported.

---

[1] García was nearing the end of his most unusual career. In late November 1898 he came to New York with a Cuban commission delegated to discuss with the United States Government problems confronting both Cubans and Americans on the island. He arrived in Washington the evening of November 30 and stopped at the Raleigh Hotel at the corner of 12th Street and Pennsylvania Avenue N.W. Though suffering from a cold contracted en route, he attended a Gridiron Club dinner the night of December 3, along with Generals Shafter, Miles, Lawton, and others, but was forced to leave early because of an attack of asthma. On December 11, he died of pneumonia in his hotel room.

Two of these were caused by dysentery and the remainder by fever.

Realizing there was little likelihood of getting cots for his men, Roosevelt encouraged them to build bunks of poles, but his success was disappointing. The tall, gaunt hunters and cowpunchers and the shorter, better-proportioned college athletes failed to respond. They lounged listlessly in their quarters, most of them housed in the little pup tents. These became steaming morasses during torrential rains and then, when the sun blazed down again, turned into ovens.

Diplomacy got little consideration when Roosevelt thought of his Riders. This he revealed in a letter to Secretary Alger:

> I am writing with the knowledge and approval of General Wheeler. We earnestly hope that you will send us—most of the regulars and, at any rate, the cavalry division, including the Rough Riders, who are as good as any regulars, and three times as good as any State troops—to Porto Rico.
>
> There are 18,000 effective men in this division. If those who were left behind were joined with them, we could land at Porto Rico in this cavalry division close to 4000 men, who would be worth easily any 10,000 National Guard, armed with black powder, Springfield or other archaic weapons.

This letter was made public, and newspapers immediately scored Roosevelt for his comparisons. Soon a cable arrived from Alger, the tone of which was in the nature of an official spanking for the ambitious colonel:

YOUR LETTER OF THE 23RD IS RECEIVED. THE REGULAR ARMY, THE VOLUNTEER ARMY, AND THE ROUGH RIDERS HAVE DONE WELL, BUT I SUGGEST THAT UNLESS YOU WANT TO SPOIL THE EFFECT AND GLORY OF YOUR VICTORY, YOU MAKE NO INDIVIDUAL COMPARISONS.

THE ROUGH RIDERS ARE NO BETTER THAN OTHER VOLUNTEERS. THEY HAD AN ADVANTAGE IN THEIR ARMS, FOR WHICH THEY OUGHT TO BE VERY GRATEFUL.

Roosevelt's hope of getting to Porto Rico was far-fetched, although he and Wheeler both seemed to think at the time they would eventually see service there. Senator Lodge was the one who conveyed the hopelessness of such an idea. He wrote Roosevelt a letter that began: "You can form no idea of the impression which your brilliant charge and splendid leadership have made on the country. You are one of the heroes of the fight and one of the most conspicuous, and everybody thinks so." Then he added:

I do not see how it is going to be possible for your regiment to go to Porto Rico, for it is stated here that no men are to be taken from the infected district and placed with fresh troops in a non-infected district like Porto Rico. I am very sorry that this should be so, but you have covered yourself with glory already and will have plenty to do in Cuba in my opinion before the work there is finished.

More tents brought into the harbor by ship were distributed on July 24. Roosevelt gave orders for those received at the Rough Rider camp to be floored. For this purpose, parties of three or four men each headed by a non-commissioned officer were sent in search of bamboo.

Church services on this day, a Sunday, were conducted by Chaplain Brown under a low tree outside Roosevelt's tent. Scores of troopers gathered there, lying or sitting around and taking advantage of what shade was available. Their strong, hard faces were constantly turned toward the minister, and all were respectfully silent while he preached.

Full rations of potatoes and onions were issued on July 25 for the first time since June. Also made available was an allowance of tainted beef that brought on an epidemic of diarrhea.

Several developments in the United States on this date would have been of interest to the Riders. The transport *Hudson* steamed into Hampton Roads flying a yellow flag at its foremast. On board were the bodies of Allyn Capron and Hamilton Fish. In New York, Troopers Edward Culver and Joseph Kline, sent back to the United States because of wounds, called on Fish's mother and told her of the manner in which her son had died. And announcement was made that Montauk Point, 116 miles from New York City, on the eastern end of Long Island, had been selected as the site for a camp in which the Army could recuperate upon its return from Cuba. The camp would be named for Colonel Charles A. Wykoff, killed on July 1 while leading the 13th Infantry up San Juan Hill.

On July 26, a visit to Morro Castle took up much of Roosevelt's day. With him went Generals Lawton and Wood, Bob Ferguson and Willie Tiffany. As they moved along the bay to its site, they were impressed with the beauty of the shores, especially the groves of palms and scarlet-flowered trees. "And the castle itself," Roosevelt wrote, "on a jutting headland, overlooking the sea and guarding the deep, narrow entrance to the bay, showed just what it was, the splendid relic of a vanished power and a vanished age." They wandered all through it, stopping to stare at its castellated battlements, its dungeons with their hideous, rusty implements of torture, and at its guns, some modern and some very old.

Medical reports for the day showed 3770 sick, 2924 down with fever. While malarial patients usually recovered quickly, the figures were alarming. August, the worst month for sickness in Cuba, was still ahead.

July 27 was routine, except for a letter Roosevelt wrote John Lewis Childs, Republican state senator from Nassau County, New York. Childs had written urging him to hurry and return to the United States so he could be elected governor. Teddy replied:

> You are most kind, but do you know that I would not be willing to leave this regiment while the war is on even for so great an office as that of Governor of New York. Do not think that I underestimate the honor; on the contrary, I place it very, very high, but I would not feel it right to leave the regiment while the war is on.

Many of the Riders who had been wounded in the fighting at Las Guásimas and San Juan had been returned to the United States and were being cared for in barracks and the hospital at Governors Island in New York. During this day, they were visited by Major Brodie, his shattered arm in a sling. With his good hand, he passed out to each Rider a five-dollar bill, explaining that it was from Colonel Roosevelt and to be spent for minor expenses and such little luxuries as they might wish to buy.

July 29 was remembered because of a notice that appeared on a bulletin board in the hospital tent. Signed by Shafter, it was addressed to General Wheeler and instructed him to make it known to the men that, as soon as the fever abated and the command was able to move, it would be sent to Long Island, New York.

A long rain occurred during the morning of July 30. The Rough Rider camp became more cut up than ever and was in a wretched condition. But the misery under foot was somewhat offset by an improvement in the food and supplies. The menu now included fresh bread, beef, tomatoes, corn, butterbeans, and cocoa. Perhaps the most welcome sight was a number of pairs of shoes and of blue flannel shirts of all sizes. The distribution of the shoes was an encouraging development in particular, for some of the men had been forced to go barefooted.

General Shafter had a special reason for wanting Teddy Roosevelt at the meeting of division and brigade commanders he called on July 31. It was held in the Governor's Palace at Santiago. The Rough Rider leader rode there with Generals Sumner and Wheeler, feeling rather proud to be included in such a group, although as successor to Wood he was fully entitled to the honor.[2]

When they were all together, Shafter got down to business quickly. His problem was the sickness now spreading so rapidly through the army. He had failed in efforts to get authorities at Washington to withdraw the troops immediately, and now the War Department was trying to force him into action he did not approve. He read a cablegram. It was from Secretary Alger and instructed him to move his troops into the interior, to as far as the end of the railroad to San Luis. Before answering this, he wanted the advice of his lieutenants.

In the ensuing discussion, opinion was unanimous: to keep the army in Cuba during the sickly season—August to October—would cause the death of thousands. There was no reason why it should not be sent north at once. Four immune regiments were on hand and could remain to see that the Spaniards got out of the island. Furthermore, no transportation to move camps inland existed, and the men were too weak to walk. As for spreading disease in the States, the troops could be kept in a detention camp until that danger was past.

So much for unanimity of thought. But how was it to be used to advantage? How could public opinion be aroused? To try to put pressure on the War Department might bring recrimination.

Then Shafter revealed why he particularly wanted Roosevelt present. The latter was a volunteer officer who soon would return

---

[2] Roosevelt fixed the date of this meeting as "about the last day of July." Other sources, including the Associated Press, placed it on August 3, although the wire service dispatch, so dated, included the notation: "delayed in transmission." In view of developments between the two dates, it would seem that the earlier of the two was correct.

to civilian life, the general pointed out. Therefore no punishment would come to him. Moreover, he had been a high government official before joining the Army, and his political connections would help. He should be the one to reach the public—maybe through a press conference. The colonel consented.[3]

Off he went, in typical Roosevelt fashion, to do a job. But Wood buttonholed him before he got away and gave him some advice: a statement in writing, maybe in the form of a letter to Shafter, would be better than a press conference.

Roosevelt accepted the suggestion. He worked diligently over the letter, reading the rough draft to the various generals and listening to their suggestions. When it was completed, it included all of the points brought out at the meeting and concluded with the paragraph:

> I write only because I cannot see our men, who have fought so bravely and who have endured hardship and danger so un-complainingly, go to destruction without striving so far as lies in me to avert a doom so fearful as it is unnecessary and un-deserved.

An Associated Press correspondent, informed of what was happening, approached Roosevelt for a copy of the letter, but the colonel refused to give him one. Instead, he took him along to see Shafter.

The general waved the letter away. "I don't want to take it," he said. "Do whatever you wish with it."

Roosevelt insisted on handing it to him. Shafter shoved it toward the reporter, and the colonel released his hold.[4]

---

[3] The records of the Society of the Army of Santiago de Cuba include the diary of Captain W. C. Brown, commanding E Troop, 1st U. S. Cavalry, who tells of talking with Roosevelt following a court-martial held the morning of August 4. He quotes the Rough Rider leader as saying he had climbed the hills around San Luis and that no suitable camp ground was to be found there, that the rain was heavier in that area than where they were presently encamped, that the problem of supply would be more difficult, and that the troops were too weak to move. He also said the colonel told him that the War Department might pigeonhole the views of the division and brigade commanders, but that if he himself could get a statement into the newspapers, he was confident such pressure would be brought upon the administration that they would be obliged to take the army north. "He realized fully the gravity of the step being taken," Brown related, "but laughingly added that he did not fear any danger of being court-martialed for it."

[4] In quoting the Roosevelt letter, the Associated Press report of the meeting of officers included this identification: "As an explanation of the situation, the following letter from Colonel Theodore Roosevelt, commanding the 1st Cavalry, to General Shafter was handed by the latter to the Associated Press for publication."

In the meantime, it was decided, possibly at Wood's suggestion, that a circular letter, or round robin, signed by all the officers, should be sent Shafter also. It stated in briefer form essentially what Roosevelt had written and included, in addition, the following accusatory paragraph:

This army must be removed at once, or perish. As the army can be safely moved now, the persons responsible for preventing such a move will be responsible for the unnecessary loss of many thousands of lives.

Wood's experience in delivering the round robin was somewhat similar to that of Roosevelt. When he presented it to Shafter, the Associated Press representative was again present. "The matter is now in your hands," Wood told the general, passing him the letter.

"I don't care whether this gentleman has it or not," Wood quoted Shafter as saying, the "gentleman" referring to the reporter.

Wood left. When he returned later, Shafter told him he had allowed the correspondent to have a copy.[5]

Before going to his cot that night, Roosevelt wrote Lodge a letter about the meeting. "The malarial fever is no more contagious than a cut finger," he stated, "yet Alger in his message to us absolutely seems to treat the yellow fever and the malarial fever as if they were alike . . . He will simply keep us here, growing weaker and weaker, until Yellow Jack does come in and we die like rotten sheep . . ."

A similar letter was addressed to Wheeler and entreated him to move the brigade north—"not next month or next week, but now, today if possible, tomorrow if possible." He pointed out that not a single case of yellow fever had occurred among its members, but that hundreds were stricken by malaria, which so weakened them that "they are in exactly the condition to die like sheep if the yellow fever really gets among them." To quarantine against malaria, he advised, would be like quarantining against toothache.

In view of what was happening in Washington even while the meeting at Santiago was in progress, it would seem Shafter's action in calling his officers together was wasted effort. Orders were issued on August 1—but not made public until a day or two

---

[5] In recounting in his autobiography the incident connected with the meeting on July 31, Roosevelt added: "Later I was much amused when General Shafter stated that he could not imagine how my letter and the round robin got out."

later—for some of Wheeler's cavalry to be forwarded to Montauk Point. "Great care should be had that no man infested with fever be sent," they read. "On the result of this shipment will depend further action in moving your command. Have a careful medical officer come with them."

Developments at Camp Wikoff were not in harmony with these orders. The site had been selected, but little else had been done. Still to be signed was a contract for the preparation of a detention camp, including necessary hospital facilities.

While preparing for the return of the cavalry, the War Department on August 2 repeated its advice to Shafter to move his army to an altitude above the fever level, at least until it could be shipped north. IT IS GOING TO BE A LONG JOB AT BEST TO GET SO MANY TROOPS AWAY, the cablegram stated.

Shafter received the message and glanced at a report lying on his desk. It placed the total sick at 4290, with 3038 cases of fever, 594 of them new.

From the standpoint of the Rough Riders, Ogden Wells put in writing what most of them were thinking:

> It is evident that unless we move soon we will not be able to move at all. It seems strange that we should be kept where we are drenched by daily rains and weakened by the hot weather when we would recuperate so fast back in the United States where we would be free from rains and have cooler weather, and where our sick could get some care.

The contract for boring wells, piping water and supplying lumber for tent and hospital floors at Montauk Point was let on this date. A woman good-doer in the neighborhood visited the site and found the air delicious, the situation ideal, but the only activity that of a few Italians at work on a sidetrack of the Long Island Rail Road.

From Shafter on August 3 the War Department received a stubborn reply about moving the troops inland. He cabled that the railroad to San Luis would take a week to repair, that it could not move more than a thousand men per day at best. He said it would be the end of August before the entire army could be transferred, even if the sick list did not increase. He also reported Lieutenant Miley had found the proposed camping ground covered with grass "as high as a man's head when riding a horse." Water would have to be pumped two miles. He concluded: "If the plan is adopted of waiting until the fever is stamped out, there will be no troops moved from here until the fever season is past, and I believe there will then be very few to move."

That morning, newspapers announced that orders had been issued for Wheeler's cavalry to return home and that other troops would follow.

At the Rough Rider camp, new uniforms were issued. Ogden Wells observed that "they are very handsome in their yellow trimmings." The major worry with him at the moment was dysentery, especially in view of advice from Dr. Church that, if he wished to recover, he would have to confine his diet to oatmeal, milk, and toast. "His prescription is rather ironical," the trooper commented in his diary, "as oatmeal and milk are not to be had at any price."

For a man prominently mentioned for political office, nothing could have been more fortunate for Teddy Roosevelt than developments on August 4. Fate seemed to have tapped him on the shoulder. On the heels of the War Department order for the initial return of troops, newspapers appeared with his letter and the round robin, both bearing his name. The public immediately gave him much of the credit for starting the move, but both praise and criticism would be his lot.[6]

Several hours after the morning newspapers appeared, the letter and round robin were received by the War Department.[7]

A conference was quickly called at the White House. When it ended, the following message was sent Shafter:

[6] Secretaries Alger and Long were critical. The former said of the letter: "It not only brought terror and anguish to half the communities and neighborhoods of the land, but it returned to Cuba in due time to spread demoralization among our troops." Long wrote in his journal: "It looks as if Roosevelt, in his impetuosity, had raised the devil getting together a town meeting of officers at Santiago and preparing the most doleful account of the condition of the soldiers there—frightening their relatives and creating anxiety all over the country, giving Spain and the Foreign Powers an idea of a setback to our army on account of the danger of an epidemic, possibly affecting unfavorably the negotiations for peace—and publishing the thing broadcast."
[7] Alger wrote of the round robin: "The publication of the round robin at that time was one of the most unfortunate and regrettable incidents of the war. This communication did not, as commonly reported, result in a selection of Montauk Point; neither did it hasten the return of the Santiago army, as every possible effort had already been made, and was then making, for the speedy repatriation of our troops."
But not everyone saw or recognized these dangers. The public in general and many newspapers applauded Roosevelt. Wrote the editor of the Florida *Times-Union and Citizen:* ". . . If there had been no Roosevelt, it is possible that no orders to move the troops would have been issued yet. Of course, the War Department intended to do so—eventually, but it acted pretty quick (sic) for a governmental outfit in starting the movement after the circular letter."

At this time, when peace is talked of, it seems strange that you should give out your cable signed by your general officers, concerning the condition of your army, to the Associated Press . . . without permission from the War Department. You did not even await a reply to your communication.

Shafter replied:

The report was given out, as I have since learned, before it reached me. I called the general officers together, to tell them what I proposed to do and to express to them my views and ask them to give me theirs. I found we all felt alike. Someone then proposed they write me a letter, setting forth their views, and I told them to do so. Meanwhile I wrote my telegram, and later it was handed in and forwarded, with the letter of the surgeons and the letter of these officers. It was not until some time after that I learned their letter had been given to the press. It was a foolish, improper thing to do, and I regret very much that it occurred . . . I have been very careful about giving to the press any information, and I will continue to do so.

On this date, the Rough Riders had two reasons for rejoicing. A payroll, their first since leaving for Cuba, was issued, and the notice was given that they would be loaded on transports for the trip back to the United States as soon as vessels could be made ready. The heat seemed unbearable.

Orders were given the Rough Riders on August 5 that they were to start the trip home on Sunday. They came at a good time, for the condition of the camp was growing steadily worse.

At Montauk Point, General Young, sufficiently recovered from the fever that had caused him to be sent back to the United States early in July, arrived to take charge. He was not disappointed with what he saw. As he afterward testified before a congressional committee, "I had more hospital facilities than we ever had in Indian fights."

The Washington *Post* on August 6 took occasion to editorialize upon the situation in Cuba and to aim at quieting the public. "Had anyone save Colonel Roosevelt written that letter to the Secretary of War, urging the transfer of the Rough Riders to Porto Rico and insisting that 4000 of them are equal to 10,000 ordinary volunteers," it stated, "he would have been dismissed with contemptuous amiability as a harmless crank. Had any other inspirited that protest against the further detention of the army at Santiago and passionately demanded its instant removal, he would have been arraigned as a disturber and a nuisance." The comment would bring numerous letters to the editor in praise of the Rough Riders and their leader.

Marching orders came at 8 A.M. August 7, but it was noon before the Riders fell in and trod the three miles to the Juragua Railroad. In the meantime, all those with new uniforms were ordered to put them on and to burn the old ones. Bedding was thrown in a pile and set afire.

At the railroad, the troops were loaded into boxcars. After a short ride, they reached Santiago. An Associated Press reporter was on hand and prepared a report that appeared in many papers of the United States the next morning:

> The 1st Volunteer Cavalry embarked on the transport *Miami* today, preparatory to sailing for home. Five of their number remain here sick, namely: Second Lieutenant William Tiffany, Troop K; Corporal Edgar A. Schwartz, Troop G; Pvt. William Hoyle, Troop E; Pvt. F. G. Whalen, Troop A; Pvt. T. D. Steadman, Troop D. These will probably leave in about ten days in care of Dr. Gonzales.
>
> The Rough Riders came to town by rail from their camp at 1 P.M. At the station, they fell into line, each company preceded by a red and white banner bearing the number of the regiment and the troop letter. Colonel Roosevelt rode at the head of the regiment as it marched down the Alameda skirting the waterfront to the dock where the *Miami* was moored.
>
> All the men looked fit but worn out. They presented a picturesque appearance. Some wore new khaki uniforms, while others were attired in heavy blue flannel shirts, with their old equipment . . . They take no tents or baggage with them.
>
> The men are ready and eager to return for the Havana campaign in the fall.

At the dock, each man was issued two months' pay and told he might go into the city. Wells was among those who went. He found provisions scarce and paid "an exorbitant price" for some guava jelly and cheese. In the course of his wanderings, he came upon a restaurant and went in and sat down at a table for the first time in two months.

The *Miami* swung out from the dock at dawn of August 8. Wells depicted the scene the Rough Riders were leaving behind:

As I sit on deck in the early morning light, a beautiful sight is stretched before me; to the north at the foot of the mountain lies the city of Santiago, while to the south stretches the bay covered with transports and merchant vessels, all flying the Stars and Stripes. The bay is long, narrow and hemmed in by high mountains, capped by small blockhouses. On the sides and in the coves are palm trees and thatched huts, which call to mind the historic quiet and laziness of the tropics. On the left, towering above the entrance of the harbor, is Morro Castle, suggestful of the medieval stronghold of the robber barons. The waves beating at its base have worn away the stone so that now they thunder into their cannons with a true Rider Haggard rumbling.

As we left our moorings and steamed slowly down the bay, the 3rd Cavalry band struck up "The Star-Spangled Banner" and, as we stood with bared heads, a mighty shout went up.

The trip north would be over a calm sea, with fresh, cool breezes. But troubles there were along the way. The *Miami* had not been long out of port when her captain approached Roosevelt, ordered by Wheeler to be responsible for conduct on board the ship. The stokers and engineers down below, the ship's officer reported, were drunk and disorderly—on whiskey given them by the Rough Riders. Teddy immediately issued an ultimatum: all whiskey voluntarily surrendered by the men would be held for them and returned when they reached the United States; all not surrendered and found would be thrown overboard. Seventy bottles were stacked away properly identified, while about twenty went into the sea.

The *Miami* was badly crowded. All the officers except Wheeler slept in an improvised shed—"not unlike a chicken coop with bunks," described Roosevelt—on the after part of the upper deck. Water and food were bad. There was no ice and few disinfectants. The sick were isolated on one portion of the deck.

The men were permitted to gamble as much as they wanted. "The loss of a month's salary was as nothing compared to keeping the men thoroughly interested and diverted," reasoned Roosevelt.

Except for the conditions on the ship, it was a leisurely voyage.

Sometimes in the evenings Wheeler joined the officers on deck and whiled away the time. Invariably they led him around to talk about the earlier war in which he had fought. Compared with that conflict, in his words, the fighting in Cuba was a mere skirmish.

On the night of August 11, death of chronic dysentery came to Quartermaster Sergeant George Walsh of A Troop. He was forty-three years old, born in England, and had joined at Whipple Barracks on May 2. His body was wrapped in a hammock the following morning and placed near a porthole with a flag spread over it. The engines were stilled while Chaplain Brown read the funeral service, after which the 3rd Cavalry band played a funeral dirge. Then the port was knocked free, "and the shotted hammock plunged heavily over the side, rushing down through the dark water to lie till the Judgment Day in the ooze that holds the timbers of so many gallant ships and the bones of so many fearless adventurers," reported Roosevelt.

Late in the afternoon of the 14th, a week after the *Miami* had left Cuba, the low sandy bluffs of the Jersey coast were sighted. That night the ship dropped anchor off Montauk Point.

Chapter 2

GLORY ENOUGH TO GO AROUND

A large crowd made up mostly of soldiers was on hand at the pier on Fort Pond Bay to greet the Riders the morning of August 15. Most of the Tampa contingent was there. Its members had been at Montauk Point for two or three days, after a brief stop at Jersey City where they received a heroes' welcome.

Excitement in the area had been in progress since the night before, when the *Miami* first was sighted drifting in to drop anchor. Much shouting and cheering rang from her decks as the quarantine officer came alongside. After conferring for some time with Roosevelt and Wheeler, he departed with a cheerful farewell: "Not tonight, boys, but first thing in the morning."

At 10:45 A.M., the *Miami* was seen to get under way and to head in toward the dock. Half an hour or so later, as the vessel neared shore, Roosevelt could be seen on the bridge beside the captain. He was waving his hat and shouting. Frequently he put a pair of binoculars to his eyes and scanned the sea of faces on the wharf. At his right side, barely reaching his shoulder, stood General Wheeler, a diminutive figure capped by a white helmet that he occasionally took off and held at arm's length.

Finally, above the noise, someone got through to Teddy: "How are you?"

His voice came booming back: "I'm in a disgracefully healthy condition! I've had a bully time and a bully fight! I feel as big and as strong as a bull moose!"

The din increased as the ship drifted in and was tied up at the pier. Deck hands looped ropes with practiced fingers. People along the wharf pushed forward, but were warded back by a military detail entrusted with the responsibility of getting the Riders safely ashore. Then the 3rd Cavalry Band—which a newspaper kindly announced "could still grind out a few blood-stirring airs"—moved down and took position at the right of the gangway. The first tune it played was "Rally Round the Flag, Boys." As the lively notes blended with the noise from the yelling throng, "Fightin' Joe" started walking off the ship. He was wearing white riding breeches, high-top boots, and a blue fatigue coat that dwarfed him. His mustache and long, pointed beard were neatly trimmed. At his side hung an enormous machete; its hilt curiously wrought in silver. The scabbard encasing it was so long the tip almost touched the ground.

A gray-haired lady pushed forward. "God bless you, General Wheeler!" she cried. "You have done gloriously!" Many in the crowd recognized her as Mrs. John A. Logan, widow of the Union general, whose son was still in Cuba.

Next came Roosevelt. His face was ruddy brown, his hair close cut. He was dressed in a well-worn uniform, not notable for its neatness. His campaign hat was fastened up on one side with the crossed-saber emblem of the Cavalry and his feet were encased in well-fitted riding boots badly in need of polish. A Colt revolver swung at his side in a holster attached to a cartridge belt filled to the last notch.

Just as Roosevelt came down the gangplank, an officer rode up on horseback and quickly alighted. The military guard escorted him through the crowd. It was General Young. The throng cheered as he shook the hand of the Rough Rider leader and hugged him to his breast—the seasoned old Indian fighter hobnobbing with the neophyte volunteer cavalryman.

Next down the gangplank came the troopers. They were in an approximation of unit formation, some limping, some so weak they had to be helped along, but all displaying a spirit of victory. The quarantine officer had found no contagious disease on board, but had diagnosed thirty-four men as suffering from malaria, diarrhea, and dysentery. Some of these would have to be removed by stretcher.

The troops came off the vessel in no alphabetical order. D Troop was first, followed by E. When F came down, led by the gallant little Captain Luna, who saluted gracefully and looked dapper in his well-worn uniform, the cheers grew deafening. Some of the applause was for Lee Sinnett, the West Virginian who had enlisted at Santa Fe early in May and had fled the Florida camp as a stowaway to appear on the firing line in Cuba, court-martial or no court-martial. Greenway, the ex-footballer looking a bit pale, was at the head of G Troop. Woodbury Kane led K Troop, the Eastern unit, its guidon ripped to tatters by Spanish bullets. He was almost black from the tropical sun, tall and erect, a striking figure, made more so by a Cuban straw hat. At his side hung a scabbardless machete, the tip protected by a strip of bacon rind. L Troop, from Indian Territory, the unit cut to pieces when Capron and Fish fell at Las Guásimas, was the last to come ashore. The band was playing "Home, Sweet Home."

Roosevelt was conducted to a horse waiting nearby. As he mounted, newspaper reporters crowded around him, hoping for comment about the political situation, but the colonel would talk only about his men. He happened to spot some A Troopers and pointed: "There go three well-known athletes and college men— Bull of Harvard and Wrenn and Larned, the tennis champions. If any man can tell them from any cowpuncher in the whole outfit, he's a dandy."

The correspondents looked at the designated troopers. They were all as brown as Indians. Larned and Wrenn had companions by the arm and were helping them along. Bull wore his hat on the back of his head, a toothbrush stuck under the band.

"It may be said that Colonel Roosevelt's men have come home in good condition, far better than could be expected, all things being considered," reported the New York *Sun*. "Nevertheless they are a worn and tired lot, and it will take lots of good air, good food, and absolute rest to bring them back to the health and strength that made them the finest regiment of volunteer cavalry that ever went forth to war."

Four days in detention, to make sure they carried no yellow fever germs, would be the lot of these fighters. Then they would go into camp for nearly a month, until fully recovered.

Good news and bad news awaited them. Among the positive developments was the announcement that Spain, on the 12th, had signed a peace protocol. From the White House, where the signing took place, word immediately was sent to the Army and Navy units in the field for all fighting to stop.[1]

---

[1] By terms of the Treaty of Paris, signed December 10, 1898, Spain relinquished her sovereignty in Cuba, ceded to the United States Porto Rico, Guam, one of the Ladrone Islands and, for the payment of $20,000,000, the Philippines. She also agreed to assume the liability of the Cuban debt amounting to about $400,000,000.

The unwelcome tidings concerned individual troopers. On August 6, an express wagon had delivered a sick, weak, and emaciated man to a home at 338 West 71st Street in New York City. Servants failed to recognize him until he called them by name. Then they realized he was Gerard Merrick Ives, Yale graduate and son of Chauncey B. Ives, prominent sculptor who had prepared the Sherman statue at Washington. Fever-ridden, the trooper was returning home from Tampa. En route, he had been too weak even to obtain food for himself. Three days later he was dead.

Hallett Alsop Borrowe, stricken with malaria and brought back on the *Olivette*, lay in a precarious condition in a cottage at Shinnecock Hills. Stanley Hollister, the champion half-miler, was only a few hours away from death by typhoid fever in the Army Hospital at Fortress Monroe, Virginia. The same ailment was on the verge of taking Alfred M. Judson, the New York broker and expert swimmer who, with Knoblauch, had dived for lost items during the landing at Daiquirí. Already the body of another victim, J. Knox Green of C Troop, first Rider to die at Montauk Point, was being prepared for shipment to his home at Rancho, Texas.

The Washington *Post* of August 18 carried a local news item that Southerners in particular read with interest:

> There was nothing of military pomp about his coming. He arrived with his son, Lieutenant Joseph W. Wheeler, about 10 P.M., walked unpretentiously up to the desk and subscribed his name as "Joseph Wheeler, United States Army."
>
> It would be quite impossible to enter the lobby at the Arlington without finding a considerable number who have known Wheeler during his sixteen years of service as a member of the House of Representatives . . .
>
> He wore a little flat straw hat, which may have been secured in Santiago or purchased from some out-of-the-way haberdasher in New York City. A black linen coat completed his appearance as a civilian, but, as he talked and moved about in his chair, the same nervous and restless man that left Washington over three months ago, the brass buttons of his military tunic peeped out from beneath, showing that he still retained his major general's uniform.

Wheeler had been called to Washington to be assigned command of the camp at Montauk Point, succeeding General Young.

The Rough Riders were released from detention on the 19th.

Many of them obtained furloughs and headed for a few hours in New York City. Among those who left on the 1:55 P.M. train was Teddy Roosevelt. He still refused to talk about politics, but newspapers noted that Congressman Lemuel Ely Quigg, prominent New York Republican, had been closeted with him at Montauk Point for more than an hour.

Oyster Bay residents got advance word that their most distinguished citizen would arrive at 6 P.M., and preparations were made accordingly. Houses were decorated. Members of the local band were hustled together. Every box and barrel that could be found was heaped into a huge pile in a vacant lot near the railway station and saturated with kerosene. Across Audrey Avenue in front of the office of the Oyster Bay *Pilot* was stretched a long, red white and blue banner bearing in huge letters, WELCOME, COLONEL! An estimated 1500 persons, the largest crowd ever assembled in the history of the community was on hand, and so were Mrs. Roosevelt and the children.

But things were not to go as planned. Shortly before the expected arrival, Mrs. Roosevelt was handed a telegram informing her that her ebullient spouse had missed the train at Jamaica and would not be in until 8 o'clock. Not a person seemed to leave after announcement of the delay was made. When the train finally rolled in with the famous passenger, there was din galore. Cannons, pistols, muskets, fireworks, torpedoes, even the whistle of the locomotive, contributed their share of noise. The pressure was so great that one little girl "was literally stripped of her frock." Roosevelt and his wife were driven home in a wagon trailed by the shouting throng.

In New York City that afternoon, a group of idlers were loitering as usual around the swanky Knickerbocker Club when a dusty figure approached its door. He was wearing a battered army hat, a loose canvas jacket, discolored canvas pants, and a disreputable pair of muddy hunting boots. A bit of yellow on each shoulder gave hint of the Cavalry, but, as the New York *Herald* reported, "the whole person was so yellow from top to bottom that Doctor Doty would have been chromo-scared had he seen him."

He was stopped by the hall porter.

"What name, sir?"

The man took off his hat, bearing sun-burned features that had brought an ecstatic air to many a drawing room during social functions before the war.

"Sergeant Craig Wadsworth, Roosevelt's Rough Riders."

It is recorded that the club's house bell immediately began ringing and continued its clamor for minutes. The idlers came to life, Scotch and sodas were poured, and excited conversation permeated the carpeted rooms and halls. Then a servant stole to the side of the dusty figure.

"Beg pardon, sir, your valet is 'ere."

So came home from the wars Craig Wadsworth, the cotillion leader and polo player who in May had surprised the Westerners at San Antonio with a bit of their own style of horsemanship.

On Sunday, the 21st, the New Yorkers in attendance at Grace Episcopal Church heard a sermon by a man who a day or two earlier had wandered in among the pews, dressed in a soldier's blouse, a mud-stained pair of trousers, and an old gray shirt. He identified himself as Chaplain Henry Brown of the Rough Riders and was promptly invited to fill the pulpit at the next service. In his homily, he gave due attention to religion, but also talked about the outfit with which he had served:

> Some seem to think we are tough riders as well as rough riders. In the early days of the recruiting of the regiment, I had occasion to go among the men at their camp fires dressed as a private, and I never heard a vulgar story, nor have I seen actions not becoming a gentleman and a soldier. I think the Rough Riders are more respectful toward religion than any other regiment. I have had as many as six hundred attend religious services at one time.

Among those at Montauk Point who were convinced the 1st Volunteers were capable riders were members of the 3rd Cavalry. When one of their horses, a vicious sorrel, threw every man in the regiment who mounted it, Tom Darnell, the Denver cowboy who had been so active in breaking mustangs at San Antonio, tamed it in an exhibition of bronco-bustin' in front of Roosevelt's tent that men talked about the rest of their lives.

A severe wind- and rainstorm struck Camp Wikoff on the 24th. Many tents, including General Wheeler's, were blown down, and for a period there was general confusion. That was the day Secretary of War Alger arrived for a two-day visit. Roosevelt had returned from Oyster Bay and was among the officers who greeted him.

The Secretary found matters at Montauk Point to his satisfaction.

even though some newspapers and social circles were complaining of conditions there, especially the great number of flies. The soldiers were eating well. Records showed that within the last few days they had been shipped 15,000 dozen eggs, 55 barrels of oatmeal, 50 boxes of lemons, 100 boxes of oranges, 206 kegs of pickle, 4800 three-pound cans of peaches, 9600 two-pound cans of pears, 4000 cans of corn, and 143,000 pounds of ice.

Before Alger left on the 26th, he and Roosevelt conferred in privacy for some time. When the colonel finally emerged, he announced that the Riders soon would be mustered out, but that, before this was done, they would ride to New York in easy stages and parade through the streets.

This day brought news that caused tears to form in the eyes of hard-featured cowboys. It was the death of Willie Tiffany, the popular, best-dressed New Yorker who had been one of the five members of the regiment left in Cuba. Brought back by ship to Boston, he died there of yellow fever after uttering as his last words, "Colonel Roosevelt is a brick." His burial would be from Old Trinity Church near his home at Newport, Rhode Island. Roosevelt and others attended, riding there in the private yacht of John Jacob Astor.

On the 31st, General Wheeler received a telegram that created excitement in every tent at Camp Wikoff. It was from Adjutant General Corbin and announced that President McKinley WILL PAY YOUR COMMAND AN INFORMAL VISIT ON SATURDAY, September 3.

Orders were sent out from the War Department on September 1 for eleven regiments, including the 1st Volunteer Cavalry, to be disbanded as soon as details could be worked out. At 6:30 o'clock that morning, the transport *City of Mexico* drifted into the harbor off Montauk Point and dropped anchor. Six hours later, down its gangplank came a figure that had all the appearances of a tired, worn-out soldier. It was General Shafter. Staff officers were there to greet him and conduct him by carriage to Wheeler's headquarters. Not a cheer was heard, not a hat lifted.

President McKinley arrived as scheduled on the 3rd, accompanied by Vice-President Garret A. Hobart, Secretary of War Alger, Attorney General John W. Griggs, and other dignitaries. The train bearing his party rolled in at 8:45 A.M. A large crowd was on hand. Nearly every officer of prominence in the camp except General Shafter, who was in detention, and General Young, who had fallen and broken his arm, was in attendance. A 21-gun salute was fired as the President appeared. The New York *Times* noted: "Colonel Roosevelt was among a group of horsemen nearby. Mr. McKinley saw him and got out of the carriage to speak to him. Colonel Roosevelt hastily dismounted and rustled with a gauntlet for fifteen seconds so that he might shake hands."

A column of carriages wound up the hill escorted by the mounted band of the 6th Cavalry. The President took off his hat and stared at the sea of white tents. His first stop was at Shafter's tent. The general, fully uniformed, his face flushed with fever, endeavored to rise from his chair.

"Don't get up, General," McKinley said, shaking hands. "You are entitled to a rest. How are you?"

"A little achy," replied Shafter, "but otherwise all right."

At the hospital, the President was conducted about by General Wheeler's daughter, Annie, who had been in Cuba as an Army nurse. She was preceded by her father, who announced in each ward: "Boys, the President has come to see you."

McKinley shook hands right and left—with soldiers, physicians, nurses, stewards, and anyone else who came near. Perspiration streamed down his face.[2] But he ignored the heat and kept walking, making a round of the kitchens, storerooms, dispensaries, and the nurses' quarters.

As noon approached, McKinley's carriage was drawn up in a hollow square formed by soldiers gathered on the parade ground. With him was Wheeler. In gentlemanly manner, the little general, his white beard glistening in the sunshine, got to his feet, doffed his hat, and announced in a tone attuned to the floors of Congress:

> The President of our great country has come here to greet the soldiers that marched so gallantly up San Juan Hill on July 1. He comes here to express the nation's thanks to you brave men. I wish to tell you that, when the President sent me here two weeks ago to command this camp, he enjoined me in the most emphatic language that I could, without regard to expense, exercise any and every authority necessary to make comfortable this body of brave men who by their courage have raised this Republic to the highest position among the great nations of the earth. I have the honor and pleasure of introducing to you the President of the United States.

[2] In New York, the temperature was recorded at 108 degrees.

McKinley arose bareheaded amid a din of cheering. When he could be heard, he requested that the soldiers keep on their hats. Then he spoke in a voice that carried far over the tented hills:

. . . I bring you the gratitude of the nation to whose history you have added by your valor a new and glorious page. You have come home after two months of severe campaigning, which has embraced assault, siege, and battle, so brilliant in achievement, so far-reaching in results as to command the unstinted praise of all your countrymen. You had the brunt of the battle on land.

. . . The brave officers and men who fell in battle and those who have died from exposure and sickness will live in immortal story, and their memories will be perpetuated in the hearts and histories of a generous people; and those who are dependent upon them will not be neglected by the government for which they so freely sacrificed their lives.

Cheering continued for fully two minutes after the President sat down. He was conducted next to General Wheeler's headquarters, where he sat under a tent flap and watched some of the Rough Riders stage a demonstration of riding that brought exclamations of surprise and approval. Then, after lunch, he was driven back to the railroad station between two lines of troops with drawn sabers. The presidential train departed at 2 P.M.

It had been a great day for Camp Wikoff. And it had been a great day for the Rough Riders, with one exception. Secretary Alger announced before leaving that the physical condition of the men would not permit them to parade in New York, as they would be mustered out of service before they would be strong enough to undergo such strain.

Church call sounded for the Rough Riders at 9 o'clock the next morning. They seated themselves on the ground around the headquarters tent and bowed their heads while Chaplain Brown opened with prayer. Then they sang hymns and repeated the Lord's prayer. There was no sermon; instead, Roosevelt stepped to a point near the chaplain and spoke in a voice that was loud and yet somehow sad:

"Before we part, I trust to have another chance to talk with you, so we'll just call this a preliminary farewell. . . . I would honestly rather have my position as colonel of this regiment than any other position on earth. Some people said to me recently,

'You must have been awfully bold to go right up that hill in front of your regiment.' I said, 'That wasn't it exactly.'"

He glanced at Brown. "I beg the chaplain's pardon, for I said, 'I had to run like hell to stay in front and keep from being run over.'"

Brown smiled as the troopers went into a delirium of shouting. When Roosevelt could be heard again, he continued:

I feel, and I know you all feel, that we are knit together by ties that can only be severed by death. Our trials, our hardships, our victories, we have all shared together, officers and men. There has been no distinction; we have all worked for and accomplished the glory of the regiment. The men who were left back in Florida did their duty as well as the men who went to Cuba, and all did it without a murmur.

We are going to keep up this organization as an inheritance to our sons. We have not finished our fighting. Our whole life is a fight. But one thing I want to warn you against. Don't attempt to pose as heroes who have come home to live on your laurels. Laurels wither in time. Don't go back and pose as heroes who have fulfilled their life duty and have nothing more to do. Get out and fight your battles in the world as bravely as you fought the nation's battles in Cuba.

I shall always do my best to keep in touch with as many of you as possible, visiting in your homes whenever opportunity offers. I want to feel that those of us who can still look back at the end of twenty years will see that each member has prospered, has become a better man, a better American; that we are as capable in fighting the battles of peace as of war.

The world will be kind to you for about ten days; everything you do will be right. After that, you will be judged by a stricter code, and if you prove worthless, you will be considered as spoiled by going to war . . .

Should there be another war, I shall endeavor to raise this regiment again, and feel certain for every vacancy there will be a hundred applicants.[3] You have demonstrated to the world that Uncle Sam has hundreds of thousands of men who are able and willing to form regiments that are simply invincible.

[3] At the outbreak of World War I, Roosevelt did attempt to get permission to reorganize his Rough Riders, promising a full regiment, but his offer was rejected, it was said, because of the objection of President Woodrow Wilson.

In closing, I only want to say that I feel a love and attachment for each and every one of you and that we are bound together by ties death alone can sever.

Applause frequently interrupted him as he spoke. When it died down at the conclusion, he turned to Brown.

"Chaplain," he said, "you have done noble work. There is no time more opportune than the present to give expression to the feeling we all bear you. You are as brave as any man in the regiment. When we went up that hill, I even caught you with a carbine in your hand. Your action on the firing line and your unrelenting care for the wounded when you would go into the midst of showers of lead to minister to the men's wants deserve the highest praise."

The cheering reached its highest peak.

Later in the day, as visitors wandered around the camp, one of them attempted to photograph Josephine. The lioness could not be induced to leave the shady side of her cage. Suddenly onto the scene strode Color Sergeant Wright, the powerful Yuma cowboy and mining engineer. He reached into the cage, picked up the snarling animal by the scruff of the neck, lifted her bodily out into the sun, and held her until the photographing was completed.

September 7 was a tragic date for "Fightin' Joe." It was the day he issued his farewell to the Cavalry Division: "My heart will always burn with increasing admiration for your courage in action, your fortitude under privation, and your constant devotion to duty in the highest sense." It was also the occasion for the removal of his headquarters tent from a spot near the railway station to the westernmost point of the island. And it brought sadness to a closely knit family.

Soon after the headquarters removal was completed, preparations were made for a swim at the nearby beach. The general's son, Thomas, a Naval Academy cadet who had served on board the cruiser *Columbia* during the Cuban campaign, and Lieutenant Newton D. Kirkpatrick of the 1st Regular Cavalry went down to the water, only 150 yards away, about 3:30 P.M. Later they were joined by the general, who took a quick dip and hurried back to his tent, mainly because of the stiff breeze blowing from sea. At 6 P.M., when the other two had not returned, he sent a corporal to tell them dinner soon would be served. In a few minutes, the corporal came rushing back in a high state of alarm. He had found no one on the beach. Search parties were hastily organized, and they continued to walk the beach, aided by lanterns after dark. Late that night the two bodies washed ashore.

In the camp on a visit at the time was a father who could offer condolences to Wheeler. It was Nicholas Fish, there in the hope of buying the horse and army kit of his late son.

On the 13th, the Riders received their last Army pay. That was the day the mustering out began. It was done a troop at a time. Somehow or other there seemed a reluctance on the part of the men to wind up their dealings with the military service. Each had to turn in his horse, carbine, blankets, and other items he had been issued and had managed to retain.

At 1 P.M., as Roosevelt sat working over papers in his tent, a committee of troopers appeared and asked if he would mind coming out for a moment. They led him to the area in which the rodeos were conducted. There, on uneven ground, sat a rough pine table and on it an object covered by a horse blanket.

Suspecting what was in store, Roosevelt was plainly moved. His bronzed face took on a deeper tinge, and through the thick lenses of his glasses moisture could be seen gathering around the eyes.

From the ranks of M Troop stepped William S. Murphy, a judge from Caddo, Indian Territory, formerly of San Antonio, a type Roosevelt referred to as a "gentleman." This man had been selected for the role he was about to play because of his reputation as one of the greatest orators in the West.

He took off his hat. He, too, had tears in his eyes. Speaking in the manner of the professional, his voice carried plainly across the assembly of Rough Riders, of black troops from the 9th and 10th Cavalry, white troopers from the 1st and 3rd and 6th, doctors, nurses, visitors, and others who had been tipped off to what was about to happen. Each word was distinctly enunciated:

Colonel, it is fitting that I, one of the troopers from the ranks of your regiment, should try to tell you as well as I can of to what is due the honor given me in making this presentation. It is well known that, while you hold your officers in the highest esteem because of their bravery, gallantry, and ability, your heart of hearts was ever with your men, whether in the tented field or in the trenches before the enemy's lines, or better still, in the trenches which your regiment captured from the enemy.

I want to tell you, sir, that one and all of us, from the highest of us to the humblest of us, will always carry with us in our hearts a pleasant and loving memory of your every act, for there has not been one among them which has not been of the kindest. As lieutenant colonel of our regiment, you first made us respect you; as our colonel, you have taught us to love you deeply, as men love men. It is our sincerest hope, now that we are about to separate, that this bronze "Bronco Buster" will sometimes make you think of us, as we shall ever think of you.

Murphy pulled back the blanket. There sat Frederic Remington's masterpiece, a two-foot statue of a cowboy clad in the conventional sombrero and chaps and clinging to a rearing pony. The animal was poised on its hind legs, its head between its forelegs, its eyes showing the desperate ugliness common to the vicious bronco. One hand of the rider was fixed firmly in the mane and the other was uplifted, grasping a rawhide quirt.

There was a moment of hushed awe as everyone stared at this standout addition to the world of art. Then Roosevelt began speaking, his voice faltering at the start:

Officers and men: I really do not know what to say to you. Nothing could possibly happen that would touch and please me as this has touched and pleased me. Trooper Murphy spoke quite truthfully when he said that my men were nearest to my heart, for while I need not say to my officers in what deep regard I hold them, they will not mind my saying that just a little bit closer come my men.

I have never tried to coddle you. I have never hesitated to call upon you to spend your blood like water and to work your muscles to the breaking point. Of course I tried to do all I could for you, as you have ever done all that you could for me. You are the best judges as to whether or not I have succeeded.

I am proud of this regiment beyond measure. I am proud of it because it is a typical American regiment, made up of typical American men. The foundation of this regiment was the bronco buster, and we have got him here in bronze. The men of the West and Southwest, horsemen, riflemen, and herders of cattle, have been the backbone of this regiment, as they are the backbone of their sections of the country. This demonstrates that Uncle Sam has nobler reserves of fighting men to call upon if the necessity arises than any other country in the world.

The West stands ready to give tens of thousands of men like you, who are only samples of what our country can produce. Besides the cowpunchers, this regiment contains men from every section of the country and from every state within the Union.

It is primarily an American regiment, and it is American because it is composed of all the races which have made America their country by adoption and those who have claimed it their country by inheritance. It gives me extreme pleasure to look around among you and see men of every occupation, men of means and men who work with their hands for a livelihood, and at the same time know that I have you for friends.

You are men of widely different pursuits. You stand here side by side. You fought shoulder to shoulder. No man asked quarter for himself, and each man went in to show that he was as good as his neighbor. That is the American spirit. You cannot imagine how proud I am of your friendship and regard.

I have a proud respect for you, because you have fighting qualities, those qualities which make men recognize you as fighters, the qualities which enable you to get into the fight. Outside of my own immediate family, I shall always feel that stronger ties exist between you and me than between me and anyone else on earth.

I realized when I took charge of you that I was taking upon myself a great responsibility. I cared for you as individuals, but did not forget that at any moment it might be necessary to sacrifice the comfort or even the lives of the individuals in order to secure the safety of the whole. You would have scorned a commander who would have hesitated to expose you to any risk.

I was bound that no other regiment should get any nearer the Spanish lines than you got, and I do not think that any other regiment did.

Prolonged cheering forced him to halt. When he could continue, his voice was louder:

We parted with many in the fight who could ill be spared, and I think that the most vivid memories that we will take away with us will not be of our own achievements, not of our own dangers, not of our own suffering, but of those whom we left on the Cuban sod and those who died in the hospitals here in the United States—the men who died from wounds and the men who, with the same devotion to country, died from disease. I cannot mention all of the names now, but three of those —Capron, O'Neill, and Fish—will suffice. They were men who died in the pride of their youthful strength, and they died for their country, like men who were proud to die.

Now, just a word more. I want to say to some of the men I see standing around not of your number—I refer to the regiments, cavalry regiments, who occupied the right and left flanks of us at Las Guásimas and San Juan—the 9th and 10th Cavalry Regiments.

Applause from the white troopers forced him to halt again. It was fully a minute before he could continue:

The Spaniards called them "Smoked Yankees," but we found them to be an excellent breed of Yankees. I am sure that I speak the sentiment of every man and officer in this assembly when I say that between you and the other cavalry regiments there is a tie which we trust will never be broken.

The cheering was louder than it had been at any time. Roosevelt waited, shifting impatiently. Even before the noise completely faded away he went on:

I should have been most deeply touched if the officers of this regiment had given me this testimonial, but, coming from you, my men, I appreciate it tenfold. It comes to me from you who shared the hardships of the campaign with me. You gave me a piece of your hardtack when I had none, and you gave me your blankets when I had none to lie upon.

To have such a gift from this peculiarly American regiment touches me more than I can say. This is something I shall hand down to my children, and I shall value it more than I do the weapons I carried through the campaign.

Now, boys, I wish to take each of you by the hand as a special privilege and to say goodbye to you individually. This is to be our farewell in camp; I hope it will not be our farewell in civil life.

When the colonel finished speaking, the men formed in line and marched past, each shaking his hand. In the line were Mr. and Mrs. Nicholas Fish.

As the last troopers approached, Roosevelt said, rather in the way of a parting remark, "I hope there won't be so many bullets when we meet again."

Among those who heard him and laughed was Pollock, the Pawnee.

"That is the first time I ever saw that man smile," Roosevelt said triumphantly.

During the afternoon, the organization of a permanent Rough Rider Association was completed. Brodie was elected president. It was the beginning of a brotherhood that would last through the years.[4]

Before the day ended, members of G, H, K, and M Troops had turned in their equipment and wound up their military service. The New York *Herald* reported: "Other troops will be mustered out tomorrow and by the next day the Rough Riders will exist only in history."

It is recorded that there was no sleeping in Camp Wikoff that night. Some of the troopers left for New York by train at 5 P.M. and others at 7:30 P.M., but many were reluctant to leave and stayed on, taking part in the last hours of a military outfit that would become a byword in history. With no orders to obey and no blankets to keep them warm, they sat around campfires, all in good mood and officers universally tolerant. As the evening wore along, the fires grew brighter and song and story louder.

An hour or so before midnight, Levi Jones, Cherokee Indian, leaped into the firelight and did a solitary dance. He was followed by two Sioux braves, who immediately brought new life to the scene. The Sioux war dance is a stamp dance. Accompanied by

[4] The first annual meeting of the Association was held at Las Vegas in June 1899. More than 600 Rough Riders, among them Roosevelt, then Governor of New York, attended. From then on reunions were held annually in August. In 1952, it was voted to hold all subsequent meetings in Las Vegas "to the last man." That "last man" was Jesse D. Langdon of Red Hook, New York. Since 1966, when Frank C. Brito of Las Cruces, New Mexico, was there with him, he has been the only member of the regiment to show up.
As of 1970, according to Frank C. Norris, director of the Rough Rider Memorial and City Museum at Las Vegas, only three members were known to be alive. They were Langdon, Brito, and Dr. George P. Hamner of Tampa, Florida.

warwhoops, it created general excitement, and soon long lines of men, the Easterner as well as the Westerner, joined in in a general uproar that went on until dawn.

The remaining troops were mustered out on the 14th. That night, the officers, led by Roosevelt, went through the routine. Missing among them was Leonard Wood, the skilled tactician who had brought order to their brief period of training, but whose abilities as a professional soldier would not permit him to remain a regimental officer. At the moment, he was amassing a fine record as Military Governor of Santiago.

On the morning of the 15th, the tall, powerful Sergeant Wright took down the colors for the last time. Forty-seven officers and 1090 men had turned in their equipment and were ready to resume their status as citizens. Their mascots already had been dispersed, "Teddy," the eagle, a gift to Roosevelt, the others sent to zoos where their care was assured.

In the late morning, the last, dawdling remnant of the regiment gathered at the railroad station. A train left shortly after noon. On it was Roosevelt, taking along with him as his house guests Surgeon Church and John McIlhenny, the New Orleans planter. They would reach Oyster Bay at 3:21 P.M.

So into history went the Rough Riders, some to be toasted in New York before making their way back to the ranches and the plains and the mountains and the trails, or to less rugged spots in the East. Others went south toward Washington, to visit the White House and other points of interest as the finale in a great experience that, for them, would not be repeated. Their life would never be the same again.

Always in their memories, praised and appreciated, would stand out a dedicated friend and stanch champion—Colonel Theodore Roosevelt, a man who throughout his amazing career would always look out for their welfare and stand behind them regardless of their personal trespasses. While the star of destiny for most of them was sinking, his was on the rise. In four months, he would be Governor of New York; in not quite two and a half years, Vice-President of the United States; in three years short one day, President. The war had changed his image from that of a bluestocking and fop to that of a man of vigorous fighting gestures and pugnacious teeth.

"Laughing Horse" was on his way.

ROSTER OF THE
1ST U. S. VOLUNTEER CAVALRY

ABBOTT, Charles G., Santa Fe, N.M.; pvt., F Troop; 28, 5 ft., 4½ ins., ruddy, gray eyes, dark brown hair; born Portsmouth, N.H.; miner; joined May 6, Santa Fe; single.

ADAIR, John M., Claremore, I.T. (Indian Territory); pvt., L Troop; dark, brown eyes, black hair; born in Fort Gibson, I.T.; farmer; joined May 14, Muskogee, I.T.; single.

ADAMS, Edgar S., San Antonio, Texas; pvt., F Troop; joined May 23, San Antonio.

ADAMS, John H., Selma, Ala.; pvt., K Troop; joined May 29, San Antonio; wounded July 1.

ADAMS, Ralph R., Yonkers, N.Y.; pvt., A Troop; joined July 27, Tampa, Fla.

ADKINS, Joseph R.; pvt., I Troop.

ADSIT, Nathaniel B., Buffalo, N.Y.; C Troop; joined June 13, Tampa.

AGNEW, Frank Vans, Kissimee, Fla.; farrier, C Troop; joined June 6, Tampa.

AKIN, James E., Dolores, Col.; pvt., G Troop; 22, 5 ft., 9½ ins., light, blue eyes, light hair; joined May 6, Santa Fe; single.

ALAMIA, John B., Port Isabel, Texas; pvt., Troop C; joined May 26, San Antonio; discharged on account of epileptic fits.

ALBERS, Heye L., Albuquerque, N.M.; pvt., F Troop; 25, 5 ft., 7 ins., fair, blue eyes, flaxen hair; born Hancock County, Ill.; barber; joined May 2, Santa Fe; single; wounded June 24.

ALBERTSON, Edward J., Santa Fe; pvt., F Troop; 23, 5 ft., 8⅞ ins., fair, gray eyes, light-brown hair; born Knox, Ohio; miner; joined May 5, Santa Fe; single; wounded June 24.

ALEXANDER, James F., Santa Fe; pvt., Troop F; 32, 5 ft., 6⅝ ins., light, gray eyes, light-brown hair; born Knox, Ohio; miner; joined May 5, Santa Fe; single.

ALEXANDER, Joseph L. B., Phoenix, Ariz.; 40, dark, black eyes, black hair; born Los Angeles, Calif.; lawyer; joined April 30, Whipple Barracks, Ariz.; married.

ALEXIS, George D., New Orleans, La.; pvt., I Troop; joined June 4, Tampa.

ALLAUN, Jacob, Sapulpa, I.T.; pvt., M Troop; joined May 14, Muskogee.

ALLEN, George L., Prescott, Ariz.; pvt., A Troop; 41, 5 ft., 7¾ ins., fair, blue eyes, iron-gray hair; born Cincinnati, Ohio; tinner; joined April 30, Whipple Barracks; married.

ALLISON, Jovillo, Bentonville, Ark.; pvt., H Troop; 22, 5 ft., 8⅝ ins., florid, blue eyes, brown hair; born Bentonville, Ark.; rancher; joined May 4, Santa Fe; single.

ALMACK, Roll, Santa Fe; pvt., E Troop; 22, 5 ft., 7⅛ ins., dark, hazel eyes, dark-brown hair; born Columbus, Ohio; laborer; joined May 6, Santa Fe; single.

AMONETTE, Albert B., Roswell, N.M.; pvt., H Troop; 21, 5 ft., 5¾ ins., ruddy, brown eyes, light hair; born Fairfield, Texas; cowboy; joined May 4, Santa Fe; single.

AMRINE, William D., Newkirk, O.T. (Oklahoma Territory); saddler, D Troop; 27, 5 ft., 7 ins., dark, brown eyes, dark-brown hair; born Salinas, Kans.; baker; joined May 5, Guthrie, O.T.; married.

ANDERSON, Arthur T., Albuquerque; pvt., G Troop; joined June 23, Santa Fe.

ANDERSON, Thomas A., San Antonio; pvt., C Troop; joined May 23, San Antonio.

ANDREWS, William C., Sulphur Springs, Texas; pvt., G Troop; joined June 23, Santa Fe.

ARENDT, Henry J., Gallup, N.M.; pvt., G Troop, transferred to I Troop May 12; 27, 5 ft., 9½ ins., fair, blue eyes, light-brown hair; born New York City; fireman; joined May 3, Santa Fe; single.

ARMIJO, George W., Albuquerque; sgt., F Troop; 20, 5 ft., 6¾ ins., fair, brown eyes, brown hair; born Valencia County, N.M.; farmer; joined May 2, Santa Fe; single; wounded June 24; member of Congress.

ARMSTRONG, Charles A., San Jose, Calif.; cpl., C Troop; wounded July 1; died of typhoid at Tampa Aug. 27.

ARMSTRONG, Charles M.; pvt., I Troop; joined June 2, Santa Fe.

ARMSTRONG, Edward C., Albuquerque; cpl., G Troop; 25, 5 ft., 10 ins., light, gray eyes, light hair; born Eldorado, Kans.; fireman; joined May 3, Santa Fe; single.

ARMSTRONG, James T.; pvt., K Troop; joined May 29, San Antonio.

ARNOLD, Edward B., Prescott; pvt., G Troop; 28, 5 ft., 10 ins., dark, gray eyes, dark-brown hair; born Los Angeles, Calif.; cowboy; joined May 3, Santa Fe; single.

ARNOLD, Henry N., New York City; pvt., A Troop; joined June 22, Tampa.

ARRINGO, G. W., Albuquerque; pvt., F Troop; wounded June 24.

ASAY, William, Safford, Ariz.; pvt., C Troop; 26, 5 ft., 5½ ins., fair, light-blue eyes, brown hair; born Salt Lake City, Utah; rancher; joined May 2, Whipple Barracks; single.

ASH, Alvin C., Raton, N.M.; pvt., G Troop; 27, 6 ft., ⅛ in., florid, blue eyes, dark-brown hair; born Travis County, Texas; cowboy; joined May 4, Santa Fe; single; wounded July 1.

ATHERTON, T. J.; pvt., F Troop; 23; born Corpus Christi, Texas; telegraph lineman; wounded June 24.

ATKINS, William T., Selma, Ala.; cpl., C Troop; joined June 4, Tampa.

AUSBURN, Charles G., New Orleans, La.; pvt., E Troop; joined May 4, Tampa.

AZBILL, John, Payson, Ariz.; pvt., A Troop; 27, 5 ft., 11 ins., fair, brown eyes, light-brown hair; born Tulare County, Calif.; cowboy; joined May 2, Whipple Barracks; single.

AZBILL, William T., Payson, Ariz.; pvt., A Troop; 29, 5 ft., 6 ins.; fair, light-blue eyes, dark-brown hair; born Santa Clara County, Calif.; cowboy; joined May 2, Whipple Barracks; single.

BABCOCK, Campbell E., Chicago Ill.; pvt., K Troop; sick of fever Aug. 19.

BABCOCK, Guy M., Cherryville, Kans.; saddler, L Troop; 19, 5 ft., 7½ ins., fair, brown eyes, dark-brown hair; born Buchanan County, Iowa; joined May 14, Muskogee, I.T.; single.

BACA, Jose M., Las Vegas, N.M.; pvt., E Troop; 37, 5 ft., 6¾ ins., dark, dark-brown eyes, black hair; born Las Vegas; cowboy; joined May 3, Santa Fe; single.

BAILEY, Robert Z., Santa Fe; pvt., F Troop; 26, 5 ft., 6¼ ins., dark, hazel eyes, black hair; born Huntington, W.Va.; cattleman; joined May 6, Santa Fe; single; wounded June 24.

BAILEY, William, Norman, O.T.; pvt., D Troop; 24, 5 ft., 7 ins., ruddy, gray eyes, black hair; born Falls County, Texas; cowboy; joined May 5, Guthrie, O.T.; married; wounded July 2.

BAILIE, Harry C., Gallup, N.M.; pvt., I Troop, transferred to G Troop; 28, 5 ft., 7¾ ins., fair, gray eyes, dark-brown hair; born Dupont, Iowa; miner; joined May 3, Santa Fe; single.

BAINTER, Abraham L., Colorado Springs, Col.; pvt., I Troop; joined May 9, San Antonio.

BAIRD, Thompson M., Thurber, Texas; pvt., M Troop; joined July 14, Tampa.

BAKER, Philip S., Clinton, Iowa; pvt., H Troop; joined June 29, Santa Fe.

BALLARD, Charles L, Roswell, N. M.; 2nd lt., M Troop; 39, 5 ft., 9 ins., dark, brown eyes,

black hair; born Hays County, Texas; cattleman and deputy U.S. marshal; joined May 7, Santa Fe; married.

BARLOW, John W., Caddo, I.T.; pvt., M Troop; joined May 14, Muskogee.

BARNARD, John C., New York City; pvt., A Troop; joined June 4, Tampa.

BARNEY, Leland, Ardmore, I.T.; pvt., M Troop; joined May 14, Muskogee.

BARRINGTON, John P., Ardmore, I.T.; pvt., M Troop; joined May 14, Muskogee.

BARTHELL, Peter K., Kingman, Ariz.; pvt., C Troop; 22, 5 ft., 9 ins., fair, light-blue eyes, light-brown hair; born Stratford, Ontario; salesman; joined May 1, Whipple Barracks; single.

BARTOO, Nelson E., Winslow, Ariz.; pvt., A Troop; 25, 5 ft., 3½ ins., fair, light-blue eyes, light-brown hair; born Potter County, Pa.; engineer; joined May 1, Whipple Barracks; single; sick in hospital from Sept. 5.

BASSAGE, Albert C., Corning, N.Y.; pvt., I Troop; joined June 25, Santa Fe.

BATCHELDER, Wallace N., Chester, Vt.; pvt., K Troop; joined July 11, Albany, N.Y.

BATES, William H.; pvt., I Troop; 22, 5 ft., 11 ins., florid, blue eyes, light hair; born Iuka, Miss.; farmer; joined May 6, Santa Fe; single.

BAWCOM, Joseph L., Bisbee, Ariz.; pvt., F Troop, transferred I Troop May 12; 28, 5 ft., 6½ ins., florid, blue eyes, brown hair; born St. Louis, Mo.; cowboy; joined May 4, Santa Fe; married.

BEAL, Andy R., Durant, I.T.; pvt., M Troop; joined May 14, Muskogee.

BEAL, Fred N., Kingfisher, O.T.; pvt., D Troop; 20, 5 ft., 10 ins., fair, blue eyes, sandy hair; born Riley County, Kans.; sailor; single; wounded June 24.

BEARD, Lyman F., Shawnee, O.T.; cpl., D Troop; 25, 6 ft., dark, blue eyes, black hair; born Wilson County, Kans.; farmer; joined May 5, Guthrie; single.

BEARD, William M., San Antonio, Texas; pvt., E Troop; joined May 28, San Antonio.

BECK, Joseph H., San Antonio; pvt., G Troop; rupture May 20, disability in line of duty.

BEEBE, Walter S., Prescott, Ariz.; pvt., B Troop; 21, 5 ft., 7 ins., fair, light-blue eyes, light-brown hair; born in Wisconsin; rancher; joined May 4, Whipple Barracks; single; stricken with fever en route to Cuba.

BEISSEL, John J., Gallup, N.M.; pvt., G Troop; 24, 5 ft., 9¼ ins., fair, blue eyes, light-brown hair; born Shenandoah, Pa.; miner; joined May 3, Santa Fe; single.

BELKNAP, Prescott H., Brookline, Mass.; pvt., A Troop; joined July 11, Boston, Mass.

BELL, Dillwyn M., Chicago; 1st sgt., L Troop; 21, 5 ft., 7¼ ins., fair, brown eyes, brown hair; born Springfield, Ill.; architect; joined May 14, Muskogee; single; wounded July 1.

BELL, John H., Santa Fe; trumpeter, F Troop; 21, 5 ft., 3⅜ ins., fair, blue eyes, brown hair; born Wichita, Kans.; plumber; joined May 2, Santa Fe; single.

BELL, Sherman, Colorado Springs, Col.; pvt., K Troop; joined May 21, San Antonio; disability June 24, line of duty.

BELL, William A., Tampa; pvt., F Troop; joined June 6, Tampa.

BENDY, Cecil C., El Paso, Texas; pvt., H Troop; 33, 5 ft., 5⅜ ins., dark, blue-gray eyes, light-brown hair; born New Orleans; Texas Ranger; joined May 4; single.

BENNETT, Edward, Cripple Creek, Col.; pvt., E Troop; 24, 5 ft., 6½ ins., fair, blue eyes, light-brown hair; born in England; miner; joined May 3, Santa Fe; single.

BENNETT, Horton A., Jackson County, Texas; wagoner, H Troop, transferred I Troop May 12; 24, 5 ft., 6¼ ins., light, blue eyes, brown hair; born Jackson County, Texas; cowboy; joined May 4, Santa Fe; single.

BENSON, Victor H.; pvt., L Troop; joined July 27, Santiago de Cuba.

BERNARD, William C., Las Vegas; pvt., E Troop, transferred to K Troop May 12; 19, 5 ft., 6 ins., dark, dark-brown eyes, dark-brown hair; born Trinidad, Col.; cowboy; joined May 3, Santa Fe; single.

BERNER, Harry E., Durant, I.T.; 1st sgt., M Troop; joined May 14, Muskogee.

BIRD, Marshall N., San Antonio; pvt., B Troop; 21, 5 ft., 7¾ ins., fair, light-brown hair, light-brown eyes; born San Jose, Calif.; newspaperman; joined May 4, Whipple Barracks; disability in line of duty.

BISHOP, Louis B., San Antonio; pvt., G Troop.

BLACK, Columbus L., Las Cruces, N.M.; pvt., H Troop; 24, 5 ft., 6½ ins., fair, blue eyes, dark hair; born Shreveport, La.; cowboy; joined May 4, Santa Fe; single.

BLACK, James S., Santa Fe; pvt., F Troop; 27, 5 ft., 7⅛ ins., fair, blue eyes, dark-brown hair; born Chicago; printer; joined May 2, Santa Fe; single.

BOAN, James F.; cpl., F Troop; wounded June 24.

BOEHNKE, John, Santa Fe; cpl., F Troop; 36, 5 ft., 7¼ ins., dark, blue eyes, black hair; born West Prussia, Germany; carpenter; joined May 2, Santa Fe; single.

BOGARDUS, Frank, Las Cruces; pvt., F Troop; 27, 5 ft., 7 ins., dark, blue eyes, dark-brown hair; born Bloomfield, Mo.; carpenter; joined May 6, Santa Fe; single.

BOGGS, Looney L., Phoenix, Ariz.; pvt., B Troop; 21, 5 ft., 11 ins., fair, light-brown eyes, light-brown hair; born Central, S.C.; rancher; joined April 20, Whipple Barracks; single; fever contracted in line of duty.

BOHLINGER, Eugene, Santa Fe; sgt., F Troop; 21, 5 ft., 10¾ ins., fair, gray eyes, light-brown hair; born St. Louis, Mo.; railroad man; joined May 2, Santa Fe; single.

BOOTH, Frank B., Albuquerque; pvt., F Troop; 22, 5 ft., 6 ins., dark, brown eyes, dark-brown hair; born Madison, Wis.; bookkeeper; joined May 5, Santa Fe; single; died Aug. 30 of wound received June 24.

BORROWE, Beekman K., Tampa; pvt., B Troop; joined June 12, Tampa; sick of disease contracted in line of duty.

BORROWE, Hallett Alsop, Jersey City, N.J.; pvt., I Troop; placed in charge of dynamite gun.

BOSCHEN, John, San Antonio; pvt., F Troop; joined May 25, San Antonio.

BOWLER, George P., New York City; pvt., C Troop; joined June 14, Tampa; sick in quarters Aug. 1–2.

BOYDSTUN, John F., Caddo, I.T.; pvt., M Troop; joined May 14, Muskogee.

BOYLE, James S., Wilder, Kans.; pvt., A Troop; 31, 5 ft., 6½ ins., fair, light-blue eyes, dark-brown hair; born Carbon County, Pa.; cowboy; joined May 3, Whipple Barracks; single; died July 2 of wound received July 1.

BRADLEY, Peter, Jerome, Ariz.; pvt., Troop C; 28, 5 ft., 9½

ins., fair, light-brown eyes, dark-brown hair; born Parkersville, W. Va; cowboy; joined May 3, Whipple Barracks; single.

BRADLEY, Thomas G., Potomac, Md.; farrier, K Troop; joined May 5, Washington, D.C.

BRADSHAW, Henry P., Clyde, Ohio; pvt., A Troop; 27, 5 ft., 11 ins., fair, light-blue eyes, dark-brown hair; born Clyde; miner; joined May 1, Whipple Barracks; single; absent sick from Aug. 15.

BRADY, Fred L., New York City; pvt., B Troop; joined June 4, Tampa.

BRADY, James B., Santa Fe; steward, Hospital Corps; dentist.

BRIERTY, Thomas; pvt., M Troop; joined July 19, Tampa.

BRANDON, Perry H., Douglas, Kans.; pvt., K Troop, transferred to D Troop July 29; joined May 5, Guthrie.

BRAUER, Lee W., Richmond, Va.; pvt., A Troop; joined July 7, Tampa.

BRAZELTON, William H., St. Louis, Mo.; pvt., G Troop; joined May 23, San Antonio.

BREEN, Timothy, Santa Fe; sgt., E Troop; 30, 5 ft., 5 ins., ruddy, gray eyes, brown hair; born in Ireland; laborer; joined May 4, Santa Fe; married; wounded July 1.

BREEN, William J., New York City; cpl., K Troop; joined May 5, Washington, D.C.

BRENNAN, Jeremiah, Santa Fe; pvt., F Troop; joined June 30, Santa Fe.

BRENNAN, John M., Santa Fe; pvt., E Troop; joined June 23, Santa Fe.

BRIGGS, Frank, Raton, N.M.; cpl., G Troop; 34, 5 ft., 8 ins., light, brown eyes, brown hair; born Camden, Pa.; laborer; joined May 3, Santa Fe; married.

BRITO, Frank C., El Paso; pvt., H Troop; 21, 5 ft., 8⅛ ins., dark, blue eyes, black hair; born

Pinos Altos, N.M.; miner, joined May 6, Santa Fe; single; malaria.

BRITO, Jose, El Paso; pvt., H Troop, transferred to I Troop May 12; 34, 5 ft., 9⅞ ins., dark, brown eyes, black hair; born El Paso; cowboy; joined May 6, Santa Fe; single

BRODIE, Alexander Oswald, Prescott; lt. col.; born New York; graduate of West Point; wounded June 24; later Governor of Arizona.

BROWN, Edwin M., San Antonio; pvt., G Troop; joined May 5, San Antonio.

BROWN, Harry R., Tampa; pvt., I Troop; joined June 7, Tampa.

BROWN, Henry A., Prescott; chaplain; rector, Church of the Advent; married.

BROWN, Hiram T., Albuquerque; pvt., E Troop, transferred to I Troop May 12; 51, 5 ft., 6⅜ ins., florid, blue eyes, iron-gray hair; born in Manchester, N.H.; electrician; joined May 4, Santa Fe; married.

BROWN, James, Gallup, N.M.; sgt., G Troop; 42, 5 ft., 4¾ ins., dark, hazel eyes, iron-gray hair; born Eyrshire, Scotland; miner; joined May 3, Santa Fe; single.

BROWN, James T., Oxford, Kans.; trumpeter, D Troop; 20, 5 ft., 6½ ins., dark, brown eyes, black hair; born Wills Point, Texas; student; joined May 5, Guthrie; single.

BROWN, John, Gallup, N.M.; pvt., G Troop, transferred to I Troop May 12; 36, 5 ft., 7 ins., florid, blue eyes, iron-gray hair; born in Ireland; gardener; joined May 3, Santa Fe; single; deserted en route to Tampa.

BROWN, Leon, Ardmore, I.T.; pvt., M Troop; joined May 14, Muskogee.

BROWN, Percy, Spring Hill, Tenn.; pvt., H Troop; joined June 4, Tampa.

BROWN, Robert, Gallup; pvt., C Troop; 35, 5 ft., 7 ins., dark, light-brown eyes, iron-gray hair; born in Scotland; miner; joined May 3, Santa Fe; single.

BROWN, Robert, Prescott; sgt., A Troop; 38, 5 ft., 8 ins., fair, blue eyes, brown hair; born New Brunswick, N.J.; cowboy; joined April 30, Whipple Barracks; single.

BRUCE, Peter R., Wagoner, I.T.; pvt., M Troop; joined May 14, Muskogee.

BRUCE, Robert H., Mineola, Texas; capt., M Troop; joined May 14, Muskogee.

BRUMLEY, Wm. H., Jr., Dolores, Col.; pvt., G Troop; 21, 5 ft., 5 ins., fair, blue eyes, light-brown hair; born Cleburne, Texas; cowboy; joined May 6, Santa Fe; single.

BRUSH, Charles A., Hanford, Calif.; pvt., I Troop; joined July 2, Santa Fe.

BRYAN, John B., Las Cruces; pvt., H Troop; 21, 5 ft., 9⅜ ins., dark, gray eyes, brown hair; born Louisville, Ky.; clerk; joined May 4, Santa Fe; single.

BUCKHOLDT, Charles, Kickapoo Springs, Texas; pvt., B Troop; joined May 25, San Antonio; ill in Siboney hospital July 10.

BUCKLIN, Elhanan W., Jamestown, N.Y.; 1st sgt., H Troop, transferred to L Troop June 8; joined June 7, Tampa.

BUGBEE, Fred W., Wilder, Kans.; pvt., A Troop; 22, 5 ft., 10 ins., fair, light-blue eyes, light-brown hair; born Oakland, Calif.; rancher; joined May 2, Whipple Barracks; single; wounded July 1.

BUGBEE, George L., Wilder, Kans.; cpl., A Troop; 28, 5 ft., 10 ins., fair, light-blue eyes, dark-brown hair; born San Francisco; trainmaster; joined May 2, Whipple Barracks; single.

BULL, Charles C., Belmont, Calif.;
pvt., A Troop; 21, 5 ft., 9 ins.,
fair, blue eyes, light-brown hair;
born San Francisco; student;
joined May 4, Whipple Barracks;
single; wounded.

BULL, Henry W., New York City;
cpl., K Troop; joined May 5,
Washington, D.C.

BULLARD, John W., Guadeloupe,
Texas; pvt., H Troop; joined
June 24, Santa Fe.

BULZING, William, Santa Fe; pvt.,
A Troop; joined June 4, Tampa;
sick in line of duty.

BUMP, Arthur L., New London,
Ohio; pvt., E Troop, transferred
from K Troop May 12; 25, 5 ft.,
11½ ins., fair, gray eyes, dark
flaxen hair; born Eau Claire,
Wis.; telephone operator; joined
May 3, Santa Fe; single;
wounded July 1.

BURDEN, I. Townsend, Jr., New
York City; pvt., K Troop.

BURDWELL, Lee, Lantry, Texas;
wagoner, K Troop; joined May
19, San Antonio.

BURGESS, George W., Green City,
Mo.; pvt., D Troop; 29, 5 ft.,
9¾ ins., dark, blue eyes, brown
hair; born Vermont, Ill.; salesman; joined May 5, Guthrie;
single.

BURKE, Edward F., Orange, N.J.;
pvt., D Troop, transferred to A
Troop July 13; joined June 4,
Tampa; sick in line of duty.

BURKS, Jesse E., Ardmore, I.T.;
pvt., M Troop; joined May 14,
Muskogee.

BURKS, Robert E., Prescott; pvt., C
Troop; 21, 5 ft., 11¼ ins., fair,
dark-brown eyes, light-brown
hair; born Hancock County, Ill.;
rancher; joined May 2, Whipple
Barracks; single.

BURRIS, Walter C., Santa Fe; pvt.,
F Troop; joined June 24, Santa
Fe.

BUTLER, James A., Albuquerque;
pvt., B Troop; joined June 24,
Tampa.

BUTLER, Peter L., Kiowa, I.T.; pvt.,
M Troop; joined May 14, Muskogee.

BYAN, John B., Las Cruces, N.M.;
pvt., H Troop.

BYRD, Samuel J. W., Muskogee;
pvt., M Troop; joined May 14,
Muskogee.

BYRNE, John, Muskogee; pvt., L
Troop, transferred to F Troop;
34, 5 ft., 7½ ins., ruddy, blue
eyes, dark-brown hair; born in
Dublin, Ireland; teamster; joined
May 14, Muskogee; single.

BYRNE, Peter F., Guthrie; pvt., D
Troop; 21, 5 ft., 7 ins., ruddy,
brown eyes, red hair; born Muscatine County, Iowa; clerk;
joined May 5, Guthrie.

BYRNES, Orlando C., Prescott; pvt.,
C Troop; 21, 5 ft., 11 ins., fair,
light-blue eyes, light-brown hair;
born Dubuque County, Iowa;
miner; joined May 2, Whipple
Barracks; single.

CALHOUN, Wesley, Durant, I.T.;
pvt., M Troop; joined May 14,
Muskogee.

CALROW, Gerald, Boerne, Texas;
pvt., D Troop; joined May 28,
San Antonio.

CAMERON, Charles H., McDonald,
Pa.; pvt., K Troop; joined June
11, Tampa.

CAMP, Cloid, Raton, N.M.; pvt.,
Troop F; 26, 5 ft., 9⅛ ins.,
light, blue eyes, sandy hair;
born Wilson County, Texas; cowboy; joined May 5, Santa Fe;
married.

CAMP, Marion, Raton, N.M.; pvt., G
Troop; 22, 5 ft., 7¼ ins., light,
gray eyes, light hair; born Wilson County, Texas; cowboy;
joined May 5, Santa Fe; single.

CAMPBELL, Douglas; pvt., K
Troop; joined June 29, Tampa.

CAMPBELL, John E., Phoenix, Ariz.;
sgt., B Troop; 31, 5 ft., 4 ins.,
light, blue eyes, brown hair;
born Pittsburgh, Pa.; farmer;

joined April 30, Whipple Barracks; single; sick in line of duty.

CAPRON, Allyn L., Fort Sill, O.T.; capt., L Troop; 26, 5 ft., 11 ins., fair, blue eyes, light-brown hair; born Brooklyn, N.Y.; U. S. Army; joined May 14, Muskogee; married; killed June 24.

CARDEN, Horace W., Ardmore, I.T.; pvt., M Troop; joined May 14, Muskogee.

CAREY, Oren E., Clanon, Iowa; pvt., L Troop; 22, 5 ft., 9 ins., fair, blue eyes, light-brown hair; born Princeton, Ill.; farmer; joined May 14, Muskogee; single.

CARLETON, William C., Tempe, Ariz.; pvt., C Troop; 21, 5 ft., 7¼ ins., fair, light-blue eyes, light-brown hair; born Genesee, Ill.; photographer; joined May 2, Whipple Barracks; single.

CARLSON, Carl, Tempe; pvt., Troop C; 26, 5 ft., 7½ ins., fair, light-blue eyes, light-brown hair; born in Sweden; farmer; joined April 30, Whipple Barracks; single.

CARPENTER, William W., Blairston, Mo.; pvt., L Troop; 26, 5 ft., 7 ins., fair, blue eyes, brown hair; born Holden, Mo.; cowboy; joined May 14, Muskogee; single; wounded July 1.

CARR, Joseph A., Washington, D.C.; 1st lt., D Troop, transferred to K Troop Sept. 5; joined April 29, Washington; wounded July 2.

CARROLL, John F., Hillsboro, Texas; pvt., K Troop; joined May 21, San Antonio.

CARTER, Arthur E., Ardmore, I.T.; pvt., M Troop; joined May 14, Muskogee.

CARTER, Joshua D., Duluth, Minn.; 36, 5 ft., 9¾ ins., fair, gray eyes, black hair; born Dubuque, Iowa; clerk; joined April 30, Whipple Barracks; single; sick in line of duty.

CARTLEDGE, Crantz, Tempe; pvt., C Troop; 20, 5 ft., 11½ ins., fair, light-blue eyes, dark-brown hair; born Colquist, Ga.; student; joined May 4, Whipple Barracks; single.

CARTNELL, Nathaniel M., Lexington, Va.; pvt., K Troop; joined May 21, San Antonio.

CASAD, Charles Darwin, Las Cruces; pvt., H Troop, transferred to I Troop May 12; 21, 5 ft., 7 ins., fair, gray eyes, light-brown hair; born Mesilla, N.M.; farmer; joined May 4, Santa Fe; single.

CASE, George, Durant, I.T.; pvt., M Troop; joined May 14, Muskogee.

CASEY, Edwin Eugene, Las Cruces; pvt., H Troop; 19, 5 ft., 6⅞ ins., florid, blue eyes, brown hair; born Orleans, Neb.; student; joined May 4, Santa Fe; single.

CASH, Walter S., Colorado Springs, Col.; sgt., K Troop; joined May 22, Washington, D.C.; wounded July 1.

CASHION, Roy V., Hennessey, O.T.; pvt., D Troop; 19, 5 ft., 7 ins., fair, brown eyes, dark-brown hair; born Baldwin, Mich.; clerk; joined May 5, Guthrie; single; killed July 1.

CASSI, Emilio, Jerome, Ariz.; trumpeter, A Troop; 27, 5 ft., 9¼ ins., fair, brown eyes, black hair; born Monte Carlo, Monaco; bandmaster; joined May 1, Whipple Barracks; single; wounded July 2.

CATE, James S., Grapevine, Texas; pvt., H Troop, transferred to I Troop May 12; 35, 5 ft., 11¾ ins., dark, gray eyes, brown hair; born Grapevine; cowboy; joined May 4, Santa Fe; single.

CAVANAUGH, Thomas F.; sgt., F Troop; 23, 5 ft., 9⅝ ins., fair, blue eyes, dark-brown hair; born Austin, Texas; clerk and cowboy; joined May 6,

Santa Fe; single; wounded June 24.

CEASE, Forrest L., Guthrie; pvt., D Troop; 22, 5 ft., 7 ins., ruddy, blue eyes, brown hair; born Butler County, Kans.; farmer; joined May 5, Guthrie; single.

CHAMBERLIN, Lowell A., Washington, D.C.; pvt., B Troop; joined July 22, Tampa.

CHAMPLIN, Fred E., Flagstaff, Ariz.; pvt., A Troop; 30, 5 ft., 10¼ ins., fair, light-blue eyes, light-brown hair; born Saginaw, Mich.; rancher; joined May 1, Whipple Barracks; single; mortally wounded July 1.

CHANNING, Roscoe H., New York City; pvt., K Troop; joined May 21, San Antonio.

CHAPIN, Guilford B., Santa Fe; wagoner, E Troop; 44, 5 ft., 3½ ins., dark, brown hair, blue eyes; born Greenbush, Ill.; guard; joined May 4, Santa Fe; single.

CHASE, Leslie C., Verdon, Neb.; pvt., D Troop; 21, 5 ft., 6¼ ins., dark, blue eyes, light-brown hair; born Westerby, Iowa; student; joined May 5, Guthrie; single.

CHERRY, Charles C., Santa Fe; pvt., F Troop; joined June 27, Santa Fe.

CHESTER, Will M., Oakwell, Texas; pvt., B Troop; joined May 19, San Antonio.

CHILCOOT, Fred, Howells, Neb.; pvt., L Troop; 23, 5 ft., 10½ ins., ruddy, blue eyes, sandy hair; born Zanesville County, Ohio; cooper; joined May 14, Muskogee; single.

CHOPETAL, Frank W., Buffalo, N.Y.; pvt., G Troop.

CHRISTIAN, Benjamin, Norfolk, Va.; pvt., B Troop; joined June 4, Tampa.

CHRISTIAN, Edward D., Tampa; pvt., F Troop; joined June 7, Tampa.

CHURCH, James Robert, Washington, D.C.; 1st lt., Hospital Corps; regimental surgeon.

CIPER, Edward G., Silver City, N.M.; trumpeter, G Troop; joined May 15, San Antonio.

CLAGETT, Jesse C., Frederick County, Md.; pvt., K Troop; joined May 5, Washington, D.C.

CLARK, Frank J., San Antonio; pvt., F Troop; joined May 28, San Antonio.

CLARK, Frank M., Hiawatha, Kans.; pvt., I Troop; joined June 27, Santa Fe.

CLARK, Ray V., Santa Fe.; farrier, F Troop; 24, 5 ft., 7⅜ ins., fair, hazel eyes, dark hair; born New Boston, Ill.; cowboy; joined May 5, Santa Fe; single; wounded.

CLARK, Winslow, Milton, Mass.; pvt., G Troop; joined May 29, San Antonio; wounded July 1.

CLEARWATER, Frank H., Brownsville, Texas; pvt., C Troop; joined May 27, San Antonio; died of typhoid Sept. 2.

CLELLAND, Calvin G., Santa Fe; pvt., F Troop; 32, 5 ft., 8¼ ins., fair, brown eyes, light-brown hair; born Indiana; rancher; joined May 6, Santa Fe; married.

CLOUD, William; pvt., E Troop, transferred to I Troop May 12; 21, 5 ft., 7⅞ ins., dark, dark-brown eyes, dark-brown hair; born Indianapolis, Ind.; car repairer; joined May 3, Santa Fe; single.

COAKLEY, Edwin, Prescott; pvt., K Troop; joined May 19, San Antonio.

COCHRAN, Charles P., Eddy, N.M.; pvt., H Troop; 26, 5 ft., 7⅝ ins., fair, blue eyes, dark-brown hair; born Lincoln County,

Mo.; cowboy; joined May 4, Santa Fe; single.

COCHRAN, Irad, Jr., Las Vegas; pvt., E Troop; 19, 5 ft., 11¾ ins., dark, brown eyes, auburn hair; born Concord, N.H.; clerk; joined May 5, Santa Fe; single; died of spinal meningitis May 26.

COCHRAN, Nicholas H., Vinita, I.T.; wagoner, L Troop; 31, 5 ft., 8½ ins., dark, brown eyes, black hair; born Sullivan County, Ind.; teamster; joined May 14, Muskogee; single.

COCHRAN, Willard M., Santa Fe; pvt., F Troop; 23, 5 ft., 6¼ ins., fair, blue eyes, dark hair; born Barber County, Kans.; rancher; joined May 6, Santa Fe; married.

COCHRAN, William O., Santa Fe; pvt., F Troop; 44, 5 ft., 6¾ ins., fair, blue eyes, brown hair; born Green County, Ind.; stockman; joined May 6, Santa Fe; married.

CODY, William F., St. Louis, Mo.; pvt., G Troop; 23, 5 ft., 9 ins., light, blue eyes, brown hair; born St. Louis; cattleman; joined May 6, Santa Fe; single.

COE, George M., Albuquerque; pvt., I Troop; joined July 2, Santa Fe.

COLBERT, Benjamin H., San Antonio; pvt., F Troop; joined May 24, San Antonio; railroad brakeman.

COLEMAN, Lockett G., St. Louis; pvt., C Troop; 20, 5 ft., 10 ins., fair, blue eyes, brown hair; born Macon, Ga.; student; joined May 4, Washington, D.C.; single.

COLEMAN, Sherrard, Santa Fe; 2nd lt., E Troop; 33, 5 ft., 4 ins., dark-brown eyes, dark-brown hair; born Louisa County, Va.; special agent for Justice Department; joined May 6, Santa Fe; married.

COLLIER, Edward G., Globe, Ariz.; pvt., B Troop; 25, 5 ft., 10 ins., fair, light-blue eyes, light-brown hair; born Chambers County, Ala.; teamster; joined May 2, Whipple Barracks; single.

COLWELL, Grant, Phoenix; pvt., B Troop; 31, 5 ft., 7½ ins., dark, dark-blue eyes, dark-brown hair; born Bolinas, Calif.; rancher; joined May 1, Whipple Barracks; single; sick in line of duty.

CONDUIT, Wentworth S., Santa Fe; corp., F Troop; joined June 27, Santa Fe.

CONE, John S., Tularosa, N.M.; saddler, H Troop; 27, 5 ft., 5⅛ ins., light-gray eyes, light-brown hair; born Grimes County, Texas; cowboy; joined May 4, Santa Fe; married.

CONLEY, Edward C., Santa Fe; pvt., F Troop; joined June 25, Santa Fe.

CONNELL, Thomas J., Bennett, Texas; pvt., H Troop; 22, 5 ft., 5¼ ins., light, blue eyes, light-brown hair; born Bennett, Texas; cowboy; joined May 6, Santa Fe; married.

CONNER, Richard C., Santa Fe; pvt., E Troop; 32, 5 ft., 7½ ins., fair, blue eyes, dark flaxen hair; born Springfield, Ill.; miner; joined May 3, Santa Fe; single.

CONOVER, Alfred J., Chickasee, I.T.; pvt., G Troop; joined June 23, Santa Fe.

CONWAY, James, San Antonio; pvt., E Troop; joined May 25, San Antonio; sick in line of duty Aug. 25.

COOK, Henry B.; pvt., K Troop; joined May 27, San Antonio.

COOK, James, Cherokee City, Ark.; pvt., L Troop; 23, 5 ft., 7¼ ins., dark, brown eyes, dark-brown hair; born Scotland

County, Mo.; blacksmith; joined May 14, Muskogee; single.

COOK, Walter M., Enid, O.T.; pvt., D Troop; 26, 5 ft., 6 ins., dark, blue eyes, black hair; born Warren County, Mo.; cattleman; joined May 5, Guthrie; single.

COOKE, Henry B.; pvt., K Troop; joined May 29, San Antonio.

COOPER, Bud G., Muskogee; pvt., M Troop; joined May 14, Muskogee.

COOPER, George B., Tampa; pvt., E Troop; joined June 4, Tampa.

CORBE, Max C., El Paso; trumpeter, K Troop, transferred from G Troop May 11; 40, 5 ft., 5¼ ins., fair, brown eyes, iron-gray hair; born Lorraine, Germany; butcher; joined May 3, Santa Fe; single.

CORBETT, Thomas F., Roswell, N.M.; pvt., H Troop; 36, 5 ft., 7¼ ins., dark, hazel eyes, black hair; born Memphis, Tenn.; cowboy; joined May 4, Santa Fe; single.

CORNISH, Thomas J., Freestone, Texas; pvt., H Troop; 41, 5 ft., 5⅝ ins., florid, blue eyes, dark-brown hair; born Freestone; cowboy; joined May 4, Santa Fe; single.

COSBY, Arthur Fortunatus, Washington, D.C.; pvt., K Troop; joined May 27, San Antonio; wounded July 1.

COTTON, Frank W., Jennings, La.; pvt., G Troop; joined June 23, Santa Fe.

COVENAUGH, Thomas F., Raton, N.M.; pvt., G Troop; wounded June 24.

COVILLE, Allen M., Topeka, Kans.; pvt., K Troop; joined May 5, Washington, D.C.

COWDEN, Elliott C., New York City; pvt., I Troop, transferred to L Troop June 7; joined May 9, Washington, D.C.

COX, Walter, Durant, I.T.; pvt., M Troop; joined May 14, Muskogee.

COYLE, Michael H., Raton, N.M.; pvt., G Troop; 21, 5 ft., 7¼ ins., dark, gray eyes, dark-brown hair; born Ashley, Pa.; laborer and cowboy; joined May 7, Santa Fe; single; wounded June 24.

CRANFORD, William, San Antonio; pvt., A Troop; 34, 5 ft., 7¾ ins., ruddy, blue eyes, dark-brown hair; born Davenport, Iowa; soldier; joined May 16, San Antonio; married.

CRAWFORD, Clinton K., Cincinnati, Ohio; pvt., H Troop; joined May 10, Tampa.

CRAWFORD, William S., Dixon, Ky.; pvt., D Troop; 25, 5 ft., 6½ ins., fair, blue eyes, light-brown hair; born Webster County, Ky.; ranchman; joined May 5, Guthrie; single.

CREECH, Hiram S., Durant, I.T.; cpl., M Troop.

CRIMMINS, Martin L., New York City; pvt., B Troop; student.

CROCKETT, Joseph B., Topeka, Kans.; pvt., G Troop, transferred to I Troop May 12; 28, 5 ft., 7½ ins., dark, brown eyes, dark hair; born Logansport, Ind.; railroad man; joined May 5, Santa Fe; married.

CRONIN, Cornelius P., Yuma, Ariz.; sgt., B Troop; 27, 5 ft., 7 ins., fair, light-blue eyes, dark-brown hair; born Boston, Mass.; county recorder; joined May 3, Whipple Barracks; single.

CROSLEY, Henry S., Guthrie; pvt., D Troop; 26, 5 ft., 8 ins., light, blue eyes, dark-brown hair; born Atchison County, Mo.; teamster; joined May 5, O.T.; married; dropped from rolls as deserter July 8.

CROSS, William E., El Reno, O.T.; pvt., D Troop; 28, 5 ft., 8¾ ins., ruddy, gray-brown eyes, dark-brown hair; born Decatur County, Iowa; farmer; joined May 5, Guthrie; single.

CROWNINSHIELD, Francis Benjamin, Marblehead, Mass.; pvt., K Troop; joined May 13, San Antonio.

CRUCIUS, George T., Montgomery, Ala.; blacksmith, K Troop; joined May 19, San Antonio.

CRUMMINS, Martin L.; pvt., B Troop; joined May 23, San Antonio.

CRUSE, James, St. Joe, Ark.; pvt., L Troop; 22, 5 ft., 8½ ins., ruddy, brown eyes, dark-brown hair; born Boone County, Kans.; farmer; joined May 14, Muskogee; single.

CULLEN, John, Santa Fe; cpl., F Troop; 33, 5 ft., 4¾ ins., dark, hazel eyes, black hair; born Troy, N.Y.; soldier; joined May 2, Santa Fe; single.

CULVER, Edward, Muskogee; pvt., L Troop; 22, 5 ft., 8¼ ins., fair, blue eyes, brown hair; born Tipper County, Miss.; cowboy; joined May 14, Muskogee; single; wounded June 24.

CUNNINGHAM, Solomon M., San Antonio; pvt., D Troop; joined May 19, San Antonio; sick in line of duty.

CURRY, George, Tularosa, N.M.; captain, H Troop; 36, 5 ft., 8⅛ ins., light, blue-gray eyes, light hair; born Bayou Sara, La.; stock raiser; joined May 7, Santa Fe; married.

CURTIS, Harry A., Boston, Mass.; pvt., A Troop; joined June 11, Tampa.

DAME, William E., Cerrillos, N.M.; 1st sgt., E Troop, transferred to F Troop as 2nd lt. July 11; 40, 5 ft., 6¾ ins., fair, blue eyes, brown hair; born Portsmouth, N.H.; miner; joined May 2, Santa Fe; married.

DAMET, John P., Alexander, S.D.; pvt., L Troop; 25, 5 ft., 5¼ ins., ruddy, blue eyes, brown hair; born Washington County, Iowa; joined May 14, Muskogee; single; wounded June 24.

DANFORTH, Clyde L., Flagstaff, Ariz.; pvt., C Troop; 30, 5 ft., 9¾ ins., fair, light-blue eyes, light-brown hair; born Eugene, Ore.; miner; joined May 2, Whipple Barracks; single.

DANFORTH, William F., Flagstaff; pvt., C Troop; 26, 5 ft., 4½ ins., fair, light-blue eyes, dark-brown hair; born Johnson County, Oregon; miner; joined May 2, Whipple Barracks; single.

DANIELS, Benjamin F., Colorado Springs, Col.; pvt., D Troop; joined May 21, San Antonio.

DARNELL, Thomas, Denver, Col.; sgt., H Troop; 27, 5 ft., 10 ins., light, blue eyes, red hair; born Denver; cowboy; joined May 6, Santa Fe; single.

DAVID, Icem J., Enid, O.T.; pvt., D Troop; 44, 5 ft., 6 ins., dark, brown eyes, dark-brown hair; born McDonough County, Ill.; machinist; joined May 5, Guthrie; married.

DAVIDSON, William A., Phoenix; sgt., B Troop; 32, 5 ft., 8 ins., fair, light-blue eyes, light-brown hair; born Cleveland, Ohio; miner; joined May 4, Whipple Barracks; single.

DAVIS, Harry A., Boston, Mass.; pvt., E Troop; joined May 25, San Antonio.

DAVIS, Henry Clay, Santa Fe; pvt., E Troop, transferred to I Troop May 12; 18, 5 ft., 6 ins., dark, brown eyes, dark-brown hair; born Santa Fe; laborer; joined May 5, Santa Fe; single.

DAVIS, James C., Wagoner, O.T.; pvt., L Troop; 22, 5 ft., 7 ins.,

fair, blue eyes, brown hair;
born Cincinnati; farmer; joined
May 14, Muskogee; single.

DAVIS, John, Tarpon Springs, Fla.;
pvt., K Troop; joined July 13,
Tampa.

DAVIS, John W., Vinita, I.T.; pvt.,
L Troop; 24, 5 ft., 7 ins., dark,
dark-brown eyes, black hair;
born Cherokee, I.T.; cowboy;
joined May 14, Muskogee;
married; wounded July 1.

DAVIS, Samuel, Sardis, Ark.; pvt.,
L Troop; 22, 5 ft., 10 ins.,
dark, dark-brown eyes, dark-
brown hair; born Washington
County, Kans.; teamster;
joined May 14, Muskogee;
single; wounded July 1.

DAWSON, Telden W., Nevada, Mo.;
pvt., L Troop; 22, 5 ft., 5¾
ins., ruddy, brown eyes, black
hair; born Nevada, Mo.;
brickmaker; joined May 14,
Muskogee; single; killed June 24.

DAY, Richard Cushing, Vinita,
I.T., 2nd lt., L Troop; 27,
6 ft., 2½ ins., fair, gray eyes,
dark-brown hair; born Miami
County, Kans.; typewriter; joined
May 14, Muskogee; single;
wounded July 1.

DAY, Robert, Santa Fe; pvt.,
B Troop; joined July 9, Tampa;
sick in line of duty.

DEAN, Dudley S., Boston, Mass.;
pvt., B Troop; 27, 5 ft., 8 ins.,
fair, light-brown eyes, flaxen
hair; born Laconia, N.H.; railroad man; joined May 5,
Washington, D.C.; single; sick
in line of duty.

DEAN, James M., Santa Fe; cpl.,
E Troop; 28, 5 ft., 8½ ins.,
florid, gray eyes, dark-brown
hair; born Lima, Ohio; clerk;
joined May 3, Santa Fe; single;
wounded June 24.

DEBLI, Joseph, Tampa; pvt., E
Troop; joined June 5, Tampa;
sick in line of duty.

DE BOHUN, John C., Santa Fe; pvt.,
F Troop; joined June 27,
Santa Fe.

DEHUMY, Gaston R., Santa Fe;
trumpeter, H Troop; joined
June 30, Santa Fe.

DE MONTELL, Oscar, Roswell,
N.M.; sgt., H Troop; 36, 5 ft.,
7¾ ins., dark, brown eyes,
black hair; born Medina,
Texas; cowboy; joined May 4,
Santa Fe; single.

DENHAM, Alexander H., Southrea,
England; pvt., D Troop; 26, 5
ft., 4½ ins., fair, blue eyes,
brown hair; born London,
England; druggist; joined May
5, Guthrie; wounded June 24;
single.

DENNEY, Robert W., Raton,
N.M.; pvt., I Troop; joined
June 27, Santa Fe.

DENNIS, David C., Nelson, Mo.;
pvt., L Troop; 24, 5 ft., 8 ins.,
fair, blue eyes, brown hair;
born Morgan County, Ky.;
farmer; joined May 14, Muskogee; single.

DETTAMORE, George Will, Clayton,
N.M.; pvt., E Troop; 32, 5 ft.,
10 ins., florid, gray eyes, dark
hair; born Green County, Tenn.;
cowboy; joined May 4, Santa
Fe; single; wounded July 1.

DETWILER, Sherman, Muscatine,
Iowa; pvt., G Troop; joined
June 27, Santa Fe.

DEVEREAUX, Horace K., Colorado
Springs, Col, 2nd lt., K
Troop; wounded July 1.

DEVOL, Harry P., San Antonio;
pvt., A Troop; died of self-in-
flicted wound Aug. 28.

DEVORE, Samuel G., Wheeling,
W.Va.; sgt., K Troop; joined May
5, Washington, D.C.; wounded
July 1.

DEWEES, John H., San Antonio;
pvt., C Troop; joined May 27,
San Antonio; sick in line of
duty.

DE ZYCHLINSKI, William T., Bismarck, N.D.; pvt., M Troop; joined July 16.

DOBSON, William H., Muskogee; pvt., L Troop; 18, 5 ft., 9½ ins., fair, gray eyes, light hair; born Tahlequah, I.T.; cowboy; joined May 14, Muskogee; single.

DODGE, George H., Denver, Col.; pvt., E Troop; 23, 5 ft., 6¾ ins., dark, hazel eyes, black hair; born Pueblo, Col.; miner; joined May 3, Santa Fe; single.

DOHERTY, George H., Jerome, I.T.; cpl., A Troop; 30, 5 ft., 6 ins., fair, dark-blue eyes, dark-brown hair; born Detroit, Mich.; carpenter; joined May 2, Whipple Barracks; killed in battle June 24.

DOLAN, Thomas Patrick, Pinos Altos, N.M.; pvt., H Troop, transferred to I Troop May 12; 23, 5 ft., 11 ins., dark, brown eyes, black hair; born Ticonderoga, N.Y.; engineer; joined May 6, Santa Fe; single.

DONALDSON, Frank; assistant surgeon.

DONNELLY, Edward, Santa Fe; cpl., F Troop; 35, 5 ft., 5⅞ ins., fair, blue eyes, flaxen hair; born Boston, Mass.; soldier; joined May 2, Santa Fe; single.

DONNELLY, Hayes, Jefferson, O.T.; farrier, I Troop; joined May 5, Santa Fe.

DONNELLY, Rutherford B. H., Jefferson, O.T.; pvt., G Troop, transferred to I Troop May 12; 21, 5 ft., 6¾ ins., fair, gray eyes, light-brown hair; born Wellington, Kans.; cowboy; joined May 5, Santa Fe; single.

DONOVAN, Freeman M., Santa Fe; pvt., E Troop; joined June 23, Santa Fe.

DORSEY, Louis, Silver City, N.M.; pvt., H Troop; 18, 5 ft., 8½ ins., ruddy, dark-brown eyes, red hair; born Silver City; miner; joined May 6, Santa Fe; single.

DOTY, George B., Santa Fe; pvt., H Troop; joined June 27, Santa Fe.

DAUGHERTY, Louis, Santa Fe; pvt., F Troop; 23, 5 ft., 5¾ ins., florid, blue eyes, dark-brown hair; born Greenwich, Ohio; telegraph operator; joined May 4, Santa Fe; single.

DOUGLAS, Arthur L., Eddy, N.M.; farrier, H Troop; 22, 5 ft., 10⅛ ins., light, hazel eyes, light hair; born Huntsville, Ala.; laborer; joined May 4, Santa Fe; single.

DOUGLAS, James, Santa Fe; pvt., F Troop; 44, 5 ft., 10¾ ins., dark, gray eyes, gray hair; born Baltimore, Md.; locksmith; joined May 5, Santa Fe; single.

DOUGLAS, James B., New York, N.Y.; pvt., E Troop; joined June 7, Tampa.

DOUTHETT, Matthew, Guthrie; pvt., D Troop; 33, 5 ft., 9½ ins.; light, blue eyes, brown hair; born Kingston on Thames, England; hotel clerk; joined May 5, Guthrie; single.

DORELL, Charles, Vinita, I.T.; pvt., M Troop; joined May 14, Muskogee.

DOWNING, Samuel, Atoka, I.T.; cpl., M Troop; joined May 14, Muskogee.

DOYLE, James, Santa Fe; sgt., F Troop; 34, 5 ft., 8¼ ins., dark, hazel eyes, dark-brown hair; born San Francisco; iron worker; joined May 2, Santa Fe; single.

DRACHMAN, Sol B., Tucson, Ariz.; pvt., B Troop; 18, 5 ft., 6 ins., sallow, dark-brown hair, dark-brown eyes; born Tucson; clerk; joined May 3, Whipple Barracks; single; sick in line of duty.

DRAPER, Durward D., Phoenix; pvt., B Troop; 30, 5 ft., 7¾ ins., fair, light-brown hair, light-brown hair, light-blue eyes; born Tallahatchie, Miss.; salesman; joined May 1, Whipple Barracks; single; sick in line of duty.

DUKE, Henry K., Lipscomb, Texas; pvt., I Troop; joined June 27, Santa Fe.

DUNCAN, Arthur G., New York City; pvt., C Troop; sick in line of duty.

DUNKLE, Fred W., East Las Vegas, N.M.; pvt., H Troop; joined June 23, Santa Fe.

DUNN, Alfred B., Calvert, Texas; pvt., G Troop; joined May 24, San Antonio.

DUNN, George M., Denver, Col.; major.

DUNNIGAN, George B., Vinita, I.T.; pvt., L Troop; 23, 5 ft., 4 ins., ruddy, blue eyes, brown hair; born Litchfield, Ill.; cowboy, joined May 14, Muskogee.

DUPUY, Joseph, Muskogee; pvt., cowboy; joined May 14, Muskogee.

DURAN, Abel B., Silver City, N.M.; pvt., H Troop; 36, 5 ft., 6 ins., dark, dark eyes, black hair; born Las Cruces, N.M.; cowboy; joined May 6, Santa Fe; married.

DURAN, Joseph L., Santa Fe; pvt., E Troop, transferred to K Troop May 12; 23, 5 ft., 6½ ins., dark, brown eyes, dark hair; born Santa Fe; barber; joined May 4, Santa Fe; single.

EADS, Wade Q., San Antonio; pvt., B Troop; joined May 21, San Antonio; sick in line of duty.

EAKIN, Alva L., Globe, Ariz.; pvt., B Troop; 29, 5 ft., 9¾ ins., fair, light-brown eyes, dark-brown hair; born Jackson County, Ill.; printer; joined May 2, Whipple Barracks; single; sick in line of duty.

EASLEY, William T., Clayton, N.M.; pvt., E Troop; 27, 5 ft., 11⅝ ins., light, gray eyes, light-brown hair; born Jackson County, Mo.; cowboy; joined May 4, Santa Fe; single.

EASTON, Stephen, Santa Fe; pvt., E Troop, trans. K Troop May 12; 28, 5 ft., 8¼ ins., dark, dark eyes, black hair; born New Mexico; gardener; joined May 5, Santa Fe; single; sick in line of duty.

EATON, Frank A., Silver City, N.M.; pvt., H Troop; 28, 5 ft., 10 ins., light, blue eyes, brown hair; born San Antonio; butcher; joined May 6, Santa Fe; married; sick in line of duty.

EBERMANN, Henry J., Chappaqua, N.Y.; sgt., H Troop; 32, 5 ft., 8 ins., fair, blue eyes, light-brown hair; born Bremen, Germany; soldier; joined May 5, Washington, D.C.; married; died of typhoid Sept. 15.

EDMUNDS, John H., Allegheny, Pa.; pvt., G Troop; 24, 5 ft., 8¾ ins., light, blue eyes, light hair; born Allegheny; cook; joined May 5, Santa Fe; single.

EDWARDS, Lawrence W.; pvt., E Troop; 34, 6 ft., ⅛ in., florid, blue eyes, steel-gray hair; born Watesboro, S.C.; laborer; joined May 4, Santa Fe; single.

EMERSON, Benjamin A., Durant, I.T.; pvt., M Troop; joined May 14, Muskogee.

EMERSON, Edwin, Jr., New York City; pvt., K Troop; joined July 12, camp near Cawai, Cuba.

EMERY, Elzie E., Shawnee, O.T.; pvt., D Troop; 28, 5 ft., 7½ ins., fair, blue eyes, dark-brown hair; born Jasper County, Iowa; grocer; joined May 5, Guthrie; single.

ENDSLEY, Guy D., Somerfield, Pa.;

pvt., F Troop; 22, 5 ft., 9½ ins., dark, gray eyes, brown hair; born Somerfield; miner; joined May 6, Santa Fe; married; died of fever in Cuba July 18.

ENGEL, Edwin P., Phoenix; pvt., C Troop; 24, 5 ft., 7¼ ins., fair, light-blue eyes, light-brown hair; born Rochester, Minn.; ranger; joined May 1, Whipple Barracks; single.

ENNIS, Richard L., Cornell, Ill.; pvt., L Troop; 25, 5 ft., 4½ ins., dark, blue eyes, dark-brown hair; born Odell, Ill.; cowboy; joined May 14, Muskogee; single.

ENYART, Silas R., Rudy, Ark.; pvt., L Troop; 27, 5 ft., 7½ ins., fair, dark-blue eyes, dark-brown hair; born Howard County, Mo.; cowboy; joined May 14, Muskogee; single; mortally wounded July 1.

ERRICKSON, M. Nichols, New York City; cpl., I Troop.

ERWIN, William T., San Antonio; pvt., F Troop; 36; joined May 28, San Antonio; baker; killed in action June 24.

EVANS, Evan, Gallup, N.M.; pvt., G Troop, trans. I Troop May 12; 36, 5 ft., 4¼ ins., florid, brown eyes, dark-brown hair; born South Wales; miner; joined May 3, Santa Fe; single.

EVANS, James R., Baldwin, Ark.; pvt., L Troop; 26, 5 ft., 5¼ ins., dark, gray eyes, brown hair; born Douglas, Mo.; farmer; joined May 14, Muskogee; single.

EWELL, Edward A., Ringgold, Texas; pvt., H Troop; 29, 5 ft., 11 ins., light, blue eyes, brown hair; born Illinois; cowboy; joined May 6, Santa Fe; married; sick in line of duty.

I.T.; pvt., M Troop; joined
FAIRMAN, Charles E., Ardmore, May 14, Muskogee.

FANDREE, Charles J., Caddo, I.T.; cpl., M Troop; joined May 14, Muskogee.

FARLEY, William, Santa Fe; pvt., F Troop; 23, 5 ft., 5¾ ins., ruddy, blue eyes, iron-gray hair; born Cleveland, Ohio; railroad man; joined May 2, Santa Fe; single.

FARRELL, Fred P., El Paso, Texas; pvt., H Troop; 21, 5 ft., 10⅜ ins., dark, gray eyes, dark-brown hair; born Jeffersonville, Ind.; laborer; joined May 4, Santa Fe; single; deserted.

FAULK, William A., Valley Falls, Kans.; pvt., D Troop; 38, 5 ft., 8¼ ins., gray eyes, sandy hair; born Whitley County, Ind.; ranchman; joined May 5, Guthrie; single.

FAUPEL, Henry F., Martington, Ill.; pvt., G Troop; 23, 5 ft., 10 ins., fair, blue eyes, dark-brown hair; born Martington; railroad man; joined May 3, Santa Fe; single.

FENNELL, William A., Reunion, Md.; pvt., E Troop; 18, 5 ft., 9¾ ins., fair, blue eyes, dark-brown hair; born Montreal, Canada; railroad clerk; joined May 3, Santa Fe; single.

FENNESSY, Thomas D., Santa Fe; sgt., F Troop; 29, 5 ft., 9½ ins., fair, blue eyes, flaxen hair; born San Francisco; telegraph operator; joined May 2, Santa Fe; single.

FERGUSON, Robert Hector Munro, New York City; 2nd lt., K Troop; joined May 5, Washington, D.C.; sick in line of duty.

FETTES, George, Antonito, Col.; pvt., E Troop; joined June 30, Santa Fe; sick in line of duty.

FISH, Hamilton, New York City; sgt., L Troop; joined May 5, Washington, D.C.; killed in action June 24.

FITCH, Roger S., Buffalo, N.Y.; pvt., G Troop; joined May 27, San Antonio.

FITZGERALD, Frank T., Tucson; pvt., B Troop; 33, 5 ft., 8¼ ins., fair, light-brown eyes, light-gray hair; born Clinton County, Iowa; miner; joined May 2, Whipple Barracks; married; sick in line of duty.

FLEMING, Clarence A.; pvt., E Troop, trans. K Troop May 12; 22, 5 ft., 7⅛ ins., dark, brown eyes, black hair; born Naples, Texas; printer; joined May 4, Santa Fe; single.

FLETCHER, Augustus C., Silver City, N.M.; pvt., H Troop; 36, 5 ft., 8¼ ins., dark, brown eyes, black hair; born Winston County, Ala.; cowboy; joined May 6, Santa Fe; single.

FLETCHER, Henry P., Green Point, Pa.; pvt., K Troop.

FLYNN, Joseph F., Albuquerque; pvt., F Troop, trans. I Troop May 12; 29, 5 ft., 5½ ins., ruddy, gray eyes, iron-gray hair; born Cranston, R.I.; cowboy; joined May 2, Santa Fe; single.

FOLEY, Henry C., Muskogee; sgt., M Troop; joined May 14, Muskogee.

FOLK, Theodore, Oklahoma City, O.T.; pvt., D Troop; 19, 5 ft., 7½ ins., light, blue-gray eyes, light-brown hair; born Austria; grocer; joined May 5, Guthrie; single.

FORCE, Peter, Selma, Ala.; pvt., C Troop; joined June 4, Tampa.

FORNOFF, Frederick, Albuquerque; pvt., G Troop; joined June 27, Santa Fe.

FORTESCUE, G. Roland, New York City; cpl., E Troop; 22, 5 ft., 6 ins., fair, blue eyes, dark-brown hair; born New York City; student; joined May 5, Washington, D.C.; single; wounded July 1.

FOSTER, John, Bisbee, Ariz.; trumpeter, B Troop; 25, 5 ft., 4½ ins., fair, light-blue eyes, dark-brown hair; born Charleston, S.C.; miner; joined May 2, Whipple Barracks; single.

FOX, Harry B., Jerome, Ariz.; pvt., A Troop; 26, 5 ft., 8¼ ins., fair, brown eyes, brown hair; born Campbelltown, Pa.; printer; joined April 30, Whipple Barracks; single.

FRANCIS, Mack, Waynesville, N.C.; pvt., E Troop; joined June 13, Tampa.

FRANTZ, Frank, Enid, Okla.; 1st lt., A Troop; 29, 5 ft., 9 ins., light, brown eyes, dark-brown hair; born Roanoke, Ill.; clerk; joined April 30, Whipple Barracks; single; wounded in action; later last territorial Governor of Oklahoma.

FREEMAN, Elisha A., Burden, Kans.; pvt., D Troop; 32, 5 ft., 9 ins., dark, blue eyes, black hair; born Wyandotte County, Kans.; cowboy; joined May 5, Guthrie; single; sick.

FREEMAN, Thomas L., Thurber, Texas; pvt., A Troop; joined June 27, Santa Fe.

FREEMAN, Will, Santa Fe; pvt., F Troop; 21, 5 ft., 4¾ ins., fair, gray eyes, dark hair; born Ypsilanti, Mich.; cigar maker; joined May 4, Santa Fe; single; wounded in action July 1.

FRENCH, Wilbur D., Safford, Ariz.; cpl., C Troop; 35, 5 ft., 5½ ins., fair, light-brown eyes, dark-brown hair; born Bethel, Vt.; rancher; joined May 2, Whipple Barracks; married.

FRENGER, Numa C., Las Cruces, N.M.; pvt., H Troop, trans. I Troop May 12; 22, 5 ft., 6 ins., dark, brown eyes, dark-brown hair; born Socorro, N.M.; clerk; joined May 6, Santa Fe; single.

FRIES, Frank D., Santa Fe; pvt., E Troop; 25, 5 ft., 6¾

ins., fair, hazel eyes, brown
hair; born Switzerland; baker;
joined May 4, Santa Fe; single.

FRITZ, William H., Windsor,
Conn.; pvt., H Troop, trans.
I Troop, May 12.

FRYE, Obey B., Flagstaff, Ariz.;
pvt., H Troop; 22, 5 ft.,
6⅜ ins., dark, brown eyes,
light-brown hair; born Paris, Ill.;
cowboy; joined May 6, Santa
Fe; single.

FULLENWEIDER, Rolla A., Raton,
N.M.; sgt., G Troop; 20, 5 ft.,
7⅞ ins., dark, black eyes, black
hair; born Brookfield, Mo.;
miner; joined May 4, Santa Fe;
single.

GALLIGHER, William D., Pawnee
City, Nebr.; pvt., F Troop; 27,
5 ft., 9⅛ ins., dark, brown eyes,
brown hair; born Pawnee City,
Neb.; blacksmith; joined May 6,
Santa Fe; single.

GAMMEL, Roy U., Jersey City, Ill.;
pvt., E Troop; joined July 5,
Santiago, Cuba.

GARDINER, John P., Boston, Mass.;
pvt., C Troop; joined May 25,
San Antonio; sick in line of
duty.

GARLAND, George W., Ardmore,
I.T.; pvt., M Troop; joined May
14, Muskogee.

GARRET, Samuel Hartley, Los Angeles, Calif.; pvt., A Troop; 22,
5 ft., 3¾ ins., fair, blue eyes,
light-brown hair; born Pottsville,
Pa.; stenographer; joined April
30, Whipple Barracks; single.

GARRISON, Elisha E., New Haven,
Conn.; trumpeter, C Troop; 26,
5 ft., 8¼ ins., fair, blue eyes,
light-brown hair; born Cincinnati,
Ohio; law clerk; joined May 7,
Washington, D.C.; single.

GASS, Conrad F., Tampa; pvt., B
Troop; joined June 13, Tampa.

GASSER, Louis, Richmond, Va.;
pvt., H Troop; 25, 5 ft., 9⅛
ins., dark, brown eyes, dark-
brown hair; born Newark, N.J.;

plumber; joined May 4, Santa
Fe; single.

GASSET, Percival, Dedham, Mass.;
sgt., I Troop; joined May 5,
Washington, D.C.

GAUGHAM, James, Phoenix; blacksmith, C Troop; 29, 5 ft., 5½
ins., dark, light-blue eyes, dark-
brown hair; born Nashville,
Tenn.; farmer; joined April 30,
Whipple Barracks.

GAVIN, Anthony, Buffalo, N.Y.;
pvt., C Troop; joined June 8,
Tampa; sick in line of duty.

GEE, Charles R., Santa Fe; blacksmith, F Troop; 27, 5 ft., 5¾
ins., fair, blue eyes, light-brown
hair; born Centerville, Mich.;
blacksmith; joined May 2, Santa
Fe; single.

GEIGER, Percy A., Durango, Col.;
pvt., F Troop, trans. I Troop
May 12; 21, 5 ft., 9⅛ ins., fair,
hazel eyes, light-brown hair;
born Davenport, Iowa; miner;
joined May 6, Santa Fe; single;
sick in line of duty.

GEORGE, Ira W., Quincy, Ill.; pvt.,
H Troop; 21, 5 ft., 8 ins., light,
blue eyes, brown hair; born
Quincy; cowboy; joined May 6,
Santa Fe; single.

GERARD, Sumner K., New York
City; sgt., C Troop; 24, 5 ft.,
10½ ins., fair, light-blue eyes,
dark hair; born Genesee, N.Y.;
law student; joined May 4,
Whipple Barracks; single.

GEVERS, Louis, Austin, Texas; pvt.,
G Troop; 34, 5 ft., 3¾ ins.,
dark, dark-brown eyes, dark-
brown hair; born St. Louis, Mo.;
miner; joined May 3, Santa Fe;
single; wounded in action July 1.

GIBBIE, William R., Las Vegas,
N.M.; pvt., E Troop; joined June
23, Santa Fe.

GIBBONS, Floyd J., Prescott; pvt.,
C Troop; 21, 5 ft., 10 ins., fair,
light-brown eyes, light-brown
hair; born Sterling, Kans.; prospector; joined May 2, Whipple
Barracks; single.

GIBBS, Henry M., Santa Fe; pvt., F Troop; 36, 5 ft., 4¾ ins., dark, blue eyes, dark-brown hair; born Swansea, South England; prospector; joined May 6, Santa Fe; single; wounded in action July 1.

GIBBS, James P., Santa Fe.; pvt., E Troop; joined June 23, Santa Fe; sick in line of duty.

GIBSON, William C., Gallup, N.M.; pvt., G Troop; joined June 27, Santa Fe.

GILLER, Alfred C., Topeka, Kans.; pvt., I Troop; joined July 2, Santa Fe.

GILMORE, Maurice E., Muskogee; pvt., L Troop; 20, 5 ft., 10¾ ins., dark, brown eyes, black hair; born Somerset, Ky.; student; joined May 14, Muskogee; single.

GIRARD, Alfred O.; sgt., I Troop; joined May 2, Washington, D.C.

GISLER, Joseph, Santa Fe; pvt., E Troop; joined June 23, Santa Fe; sick in line of duty.

GLESSNER, Otis, Santa Fe; pvt., F Troop; joined June 25, Santa Fe; wounded in action July 1.

GLOVER, William H., Liberty, Texas; pvt., A Troop; joined July 10, Tampa.

GOLDBERG, Samuel, Santa Fe; cpl., F Troop; 22, 5 ft., 5 ins., fair, hazel eyes, dark-brown hair; born Russia; clerk; joined May 2, Santa Fe; single; wounded in action July 1.

GOOCH, John R., Santa Fe; pvt., F Troop, trans. I Troop May 12; 21, 5 ft., 9⅞ ins., fair, brown eyes, dark hair; born Santa Fe; gardener; joined May 5, Santa Fe; single; sick in line of duty.

GOODRICH, Benjamin H., Santa Fe; pvt., I Troop; joined May 4, Santa Fe; sick in line of duty.

GOODRICH, David M., Cambridge, Mass.; 2nd lt., D Troop; 21, 6 ft., ½ in., fair, brown eyes, dark-brown hair; born Akron, Ohio; student; joined May 4, Washington, D.C.; single.

GOODWIN, James C., Tempe, Ariz.; pvt., C Troop; 34, 5 ft., 6¾ ins., dark, light-blue eyes, dark-brown hair; born Ralls County, Mo.; rancher; joined May 4, Whipple Barracks; single.

GOODWIN, John, Gallup, N.M.; pvt., G Troop; 22, 5 ft., 8⅛ ins., fair, blue eyes, light-brown hair; born Johnstown, Pa.; plumber; joined May 3, Santa Fe; single.

GOODWIN, Richard E., Phoenix; saddler, B Troop; 27, 5 ft., 11¼ ins., fair, light-blue eyes, dark-brown hair; born Fresno County, Calif.; miner; joined May 2, Whipple Barracks; single.

GORDON, Johnson, Birmingham, Ala.; pvt., M Troop.

GOSLING, Frederick W., Bedfordshire, England; pvt., H Troop; joined June 11, Tampa; died in hospital Aug. 19.

GOSS, Conrad F., Tampa; pvt., B Troop.

GOUGHAN, James, Phoenix; pvt., C Troop.

GREEN, Charles H., Albuquerque; pvt., D Troop.

GREEN, Henry Clay; pvt., E Troop; 28, 6 ft., 2⅞ ins., dark, gray eyes, dark-brown hair; born North Carolina; mining engineer; joined May 4, Santa Fe; single; killed in action July 1.

GREEN, John D., Santa Fe; pvt., F Troop; joined June 27, Santa Fe.

GREEN, J. Knox, Rancho, Texas; pvt., G Troop; died at Montauk Point Aug. 15.

GREEN, John Wesley, Gallup, N.M.; 1st lt., G Troop; 37, 5 ft., 9 ins., dark, hazel eyes, black hair; born Columbus, Ohio; soldier; joined May 7, Santa Fe; married.

GREENLEY, James T., Prescott; sgt., A Troop; 39, 5 ft., 8¾ ins., fair, light-blue eyes, light-brown hair; born Peter County, Mo.; blacksmith; joined May 2,

Whipple Barracks; wounded in action July 1.

GREENWALD, Samuel, Arcata, Calif.; sgt., A Troop; 37, 5 ft., 5¼ ins., dark, blue eyes, black hair; born Yorka, Calif.; clerk; joined April 30, Whipple Barracks; single.

GREENWAY, John C., Hot Springs, Ark.; 1st lt., A Troop; wounded June 24; sick in line of duty.

GREENWOOD, William W., Prescott; 1st sgt., A Troop; 44, 5 ft., 6¼ ins., light, light-blue eyes, brown hair; born Troy, N.Y.; miner; joined April 30, Whipple Barracks; single; wounded July 1.

GREGORY, Walter T., Phoenix; cpl., B Troop; 25, 5 ft., 6¾ ins., fair, dark-blue eyes, dark-brown hair; born Cheyenne, Wyo.; reporter; joined April 30, Whipple Barracks; single; sick in line of duty.

GREENWALD, Samuel, Prescott; 2nd lt., I Troop; joined April 30, Whipple Barracks.

GRIFFIN, Arthur J., Santa Fe; trumpeter, E Troop; 24, 5 ft., 7 ins., fair, blue eyes, light hair; born Santa Fe; clerk; joined May 3, Santa Fe; single.

GRIFFIN, Walter W., Globe, Ariz.; pvt., A Troop; 36, 5 ft., 7½ ins., fair, light-blue eyes, dark-brown hair; born Prince Georges County, Md.; cowboy; joined May 2, Whipple Barracks; single; sick in line of duty.

GRIFFIN, William Elkins, Santa Fe; 1st lt., E Troop; 31, 5 ft., 6½ ins., light, gray eyes, light-brown hair; born Santa Fe; clerk; joined May 6, Santa Fe; married.

GRIFFITH, Ezra E., Sepulpa, I.T.; pvt., M Troop; joined May 14, Muskogee.

GRIGG, John G., San Antonio; pvt., E Troop; joined May 16, San Antonio.

GRIGSBY, Braxton, New York City; pvt., E Troop; joined May 30, San Antonio; sick in line of duty.

GRIGSBY, James B., Deming, N.M.; pvt., H Troop; 24, 5 ft., 9 ins., dark, brown eyes, dark-brown hair; born Homer, La.; cowboy; joined May 6, Santa Fe; single.

GRINDELL, Thomas F., Tempe, Ariz.; sgt., C Troop; 26, 5 ft., 8½ ins., fair, brown eyes, dark-brown hair; born Plattsville, Wis.; teacher; joined April 30, Whipple Barracks; single.

GROVES, Oscar, Raton, N.M.; pvt., G Troop; 23, 5 ft., 6⅞ ins., dark, blue eyes, dark-brown hair; born Atcheson, Kans.; florist; joined May 5, Santa Fe; single.

GURNEY, Frank W., Tampa; pvt., B Troop; joined June 12, Tampa.

GUTILIUS, Nevin P., Tularosa, N.M.; sgt., H Troop; 44, 5 ft., 3¾ ins., ruddy, brown eyes, gray hair; born Gettysburg, Pa.; miner; joined May 5, Santa Fe; single.

HADDEN, David A., San Antonio; pvt., E Troop; joined May 12, San Antonio; sick in line of duty.

HAEFNER, George V., Gallup, N.M.; farrier, G Troop; 21, 5 ft., 8⅞ ins., dark, hazel eyes, dark-brown hair; born Marissa, Ill.; miner; joined May 3, Santa Fe; single.

HAEFNER, Henry J., Gallup, N.M.; pvt., G Troop; 23, 5 ft., 6¼ ins., dark, brown eyes, dark-brown hair; born Marissa, Ill.; miner; joined May 3, Santa Fe; single; mortally wounded June 24.

HALE, Edward, Santa Fe; cpl., F Troop; 22, 5 ft., 6 ins., fair, blue eyes, brown hair; born Holt County, Mo.; fireman; joined May 2, Santa Fe; single.

HALEY, Robert M., Wagoner, I.T.; pvt., L Troop; 25, 5 ft., 5½ ins., dark, dark-brown eyes, dark-brown hair; born Perry, Mo.; machinist; joined May 14, Muskogee; single.

HALL, Edward C., New Haven, Conn.; pvt., C Troop; joined June 27, Washington, D.C.

HALL, James T., Wagoner, I.T.; pvt., M Troop; joined May 14, Muskogee.

HALL, Joel Rexford, Seattle, Wash.; pvt., B Troop; 28, 5 ft., 7¼ ins., fair, light-brown eyes, dark-brown hair; born Syracuse, N.Y.; rancher; joined May 2, Whipple Barracks; single; killed in battle July 1.

HALL, John, Durant, I.T.; farrier, M Troop; joined May 14, Muskogee.

HALL, John M., Phoenix; pvt., B Troop; 27, 5 ft., 6 ins., fair, dark-blue eyes, dark-brown hair; born Wallace, Texas; letter carrier; joined May 1, Whipple Barracks; single; wounded July 1.

HALL, John P., Williamson County, Texas; pvt., E Troop; 22, 5 ft., 8¼ ins., fair, gray eyes, dark-brown hair; born Williamson, Texas; cowboy; joined May 4, Santa Fe; single; wounded July 1.

HALL, Thomas W.; 1st lt., adjutant, regimental quartermaster; resigned Aug. 1.

HAMILTON, James C., Roswell, N.M.; cpl., H Troop; 23, 5 ft., 8⅞ ins., dark, blue eyes, light-brown hair; born Allegheny County, Pa.; cowboy; joined May 4, Santa Fe; single.

HAMILTON, James Monroe, Deming, N.M.; pvt., H Troop; 24, 5 ft., 3⅞ ins., dark, blue eyes, brown hair; born San Francisco; cowboy; joined May 6, Santa Fe; single.

HAMILTON, Thomas, Jerome, Ariz.; blacksmith, A Troop; 28, 5 ft., 10 ins., white, blue eyes, dark-brown hair; born Rockford, Ill.; blacksmith; joined April 30, Whipple Barracks; single.

HAMILTON, Troy, Hartshorne, I.T.; pvt., M Troop; joined May 14, Muskogee.

HAMILTON, Warden W., Chicago; pvt., E Troop; joined June 28, Santa Fe.

HAMMER, John S., San Antonio; pvt., B Troop; joined May 21, San Antonio; wounded July 1.

HAMNER, George, Santa Fe; pvt., F Troop; 24, 5 ft., 6⅝ ins., dark, gray eyes, dark-brown hair; born Favor's Mills, Va.; joined May 6, Santa Fe; single.

HANSON, Ivan M., Phoenix; pvt., C Troop; 21, 5 ft., 7¼ ins., dark-brown eyes, dark-brown hair; born Bates County, Mo.; farmer; joined May 2, Whipple Barracks; single.

HANSON, William, Prescott; pvt., C Troop; 34, 5 ft., 7 ins., fair, blue eyes, flaxen hair; born in Denmark; cowboy; joined April 30, Whipple Barracks; single.

HARDING, John D., Socorro, N.M.; pvt., E Troop; sick in line of duty.

HARKNESS, Daniel D., Las Vegas; pvt., E Troop; 21, 5 ft., 8¼ ins., light, blue eyes, brown hair; born Crawford, Iowa; plumber; joined May 3, Santa Fe; single.

HARMSON, Frank W., Tucson, Ariz.; farrier and blacksmith, B Troop; 27, 5 ft., 8 ins., fair, light-brown eyes, reddish-brown hair; born St. Joseph, Mo.; bricklayer; joined May 1, Whipple Barracks; single; sick in line of duty.

HARNER, Frank J., Prescott; trumpeter, A Troop; 24, 5 ft., 2¾ ins., fair, blue eyes, dark-brown hair; born Tucson; cowboy; joined April 30, Whipple Barracks; single; sick in line of duty.

HARRIS, Chester, Muskogee; pvt., M Troop; joined May 14, Muskogee.

HARTLE, Albert C., Santa Fe; pvt., F Troop; 26, 5 ft., 3¾ ins., fair, blue eyes, red hair; born Ontario, Canada; cook; joined May 2, Santa Fe; single; wounded June 24.

HARTZELL, Ira C., Phoenix; pvt.,

B Troop; 21, 5 ft., 10¼ ins.,
fair, light-blue eyes, light-brown
hair; born Greenville, Ohio;
rancher; joined April 30, Whipple Barracks; single; sick in line
of duty.

HASKELL, Ernest Eddy; acting 2nd
lt.; on leave from West Point.

HATCH, Charles P., Newport, R.I.;
pvt., D Troop.

HAWES, Frederick W., Denison,
Texas; pvt., M Troop; joined
July 8, Tampa.

HAWES, George P., Jr., Richmond,
Va.; pvt., A Troop; joined June
27, Tampa.

HAWKINS, Charles D., Vinita, I.T.;
pvt., L Troop; 28, 5 ft., 10½
ins., dark, gray eyes, black hair;
born Kansas County, Kans.; cowboy; joined May 14, Muskogee;
single.

HAWKINS, Morency A., Tioga,
Texas; sgt., M Troop; joined
May 14, Muskogee.

HAWLEY, Elmer, Phoenix; sgt., B
Troop; 33, 5 ft., 8 ins., fair,
light-blue eyes, dark-brown hair;
born Valparaiso, Ind.; farmer;
joined April 30, Whipple Barracks; married; sick in line of
duty.

HAYDON, Roy F., Prescott; pvt., B
Troop; 27, 5 ft., 9¾ ins., fair,
light-blue eyes, light-brown hair;
born London, England; cowboy;
joined May 2, Whipple Barracks;
single; sick in line of duty.

HAYES, Frank P., San Antonio; 2nd
lt., L Troop; joined May 14,
Muskogee.

HAYMON, Edward G. B., Chicago;
pvt., A Troop; joined July 11.

HAYNES, Jacob M., Newkirk, O.T.;
pvt., D Troop; joined May 28,
San Antonio.

HAYWOOD, Henry H., New York
City; sgt., K Troop; joined May
5, Washington D.C.; mortally
wounded July 1.

HEAGART, Rudolph H., Vinita, I.T.;
pvt., L Troop; 18, 5 ft., 8 ins.,
ruddy, brown eyes, dark-brown

hair; born Vinita; cowboy; joined
May 14, Muskogee; single.

HEALEY, Frank F., Brooklyn, N.Y.;
pvt., G Troop; joined June 14,
Tampa.

HEARD, Judson, Pecos City, Texas;
pvt., E Troop; joined July 8,
Tampa.

HEDRICK, Ben; pvt., F Troop; 21,
5 ft., 7½ ins., fair, brown eyes,
dark hair; born Sherman,
Texas; laborer; joined May 4,
Santa Fe; single.

HEITMAN, Charles E., Phoenix;
cpl., B Troop; 23, 5 ft., 8½
ins., fair, dark-blue eyes, dark-
brown hair; born Spencer, Ind.;
machinist; joined April 30, Whipple Barracks; single.

HENDERLEIDER, Jerome W., Saranac, Mich.; pvt., L Troop; 25,
5 ft., 9½ ins., ruddy, blue eyes,
dark-brown hair; born Saranac;
mason; joined May 14, Muskogee; single; sick in line of duty.

HENDERSON, John, Gallup, N.M.;
pvt., G Troop; 23, 5 ft., 5¾
ins., fair, blue eyes, dark-brown
hair; born Thomastown, Pa.;
miner; joined May 3, Santa Fe;
single; wounded July 1.

HENDERSON, Sibird B., Globe,
Ariz.; pvt., B Troop; 30, 5 ft.,
4 ins., fair, light-blue eyes, light-
brown hair; born Doniphan,
Kans.; cowboy; joined May 4,
Whipple Barracks; single; sick in
line of duty.

HENDRICKS, Milo A., Whitefield,
I.T.; pvt., L Troop; 21, 5 ft.,
6½ ins., dark, gray eyes, brown
hair; born Choctaw Nation, I.T.;
student; joined May 14, Muskogee; single; mortally wounded
July 1.

HENLEY, King C., Winslow, Ariz.;
sgt., A Troop; 43, 5 ft., 10¾
ins., fair, light-blue eyes, light-
brown hair; born Henderson
County, N.C.; miner; joined May
1, Whipple Barracks; single.

HENSHAW, Laten R., El Paso,
Texas; pvt., G Troop; joined
May 23, San Antonio.

HERMEYER, Ernest H., Roswell, N.M.; pvt., H Troop; 29, 5 ft., 8⅞ ins., dark, blue eyes, brown hair; born in Germany; laborer; joined May 4, Santa Fe; single.

HEROLD, Philip M., Phoenix; pvt., C Troop; 24, 5 ft., 7 ins., fair, light-blue eyes, light-brown hair; born Seneca, Kans.; bookkeeper; joined May 2, Whipple Barracks; single.

HERRIG, Frederick, Kalispel, Mont.; cpl., K Troop; joined May 13, San Antonio.

HERRING, Leary O., Fowler, Col.; pvt., H Troop; 26, 5 ft., 6 ins., light, blue eyes, brown hair; born Newbern, N.C.; cowboy; joined May 6, Santa Fe; single.

HERSEY, Henry B., Santa Fe; major; born in Vermont.

HEYWOOD, John P., Tampa; pvt., B Troop; joined July 5, Tampa.

HICKEY, Walter, Nashua, N.H.; pvt., F Troop; 21, 5 ft., 8¾ ins., ruddy, blue eyes, brown hair; born Nashua; shoemaker; joined May 2, Santa Fe; single.

HIGGINS, Thaddeus, New York City; sgt., K Troop; joined May 5, Washington, D.C.

HILDEBRAND, Louis T., Prescott; pvt., B Troop; 23, 5 ft., 4½ ins., fair, light-blue eyes, dark-brown hair; born New Orleans, La.; butcher; joined May 4, Whipple Barracks; single; sick in line of duty.

HILDRETH, Fenn S., Tucson; pvt., B Troop; 23, 5 ft., 6 ins., fair, dark-blue eyes, dark-brown hair; born Ukiah, Calif.; pharmacist; joined May 2, Whipple Barracks; single; sick in line of duty.

HILL, Calvin, Pawnee, O.T.; cpl., D Troop; 38, 5 ft., 7 ins., sandy, blue eyes, sandy hair; born Cannon County, Tenn.; rancher; joined May 5, Guthrie; married.

HILL, Edwin M., Tecumseh, O.T.; pvt., D Troop; 27, 5 ft., 11½ ins., dark, blue eyes, dark-brown hair; born Warren County, Mo.; farmer; joined May 5, Guthrie; single; wounded June 24.

HILL, Frank A., Raton, N.M.; saddler, G Troop; 29, 6 ft., ⅜ in., dark, blue eyes, brown hair; born Livingston County, Mo.; harness-maker; joined May 2, Santa Fe; single.

HILL, Grant, Santa Fe; farrier, E Troop; 30, 5 ft., 6½ ins., fair, light-blue eyes, light hair; born Martinsville, Ill.; clerk; joined May 3, Santa Fe; single.

HILL, Ira A., Newkirk, O.T.; sgt., D Troop; 23, 5 ft., 7 ins., dark, blue eyes, dark-brown hair; born Grand Isle, Vt.; lawyer; joined May 5, Guthrie; single.

HILL, Jefferson, Santa Fe; wagoner, F Troop; 25, 5 ft., 9⅜ ins., florid, blue eyes, dark hair; born Jefferson City, Mo.; teamster; joined May 4, Santa Fe; single.

HILL, Wesley, Tempe, Ariz.; cpl., C Troop; 21, 5 ft., 5¼ ins., fair, dark-brown eyes, dark-brown hair; born Dundee, Ill.; schoolteacher; joined May 2, Whipple Barracks; single; sick in line of duty.

HIXON, Thomas L., Las Vegas; cpl., E Troop; 28, 5 ft., 10¼ ins., florid, hazel eyes, light hair; born Lexington, Mo.; railroad man; joined May 3, Santa Fe; single.

HODGDON, Charles E., Prescott; pvt., A Troop; 29, 5 ft., 8¼ ins., fair, blue eyes, dark-brown hair; born Pelatima, Calif.; miner; joined April 30, Whipple Barracks; single.

HOFFMAN, Fred, Pueblo, Col.; pvt., A Troop; joined May 22, San Antonio.

HOFFMAN, George B., Somerville, N.C.; pvt., M Troop; joined June 11, Tampa.

HOGAN, Daniel L., Flagstaff, Ariz.; pvt., A Troop; 31, 5 ft., 7¼ ins., fair, light-blue eyes, dark-brown hair; born Syracuse, N.Y.;

prospector; joined May 1, Whipple Barracks; single.

HOGAN, Michael, Santa Fe; pvt., F Troop, trans. I Troop May 12; 30, 5 ft., 7⅜ ins., fair, hazel eyes, dark-brown hair; born in Massachusetts; teamster; joined May 4, Santa Fe; single.

HOGLE, Will H., Santa Fe; pvt., E Troop; 22, 5 ft., 6½ ins., florid, gray eyes, dark-brown hair; born Marshalltown, Iowa; clerk; joined May 3, Santa Fe; single; sick in line of duty.

HOKEY, Charles J., Krebs, I.T.; trumpeter, M Troop; joined May 14, Muskogee.

HOLDEN, Prince A., Grayson County, Texas; pvt., E Troop, trans. K Troop May 12: 26, 5 ft., 7⅝ ins., florid, hazel eyes, flaxen hair; born Springfield, Ill.; cowboy; joined May 3, Santa Fe; single.

HOLDERMAN, Bert T., Artopa, Kans.; pvt., L Troop; 28, 5 ft., 5¾ ins., fair, gray eyes, brown hair; born Fort Gibson, I.T.; farmer; joined May 14, Muskogee; single.

HOLLISTER, L. Stanley, Santa Barbara, Calif.; pvt., A Troop; 24, 5 ft., 10¼ ins., fair, brown eyes, dark-brown hair; born Santa Barbara; student; joined May 4, Whipple Barracks; single; wounded July 2, died of typhoid Aug. 17.

HOLMES, Thomas M., Newkirk, O.T.; pvt., D Troop; 23, 5 ft., 9¾ ins., fair, blue eyes, brown hair; born Correctionville, Iowa; farmer; joined May 5, Guthrie; single; wounded July 1.

HOLT, Everett E., Coffeyville, Kans.; pvt., F Troop; 31, 5 ft., 5 ins., dark, blue eyes, fair hair; born Turkey Creek, Kans.; cowboy; joined May 6, Santa Fe; single.

HOLT, Harrison J., Cambridge, Mass.; pvt., D Troop; 22, 5 ft., 10¾ ins., fair, blue eyes, brown

hair; born Portland, Me.; student; joined May 5, Guthrie; single.

HOLTZSCHUE, Carl, Sabetha, Kans.; cpl., A Troop; 25, 5 ft., 7½ ins., fair, dark-blue eyes, dark-brown hair; born St. Joseph, Mo.; prospector; joined April 30, Whipple Barracks; single; sick in line of duty.

HONEYCUTT, James V., Shawnee, O.T.; pvt., D Troop; 23, 5 ft., 6½ ins., dark, dark-brown eyes, black hair; born Pawnee County, Neb.; farmer; joined May 5, Guthrie; single.

HONEYMAN, John D., San Antonio; cpl., A Troop.

HOOD, John B., New York City; pvt., E Troop; joined June 6, Tampa; sick in line of duty.

HOPPING, Charles O., Santa Fe; pvt., F Troop; 24, 5 ft., 6 ins., dark, brown eyes, dark-brown hair; born Burlington, Iowa; moulder; joined May 6, Santa Fe; single.

HOUCHIN, Willis C., Durant, I.T.; pvt., M Troop; joined May 14, Muskogee.

HOUSTON, Robert C., Hillsboro, N.M.; pvt., H Troop; joined July 2, Santa Fe.

HOWARD, John L., St. Louis; cpl., A Troop; 25, 5 ft., 7¼ ins., fair, light-blue eyes, light-brown hair; born St. Louis County, Mo.; teamster; joined May 3, Whipple Barracks; single.

HOWARD, John S., Boerne, Texas; pvt., D Troop; joined May 28, San Antonio.

HOWELL, William, Muskogee; pvt., M. Troop; joined May 14, Muskogee.

HOWELL, William S. E., Cerrillos, N.M.; farrier, E Troop; 33, 5 ft., 8¼ ins., florid, blue eyes, brown hair; born Monroe County, Mo.; miner; joined May 5, Santa Fe; single.

HOWLAND, Harry, Flagstaff; pvt.,

C Troop; 36, 5 ft., 4¾ ins., fair, light-blue eyes, light-brown hair; born Fulton County, Ohio; rancher; joined May 1, Whipple Barracks; single.

HUBBEL, John D., Boston, Mass.; pvt., A Troop; joined July 22, Santiago; sick in line of duty.

HUBBELL, William C., Nogales, Ariz.; pvt., C Troop; joined May 19, San Antonio; railway mail clerk.

HUDSON, Arthur L., Santa Fe; pvt., E Troop; 22, 5 ft., 3½ ins., dark, gray eyes, dark-brown hair; born Chilicothe, Ohio; jeweler; joined May 3, Santa Fe; single.

HUFFMAN, Lawrence E., Las Cruces, N.M.; pvt., A Troop; joined June 29, Santa Fe.

HUGHES, David L., Tucson; cpl., B Troop; 25, 5 ft., 8½ ins., fair, light-brown eyes, dark-brown hair; born Tucson; black-smith; joined May 2, Whipple Barracks; single; wounded July 1.

HUGHES, Frank, Vinita; pvt., L Troop; 21, 5 ft., 8 ins., dark, brown eyes, dark-brown hair; born Pulaski County, Mo.; farmer; joined May 14, Muskogee; single.

HUGHES, Garfield, Albuquerque; 2nd sgt., F Troop; 18, 5 ft., 9⅜ ins., fair, brown eyes, brown hair; born Marysville, Kans.; student; joined May 2, Santa Fe; single.

HUGHES, William E., Vinita; pvt., L Troop; 19, 5 ft., 6¾ ins., fair, blue eyes, light-brown hair; born Maries County, Mo.; farmer; joined May 14, Muskogee; single.

HULME, Robert A., El Reno, O.T.; pvt., D Troop, trans. K Troop May 11; 21, 5 ft., 8½ ins., dark, blue eyes, black hair; born Alberton, Ga.; baggage clerk; joined May 5, Guthrie; single.

HULSKOTTER, John, Santa Fe; pvt., E Troop; 34, 5 ft., 4½ ins., fair, blue eyes, sandy hair; born New York City; miner; joined May 2, Santa Fe; single.

HUNT, Leroy R., Cincinnati; pvt., H Troop; joined May 25, San Antonio.

HUNTER, Charles E., Enid, O.T.; sgt., D Troop; 42, 5 ft., 4 ins., ruddy, brown eyes, dark-brown hair; born Brooklyn, N.Y.; real estate dealer; joined May 5, Guthrie; married.

HUNTER, Paul W., Chandler, O.T.; sgt., D Troop; 27, 5 ft., 7½ ins., dark, brown eyes, dark-brown hair; born Atchison, Kans.; farmer; joined May 5, Guthrie; single.

HUSON, Willis O., Yuma, Ariz.; 1st sgt., C Troop; 34, 5 ft., 7¾ ins., fair, dark-brown eyes, dark-brown hair; born Waucoma, Iowa; lawyer; joined May 2, Whipple Barracks; single; sick in line of duty.

HUSTON, Robert B., Guthrie; capt., D Troop; 34, 5 ft., 9 ins., ruddy, blue eyes, sandy hair; born Hamilton, Ohio; lawyer; joined May 5, Guthrie; married; sick in line of duty.

HUTCHASON, Joseph M., Jimtown, Tenn.; pvt., E Troop; joined June 4, Tampa.

HUTCHISON, William M., Santa Fe; pvt., E Troop; 25, 5 ft., 7¼ ins., fair, dark-blue eyes; brown hair; born Arnot, Pa.; miner; joined May 3, Santa Fe; single.

IRVINE, Wm. T.; killed in battle June 24.

ISBELL, Thomas J., Vinita; pvt., L Troop; 23, 5 ft., 7¼ ins., ruddy, brown eyes, red hair; born Fort Gibson, I.T.; cowboy; joined May 4, Muskogee; single.

ISHLER, Shelby F., Horton, Kans.; pvt., D Troop; 21, 5 ft., 8 ins., fair, gray eyes, light-brown hair; born Martinsville, Ill.; boilermaker; joined May 5, Guthrie; single.

IVES, Gerard Merrick, New York City; pvt., K Troop; joined June 9, Tampa; died of typhoid fever Aug. 9.

IVY, Charles B., Waco, Texas; pvt., D Troop; joined May 23, San Antonio.

JACKSON, Charles B., Prescott; pvt., A Troop; 26, 5 ft., 9 ins., fair, light-blue eyes, dark-brown hair; born Hillsdale, Mich., rancher; joined May 1, Whipple Barracks; single; wounded July 1.

JACKSON, Cade C., Flagstaff; cpl., A Troop; 21, 5 ft., 7 ins., fair, light-blue eyes, brown hair; born Erath County, Texas; horseman; joined May 1, Whipple Barracks; single.

JACKSON, John N., Caddo, I.T.; cpl., M Troop; joined May 14, Muskogee.

JACKSON, John W., Jerome, Ariz.; pvt., A Troop; 29, 5 ft., 5¼ ins., fair, dark-blue eyes, light-brown hair; born Marshall, Texas; carpenter; joined May 1, Whipple Barracks; single.

JACOBUS, Charles W., Santa Fe; pvt., E Troop; joined June 23, Santa Fe.

JAMES, William F., San Antonio; pvt., K Troop; joined May 13, San Antonio.

JAMES, Frank W., Marion County, Ga.; pvt., Troop H; joined May 19, San Antonio.

JAMES, William T., Jeroma, Ariz.; pvt., B Troop; 28, 5 ft., 9¼ ins., fair, light-blue eyes, dark-brown hair; born Fitchburg, Mass., miner; joined May 4, Whipple Barracks; single; sick in line of duty.

JENKINS, Micah J., Young's Island, S.C.; major; formerly in U.S. regular service.

JOHNS, William S., Thomasville, Mo.; pvt., L Troop; 33, 5 ft., 8 ins., dark, blue eyes, dark-brown hair; born Spender, Ind., carpenter; joined May 14, Muskogee; single.

JOHNSON, Albert John, Raton, N.M.; pvt., G Troop; 29, 5 ft., 9½ ins., florid, blue-gray eyes, dark flaxen hair; born New York City; miner; joined May 3, Santa Fe; single.

JOHNSON, Albert Sidney, Oklahoma City, O.T.; 2nd lt., M Troop; joined May 14, Muskogee; sick in line of duty.

JOHNSON, Anton E., Prescott; pvt., B Troop; 27, 5 ft., 3¼ ins., fair, light-blue eyes, light-brown hair; born Round Nally, Utah; cowboy; joined May 3, Whipple Barracks; single; sick in line of duty.

JOHNSON, Bankston, Caddo, I.T.; pvt., M Troop; joined May 14, Muskogee.

JOHNSON, Charles, Lund, Sweden; pvt., H Troop; joined June 4, Tampa.

JOHNSON, Charles L., Ardmore, I.T.; pvt., M Troop; joined May 14, Muskogee.

JOHNSON, Harry F., Beaumont, Texas; pvt., H Troop; joined June 29, Tampa.

JOHNSON, John W., Kingman, Ariz.; pvt., A Troop; 34, 5 ft., 8 ins., fair, light-blue eyes, dark-brown hair; born Boston, Mass.; miner; joined May 2, Whipple Barracks; single; sick in line of duty.

JOHNSON, Lewis L., Beaumont, Texas; pvt., H Troop; joined June 29, Tampa.

JOHNSON, Nova A., Roswell, N.M.; cpl., H Troop; 37, 6 ft., 1¼ ins., fair, blue eyes, black hair; born Sullivan County, Mo.; laborer; joined May 5, Santa Fe; single.

JOHNSTON, Charles E., San Antonio; pvt., E Troop; joined May 16, San Antonio; sick in line of duty.

JOHNSTON, Edward W., Cushing, O.T.; pvt., D Troop; 19, 5 ft., 7¾ ins., fair, blue eyes, brown hair; born Brock, Neb.; schoolteacher; joined May 5, Guthrie; single; wounded July 1.

JOHNSTON, Gordon, Birmingham, Ala.; pvt., M Troop; joined July 8, Tampa.

JONES, Albert M., Santa Fe; sgt., E Troop; 28, 5 ft., 8⅜ ins., florid, blue eyes, dark-brown hair; born Warrenton, Va.; clerk; joined May 6, Santa Fe; single.

JONES, Charles L., McAlester, I.T.; pvt., M Troop; joined May 14, Muskogee.

JONES, George F., El Paso, Texas; pvt., H Troop; joined May 14, San Antonio.

JONES, Levi, Vinita, I.T.; pvt., L Troop; 24, 5 ft., 7⅜ ins., copper, dark-brown eyes, black hair; born Cherokee Nation, I.T.; cowboy; joined May 14, Muskogee; single.

JONES, Thomas B., Santa Fe; pvt., E Troop; 33, 5 ft., 6¼ ins., dark, hazel eyes, dark-brown hair; born Livingston County, Mich.; cowboy; joined May 3, Santa Fe; married.

JONES, William G., Ardmore, I.T.; pvt., M Troop; joined May 14, Muskogee.

JONES, William H., Raton, N.M.; pvt., G Troop; 28, 5 ft., 6½ ins., dark, brown eyes, dark-brown hair; born Fairbury, Ill., miner; joined May 5, Santa Fe; single.

JOPLING, Cal, Hamilton County, Texas; pvt., H Troop; 22, 5 ft., 8 ins., dark, gray eyes, light-brown hair; born Hamilton County; cowboy; joined May 4, Santa Fe; single.

JORDAN, Andrew M., Rossa, Texas; pvt., D Troop; 22, 5 ft., 8¾ ins., fair, blue eyes, light-brown hair; born Clayton, Texas; railroad man; joined May 5, Guthrie; single.

JORDAN, Eldridge E., Phoenix; cpl., C Troop; 23, 5 ft., 10¼ ins., fair, dark-brown eyes, dark-brown hair; born Glen Rose, Texas; rancher; joined April 30, Whipple Barracks; single.

JOYCE, Walter, Ross, Ohio; pvt., D Troop; 27, 5 ft., 8¾ ins., fair, bluish-brown eyes, dark-brown hair; born Butler County, Ohio; teacher; joined May 5, Guthrie; single.

JUDSON, Alfred M., New York City; pvt., E Troop; joined May 24, San Antonio; died of typhoid Aug. 17.

KANE, Woodbury, New York City; 1st lt., K Troop; joined May 5, Washington, D.C.

KANIA, Frank, Jamestown, N.D.; pvt., G Troop; 21, 5 ft., 11¾ ins., dark, brown eyes, dark-brown hair; born Jamestown; miner; joined May 3, Santa Fe; single.

KANSKY, Joseph F., Tacoma, Wash.; sgt., H Troop, trans. I Troop May 12; 32, 5 ft., 5 ins., dark, blue eyes, light-brown hair; born in Austria; soldier; joined May 6, Santa Fe; single.

KASTENS, Harry E., Winslow, Ariz.; cpl., C Troop; 22, 5 ft., 8½ ins., fair, light-blue eyes, dark-brown hair; born Berkeley, Calif.; mechanic; joined May 1, Whipple Barracks; single.

KEAN, John R., Maxwell, Ontario; pvt., L Troop; 34, 5 ft., 7½ ins., dark, blue eyes, dark-brown hair; born Canning, Nova Scotia; blacksmith; joined May 14, Muskogee; wounded June 24.

KEARNS, Edward L., Tampa; pvt., M Troop; joined Aug. 2, Tampa.

KEELEY, Bert T., Lamy, N.M.;
pvt., G Troop; joined June 27,
Santa Fe.

KEHOE, Michael J., Ottawa,
Canada; pvt., H Troop; 27,
5 ft., 11 ins., dark, blue eyes,
brown hair; born Ottawa;
electrician; joined May,
Santa Fe; single.

KEIR, Alex S., Bisbee, Ariz.;
pvt., B Troop; 33, 5 ft., 8¼
ins., fair, light-blue eyes, light-
brown hair; born San Bernadino, Calif.; furrier; joined
May 2, Whipple Barracks;
single; sick in line of duty.

KEITHLEY, Luther M., Hartshorne,
I.T.; saddler, M Troop;
joined May 14, Muskogee.

KEITHLEY, Ora E., Hartshorne,
I.T.; pvt., M Troop; joined
May 14, Muskogee.

KELLY, John M., El Paso, Texas;
pvt., H Trooop; 40, 5 ft., 6¼
ins., dark, gray eyes, black
hair; born Cincinnati; clerk;
joined May 4, Santa Fe;
single.

KELLY, William H., Las Vegas;
1st lt., H Troop; 42, 5 ft., 6⅝
ins., light, blue eyes, gray hair;
born Philadelphia, Pa.; clerk;
joined May 7, Santa Fe;
married.

KELM, Amandus, Silver City,
N.M.; pvt., H Troop; 21, 5 ft.,
9 ins., light, blue eyes, brown
hair; born Berlin, Germany;
plumber; joined May 6, Santa
Fe; single.

KENDALL, Harry J., Colesburg,
Ky.; pvt., H Troop; joined
June 28, Santa Fe.

KENNEDY, Stephen A., Santa
Fe; pvt., F Troop; joined
June 28, Santa Fe.

KENNIA, Frank; pvt., K Troop;
joined May 3, Santa Fe.

KERNEY, George M., Globe, Ariz.;
wagoner, F Troop, trans. I
Troop May 12; 43, 5 ft.,
6½ ins., ruddy, blue eyes,
brown hair; born Philadelphia,
Pa.; miner; joined May 2,
Santa Fe; single.

KERR, George, Jr., East
Downington, Pa.; pvt.,
K Troop; joined May 7,
Washington, D.C.

KEYES, Maxwell, San Antonio; 2nd
lt., F Troop; 24, 5 ft., 10¾
ins., dark, brown eyes, dark-
brown hair; born Fort Sill,
I.T.; soldier; joined May 6,
Santa Fe; single.

KING, George C., Prescott; pvt.,
B Troop; 24, 5 ft., 6 ins., fair,
light-blue eyes, light-brown
hair; born Sacramento, Calif.;
packer; joined May 2, Whipple
Barracks; single; sick in line of
duty.

KING, Henry A., Manistee, Mich.;
pvt., G Troop; 28, 5 ft., 5¾
ins., ruddy, gray eyes, brown
hair; born Manistee; teamster;
joined May 6, Santa Fe;
single.

KING, Harry Bruce, Raton, N.M.;
pvt., F Troop; 26, 5 ft., 7¼
ins., dark, brown eyes, light-
brown hair; born New York
City; carpenter; joined May 4,
Santa Fe; single.

KING, Herbert A., Santa Fe; sgt.,
F Troop; 23, 5 ft., 10 ins.,
fair, blue eyes, brown hair;
born Toronto, Canada; fireman;
joined May 2, Santa Fe;
single.

KING, John, McAlester, I.T.;
farrier, M Troop; joined May
14, Muskogee.

KINGSLEY, Charles E., Las Vegas;
pvt., E Troop; 39, 5 ft., 8⅝
ins., dark, blue eyes, black
hair; born Syracuse, N.Y.;
railroad man; joined May 5,
Santa Fe; married.

KINKADE, Elijah S., Muskogee;
pvt., L Troop; 36, 5 ft., 11
ins., dark, light-blue eyes,
dark-brown hair; born Saline
County, Mo.; cowboy;
joined May 14, Muskogee;
single.

KINNEBRUGH, Ollie A., Decatur, Texas; pvt., H Troop; 26, 5 ft., 8¼ ins., dark, brown eyes, brown hair; born in Arkansas; cowboy; joined May 4, Santa Fe; single.

KINNEY, Mike, Imlay, Mich.; blacksmith, L Troop; 30, 5 ft., 9½ ins., dark, blue eyes, black hair; born St. Clair County, Mich.; cowboy; joined May 14, Muskogee; single; sick in line of duty.

KIRCH, Henry, Gallup, N.M.; cpl., G Troop; 23, 5 ft., 5 ins., dark, hazel eyes, dark-brown hair; born New York City; car inspector; joined May 3, Santa Fe; single.

KISSAM, William A., New York City; pvt., E Troop; joined June 6, Tampa.

KLINE, Joe A., Vinita, I.T.; pvt., L Troop; 26, 5 ft., 7½ ins., fair, blue eyes, brown hair; born Ottumwa, Iowa; printer; joined May 14, Muskogee; single; wounded July 1.

KLINE, John S., San Marcial, N.M.; pvt., G Troop; joined June 27, Santa Fe.

KLINGMAN, Adam H., Flagstaff, Ariz.; sgt., C Troop; 30, 5 ft., 9 ins., fair, light-brown eyes, light-brown hair; born Wayne County, Ind.; cowboy; joined May 1, Whipple Barracks; single.

KNAPP, Edgar A., Elizabeth, N.J.; pvt., E Troop; joined May 30, San Antonio.

KNOBLAUCK, Charles E., New York City; cpl., E Troop; joined May 30, San Antonio.

KNOBLAUCK, George W., New York City; trumpeter, K Troop; joined May 11, San Antonio.

KNOX, Robert G., Clinton, La.; pvt., K Troop.

KNOX, William Frank; pvt., D Troop; joined June 4, Tampa.

KREVT, Robert G.; pvt., L Troop; joined July 9, Santiago.

KYLE, Yancey, McAlester, I.T.; pvt., M Troop; joined May 14, Muskogee; died of typhoid at Tampa July 5.

LAIRD, Emmett, Albuquerque, N.M.; pvt., D Troop.

LAIRD, Thomas J., Prescott; pvt., B Troop; 34, 5 ft., 9¾ ins., fair, light-blue eyes, reddish-brown hair; born Monford, Wis.; miner; joined May 2, Whipple Barracks; single; sick in line of duty.

LAMOTTE, Henry, Williamsburg, Mass.; major, Hospital Corps; wounded July 2.

LAND, Oscar N., Denver, Col.; pvt., E Troop, trans. K Troop May 12; 21, 5 ft., 10⅝ ins., light, dark-blue eyes, dark flaxen hair; born Boonesboro, Ark.; laborer; joined May 3, Santa Fe; single.

LANE, Edward K., Chitopa, Kans.; pvt., L Troop; 27, 5 ft., 11 ins., fair, light-blue eyes, brown hair; born Washington County, Pa.; cowboy; joined May 14, Muskogee; single.

LANE, Sanford G., Sapulpa, I.T.; pvt., M Troop, trans. L Troop June 8; joined May 14, Muskogee.

LANGDON, Jesse D., Fargo, N.D.; pvt., K Troop; joined May 7, Washington, D.C.

LANGSTON, John S., Carrillos, N.M.; sgt., E Troop; 31, 5 ft., 8⅞ ins., fair, gray eyes, brown hair; born Piqua, Ohio; railroad conductor; joined May 2, Santa Fe; married.

LANKFORD, Jerome W., White Hills, Ariz.; wagoner, C Troop; 38, 5 ft., 7 ins., fair, light-blue eyes, light-brown hair; born Grayson County, Texas; miner; joined May 2, Whipple Barracks; single.

LANNON, John, Hillsboro, Texas;

pvt., H Troop; joined June 28, Santa Fe.

LARNED, William A., Summit, N.J.; pvt., A Troop; joined June 4, Tampa.

LARSEN, Louis; pvt., F Troop; 25, 5 ft., 10¾ ins., florid, blue eyes, light hair; born Aalborg, Denmark; laborer; joined May 6, Santa Fe; single; sick in line of duty.

LARSON, Anton, Silverton, Col.; pvt., G Troop; 42, 5 ft., 9¼ ins., florid, gray eyes, light-brown hair; born in Sweden; miner; joined May 3, Santa Fe; single.

LAVELLE, Nolan Z., San Antonio; pvt., F Troop; joined May 24, San Antonio.

LAWRENCE, Richard, La Porte, Ind.; pvt., L Troop; 23, 5 ft., 9 ins., ruddy, blue eyes, light-brown hair; born La Porte; cowboy; joined May 14, Muskogee; single.

LAWSON, Frank H., Las Cruces, N.M.; pvt., H Troop; 28, 5 ft., 6½ ins., dark, blue eyes, dark hair; born Matagorda, Texas; rancher; joined May 6, Santa Fe; single.

LEACH, John M., Santa Fe; pvt., F Troop; joined June 27, Santa Fe.

LEAHY, David J., Raton N.M.; 2nd lt., G Troop; 31, 5 ft., 11 ins., light, blue eyes, light hair; born in Illinois; attorney at law; joined May 7, Santa Fe; single; wounded July 1.

LEDWIDGE, Thomas P., Santa Fe; cpl., E Troop; 28, 5 ft., 6 ins., fair, blue eyes, dark-brown hair; born Salem, Ill.; carpenter; joined May 3, Santa Fe; single.

LEE, Jerry F., Globe, Ariz.; cpl., B Troop; 5 ft., 5½ ins., fair, light-blue eyes, dark-brown hair; born Wilmington, Del.; cook; wounded July 1.

LEE, Joseph Jenkins, Knoxville,

Md.; pvt., K Troop; joined May 19, San Antonio; sick in line of duty.

LEE, Robert E., Dona Ana, N.M.; trumpeter, E Troop; 28, 5 ft., 4⅝ ins., dark, brown eyes, dark-brown hair; born Dona Ana; cowboy; joined May 6; single.

LEFFERT, Charles E., Santa Fe; pvt., F Troop; 19, 5 ft., 6 ins., fair, blue eyes, flaxen hair; born Logansport, Ind.; machinist; joined May 2, Santa Fe; single.

LEFORS, Jefferson Davis, Prescott; pvt., A Troop; 37, 5 ft., 7¾ ins., fair, brown eyes, brown hair; born Arkansas County, Ark.; miner; joined April 30, Whipple Barracks; single.

LENTZ, Edward, Bowling Green, Ohio; pvt., L Troop; 30, 5 ft., 8½ ins., fair, blue eyes, light-brown hair; born Will County, Ill.; carpenter; joined May 14, Muskogee.

LEROY, Arthur M., Prescott; sgt., A Troop; 41, 5 ft., 8¼ ins., fair, blue eyes, grayish-brown hair; born Boston, Mass.; cowboy; joined April 30, Whipple Barracks.

LE STOURGEON, E. Guy, San Antonio; pvt., F Troop; joined May 27, San Antonio.

LEWIS, Adelbert, Beaver County, Utah; pvt., H Troop; joined June 6, Tampa.

LEWIS, Edward S., Las Vegas; trumpeter, E Troop; 19, 5 ft., 6¼ ins., dark, gray eyes, dark hair; born Roswell, N.M.; laborer; joined May 3, Santa Fe; single.

LEWIS, Frank A., Newark, N.J.; pvt., L Troop; joined July 2, Santiago.

LEWIS, James, Silver City, N.M.; pvt., E Troop; joined June 30, Tampa.

LEWIS, Taylor B., Las Cruces, N.M.; wagoner, H Troop; 39,

5 ft., 7⅜ ins., florid, blue eyes, sandy hair; born Blountsville, Ala.; miner; joined May 5, Santa Fe; single.

LEWIS, William F., Congress, Ariz.; pvt., A Troop; 37, 5 ft., 5¼ ins., fair, dark-brown eyes, dark-brown hair; born Dodgeville, Wis.; cowboy; joined May 3, Whipple Barracks; single.

LIE, Frederick K., Oregon, N.M.; cpl., K Troop; joined May 13, San Antonio.

LIGGETT, Edward, Jerome, Ariz.; pvt., A Troop; 30, 5 ft., 8½ ins., fair, brown eyes, brown hair; born Eagleville, Pa.; teamster; joined May 2, Whipple Barracks; single; mortally wounded June 24.

LIGON, Robert E., Beaumont, Texas; pvt., H Troop; joined May 25, San Antonio.

LINCOLN, Malcolm D., Lucknow, I.T.; pvt., G Troop; joined June 25, Santa Fe.

LISK, Guy M., Santa Fe; pvt., F Troop; 27, 6 ft., ½ in., dark, hazel eyes, dark-brown hair; born Blandensville, Ill.; schoolteacher; joined May 2, Santa Fe; single.

LITTLE, Rollie L., West Fork, Ark.; pvt., L Troop; 25, 5 ft., 10¾ ins., ruddy, dark-brown eyes, black hair; born Campton, Ky.; cowboy; joined May 14, Muskogee; single.

LITTLETON, Elias M., Springer, N.M.; pvt., G Troop; joined June 25, Santa Fe.

LIVINGSTON, Thomas Cambridge, Hamilton County, Texas; pvt., E Troop; 37, 5 ft., 7⅜ ins., florid, blue eyes, iron-gray hair; born Hamilton County; cowboy; joined May 3, Santa Fe; single.

LLEWELLYN, Morgan O. B., Las Cruces, N.M.; cpl., H Troop; 19, 6 ft., ⅞ in., dark,

dark-brown eyes, brown hair; born Omaha, Neb.; student; joined May 4, Santa Fe; single.

LLEWELLYN, William H. H., Las Cruces, N.M.; capt., G Troop; 45, 6 ft., florid, brown eyes, brown hair; born Monroe, Wis.; attorney at law; joined May 7, Santa Fe; sick in line of duty.

LLOYD, William E., Durant, I.T.; sgt., M Troop; joined May 14, Muskogee.

LOGUE, David, Leavenworth, Kans.; pvt., B Troop; 26, 5 ft., 4 ins., fair, light-blue eyes, dark-brown hair; born Springfield, Mo.; miner; joined May 4, Whipple Barracks; single; killed in battle July 1.

LONG, Benjamin A., New York City; saddler, K Troop; joined May 7, Washington, D.C.; wounded July 1.

LOUGHMILLER, Edgar F., Oklahoma City, O.T.; pvt., D Troop; 24, 5 ft., 7¼ ins., light, dark-blue eyes, brown hair; born Easton, Kans.; ranchman; joined May 5, Guthrie; single.

LOVE, Henry K., Tecumseh, O.T.; pvt., D Troop; 31, 5 ft., 8¼ ins., fair, gray eyes, brown hair; born Keokuk, Iowa; clerk; joined May 5, Guthrie; single; sick in line of duty.

LOVE, William J., Jersey City, N.J.; pvt., G Troop, trans. I Troop May 12; 27, 5 ft., 9⅝ ins., dark, brown eyes, dark-brown hair; born Las Vegas; cowboy; joined May 3, Santa Fe; single.

LOVELACE, Carl, Waco, Texas; pvt., Troop D.

LOWE, Frank, Santa Fe; pvt., E Troop; joined June 30, Santa Fe.

LOWITZKI, Hyman S., Santa Fe; pvt., E Troop; 24, 5 ft., 3¼ ins., dark, blue eyes, dark-brown hair; born New York City; livery; joined May 3, Santa Fe; single.

LUDY, Daniel, Las Vegas, N.M.; pvt., E Troop; 32, 5 ft., 6¼ ins., ruddy, blue eyes, light-brown hair; born Emporia, Kans.; cowboy; joined May 3, Santa Fe; single.

LUNA, Maximiliano, Santa Fe; capt., F Troop; 27, 5 ft., 4½ ins., dark, brown eyes, black hair; born Las Lunas, N.M.; insurance agent; joined May 6, Santa Fe; married.

LUSK, Henry K., El Reno, O.T.; pvt., D Troop; 29, 5 ft., 9½ ins., dark, blue eyes, dark-brown hair; born Middleville, Mich.; laborer; joined May 5, Guthrie; single.

LUTHER, Arthur A., Paterson, N.J.; farrier, D Troop; 26, 5 ft., 8½ ins., dark, brown eyes, black hair; born Green County, Ind.; veterinary surgeon; joined May 5, Guthrie; single.

LUTZ, Eugene A., Raton, N.M.; pvt., G Troop; 22, 5 ft., 8⅝ ins., dark, blue eyes, dark-brown hair; born Randolph County, W.Va.; machinist; joined May 5, Santa Fe; single; sick in line of duty.

LYLE, James C., Georgetown, Col.; pvt., G Troop; 23, 5 ft., 8¼ ins., light, gray eyes, light hair; born Lafayette, Wis.; butcher; joined May 6, Santa Fe; single.

LYNCH, Charles S., Caddo, I.T.; cpl., M Troop; joined May 14, Muskogee.

MCADAMS, Joel H., Mount Pelia, Tenn.; pvt., H Troop; joined July 2, Santa Fe.

MCADAMS, Richard P., Mount Pelia, Tenn.; pvt., H Troop; joined July 2, Santa Fe.

MCANDREW, John, Congress Junction, Ariz.; cpl., C Troop; 33, 5 ft., 9½ ins., fair, blue

eyes, dark-brown hair; born Pittston, Pa.; attorney at law; joined April 30, Whipple Barracks; married.

MCCAA, Columbus Haile, Gallup, N.M.; pvt., G Troop; 37, 5 ft., 5¼ ins., ruddy, gray eyes, iron-gray hair; born Franconia, Ala.; farmer; joined May 6, Santa Fe; single.

MCCABE, Frederick Howard, Santa Fe; pvt., E Troop; 20, 5 ft., 8¼ ins., light, gray eyes, brown hair; born Santa Fe; clerk; joined May 3, Santa Fe; single.

MCCABE, George J., Bisbee, Ariz.; cpl., B Troop; 30, 5 ft., 7¾ ins., fair, light-brown eyes, iron-gray hair; born Delphos, Ohio; miner; joined May 2, Whipple Barracks; single; sick in line of duty.

MCCAMISH, Andrew L., Bethel, Kans.; pvt., L Troop; 27, 5 ft., 8¾ ins., fair, blue eyes, light-brown hair; born Wyandotte County, Kans.; cowboy; joined May 14, Muskogee; single.

MCCANN, Walter J., Phoenix, Ariz., pvt., B Troop; 30, 5 ft., 6¾ ins., fair, light-blue eyes, light-brown hair; born Wicklow, Canada; clerk; joined April 30, Whipple Barracks; single; injured en route to Cuba.

MCCARTER, George A., Safford, Ariz.; cpl., A Troop; 38, 5 ft., 7¾ ins., fair, light-brown eyes, iron-gray hair; born Erie County, Pa.; cowboy; joined May 2, Whipple Barracks; single.

MCCARTHY, Calvin, Phoenix, Ariz.; cpl., B Troop; 23, 5 ft., 10¼ ins., fair, light-blue eyes, light-brown hair; born Pittsburgh, Pa.; cook; joined April 30, Whipple Barracks; single; sick in line of duty.

MCCARTHY, Frederick J., Mentzville, Mo.; pvt., H Troop; joined June 25, Santa Fe.

McCARTHY, Frank M., Flagstaff, Ariz.; pvt., A Troop; 30, 5 ft., 7 ins., fair, light-brown eyes, light-brown hair; born Piatt County, Ill.; rancher; joined May 1, Whipple Barracks; single.

McCARTHY, George H., Los Angeles, Calif.; pvt., G Troop; 26, 5 ft., 10½ ins., fair, brown eyes, black hair; born Pittsburgh, Pa.; barber; joined May 3, Santa Fe; single.

McCLINTOCK, James H., Phoenix, Ariz.; capt., B Troop; 38; born Sacramento, Calif.; wounded June 24.

McCLURE, David V., Oklahoma City, O.T.; cpl., D Troop; 18, 5 ft., 6½ ins., light, hazel eyes, light-brown hair; born Atoka, I.T.; ranchman; joined May 5, Guthrie; single.

McCOY, John, Monrovia, Calif.; pvt., F Troop; 24, 5 ft., 7⅛ ins., dark, brown eyes, dark hair; born Peru, Ind., laborer; joined May 4, Santa Fe; married.

McCULLOCH, Samuel T., Springer, N.M.; pvt., G Troop; 21, 5 ft., 4⅞ ins., fair, blue eyes, brown hair; born Huntington, Pa.; cowboy; joined May 5, Santa Fe; single.

McCURDY, Frank Allen, Philadelphia, Pa.; pvt., F Troop; joined May 29, San Antonio.

McCURDY, John, Philadelphia, Pa.; pvt., F Troop; joined May 29, San Antonio.

McDANIEL, Thomas E., Muskogee, I.T.; pvt., M Troop; joined May 14, Muskogee.

McDONALD, Asa W., Bearing Cross, Ark.; pvt., L Troop; 26, 5 ft., 9½ ins., fair, brown eyes, brown hair; born Shelby, Ill.; fireman; joined May 14, Muskogee; single.

McDONALD, Frank R., Oolagah, I.T.; pvt., Troop L; 28, 5 ft., 7 ins., dark, light-brown eyes, dark-brown hair; born Keysport, Ill.; laborer; joined May 14, Muskogee; single; wounded July 1.

McDOWELL, John C., Santa Fe; pvt., E Troop; joined June 25, Santa Fe.

McFIE, Ralph E., pvt., E Troop; 20, 5 ft., 10⅛ ins., fair, hazel eyes, dark flaxen hair; born Coulterville, Ill.; clerk; joined May 3, Santa Fe; single.

McGARR, Charles L., Phoenix, Ariz.; cpl., A Troop; 28, 5 ft., 5¾ ins., fair, brown eyes, dark-brown hair; born Tucson, Ariz.; soldier; joined April 30, Whipple Barracks; single.

McGEHEE, Matthew T., Raton, N.M.; sgt., G Troop; 37, 5 ft., 8¼ ins., dark, blue eyes, dark-brown hair; born Bradley County, Ark.; nurseryman; joined May 4, Santa Fe; single.

McGINNIS, Schuyler A., Newkirk, O.T.; 1st lt., D Troop; 30, 5 ft., 11½ ins., ruddy, blue eyes, black hair; born Coffey County, Kans.; lawyer; joined May 5, Guthrie; married.

McGINTY, Joseph E., Tucson, Ariz.; wagoner, B Troop; 23, 5 ft., 6¼ ins., fair, light-blue eyes, dark-brown hair; born Morehouse County, La.; carpenter; joined May 1, Whipple Barracks; single.

McGINTY, William, Shipaupi, I.T.; pvt., D Troop, trans. K Troop May 11; 27, 5 ft., 5 ins., fair, blue eyes, sandy hair; born Harrison County, Mo.; cowboy; joined May 5, Guthrie; single.

McGOWAN, Alexander, Gallup, N.M.; pvt., G Troop; joined May 3, Santa Fe; born in Scotland; miner; single.

McGREGOR, Herbert P., Santa Fe; pvt., F Troop; 29, 5 ft., 8½ ins., florid, dark eyes,

brown hair; born Kittanning,
Pa.; clerk; joined May 2,
Santa Fe; single; wounded
July 1.

McGuire, James E., Chelsea,
I.T.; pvt., L Troop; 21, 5 ft.,
5½ ins., dark, brown eyes,
black hair; born Craig County,
Va.; cowboy; joined May 14,
Muskogee; single; sick in line
of duty.

McIlhenny, John A., New
Orleans, La.; 2nd lt., E Troop;
joined May 19, San Antonio;
sick in line of duty.

McKay, Charles F., Santa Fe;
pvt., E Troop; 26, 5 ft., 9¼
ins., fair, blue eyes, light hair;
born Leavenworth, Kans.;
printer; joined May 3, Santa
Fe; single.

McKay, James; Vinita, I.T.; cpl.,
L Troop; 28, 5 ft., 6¼ ins.,
fair, blue eyes, brown hair;
born Youngstown, Ohio; farmer;
joined May 14, Muskogee;
single.

McKay, William J., Oshkosh,
Wis.; pvt., K Troop; joined
May 13, San Antonio.

McKinley, Charles E., Cerrillos,
N.M.; pvt., E Troop; 29, 5 ft.,
10¼ ins., florid, gray eyes,
black hair; born West Liberty,
W.Va.; laborer; joined May 4,
Santa Fe; single; wounded,
July 1.

McKinney, Frank G., Harrison,
Ark.; pvt., G Troop; 23, 5 ft.,
6½ ins., dark, gray eyes,
light-brown hair; born
Franklin County, Ark.; railroad
man; joined May 3, Santa Fe;
single.

McKinney, Oliver, Canon City,
Col.; pvt., G Troop; 21, 5 ft.,
9⅝ ins., dark, gray eyes, light-
brown hair; born Canon City;
laborer; joined May 5, Santa
Fe; single.

McKinnon, Samuel, Madrid, N.M.;
pvt., E Troop; 21, 5 ft., 11¼
ins., ruddy, dark-blue eyes,

dark-brown hair; born Braids-
wood, Ill.; miner; joined May
3, Santa Fe; single.

McMaster, Frederick D.; pvt.,
K Troop; sick in line of duty.

McMillen, Albert Campbell, New
York City; pvt., B Troop;
joined May 23, San Antonio.

McMillen, Robert L., Shawnee,
O.T.; pvt., D Troop; 25, 5 ft.,
9½ ins., dark, dark-brown
eyes, black hair; born Nevada
County, Ark.; clerk; joined
May 5, Guthrie; single;
wounded July 1.

McMullen, John, Ardmore, I.T.;
wagoner, M Troop; joined
May 14, Muskogee.

McMullen, Samuel J., St. Louis,
Mo.; pvt., G Troop; 27, 5 ft.,
8¾ ins., florid, gray eyes, dark
flaxen hair; born Milwaukee,
Wis.; fireman; joined May 3,
Santa Fe; single.

McMurtry, George G., Pittsburgh,
Pa.; pvt., D Troop.

McPherson, Charles E., Caddo,
I.T.; pvt., M Troop; joined
May 14, Muskogee.

McSparron, John, Gallup, N.M.;
cpl., G Troop; 38, 5 ft., 5⅜
ins., dark, brown eyes, iron-
gray hair; born in England;
miner; joined May 3, Santa Fe;
single; wounded July 1.

Madden, Charles E., Broken,
I.T.; pvt., M Troop; joined
May 14, Muskogee.

Madsen, Christian, El Reno, O.T.;
regimental quartermaster sergeant; sick in line of duty.

Mahan, Lloyd L., Cerrillos, N.M.;
pvt., E Troop; 22, 6 ft., ⅝ in.,
light, blue eyes, light-brown
hair; born Hymera, Ind.; miner;
joined May 5, Santa Fe;
single.

Maloon, Winthrop L.; pvt., K
Troop; joined May 5, Washington, D.C.

Mann, Eugene M., Omaha, Neb.;
pvt., G Troop; 33, 5 ft., 7¾

ins., dark, hazel eyes, dark-brown hair; born in Iowa; joined May 3, Santa Fe; single.

MARINE, Rufus H., Flagstaff, Ariz.; pvt., A Troop; 24, 5 ft., 7 ins., fair, light-brown eyes, light-brown hair; born Green Castle, Miss.; cowboy; joined May 1, Whipple Barracks; single; sick in line of duty.

MARION, Frank, Muskogee, I.T.; trumpeter, M Troop; joined May 14, Muskogee.

MARSHALL, Creighton G., Washington, D.C.; wagoner, K Troop; joined May 5, Washington.

MARTI, Frank, Jerome, Ariz.; sgt., C Troop; 31, 5 ft., 4½ ins., fair, light-brown eyes, light-brown hair; born Berne, Switzerland; cowboy; joined May 2, Whipple Barracks; single.

MARTIN, Denry D., Cerrillos, N.M.; pvt., E Troop; 25, 5 ft., 9 ins., florid, gray eyes, dark-brown hair; born Harrison County, Mo.; bridge builder; joined May 4, Santa Fe; single.

MARTIN, John, Decatur, Ill.; pvt., E Troop; 26, 5 ft., 8⅛ ins., fair, hazel eyes, dark hair; born Streaton, Ill.; miner; joined May 5, Santa Fe; single.

MARTIN, Robert Lee, Santa Fe; pvt., H Troop; 27, 5 ft., 9⅝ ins., light, hazel eyes, light-brown hair; born Maries County, Mo.; cowboy; joined May 4, Santa Fe; single.

MARTIN, Thomas, Santa Fe; pvt., F Troop; 36, 5 ft., 10⅛ ins., dark, dark-brown eyes, black hair; born Fairfield, Iowa; horseshoer; joined May 2, Santa Fe; single.

MARVIN, William E., Yuma, Ariz.; pvt., C Troop; 29, 5 ft., 6½ ins., fair, light-blue eyes, dark-brown hair; born Milan, Mich.; surveyor; joined May 2, Whipple Barracks; single.

MASON, David P., Brownsville, Texas; pvt., C Troop; joined May 22, San Antonio.

MASSIE, James A., Santa Fe; 1st lt., Hospital Corps.

MATTOCKS, William L., Santa Fe; sgt., F Troop; 22, 5 ft., 8¾ ins., fair, blue eyes, dark-brown hair; born Jackson County, Iowa; printer; joined May 2, Santa Fe; single.

MAVERICK, Lewis, San Antonio; pvt., K Troop; joined May 15, San Antonio.

MAXEY, James H., Yuma, Ariz.; QM sgt., C Troop; 31, 5 ft., 10¾ ins., fair, light-brown eyes, dark-brown hair; born Marion, Ill.; cowboy; joined May 2, Whipple Barracks; single.

MAY, James A., Safford, Ariz.; pvt., A Troop; 32, 5 ft., 11¾ ins., fair, light-brown eyes, reddish-brown hair; born Amador, Calif.; cowboy; joined May 2, Whipple Barracks; single; sick in line of duty.

MAYTUBBY, Bud, Caddo, I.T.; pvt., M Troop; joined May 14, Muskogee.

MEAGHER, Henry, El Reno, O.T.; cpl., D Troop; 20, 5 ft., 7½ ins., fair, blue eyes, dark-brown hair; born Canadian County, O.T.; ranchman; joined May 5, Guthrie; single; wounded July 1.

MEAGHER, Thomas F., Muskogee; pvt., L Troop; 20, 5 ft., 10 ins., dark, blue eyes, black hair; born Muskogee; student; joined May 14, Muskogee; wounded June 24.

MENGER, Otto F., Clayton, N.M.; cpl., E Troop; 28, 6 ft., 2¼ ins., florid, blue eyes, brown hair; born Mora, N.M.; clerk; joined May 4, Santa Fe; single; wounded July 1.

MERCHANT, James E., Cerrillos, N.M.; pvt., E Troop; 27, 5 ft., 7¼ ins., fair, blue eyes, sandy hair; born Boonesboro, Iowa; miner; joined May 3, Santa Fe; married.

MERRITT, Fred M., Tucson, Ariz.; pvt., B Troop; 24, 5 ft., 8 ins., fair; born Florence, Ariz.; miner; joined May 2, Whipple Barracks; sick in line of duty.

MERRITT, William W., Red Oak, Iowa; pvt., B Troop; joined July 3, Tampa.

MEYERS, Fred P., Gallup, N.M.; 1st sgt., G Troop; 33, 5 ft., 7⅞ ins., fair, gray eyes, dark-brown hair; born Napole, N.Y.; painter; joined May 4, Santa Fe; married; wounded July 1.

MIDDLETON, Clifton C., Globe, Ariz.; pvt., B Troop; 21, 5 ft., 4½ ins., fair; born Globe; miner; joined May 2, Whipple Barracks; single; sick in line of duty.

MILLER, Boot, Chelsea, I.T.; pvt., L Troop; 26, 5 ft., 7 ins., dark, blue eyes, brown hair; born in Texas; cowboy; joined May 14, Muskogee; married.

MILLER, David R.; pvt., I Troop; joined June 29, Santa Fe.

MILLER, Edwin H., Junction City, Kans.; pvt., I Troop; joined May 19, San Antonio.

MILLER, Frank P., Los Angeles, Calif.; pvt., G Troop; 24, 5 ft., 9⅞ ins., dark, brown eyes, brown hair; born Plattsburg, Mo.; fireman; joined May 3, Santa Fe; single.

MILLER, Jacob H., Needles, Calif.; pvt., I Troop; joined June 25, Santa Fe.

MILLER, John S.; pvt., E Troop; 44, 5 ft., 8¾ ins., dark, blue eyes, light-brown hair; born Cherokee Nation; cowboy; joined May 3, Santa Fe; married; died of yellow fever at Siboney July 16.

MILLER, Raleigh L., Pueblo, Col.; sgt., G Troop; 22, 5 ft., 6¼ ins., fair, blue eyes, light hair; born Richmond, Va.; clerk; joined May 5, Santa Fe; single.

MILLER, Roscoe Benjamin, Guthrie, O.T.; pvt., D Troop; 18, 5 ft., 9 ins., fair, gray eyes, light-brown hair; born Fort Scott, Kans.; joined May 5, Guthrie; single; sick in line of duty.

MILLER, Samuel, Roswell, N.M.; pvt., H Troop; 28, 5 ft., 8 ins., ruddy, blue eyes, light-brown hair; born Jack County, Texas; cowboy; joined May 4, Santa Fe; single.

MILLER, Theodore Westwood, Akron, Ohio; pvt., D Troop; joined June 4, Tampa; mortally wounded July 1.

MILLER, Volney Dorsey, Guthrie, O.T.; pvt., D Troop; 25, 5 ft., 7¼ ins., dark, brown eyes, black hair; born Barton County, Kans.; engineer; joined May 5, Guthrie; single.

MILLS, Charles E., Cedar Rapids, Iowa; pvt., A Troop; joined June 5, Tampa.

MILLS, John B., Santa Fe; pvt., F Troop; 28, 5 ft., 6 ins., ruddy, blue eyes, light-brown hair; born Belfast, Ireland; cabinet maker; joined May 2, Santa Fe; single.

MISNER, Jackson Harvey, Bisbee, Ariz.; pvt., B Troop; 24, 5 ft., 9 ins., fair, light-brown eyes, dark-brown hair; born Dayton, Ohio; locomotive fireman; joined May 2, Whipple Barracks; single; sick in line of duty.

MITCHELL, Mason, New York City; pvt., K Troop; joined May 12, San Antonio; wounded July 1.

MITCHELL, William, Wagoner, I.T.; pvt., M Troop; joined May 14, Muskogee.

MITCHELL, William A., El Paso, Texas; sgt., H Troop; 30, 6 ft., 1 in., fair, blue eyes, dark-brown hair; born Huntsville, Mo.; cowboy; joined May 5, Santa Fe; single.

MITCHELL, William H., Salem,

Mass.; pvt., D Troop; 35, 5
ft., 7¼ ins., dark, blue eyes,
dark-brown hair; born Salem;
joined May 5, Guthrie; single.

MOFFETT, Edward B., Yuma,
Ariz.; pvt., C Troop; 24, 5 ft.,
8¼ ins., fair, light-blue eyes,
dark-brown hair; born Visalia,
Calif.; engineer; joined May 2,
Whipple Barracks; single.

MOHLER, Jacob S., Gallup, N.M.;
QM sgt., G Troop; 31, 5 ft.,
5 ins., light, blue eyes, brown
hair; born Carlisle, Pa.; hotel-
keeper; joined May 3, Santa
Fe; single.

MONCKTON, William J., San
Antonio; pvt., H Troop;
joined May 2, San Antonio.

MONTGOMERY, Lawrence N.; pvt.,
K Troop; joined May 12, San
Antonio; sick in line of duty.

MOONEY, Thomas A., Silver
City, N.M.; pvt., H Troop;
22, 6 ft., ½ in., light, blue
eyes, light-brown hair; born
Saguache County, Col.; cowboy;
joined May 6, Santa Fe;
single.

MOORE, John J., Vinita, I.T.; pvt.,
L Troop; 21, 5 ft., 9½ ins.,
dark, brown eyes, black hair;
born Cherokee Nation, I.T.;
clerk; joined May 14, Muskogee;
single.

MOORE, Roscoe B., Raton, N.M.;
pvt., I Troop; joined June 30,
Santa Fe.

MORAN, Daniel, Gallup, N.M.;
pvt., G Troop; 41, 5 ft., 5¼
ins., light, brown eyes, dark-
brown hair; born Pittsburgh,
Pa.; miner; joined May 3,
Santa Fe; single.

MORAN, Thomas, Fort Sill, O.T.;
farrier, D Troop; 37, 5 ft.,
4½ ins., fair, gray eyes,
dark-brown hair, born Leeds,
England; soldier; joined May 5,
Guthrie.

MORAN, William J., Cerrillos,
N.M.; pvt., E Troop; 32,
5 ft., 5¼ ins., ruddy, hazel

eyes, dark-brown hair; born
Shamokin, Pa.; miner; joined
May 3, Santa Fe; married.

MORGAN, Francis Lee, White
Hills, Ariz.; saddler, C Troop;
26, 5 ft., 6¼ ins., fair, blue
eyes, brown hair; born Makanda,
Ill.; laborer; joined April 30,
Whipple Barracks; single.

MORGAN, Morton M., Silver City,
N.M.; cpl., H Troop; 29, 5 ft.,
10½ ins., fair, blue eyes,
light hair; born Hazelton, Ind.;
watchmaker; joined May 7,
Santa Fe; single.

MORGAN, Schuyler C., Hazard,
Ky.; pvt., G Troop; 29, 5 ft.,
8¾ ins., fair, blue eyes, light-
brown hair; born Hazard;
saddler; joined May 6, Santa
Fe; single.

MORGAN, Ulysses G., Hazard, Ky.;
pvt., G Troop; 30, 5 ft., 7½
ins., light, blue eyes, brown
hair; born Hazard; clerk; joined
May 5, Santa Fe; single.

MORRELL, Robert W., Elizabeth,
N.J.; pvt., M Troop; joined
June 11, Muskogee; sick in
line of duty.

MORRIS, Ben F., Raton, N.M.;
pvt., I Troop; joined June 29,
Santa Fe.

MORRISON, Amaziah B., Las Vegas,
N.M.; pvt., E Troop; 40, 5 ft.,
9¼ ins., dark, gray eyes,
brown hair; born Coffeeleo,
Tenn.; minister; joined May 5,
Santa Fe; married.

MORRISON, John V., Springerville,
Ariz.; sgt., H Troop, trans. I
Troop May 12; 37, 5 ft.,
3⅞ ins., florid, blue eyes,
brown hair; born Chicago, Ill.;
cattleman; joined May 6,
Santa Fe; single.

MORSE, Raymond; sgt., G Troop;
25, 5 ft., 4¾ ins., florid, blue
eyes, dark-brown hair; born
Springfield, Mass.; bricklayer;
joined May 3, Santa Fe;
single.

MULLEN, John, Chicago, Ill.;

cpl., E Troop; 26, 5 ft., 6½ ins., dark, gray eyes, dark-brown hair; born Chicago; miner; joined May 3, Santa Fe; single; wounded July 1.

MULLEN, J. Oscar, Tempe, Ariz.; pvt., C Troop; 21, 6 ft., ¼ in., fair, dark-brown eyes, dark-brown hair; born Butte County, Calif.; rancher; joined May 2, Whipple Barracks; single.

MULLER, Frederick, Santa Fe; capt., E Troop; 35, 5 ft., 6¾ ins., light, light-blue eyes, light-brown hair; born Winterbach, Wertumburg, Germany; county collector; joined May 6, Santa Fe; married.

MUNGER, William C., Santa Fe; pvt., E Troop; joined July 2, Santa Fe; sick in line of duty.

MUNN, Edward, Elizabeth, N.J.; pvt., D Troop.

MURCHIE, Guy, Calais, Maine; pvt., A Troop; 25, 5 ft., 10¼ ins., fair, blue eyes, flaxen hair; born Calais; student; joined May 4, Whipple Barracks; single.

MURPHY, James E., St. Mark, Texas; pvt., B Troop; 27, 5 ft., 8 ins., dark, dark-brown eyes, dark-brown hair; born Longview, Texas; cowboy; joined May 3, Whipple Barracks; single; wounded July 1.

MURPHY, William S., Caddo, I.T.; pvt., M Troop; joined May 14, Muskogee.

MURRAY, Frank, Roswell, N.M.; cpl., H Troop; 34, 5 ft., 7⅜ ins., dark, gray eyes, dark-brown hair; born Sansaba, Texas; cowboy; joined May 4, Santa Fe; single.

MURRAY, George F., Deming, N.M.; pvt., H Troop; joined June 30, Santa Fe.

MUXLOW, Lorrin D., Guthrie; wagoner, D Troop; 29, 5 ft., 9 ins., dark, brown eyes, black hair; born Denver, Col.; liveryman; joined May 5, Guthrie; single.

NASH, Henry W., Young, Ariz.; sgt., A Troop; 29, 5 ft., 6¾ ins., fair, dark-brown eyes, dark-brown hair; born Mount Sterling, Ind.; cowboy; joined May 2, Whipple Barracks; single; sick in line of duty.

NEAL, John M., Santa Fe; pvt., F Troop; joined June 27, Santa Fe.

NEFF, Nettleton, Cincinnati, Ohio; pvt., H Troop; joined May 29, San Antonio.

NEHMER, Charles A., Chicago, Ill.; farrier, F Troop; 32, 5 ft., 4 ins., light, blue eyes, dark-brown hair; born Martinbergh, Germany; blacksmith; joined May 2, Santa Fe; single.

NEHMER, William J., Silver City, N.M.; pvt., H Troop; 30, 5 ft., 4 ins., light, blue eyes, brown hair; born Stettin, Germany; soldier; joined May 6, Santa Fe; single.

NESBIT, Otto W., Santa Fe; pvt., F Troop; joined June 23, Santa Fe.

NETTLEBLADE, Adolph F., Cerrillos, N.M.; pvt., E Troop; 31, 5 ft., 5⅞ ins., dark, brown eyes, dark-brown hair; born in Sweden; painter; joined May 5, Santa Fe; single.

NEVILLE, George A., Yuma, Ariz.; pvt., C Troop; 40, 6 ft., 1 in., fair, light-blue eyes, dark-brown hair; born Pike County, Ill.; cowboy; joined May 2, Whipple Barracks; single.

NEWCOMB, Marcellus L., Waukomis, O.T.; pvt., D Troop; 23, 5 ft., 6 ins., dark, blue eyes, black hair; born Steuben County, N.Y.; cattleman; joined May 5, Guthrie; single; wounded June 24.

NEWITT, George W., Santa Fe; pvt., F Troop; joined June 25, Santa Fe.

NEWHONE, Thomas M., Phoenix, Ariz.; pvt., C Troop; 35, 5 ft.,

10¾ ins., fair, light-blue eyes, dark-brown hair; born Pike County, Ill.; rancher; joined May 1, Whipple Barracks; single; died of typhoid Aug 4.

NICHOLS, Errickson N., New York City; cpl., I Troop; joined June 20, Tampa.

NICHOLS, Frederick E., Purcell, I.T.; pvt., M Troop; joined May 14, Muskogee.

NICHOLS, Ode C., Durant, I.T.; 1st lt., M Troop; joined May 14, Muskogee.

NICHOLSON, Charles P., Baltimore, Md.; pvt., K Troop; joined May 11, San Antonio; sick in line of duty.

NICKELL, William E., Santa Fe; pvt., F Troop; 18, 5 ft., 9½ ins., florid, blue eyes, brown hair; born Topeka, Kans.; stage driver; joined May 6, Santa Fe; single.

NOBLES, William H., Silver City, N.M.; pvt., H Troop; 32, 5 ft., 7¼ ins., dark, blue eyes, dark hair; born Zanesville, Ohio; plumber; joined May 6, Santa Fe; single.

NOISH, John, Raton, N.M.; pvt., G Troop; 22, 5 ft., 7 ins., florid, blue eyes, dark-red hair; born in Scotland; miner; joined May 3, Santa Fe; single.

NORMAN, Maxwell, Newport, R.I.; cpl., K Troop; joined May 7, Washington, D.C.

NORRIS, Edmund S., Guthrie, O.T.; pvt., K Troop; joined May 13, San Antonio.

NORRIS, George, Kingfisher, O.T.; cpl., D Troop; 21, 5 ft., 6 ins., dark, dark-brown eyes, brown hair; born Shelbina, Mo.; teacher; joined May 5, Guthrie; single.

NORTH, Franklin H., New York City; pvt., I Troop; joined Aug. 1, Tampa.

NORTON, Edward G., Phoenix; QM sgt., B Troop; 22, 5 ft.,

11¼ ins., fair, light-blue eyes, dark-brown hair; born Vicksburg, Miss.; nurseryman; joined April 30, Whipple Barracks; single; sick in line of duty.

NORTON, Gould G., Tampa; pvt., B Troop; joined June 29, Tampa; sick in line of duty.

NORTON, John W., Lockport, Ill.; pvt., C Troop; joined June 8, Tampa.

NORTON, Oliver B.; pvt., B Troop; joined May 2, San Antonio; killed in battle July 1.

NOYES, Sam W., Tucson; sgt., C Troop; 22, 5 ft., 10¼ ins., fair, dark-brown eyes, dark-brown hair; born Fort Sanders, Wyo.; insurance agent; joined May 2, Whipple Barracks; single; sick in line of duty.

O'BRIEN, Edward, Jerome, Ariz.; pvt., A Troop; 32, 5 ft., 10½ ins., fair, light-blue eyes, dark-brown hair; born Charlestown, Mass., miner; joined May 3, Whipple Barracks; single; wounded July 2.

O'DELL, William W., Parkersburg, W.Va.; pvt., G Troop, trans. I Troop May 12; 29, 5 ft., 8¾ ins., fair, brown eyes, dark-brown hair; born Parkersburg; railroad man; joined May 3, Santa Fe; single.

O'LEARY, Daniel, Tempe, Ariz.; pvt., C Troop; 24, 5 ft., 5¾ ins., fair, light-blue eyes, dark-brown hair; born Port Credit, Ontario, Canada; farmer; joined April 30, Whipple Barracks; single.

O'NEAL, Thomas, Springer, N.M.; wagoner, G Troop; 33, 5 ft., 7¼ ins., florid, blue-gray eyes, dark-brown hair; born Macon County, Ill.; cowboy; joined May 5, Santa Fe; single.

O'NEIL, John; pvt., E Troop; 29, 5 ft., 5 ins., fair, blue eyes, red hair; born Scranton, Pa.; miner; joined May 3, Santa Fe; single; died of dysentery Aug. 3.

O'NEILL, William O., Prescott; capt., A Troop; 38, 5 ft., 10½ ins., dark, brown eyes, dark-brown hair; born in Ireland; lawyer; joined April 29, Whipple Barracks; married; killed in action July 1.

ORME, Norman L., Phoenix; pvt., B Troop; 22, 5 ft., 6¾ ins., fair, light-brown eyes, dark-brown hair; born Rockwell County, Texas; post office clerk; joined May 1, Whipple Barracks; single; wounded June 24.

OSBORNE, George, Australia; pvt., A Troop; joined June 4, Tampa.

OSKISON, Richard L., Vinita, I.T.; pvt., L Troop; 21, 5 ft., 8½ ins., ruddy, brown eyes, light-brown hair; born in Cherokee Nation, I.T.; cowboy; joined May 14, Muskogee; single.

OTT, Charles H., Silver City, N.M.; cpl., H Troop; 20, 5 ft., 10 ins., light, blue eyes, dark hair; born Silver City; printer; joined May 6, Santa Fe; single.

OWENS, Clay T., El Paso, Texas; pvt., H Troop; 28, 5 ft., 10¼ ins., dark, gray eyes, light-brown hair; born Ellis County, Texas; joined May 4, Santa Fe; single.

OWENS, Edward L., Vinita, I.T.; pvt., L Troop; 23, 5 ft., 4¾ ins., fair, blue eyes, dark-brown hair; born in Richland, Ohio; cowboy; joined May 14, Muskogee; single.

OWENS, John M., Oologah, I.T.; pvt., M Troop; joined May 14, Muskogee.

OWENS, William A., Jerome, Ariz.; pvt., B Troop; 24, 5 ft., 8¼ ins., fair, light-brown eyes, dark-brown hair; born Wilson County, Texas; miner; joined May 1, Whipple Barracks; married; sick in line of duty.

PACE, John, Bentonville, Ark.; pvt., H Troop; 23, 5 ft., 6⅜ ins., dark, blue eyes, light-brown hair; born Bentonville; cowboy; joined May 4, Santa Fe; single.

PAGE, John F., Wayland, Iowa; pvt., D Troop; 34, 5 ft., 9¾ ins., dark, blue eyes, dark-brown hair; born Marshalltown, Iowa; engineer; joined May 5, Guthrie; single.

PAGE, John F., Alva, O.T.; pvt., D Troop.

PAGE, William, Richenbar, Ariz.; pvt., A Troop; 28, 5 ft., 10 ins., fair, light-blue eyes, dark-brown hair; born Ottumna, Iowa; miner; joined May 2, Whipple Barracks; single.

PALMER, Orlando G., Ponca City, O.T.; 1st sgt., D Troop; 33, 5 ft., 8 ins., light, brown eyes, light-gray hair; born Linn County, Iowa; schoolteacher and lawyer; joined May 5, Guthrie; married.

PALMER, William F., Shawnee, O.T.; pvt., D Troop; 24, 5 ft., 6½ ins., dark, brown eyes, dark-brown hair; born Washington, Ind.; railroad man; joined May 5, Guthrie; single.

PARKER, John W., Safford, Ariz.; pvt., Troop C; 21, 5 ft., 8¾ ins., fair, light-brown eyes, dark-brown hair; born Lonoke County, Ark.; cowboy; joined May 2, Whipple Barracks; single.

PARKER, Ora E., Dickens, Iowa; pvt., L Troop; 26, 5 ft., 8½ ins., fair, blue eyes, light-brown hair; born New York City; engineer; joined May 14, Muskogee; single; wounded in action July 1.

PARMELE, Charles A., Santa Fe; pvt., F Troop; joined June 28, Santa Fe.

PARNELL, Bud, Muskogee; pvt., L Troop; 26, 5 ft., 10 ins., fair, blue eyes, light hair; born Atlanta, Ga.; cowboy; joined May 14, Muskogee; single.

PARRISH, Robert J., Clayton, N.M.; pvt., E Troop; 22, 5 ft., 5½ ins., florid, hazel eyes, dark hair; born Waukegan, Ill.; cowboy; joined May 4, Santa Fe; single.

PARSONS, Cragg, Ardmore, I.T.; blacksmith, M Troop; joined May 14, Muskogee.

PATE, Stephen A. Tucson, Ariz.; QM sgt., B Troop; 38, 5 ft., 9½ ins., dark, light-brown eyes, dark-brown hair; born Clermont, Ohio; rancher; joined May 2, Whipple Barracks; single; wounded July 1.

PATTERSON, Hal A., Selma, Ala.; pvt., B Troop; joined June 4, Tampa; sick in line of duty.

PATTERSON, Robert S., Safford, Ariz.; 1st lt., C Troop; 30, 5 ft., 7 ins., fair, light-brown eyes, dark-brown hair; born Blair County, Pa.; rancher; joined May 2, Whipple Barracks; single; sick in line of duty.

PAXTON, Frank, Safford, Ariz.; pvt., A Troop; 24, 5 ft., 8½ ins., fair, light-blue eyes, dark-brown hair; born Barton County, Mo.; cowboy; joined May 2, Whipple Barracks; single.

PAYNE, Forest B., Phoenix; pvt., C Troop; 22, 5 ft., 8¾ ins., fair, light-brown eyes, light-brown hair; born Sweet Springs, Mo.; salesman; joined May 1, Whipple Barracks; single.

PEABODY, Harry, Raton, N.M.; pvt., G Troop; 23, 5 ft., 6 ins., dark, blue eyes, brown hair; born Brookfield, Mo.; cook; joined May 5, Santa Fe; single.

PEARSALL, Paul S., New York City; pvt., A Troop; joined Aug. 6, Tampa.

PEARSON, Rufus W., Phoenix; sgt., C Troop; 21, 5 ft., 9½ ins., fair, light-brown eyes, light-brown hair; born Flat Creek, Tenn.; lawyer; joined April 30, Whipple Barracks; married.

PECK, John C., Santa Fe; pvt., B Troop; joined July 2, Santa Fe.

PEMBERTON, Thomas W., Jr., Phoenix; cpl., B Troop; 22, 5 ft., 10¾ ins., fair, light-brown eyes, light-brown hair; born Chicago, Ill.; electrician; joined April 30, Whipple Barracks; single; sick in line of duty.

PENNINGTON, Elijah, San Antonio; pvt., G Troop; joined May 29, San Antonio.

PERRY, Arthur L., Santa Fe; trumpeter, F Troop; 21, 5 ft., 4½ ins., fair, blue eyes, brown hair; born Baton Rouge, La.; printer; joined May 2, Santa Fe; single; wounded July 1.

PERRY, Arthur R., Phoenix; sgt., C Troop; 34, 5 ft., 11¾ ins., dark, dark-brown eyes, dark-brown hair; born Devonshire, England; contractor; joined May 1, Whipple Barracks; single.

PERRY, Charles B., Perry's Landing, Texas; pvt., A Troop; joined May 21, San Antonio; wounded in action July 2.

PETTIT, Louis P., Flagstaff, Ariz.; pvt., A Troop; 30, 5 ft., 9¾ ins., fair, dark-blue eyes, light-brown hair; born Sacramento, Calif.; rancher; joined May 1, Whipple Barracks; single.

PETTY, Archibald, Gallup, N.M.; pvt., G Troop; 19, 5 ft., 6 ins., fair, hazel eyes, reddish hair; born Nashville, Tenn.; miner; joined May 3, Santa Fe; single.

PHILIP, Hoffman, Washington, D.C.; pvt., A Troop; joined June 4, Tampa.

PHILPOT, Leigh T., Bryson, Ky.;
pvt., L Troop; 25, 5 ft., 11½
ins., ruddy, blue eyes, dark-
brown hair; born Clay County,
Ky.; cowboy; joined May 14,
Muskogee; single.

PHIPPS, Thomas W., Bland, N.M.;
pvt., G Troop; joined June 23,
Santa Fe.

PHYSIOC, Willis J., Columbia, S.C.;
cpl., H Troop; 22, 5 ft., 8¼
ins., fair, blue eyes, dark-brown
hair; born Columbia; soldier;
joined May 5, Washington,
D.C.; single.

PIERCE, Howard, Chicago, Ill.;
pvt., G Troop, trans. I Troop
May 12; 23, 5 ft., 3½ ins.,
dark, brown eyes, black hair;
born Chicago; railroad man;
joined May 3, Santa Fe;
single.

PIERCE, Harry B., Central City,
N.M.; pvt., A Troop; joined
June 23, Santa Fe.

PIERSOL, James M., Osborne, Mo.;
pvt., H Troop; joined June 30,
Santa Fe.

PIPER, Edward G., Silver City,
N.M.; trumpeter, G Troop.

PIPKIN, Price; pvt., H Troop; 33,
5 ft., 5 ins., dark, blue eyes,
brown hair; born in Arkansas;
cowboy; joined May 6; single.

PIPKINS, Virgil A., Broken, I.T.;
pvt., M Troop; joined May 14,
Muskogee.

PLATT, Clay, San Antonio;
trumpeter.

POE, Nathaniel M., Adair, I.T.;
pvt., L Troop; 21, 5 ft., 7 ins.,
fair, blue eyes, light-brown hair;
born Allamolt, Kans.; cowboy;
joined May 14, Muskogee; single;
wounded June 24.

POEY, Alfred; pvt., K Troop;
joined July 21, Washington, D.C.

POLLAK, Albin Jay, Yountville,
Calif.; pvt., K Troop; sick in
line of duty.

POLLOCK, Horatio C., Phoenix,
Ariz.; pvt., B Troop; joined
July 3, Tampa.

POLLOCK, John F., Tularosa, N.M.;
trumpeter, H Troop; 34, 5 ft.,
11⅛ ins., dark, blue eyes,
dark-brown hair; born Hardin,
Tenn.; cowboy; joined May 4,
Santa Fe; married.

POLLACK, William J., Pawnee,
O.T.; pvt., D Troop; 28, 5 ft.,
8 ins., dark, dark-brown eyes,
black hair; born in Nebraska;
artist; joined May 5, Guthrie;
single.

POMEROY, Fred A., Kingman,
Ariz.; farrier and blacksmith,
B Troop; 22, 5 ft., 8¼ ins.,
fair, light-blue eyes, light-brown
hair; born Dakota, Calif.;
accountant; joined May 2,
Whipple Barracks; single; sick
in line of duty.

POND, Ashley, Detroit, Mich.;
pvt., C Troop; joined June 21,
Washington, D.C.; sick in line
of duty.

POOLE, Wilbert L., Durant, I.T.;
sgt., M Troop; joined May 14,
Muskogee.

POWELL, Lory H., Roswell, N.M.;
pvt., H Troop; 24, 5 ft., 9½ ins.,
fair, hazel eyes, light hair; born
Winola, Miss.; farmer; joined
May 4, Santa Fe; single.

POWERS, Albert, Santa Fe; cpl.,
F Troop; 29, 5 ft., 5⅝ ins.,
ruddy, gray eyes, dark-brown
hair; born Philadelphia, Pa.;
plumber; joined May 5, Santa
Fe; single; wounded July 1.

PRENTICE, Royal A., Las Vegas,
N.M.; sgt., E Troop; 21, 5 ft.,
7 ins., fair, light-gray eyes,
brown hair; born Cooperstown,
N.Y.; joined May 3, Santa Fe;
stenographer; single.

PRESTON, Robert A., Stiles, Texas;
pvt., G Troop; joined May 24,
San Antonio.

PRICE, Benjamin W., Eufaula, I.T.;
pvt., L Troop; 26, 5 ft., 4¾
ins., ruddy, brown eyes,
brown hair; born Sebastian
County, Kans.; farmer; joined
May 14, Muskogee; single.

PRICE, Stewart R., Plattsburg, Mo.;
cpl., E Troop, trans. I Troop
May 12; 22, 5 ft., 11¾ ins.,
fair, hazel eyes, dark-brown
hair; born Plattsburg; lawyer;
joined May 4, Santa Fe;
single.

PROCTER, Joseph H., Pawnee,
O.T.; pvt., D Troop; 22, 5 ft.,
11¾ ins., ruddy, blue eyes,
dark hair; born Madison
County, Iowa; farmer; joined
May 5, Guthrie; single.

PROFFITT, William B., Prescott;
pvt., B Troop; 24, 5 ft., 11¾
ins., dark, light-blue eyes, dark-
brown hair; born Madison
County, Texas; rancher; joined
May 1, Whipple Barracks;
single; sick in line of duty.

PRONGER, Norman W., Silver City,
N.M.; pvt., H Troop; 24, 5
ft., 7¼ ins., dark, blue eyes,
brown hair; born in England;
miner; joined May 6, Santa
Fe; single.

PULLEY, William O., Marion, Ill.;
pvt., L Troop; 5 ft., 8 ins.,
dark, blue eyes, black hair;
born Taney County, Mo.;
cowboy; joined May 14,
Muskogee; single.

QUAID, William, Jr., Newbury,
N.Y.; pvt., K Troop; joined
May 5, Washington, D.C.

QUIER, Frank T., Santa Fe;
cpl., F Troop; 21, 5 ft., 4¾
ins., fair, blue eyes, fair hair;
born Larned, Kans.; teamster;
joined May 2, Santa Fe; single.

QUIGG, George H., Gallup, N.M.;
pvt., G Troop; joined June 27,
Santa Fe.

QUINN, Walter D., San Marcial,
N.M.; pvt., G Troop; joined
June 27, Santa Fe.

RADCLIFF, William; Gallup, N.M.;
pvt., G Troop.

RAFALOWITZ, Hyman, Philadelphia,
Pa.; pvt., F Troop; 30, 5 ft.,
4 ins., dark, hazel eyes, dark-
brown hair; born in Russia;
horsemen; joined May 4,
Santa Fe; single.

RAGLAND, Robert C., Guthrie;
pvt., G Troop; 21, 5 ft., 8 ins.,
dark, gray eyes, black hair;
born in Mulberry Grove, Ill.;
butcher; joined May 5, Santa
Fe; single.

RAMSEY, Homer M., Pearsall,
Texas; pvt., E Troop; joined
May 27, San Antonio; wounded
July 1.

RANDEBAUGH, James D., Flagstaff,
Ariz.; pvt., A Troop; 26, 5 ft.,
10¼ ins., fair, dark-brown
eyes, dark-brown hair; born
Morris County, Kans.; rancher;
joined May 1, Whipple Barracks; single.

RANDOLPH, Joseph A., Waukomis,
O.T.; sgt., D Troop; 39, 5 ft.,
10 ins., fair, blue eyes, brown
hair; born Ottawa, Iowa; cattleman; joined May 5, Guthrie;
married.

RANLETT, Charles J., New York
City; pvt., I Troop; joined
June 4, Tampa.

RAPP, Adolph, San Antonio;
pvt., A Troop; joined May 21,
San Antonio.

RATCLIFFE, William, Gallup,
N.M.; pvt., G Troop; 32, 5 ft.,
7⅞ ins., dark, gray eyes,
auburn hair; born Ironton,
Ohio; miner; joined May 6,
Santa Fe; single.

RAUDEBAUGH, James D., Flagstaff,
Ariz.; pvt., A Troop.

RAULETT, Charles, New Orleans,
La.; pvt., I Troop.

RAYBURN, Harry C., Camden,
Iowa; pvt., C Troop; joined
June 28, Santa Fe.

RAYMOND, Millard Lee, Santa Fe;
pvt., F Troop; 23, 5 ft., 4½
ins., dark, blue eyes, dark-brown
hair; born Ollumwa, Iowa;
cowboy; joined May 4, Santa
Fe; single.

REAY, Scott, Blackwell, O.T.;

sgt., D Troop; 23, 5 ft., 10 ins., dark, blue-gray eyes, dark-brown hair; born Elk County, Kans.; farmer; joined May 5, Guthrie; single.

REBENTISCH, Adolph, San Antonio; pvt., F Troop; joined May 19, San Antonio; wounded June 24.

REBER, William R.; sgt., E Troop; 30, 5 ft., 5⅞ ins., ruddy, blue eyes, light-brown hair; born St. Louis, Mo.; lawyer; joined May 4, Santa Fe; single; wounded July 1.

REED, Clifford L., Santa Fe; pvt., F Troop; 21, 5 ft., 5⅝ ins., fair, gray eyes, dark-brown hair; born Hamilton County, Ohio; cowboy; joined May 6, Santa Fe; single; wounded June 24.

REED, Colton, San Antonio; pvt., K Troop; joined May 28, San Antonio.

REED, George W., Tucson, Ariz.; farrier, C Troop, 27, 5 ft., 7¼ ins., fair, light-brown eyes, light-brown hair; born Ritchie, W.Va., laborer; joined May 2, Whipple Barracks; single; sick in line of duty.

REED, Harry B., Santa Fe; pvt., F Troop; 23, 5 ft., 7 ins., fair, blue eyes, light-brown hair; born Mount Carroll, Ill.; tinner; joined May 2, Santa Fe; single.

REGAN, John J., Beaumont, Texas; pvt., H Troop; joined June 29, Tampa.

REID, Robert W., Raton, N.M.; pvt., G Troop; 25, 5 ft., 7½ ins., dark, blue eyes, light-brown hair; born Decatur, Ill.; railroad man; joined May 5, Santa Fe; single; wounded June 24.

REID, William S., Raton, N.M.; blacksmith, G Troop; 33, 5 ft., 11⅞ ins., dark, blue eyes, brown hair; born Decatur, Ill.; blacksmith; joined May 5, Santa Fe; single.

REIDY, John, Ottawa, Kans.; pvt., H Troop.

RENNER, Charles L., Santa Fe; pvt., F Troop; 25, 5 ft., 7½ ins., fair, brown eyes, dark-brown hair; born Baden, Germany; confectioner; joined May 2, Santa Fe; single.

REYER, Adolph T., Santa Fe; pvt., F Troop; joined July 2, Santa Fe.

REYNOLDS, Benjamin F., Ardmore, I.T.; pvt., M Troop; joined May 14, Muskogee.

REYNOLDS, Edwin L., Santa Fe; pvt., F Troop; 24, 5 ft., 8⅝ ins., dark, blue eyes, brown hair; born Cheyenne, Wyo.; miner; joined May 6, Santa Fe; single.

REYNOLDS, Lewis, Kingman, Ariz.; pvt., A Troop; 33, 5 ft., 7½ ins., fair, light-blue eyes, dark-brown hair; born Bedford, Ill.; cowboy; joined May 1, Whipple Barracks; single; mortally wounded July 1.

RHOADES, John D., Hennessey, O.T.; cpl., D Troop; 26, 5 ft., 8⅞ ins., dark, brown eyes, black hair; born Warwick County, Ind.; farmer; joined May 4, Guthrie; single; wounded June 24.

RHODES, Samuel H., Tonto Basin, Ariz.; sgt., A Troop; 31, 5 ft., 11½ ins., fair, light-blue eyes, dark-brown hair; born Vissalia, Calif.; cowboy; joined May 1, Whipple Barracks; single; sick in line of duty.

RICE, Lee C., Santa Fe; pvt., F Troop; joined June 23, Santa Fe.

RICH, Allen K., Fort Gibson, I.T.; pvt., L Troop; 22, 5 ft., 9¼ ins., fair, brown eyes, dark-brown hair; born Clay, Tenn.; farmer; joined May 14, Muskogee; single.

RICHARDS, Richard, Albuquerque, N.M.; pvt., G Troop; joined June 23, Santa Fe.

RICKETTS, Basil N., New York
City; sgt., I Troop; joined
May 5, Washington, D.C.;
wounded in action July 1.

RICKETTS, William L., Phoenix,
Ariz.; pvt., C Troop; 21, 5 ft.
8½ ins., fair, light-brown eyes,
dark-brown hair; born Lynneville,
Ind.; rancher; joined May 1,
Whipple Barracks; single; sick
in line of duty.

REIDY, John, Ottawa, Kans.; pvt.,
I Troop; joined June 27,
Santa Fe.

RINEHART, Robert, Phoenix, Ariz.;
pvt., B Troop; joined May 19,
San Antonio; sick in line of
duty.

RITCHIE, James D., Gallup, N.M.;
cpl., G Troop; 33, 5 ft., 6¼
ins., dark, gray eyes, dark-
brown hair; born in Scotland;
miner; joined May 3, Santa
Fe; single.

ROBERSON, James R., Belle County,
Texas; 32, 5 ft., 9⅝ ins., florid,
blue eyes, sandy hair; born
Belle County; cowboy; joined
May 4, Santa Fe; single.

ROBERTS, Frank S., San Antonio;
pvt., B Troop; joined May 21,
San Antonio.

ROBERTS, John P., Clayton, N.M.;
pvt., E Troop; 32, 5 ft., 5⅞
ins., florid, light-brown eyes,
dark-brown hair; born Norfolk,
Va.; contractor; joined May 4,
Santa Fe; single.

ROBERTS, Thomas, Golden, N.M.;
pvt., E Troop; 43, 5 ft., 6 ins.,
florid, blue eyes, iron-gray
hair; born Washington D.C.;
miner; joined May 4, Santa
Fe; single.

ROBERTS, William J., Vinita, I.T.;
pvt., L Troop; 29, 5 ft., 6¼
ins., ruddy, brown eyes, black
hair; born Cherokee County,
Ga.; farmer; joined May 14,
Muskogee; single.

ROBERTSON, George W., Muskogee;
pvt., L Troop; 25, 5 ft., 11 ins.,
ruddy, brown eyes, dark-brown

hair; born in Kentucky; cowboy;
joined May 14, Muskogee; single.

ROBINSON, Frank P.; pvt., L Troop;
43, 5 ft., 7¼ ins., ruddy,
brown eyes, sandy hair; born
Hancock County, Ill.; farmer;
joined May 14, Muskogee;
single.

ROBISON, John F.; pvt., E Troop;
killed in action July 2.

ROBINSON, Kenneth Douglas, New
York City; pvt., K Troop;
wounded in action July 1.

ROBINSON, John F.; pvt., E Troop;
28, 5 ft., 7⅝ ins., dark, blue-
gray eyes, dark-brown hair;
born Louisville, Ky.; cowboy;
joined May 4, Santa Fe;
single; killed in action July 2.

RODERER, John N., Prescott; pvt.,
C Troop; 18, 5 ft., 8 ins., fair,
brown eyes, brown hair; born
Weiden, Germany; baker;
joined May 3, Whipple Barracks; single.

RODGERS, Joseph J., Tillon, Ark.;
pvt., L Troop; 27, 5 ft., 7
ins., fair, brown eyes, sandy
hair; born Phillips County,
Ark.; cowboy; joined May
14, Muskogee; single; wounded
in action July 1.

ROEDIGER, August, Charlotte,
N.C.; pvt., H Troop; 34, 5
ft., 5 ins., dark, blue eyes,
dark hair; born Charlotte;
soldier; joined May 6,
Santa Fe; single.

ROGERS, Albert, Santa Fe;
pvt., F Troop; joined June 27,
Santa Fe.

ROGERS, Joseph J., Tillon,
Ark.; pvt., L Troop; wounded
in action July 1.

ROGERS, Leo G., Bogart, Mo.;
saddler, F Troop; 21, 6 ft., ⅜
in., dark, hazel eyes, dark-
brown hair; born Carroll
County, Mo.; laborer; joined
May 2, Santa Fe; single.

ROLAND, George, Deming, N.M.;
pvt., G Troop; 27, 5 ft., 9 ins.,
fair, blue eyes, brown

hair; cowboy; joined May 31, San Antonio; married; wounded in action June 24.

RONALDS, Reginald, New York City; sgt., K Troop; joined May 5, Washington, D.C.

ROOSEVELT, Theodore, New York City; colonel.

ROSE, Lewis W., Los Angeles, Calif.; pvt., M Troop; joined July 9, Tampa.

ROSE, Michael C., Silver City, N.M.; pvt., H Troop; 26, 5 ft., 6⅝ ins., light, gray eyes, brown hair; born Graham, N.C.; bookbinder; joined May 6, Santa Fe; single.

ROSS, William E., Ardmore, I.T.; pvt., M Troop; joined May 14, Muskogee.

ROUSE, John L., Durant, I.T.; pvt., M Troop; joined May 14, Muskogee.

ROWDIN, John E., Phoenix, Ariz.; pvt., C Troop; 28, 5 ft., 5¼ ins., fair, light-blue eyes, dark-brown hair; born Richmond, Va.; cowboy; joined May 2, Whipple Barracks; single.

RUPERT, Charles W., Prescott; pvt., C Troop; 32, 5 ft., 5½ ins., dark, blue eyes, dark-brown hair; born Scranton, Pa.; teamster; joined April 30, Whipple Barracks; single.

RUSSELL, Albert P., El Reno, O.T.; pvt., D Troop; 26, 5 ft., 10¾ ins., ruddy, blue eyes, dark hair; born Pike County, Ala.; soldier; joined May 5, Guthrie; single.

RUSSELL, Arthur L., Santa Fe; pvt., F Troop; 21, 5 ft., 5¾ ins., fair, blue eyes, brown hair; born Wausau, Wis.; plasterer; joined May 2, Santa Fe; single; wounded in action June 24.

RUSSELL, Daniel, Goodland, I.T.; pvt., L Troop; 21, 5 ft., 10 ins., dark, dark-brown eyes, black hair; born Choctaw Nation, I.T.; cowboy; joined May 14, Muskogee; single.

RUSSELL, Marcus D., Troy, N.Y.; pvt., G Troop; joined May 27, San Antonio; killed in action June 24.

RUSSELL, Walter L., Caddo, I.T.; pvt., M Troop; joined May 14, Muskogee.

RUSSIG, Max; pvt., I Troop; joined June 13, Tampa.

RUTHERFORD, Bruce H., Pana, Ill.; pvt., H Troop; joined June 22, Tampa.

RYAN, John E., Santa Fe; pvt., E Troop; 39, 5 ft., 6½ ins., dark, dark-brown eyes, iron-gray hair; born St. Louis, Mo.; railroad man; joined May 3, Santa Fe; single; wounded in action July 1.

RYNERSON, William L., Las Cruces, N.M.; QM sgt., H Troop; 23, 5 ft., 8½ ins., dark, black eyes, dark hair; born Las Cruces; detective; joined May 4, Santa Fe; single.

ST. CLAIR, Edward C., New Orleans, La.; pvt., H Troop; 33, 5 ft., 5 ins., dark, brown eyes, brown hair; born New Orleans; packer; joined May 6, Santa Fe; single.

SANDOVAL, Joe T., Santa Fe; saddler, E Troop; 32, 5 ft., 5⅛ ins., dark, black eyes, dark-brown hair; born Santa Fe; saddler; joined May 4, Santa Fe; married.

SANDS, George H, South New Berlin, N.Y.; sgt., D Troop; 27, 5 ft., 6½ ins., fair, light-blue eyes, brown hair; born Utica, N.Y.; painter; joined May 5, Guthrie; single.

SANTO, William T., Chouteau, I.T.; pvt., L Troop; 31, 5 ft., 7⅛ ins., dark, blue eyes, brown hair; born Stevens County, Texas; cowboy; joined May 14, Muskogee; single; killed in action July 1.

SAUCIER, Harry S., New Orleans, La.; pvt., H Troop; joined May 28, San Antonio.

SAUNDERS, William H., Salem, Mass.; pvt., B Troop; joined May 4, Washington, D.C.; sick in line of duty.

SAVILLE, Michael, Chicago; pvt., G Troop; 29, 5 ft., 7¾ ins., florid, blue eyes, brown hair; born Chicago, Ill.; machinist; joined May 3, Santa Fe; single.

SAWYER, Benjamin, Hillsboro, Ill.; pvt., H Troop; joined June 23, Santa Fe.

SAYERS, Samuel E., Yuma, Ariz.; pvt., C Troop; joined May 19, San Antonio.

SAYRE, Hal, Jr., Denver, Col.; 2nd lt., C Troop; 22, 5 ft., 10½ ins., fair, gray eyes, light-brown hair; born Central City, Col.; student; joined May 17, San Antonio; single.

SCANLON, Edward, Cerrillos, N.M.; pvt., E Troop; 23, 5 ft., 7⅞ ins., florid, gray eyes, red hair; born New York City; clerk; joined May 5, Santa Fe; single; died of typhoid Oct. 3 while awaiting muster-out.

SCHAFER, George, Pinos Altos, N.M.; pvt., H Troop; 21, 5 ft., 7¼ ins., dark, brown eyes, dark-brown hair; born Pinos Altos; cowboy; joined May 6, Santa Fe; married.

SCHARF, Charles A., Flagstaff, Ariz.; pvt., C Troop; 24, 5 ft., 5 ins., fair, light-blue eyes, light-brown hair; born Butler County, Kans.; farmer; joined May 1, Whipple Barracks; single.

SCHARNHORSE, Carl J., Jr., Santa Fe; pvt., F Troop, trans. I Troop May 12; 22, 5 ft., 4 ins., dark, blue eyes, brown hair; born Del Norte, Col.; cowboy; joined May 6, Santa Fe; single.

SCHENCK, Frank W., Grand Island, Neb.; pvt., B Troop; 29, 5 ft., 7¾ ins., fair, light-blue eyes, light-brown hair; born Cincinnati, Ohio; cook; joined May 3,

Whipple Barracks; single; sick in line of duty.

SCHMUTZ, John C., Germantown, Ohio; pvt., D Troop; joined May 23, San Antonio; sick.

SCHNEPPLE, William C., Santa Fe; pvt., E Troop; 19, 5 ft., 6½ ins., fair, blue eyes, brown hair; born Santa Fe; clerk; joined May 3, Santa Fe; single.

SCHULZ, Theodore E., Tampa; pvt., M Troop; joined June 17, Muskogee.

SCHUPP, Eugene, Santa Fe; pvt., D Troop.

SCHUTT, Henry, Warren, Pa., pvt., H Troop; joined June 8, Tampa.

SCHWARTZ, Edgar A.; cpl., G Troop.

SCHWEIZER, Jacob, El Reno, O.T.; 2nd lt., D Troop; 38, 5 ft., 10 ins., fair, blue eyes, light-brown hair; born Baden, Germany; soldier; joined May 5, Guthrie; married.

SCOBEY, Arthur E., Wills Point, Texas; pvt., L Troop; 27, 5 ft., 10 ins., dark, brown eyes, dark-brown hair; born Williamson, Ill.; cowboy; joined May 14, Muskogee; single; wounded in action July 1.

SCOTT, Cliff D., Clifton, O.T.; pvt., D Troop; 26, 5 ft., 6¾ ins., dark, brown eyes, dark-brown hair; born Allen County, Kans.; printer; joined May 5, Guthrie; single.

SCROGGINS, Oscar, Logan County, Ill.; 25, 5 ft., 8⅜ ins., dark, light-brown eyes, black hair; born Logan County, Ill.; farmer; joined May 4, Santa Fe; single.

SCUDDER, William M., Phoenix, Ariz.; pvt., C Troop; 21, 5 ft., 10½ ins., fair, blue eyes, brown hair; born Chicago, Ill.; student; joined May 4, Washington, D.C.; single; sick in line of duty.

SCULL, Guy H., Boston, Mass.; pvt., C Troop; 21, 5 ft., 11 ins., fair, blue eyes, brown hair; born

Boston; student; joined May 4, Washington, D.C.; single.

SEADERS, Ben F., Las Vegas, N.M.; pvt., E Troop; 25, 6 ft., ¾ in., gray eyes, brown hair; born Crawford County, Ill.; cowboy; joined May 3, Santa Fe; single.

SEAVER, George H., Muskogee; pvt., L Troop; 20, 5 ft., 8½ ins., dark, brown eyes, dark-brown hair; born St. Joseph, Mo.; clerk; joined May 14, Muskogee; single; wounded in action July 2.

SELLERS, Henry J., Williams, Ariz.; pvt., A Troop; 32, 5 ft., 4 ins., brown eyes, brown hair; born San Benito, Calif.; cowboy; joined April 30, Whipple Barracks; single.

SELLS, Henry, Flagstaff, Ariz.; pvt., A Troop; 33, 5 ft., 4½ ins., fair, light-blue eyes, light-brown hair; born Wittenburg, Germany; cook; joined May 1, Whipple Barracks; single.

SENNETT, Lee, Marysville, W.Va.; pvt., H Troop.

SENNETT, James B., Santa Fe; pvt., F Troop; joined June 8, Santa Fe.

SETTLE, Green A., Jackson County, Ky.; 38, 5 ft., 9 ins., light, dark-blue eyes, dark hair; born Jackson County, Ky.; soldier; joined May 6, Santa Fe; single.

SEWALL, Henry F., New York City; pvt., A Troop; joined Aug. 6, Tampa.

SEXSMITH, William, Yuma, Ariz.; pvt., C Troop; 28, 5 ft., 10½ ins., fair, dark-blue eyes, light-brown hair; born Fayette County, Ky.; rancher; joined May 2, Whipple Barracks; single.

SHACKELFORD, Marcus L., Jerome, Ariz.; pvt., C Troop; 25, 5 ft., 7¼ ins., fair, dark-blue eyes, dark-brown hair; born Reno County, Calif; rancher; joined May 1, Whipple Barracks; single.

SHANAFELT, Dick, Perry, O.T.; pvt., D Troop; 19, 5 ft., 10 ins., gray-blue eyes, dark-brown hair;

born Franklin County, Mo.; newsdealer; joined May 5, Guthrie; single.

SHANKS, Lee P., Paducah, Ky.; pvt., A Troop; joined May 19, San Antonio.

SHANNON, Charles W., Raton, N.M.; pvt., G Troop; 26, 5 ft., 10⅛ ins., light, gray eyes, light hair; born Salisburg, Mo.; brakeman; joined May 5, Santa Fe; single.

SHARLAND, George H., Santa Fe; pvt., F Troop; 27, 5 ft., 3 ins., fair, blue eyes, brown hair; born London, England; laborer; joined May 6, Santa Fe; single.

SHARP, Emerson E., Wanamaker, Tenn.; pvt., H Troop; 30, 5 ft., 10⅞ ins., light, blue eyes, dark hair; born Wanamaker; farmer; joined May 6, Santa Fe; single.

SHARP, Walter L., Chicago, Ill.; pvt., L Troop; joined June 7, Tampa.

SHAW, James A., Prescott; pvt., A Troop; 31, 5 ft., 11 ins., fair, light-blue eyes, dark-brown hair; born Shelbyville, Ill.; cowboy; joined May 2, Whipple Barracks; single.

SHAW, John F., Scott County, Iowa; pvt., H Troop; 24, 5 ft., 9 ins., florid, blue eyes, red hair; born Scott County, Iowa; rancher; joined May 4, Santa Fe; single.

SHEARD, Uriah, El Paso, Texas; farrier, H Troop; 41, 5 ft., 8⅜ ins., florid, blue eyes, brown hair; born Brockner County, Ohio; cowboy; joined May 4, Santa Fe; single.

SHERMAN, Horace E., Santa Fe; 1st sgt., F Troop; 29, 5 ft., 11¾ ins., fair, blue eyes, brown hair; born Elroy, Wis.; soldier; joined May 2, Santa Fe; married.

SHIELDS, William G., Santa Fe; pvt., F Troop; 27, 5 ft., 8 ins., fair, light eyes, dark-brown hair; born Dayton, Ohio; railroad man; joined May 2, Santa Fe; single.

SHIPP, Edward M., Kingfisher, O.T.; pvt., D Troop; 25, 5 ft., 9 ins., fair, blue eyes, light-brown hair; born Paulding County, Ga.; laborer; joined May 5, Guthrie; single; sick in line of duty.

SHOCKEY, James M., Perry, O.T.; cpl., D Troop; 23, 5 ft., 9 ins., dark, blue-gray eyes, black hair; born Montgomery, Kans.; ranchman; joined May 5, Guthrie; single.

SHOEMAKER, John, Phoenix, Ariz.; pvt., C Troop; 29, 5 ft., 11½ ins., fair, light-brown eyes, black hair; born Scott County, Va.; cowboy; joined May 2, Whipple Barracks; single.

SIMMONS, Charlie M., Raton, N.M.; pvt., G Troop; 25, 5 ft., 9¾ ins., light, brown eyes, dark-brown hair; born Cherokee, Iowa; farmer; joined May 6, Santa Fe; single.

SIMMS, William M., Vinita, I.T.; pvt., L Troop; 35, 5 ft., 7¼ ins., ruddy, blue eyes, brown hair; born New York City; farmer; joined May 14, Muskogee; single; wounded in action July 1.

SIMPSON, William Sloan, Dallas, Texas; cpl., D Troop; 21, 5 ft., 9¾ ins., fair, brown eyes, brown hair; born Weatherford, Texas; student; joined May 5, Guthrie; single.

SINNETT, James B, Santa Fe; pvt., F Troop.

SINNETT, Lee, Maizeville, W.Va.; pvt., G Troop; 21, 5 ft., 7½ ins., fair, gray eyes, dark hair; born Marysville, W.Va.; railroad man; joined May 5, Santa Fe; single.

SKELTON, James Wesley, Trinity Mills, Texas; pvt., L Troop; 25, 5 ft., 7½ ins., ruddy, dark-brown eyes, dark-brown hair; born Collins County, Texas; laborer; joined May 14, Muskogee; single.

SKINNER, Arthur V., Santa Fe; pvt., E Troop; 22, 5 ft., 5¼ ins., fair, gray eyes, dark-brown hair; born Georgetown, Col.; carpenter; joined May 3, Santa Fe; married.

SKIPWITH, John G., Santa Fe; pvt., F Troop; joined June 8, Santa Fe.

SKOGSBERG, Charles G., Safford, Ariz.; pvt., C Troop; 21, 5 ft., 9 ins., fair, light-blue eyes, dark-brown hair; born in Sweden; cowboy; joined May 2, Whipple Barracks; single.

SLAUGHTER, Benjamin, San Antonio; pvt., G troop; joined June 6, Tampa.

SLEVIN, Edward, Tampa; pvt., E Troop; joined June 4, Tampa.

SLOAN, Samuel P., South McAlester, I.T.; pvt., M Troop; joined May 14, Muskogee.

SLOAN, Thomas M., Phoenix; pvt., C Troop; joined June 18, Tampa.

SMITH, Bert, Vinita, I.T.; pvt., L Troop; 69, 5 ft., 6⅜ ins., dark, blue eyes, dark-brown hair; born Vinita; cowboy joined May 14, Muskogee; single.

SMITH, Clarke T., Philadelphia, Pa.; pvt., K Troop, joined July 8, Philadelphia.

SMITH, Fred, Guthrie; pvt., D Troop; 23, 5 ft., 9 ins., fair, blue eyes, light-brown hair; born New York City; cook; joined May 5, Guthrie.

SMITH, George L., Frankfort, Mich.; pvt., K Troop; joined May 23, San Antonio.

SMITH, Joseph L., Caddo, I.T.; cpl., M Troop; joined May 14, Muskogee.

SMITH, Joseph S., Philadelphia, Pa., pvt., K Troop; joined May 13, San Antonio.

SMITH, Race W., San Antonio; pvt., B Troop; joined May 21, San Antonio; mortally wounded in action July 2.

SMITH, Sylvester S., Vinita, I.T.;

pvt., L Troop; 38, 5 ft., 4½ ins., dark, blue eyes, brown hair; born Cherokee Nation, I.T.; farmer; joined May 14, Muskogee; single.

SNODDERLY, William L., Bisbee, Ariz.; pvt., B Troop; 27, 5 ft., 7¼ ins., fair, light-brown eyes, dark-brown hair; born Knoxville, Tenn.; miner; joined May 2, Whipple Barracks; single; sick in line of duty.

SOMERS, Fred B., Prescott; trumpeter, C Troop; 27, 5 ft., 6¾ ins., fair, light-brown eyes, light-brown hair; born Detroit, Mich.; lawyer; joined May 1, Whipple Barracks; single; sick in line of duty.

SOMERS, Willis E., Raton, N.M.; pvt., G Troop; 21, 5 ft., 8⅜ ins., fair, hazel eyes, light-brown hair; born Williamsport, Pa.; carpenter; joined May 5, Santa Fe; single.

SPENCER, Arthur P., Santa Fe; cpl., F Troop; 19, 5 ft., 6 ins., fair, hazel eyes, brown hair; born Council Grove, Kans.; printer; joined May 2, Santa Fe; single.

SPENCER, Edward J., Clay County, Texas; pvt., F Troop, trans. I Troop May 12; joined May 2, Santa Fe.

STALEY, Francis M., Waukomis, O.T.; pvt., D Troop; 23, 5 ft., 7¾ ins., fair, blue eyes, light-brown hair; born Jackson County, Mo.; farmer; joined May 5, Guthrie.

STANTON, Richard H., Phoenix; pvt., B Troop; 24, 5 ft., 9½ ins., fair, light-blue eyes, light-brown hair; born New York City; policeman; joined April 30, Whipple Barracks; single; sick in line of duty.

STARK, Wallace J., Safford, Ariz.; pvt., A Troop; 21, 5 ft., 8¼ ins., fair, light-blue eyes, light-brown hair; born Barton County, Mo.; cowboy; joined May 2, Whipple Barracks; single.

STAUB, Louis E., Santa Fe; pvt., F Troop; 36, 5 ft., 5½ ins., fair, gray eyes, dark-brown hair; born Canton, Ohio; barber; joined May 2, Santa Fe; single.

STEADMAN, T. D.; pvt., D Troop

STECKER, Ernest, Los Angeles, Calif.; sgt. major.

STELZRIEDE, John A. W., Tempe, Ariz.; trumpeter, C Troop; 21, 6 ft., 1 in., fair, dark-blue eyes, light-brown hair; born Belleville, Ill.; section foreman for railroad; joined April 30, Whipple Barracks; single.

STEFENS, Luke B., Rio Vista, I.T.; pvt., L Troop; 22, 5 ft., 10¾ ins., fair, blue eyes, light-brown hair; born Bedford, Ark.; teacher; joined May 14, Muskogee; single.

STEPHENS, Oregon, Purdy, I.T.; pvt., E Troop; 36, 5 ft., 6¼ ins., dark, light-brown hair, brown eyes; born Holt County, Ga.; cowboy; joined May 3, Santa Fe; single.

STEVENS, Joseph Sampson, Newport, R.I.; cpl., K Troop; joined May 5, Washington, D.C.

STEWART, Clyde H., Pawnee, O.T.; pvt., D Troop; 20, 5 ft., 8½ ins., dark, blue eyes, dark hair; born Nemaha County, Kans.; joined May 5, Guthrie; typesetter; single.

STEWART, Henry J., Caddo, I.T.; pvt., M Troop; joined May 14, Muskogee; died in hospital Aug. 26.

STEWART, Luther L., Raton, N.M.; cpl., G Troop; 24, 5 ft., 8¾ ins., fair, blue eyes, brown hair; born Roanoke, Va.; saloonkeeper; joined May 5, Santa Fe; single; wounded in action June 24.

STEWART, Newton, El Paso, Texas; pvt., H Troop; 22, 5 ft., 8⅞ ins., florid, hazel eyes, dark hair; born Ellis County, Texas; butcher; joined May 4, Santa Fe; single.

STEWART, W. Walton, Selma, Ala.; pvt., B Troop; joined June 4, Tampa; sick in line of duty.

STIDHAM, Theodore E., Eufaula, I.T.; pvt., L Troop; 26, 5 ft., 7¾ ins., dark, dark-brown eyes, black hair; born in I.T.; cowboy; joined May 14, Muskogee; single.

STILLSON, Earl, Topeka, Kans.; pvt., G Troop; joined June 27, Santa Fe.

STOCKBRIDGE, Arthur J., Santa Fe; pvt., F Troop; 23, 5 ft., 9 ins., light, brown eyes, brown hair; born Trinidad, Col.; farmer; joined May 5, Santa Fe; single.

STOCKTON, Richard, Elizabeth, N.J.; pvt., K Troop; joined May 26, San Antonio.

STORMS, Morris J., Roswell, N.M.; pvt., H Troop; 24, 5 ft., 11⅞ ins., dark, brown eyes, auburn hair; born Madison County, Ky.; cowboy; joined May 4, Santa Fe; single.

SULLIVAN, Patrick J., Prescott; pvt., A Troop; 30, 5 ft., 8¾ ins., blue eyes; light-brown hair; born Sidney, Ohio; barber; joined June 30, Whipple Barracks; married.

SULLIVAN, William J., Silver City, N.M.; pvt., H Troop; 34, 5 ft., 4½ ins., ruddy, hazel eyes, dark-brown hair; born Manchester, Va.; laborer; joined May 6, Santa Fe; single.

SWAN, George D., Gallup, N.M.; pvt., G Troop; 32, 5 ft., 8½ ins., light, hazel eyes, dark-brown hair; born Bowling Green, Ohio; butcher; joined May 3, Santa Fe; single.

SWEARINGER, George, Maysville, Mo.; pvt., L Troop; 23, 5 ft., 8½ ins., fair, blue eyes, light hair; born Maizeville, Mo.; teamster; joined May 14, Muskogee; single.

SWEET, Philip K., New York City; sgt., K Troop; joined May 7, Washington, D.C.; sick in line of duty.

SWETNAM, John W., Globe, Ariz.; pvt., B Troop; 24, 5 ft., 10¼ ins., fair, light-brown eyes, light-brown hair; born Wolfe County, Ky.; cowboy; joined May 4, Whipple Barracks; single; killed in action July 1.

SYKES, Marion, Muskogee; pvt., M Troop; joined May 14, Muskogee.

TAILOR, James B., Ardsley on Hudson, N.Y.; cpl., K Troop; joined May 5, Washington, D.C.

TAIT, John H., Raton, N.M.; pvt., G Troop, trans. I Troop May 12; 25, 5 ft., 8 ins., light, blue eyes, light-brown hair; born Chicago, Ill.; fireman; joined May 5, Santa Fe; single.

TALMAN, Frank U., South McAlester, I.T.; cpl., M Troop; joined May 14, Muskogee.

TAUER, William L., Ponca City, O.T.; pvt., D Troop; 21, 5 ft., 6½ ins., dark, blue-gray eyes, dark hair; born Fort Worth, Texas; laborer; joined May 5, Guthrie; single.

TANGEN, Edward, Santa Fe; pvt., F Troop; 29, 5 ft., 7¼ ins., ruddy, blue eyes, brown hair; born Hancock, Mich., laborer; joined May 2, Santa Fe; single.

TAYLOR, Berry F., Las Vegas; sgt., E Troop; 35, 5 ft., 10¾ ins., dark, dark eyes, dark hair; born in Cuba; actor; joined May 3, Santa Fe; single.

TAYLOR, Warren P., Hillsboro, Texas; pvt., L Troop; 36, 5 ft., 10¼ ins., dark, dark-brown eyes, black hair; born Guntersville, Ala.; painter; joined May 14, Muskogee; single.

TAYLOR, William R., New York City; pvt., E Troop; joined June 4, Tampa.

TEMPLE, Frank, Lafayette, Ind.; pvt.; F Troop; 44, 5 ft., 6⅛ ins., dark, hazel eyes, dark-brown hair; born Lafayette; laborer; joined May 2, Santa Fe; sick in line of duty.

TEST, Clarence L., Austin, Texas; pvt., K Troop; joined May 10, Mt. Gretna, Pa.

THOMAS, Albert M., Guthrie; pvt., D Troop; 21, 5 ft., 9¾ ins., dark, black hair; born Dallas, Texas; marshal; joined May 5, Guthrie; married.

THOMAS, Jesse C., Caddo, I.T.; pvt., M Troop; joined May 14, Muskogee.

THOMAS, John R., Jr., Muskogee; 1st lt., L Troop; 22, 5 ft., 11 ins., fair, brown eyes, brown hair; born Metropolis, Ill.; clerk; joined May 14, Muskogee; single; wounded in action June 24.

THOMAS, Neal, Aztec, N.M.; pvt., G Troop; joined May 29, San Antonio.

THOMAS, Rufus K., Boston, Mass.; pvt., A Troop; joined June 28, Washington, D.C.

THOMAS, Theodore C., Leavenworth, Kans.; pvt., H Troop; joined June 18, Tampa.

THOMPSON, Alexander M., Deming, N.M.; pvt., H Troop; 22, 5 ft., 7⅞ ins., light, gray eyes, light-brown hair; born Georgetown, N.M.; cattleman; joined May 6, Santa Fe.

THOMPSON, Charles, Mercer County, W.Va.; pvt., F Troop; 24, 5 ft., 6¼ ins., fair, blue eyes, dark-brown hair; born Mercer County; miner; joined May 2, Santa Fe; single.

THOMPSON, Frank M., Aztec, N.M.; pvt., G Troop; 27, 5 ft., 6 ins., florid, blue eyes, flaxen hair; born Des Moines, Iowa; laborer; joined May 3, Santa Fe; single.

THOMPSON, George; pvt., I Troop; joined June 24, Santa Fe.

THOMPSON, Joseph F., Jr., Washington, D.C.; pvt., A Troop; joined June 24, Washington, D.C.

THOMPSON, Sylvester V.; pvt., L Troop; 27, 5 ft., 10¾ ins., ruddy, blue eyes, brown hair; born Camblin County, Mo.; cowboy; joined May 14, Muskogee; single; wounded in action July 1.

THORPE, Henry H., Southampton, L.I.; pvt., K Troop; joined May 5, Washington, D.C.

TIFFANY, William, New York City; lt., K Troop; joined May 5, Washington, D.C.; died of typhoid Aug. 26.

TILKIE, Charles M., Chicago, Ill.; pvt., B Troop; joined June 23, Tampa.

TOLAND, Jesse T.; Bisbee, Ariz.; pvt., B Troop; 23, 5 ft., 9 ins., fair, blue eyes, dark-brown hair; born St. Helena, Calif.; cook; joined May 2, Whipple Barracks; single; sick in line of duty.

TOMLINSON, Leroy E., Prescott; pvt., B Troop; 21, 5 ft., 11 ins., fair, light-brown eyes, dark-brown hair; born Trenton, Mo.; painter; joined May 4, Whipple Barracks; single; died of fever June 23.

TORBETT, John G.; pvt., E Troop; trans. I Troop May 12; 30, 5 ft., 6 ins., dark, brown eyes, black hair; born in Scotland; miner; joined May 3, Santa Fe; single.

TOWNSEND, Albert B., Prescott; pvt., B Troop; 24, 5 ft., 8½ ins., fair, light-brown eyes, light-brown hair; born New York State; lineman; joined May 2, Whipple Barracks; single.

TOWNSEND, Charles M., Faribault, Minn., pvt., I Troop; joined June 23, Santa Fe.

TOY, J. Frederick, Philadelphia, Pa.; pvt., K Troop; joined May 10, Mount Gretna, Pa.

TRAVIS, Grant, Aztec, N.M.; pvt., G Troop; 36, 5 ft., 10⅞ ins., dark, blue eyes, dark-brown hair; born Canal Winchester, Ohio; teacher; joined May 6, Santa Fe; single.

TRAYNOR, William S., Wilcox, Ariz.; pvt., H Troop; joined June 4, Tampa.

TRITZ, William H., Windsor, Conn.; pvt., H Troop; 23, 5 ft., 7 ins., dark, blue eyes, dark hair; born Windsor; carpenter; joined May 6, Santa Fe; married.

TROWBRIDGE, Lafayette, Prescott; cpl., C Troop; 25, 5 ft., 5 ins., fair, brown eyes, brown hair; born Johnson County, Wis.; cook; joined April 30, Whipple Barracks; married.

TRUMAN, George E., San Antonio; pvt., B Troop; joined May 28, San Antonio; sick in line of duty.

TRUMP, Norman O., Santa Fe; pvt., F Troop; 28, 5 ft., 9¾ ins., dark, brown eyes, dark-brown hair; born Worth County, Mo.; cowboy; joined May 2, Santa Fe; single.

TUDOR, J. William, Jr., Boston, Mass.; pvt., K Troop; joined May 5, Washington, D.C.

TUTTLE, Arthur L., Safford, Ariz.; pvt., A Troop; 21, 5 ft., 10¾ ins., fair, dark-blue eyes, light-brown hair; born Safford; cowboy; joined May 2, Whipple Barracks; single.

TWYMAN, John L., Raton, N.M.; pvt., I Troop; joined June 27, Santa Fe.

TYLER, Edwin, Ardmore, I.T.; blacksmith, M Troop; joined May 14, Muskogee.

UTTLING, Charles H., Phoenix; sgt., B Troop; 30, 5 ft., 10½ ins., fair, light-blue eyes, light-brown hair; born Nova City, Calif.; cowboy; joined April 30, Whipple Barracks; single; sick in line of duty.

UNDERWOOD, Clarence H., Colorado Springs, Col.; Trumpeter, I

Troop; joined May 19, San Antonio.

VANCE, William E., Austin, Texas; pvt., C Troop; joined May 21, San Antonio.

VANDERSLICE, James E., Enid, O.T.; pvt., D Troop; 28, 5 ft., 9 ins., light, blue eyes, dark-brown hair; born Doniphan County, Kans.; laborer; joined May 5, Guthrie; single.

VAN HORN, Eustus E., Halstead, Kans.; pvt., G Troop; 23, 6 ft., ⅝ in., florid, blue eyes, brown hair; born Halstead; laborer; joined May 3, Santa Fe; single.

VAN SCHAICK, Henry S., New York City; cpl., K Troop; joined May 7, Washington, D.C.

VAN SICLEN, Frank, Safford, Ariz.; pvt., A Troop; 27, 5 ft., 6 ins., fair, blue eyes, dark-brown hair; born Ingham County, Mich.; cowboy; joined May 2, Whipple Barracks; single; sick in line of duty.

VAN TREESE, Louis H., Tucson, Ariz.; pvt., B Troop; 21, 5 ft., 7 ins., fair, light-brown eyes, dark-brown hair; born Greenville, Ill.; clerk; joined May 2, Whipple Barracks; single, sick in line of duty.

VAN VALEN, Alexander L., Poughkeepsie, N.Y.; pvt., D Troop; joined June 4, Tampa.

VENABLE, Warner M., Stephenville, Texas; pvt., K Troop; joined June 22, Tampa.

VICKERS, John W., South McAlester, I.T.; pvt., M Troop; joined May 14, Muskogee.

VINES, Jesse G., Phoenix; pvt., C Troop; 21, 5 ft., 9¼ ins., fair, light-blue eyes, light-brown hair; born San Bernadino, Calif.; cowboy; joined May 1, Whipple Barracks; single.

VINNEDGE, George E., Santa Fe; pvt., F Troop; 23, 5 ft., 9¾ ins., fair, blue eyes, black hair; born

born Indianapolis, Ind.; railroad man; joined May 2, Santa Fe; single.

VYNE, Nicholas A., Emporia, Kans.; sgt., G Troop; 32, 5 ft., 8⅛ ins., blue eyes, light-brown hair; born Ottawa, Mich.; miner; joined May 4, Santa Fe; married.

WADSWORTH, Craig W., Genesee, N.Y.; sgt., K Troop; joined May 5, Washington, D.C.

WAFFENSMITH, William H., Raton, N.M.; sgt., I Troop; joined June 29, Santa Fe.

WAGER, Oscar G., Jerome, Ariz.; pvt., A Troop; 20, 5 ft., 7½ ins., dark, dark-brown eyes, black hair; born Wager, Ark.; cowboy; joined May 2, Whipple Barracks; single.

WAGGONER, Curtis C., Roswell, N.M.; pvt., H Troop; 31, 5 ft., 6 ins., ruddy, gray eyes, brown hair; born Crawford County, Ill.; cowboy; joined May 4, Santa Fe; married.

WAGGONER, Daniel G., Roswell, N.M.; pvt., H Troop; 26, 5 ft., 7⅜ ins., dark, blue eyes, light-brown hair; born in Kansas; cowboy; joined May 5, Santa Fe; married.

WAGNER, John D., Caddo, I.T.; pvt., M Troop; joined May 14, Muskogee.

WAGNER, William W., Bland, N.M.; pvt., E Troop; 30, 5 ft., 4½ ins., dark, gray eyes, brown hair; born Erie, Pa.; miner; joined May 3, Santa Fe; single.

WALLACE, Alexander H.; pvt., A Troop; joined May 28, San Antonio; died of typhoid Aug. 31.

WALLACE, Walter D., Flagstaff, Ariz.; pvt., A Troop; 25, 5 ft., 8¼ ins., fair, dark-brown eyes, dark-brown hair; born Hamblin County, Tenn.; rancher; joined May 1, Whipple Barracks; single; sick in line of duty.

WALLACE, William F., Flagstaff;

pvt., A Troop; 21, 5 ft., 8¼ ins., fair, light-blue eyes, light-brown hair; born Ontaria, Canada; cowboy; joined May 1, Whipple Barracks; single; wounded in action July 1.

WALLACK, Robert R., Washington, D.C.; pvt., C Troop; joined May 19, San Antonio.

WALLAR, John H., Prescott; wagoner, A Troop; cowboy; wounded in action June 24.

WALLER, Edward C.; cpl., E Troop; 21, 5 ft., 11½ ins., dark, brown eyes, dark-brown hair; born Chicago, Ill.; student; joined May 5, Washington, D.C.; single; wounded in action July 2.

WALLER, John H., Prescott; wagoner, A Troop; 44, 5 ft., 7 ins., fair, blue eyes, dark-brown hair; born Highland County, Ohio; cowboy; joined April 30, Whipple Barracks; single; wounded in action July 1.

WALSH, George, San Francisco; sgt., A Troop; 43, 5 ft., 9 ins., fair, light-blue eyes, brown hair; born Manchester, England; painter; joined May 2, Whipple Barracks; died at sea of dysentery Aug. 11.

WALSH, John, Santa Fe; pvt., F Troop; joined June 25, Santa Fe.

WALTERS, Jesse, Phoenix; trumpeter, B Troop; 21, 5 ft., 8½ ins., fair, light-brown eyes, light-brown hair; born Bollarrat, Col.; locomotive engineer; joined May 2, Whipple Barracks; single; sick in line of duty.

WARD, Frank, Globe, Ariz.; pvt., B Troop; 38, 5 ft., 8½ ins., fair, light-blue eyes, light-brown hair; born Edinburgh, Scotland; rancher; joined May 4, Whipple Barracks; married.

WARDEN, John L., New York City; pvt., K Troop.

WARDWELL, Louis C., Jr., Santa Fe; pvt., F Troop; 20, 5 ft.,

6½ ins., fair, blue eyes, dark-brown hair; born Pueblo, Col.; cowboy; joined May 2, Santa Fe; single.

WARFORD, David E., Globe, Ariz.; pvt., B Troop; 21, 5 ft., 3½ ins., fair, light-brown eyes, dark-brown hair; born Troy, N.Y.; cowboy; joined May 4, Whipple Barracks; single; wounded in action July 1.

WARREN, George W., Santa Fe; pvt., E Troop; joined June 25, Santa Fe.

WARREN, Hedrick M., Phoenix; cpl., C Troop; 21, 5 ft., 9½ ins., fair, light-blue eyes, light-brown hair; born Pueblo, Col.; rancher; joined May 1, Whipple Barracks; single.

WARREN, Paul, Santa Fe; pvt., F Troop; 29, 5 ft., 7½ ins., ruddy, blue eyes, dark-brown hair; born Quincy, Ill.; cowboy; joined May 2, Santa Fe; single.

WATERBURY, Eugene W., Tucson, Ariz.; cpl., B Troop; 24, 5 ft., 6½ ins., fair, light-blue eyes, light-brown hair; born Muskegan, Mich.; hotel clerk; joined May 2, Whipple Barracks; single.

WATROUS, Charles E., Santa Fe; pvt., F Troop; 32, 5 ft., 7⅜ ins., dark, blue eyes, sandy hair; born Watrous, N.M.; farmer; joined May 5, Santa Fe; single.

WAYLAND, T. J., Williams, Ariz.; pvt., A Troop; 41, 5 ft., 7¾ ins., blue eyes, dark-brown hair; born Sherman, Texas; cowboy; joined April 30, Whipple Barracks; single; sick in line of duty.

WEAKLEY, Horace W., Santa Fe; 1st lt., F Troop; 29, 5 ft., 10 ins., fair, hazel eyes, brown hair; born Shelbyville, Ind.; mining engineer; joined May 6, Santa Fe; single.

WEATHERS, Bruce C., Safford, Ariz.; cpl., C Troop; 33, 5 ft., 9¼ ins., fair, light-blue eyes, light-brown hair; born Browns-ville, Ind.; cowboy; joined May 2, Whipple Barracks; single.

WEAVER, Otis B., Mount Vernon, Texas; sgt., M Troop; joined May 14, Muskogee.

WEBB, Adelbert D., Safford, Ariz.; pvt., A Troop; 30, 5 ft., 10½ ins., fair, light-brown eyes, light-brown hair; born Jefferson, Ohio; cowboy; joined May 1, Whipple Barracks; single; sick in line of duty.

WEBB, Gerald A., Guthrie; sgt., D Troop; 26, 5 ft., 9¾ ins., fair, blue eyes, light-brown hair; born Lyonsville, Iowa; soldier; joined May 5, Guthrie; single.

WEBB, William W., Mesquite, Texas; pvt., B Troop; 30, 5 ft., 5½ ins., fair, light-blue eyes, dark-brown hair, born Dallas, Texas; cowboy; joined May 3, Whipple Barracks; single; sick in line of duty.

WEBER, Beauregard, Santa Fe; pvt., F Troop; 30, 5 ft., 6¾ ins., fair, blue eyes, sandy hair; born St. Louis, Mo.; prospector; joined May 6, Santa Fe; single.

WEBSTER, David, Durant, I.T.; pvt., M Troop; joined May 14, Muskogee.

WEIL, Henry J., Kingman, Ariz.; pvt., A Troop; 22, 5 ft., 6 ins., fair, light-blue eyes, flaxen hair; born San Francisco; clerk; joined May 1, Whipple Barracks; single.

WEITZEL, John F., Newkirk, O.T.; pvt., D Troop; 19, 5 ft., 4½ ins., fair, blue-gray eyes, dark-brown hair; born Cowley County, Kans.; joined May 5, Guthrie; single.

WELCH, Anthony, Durango, Col.; pvt., G Troop; 23, 5 ft., 6⅜ ins., florid, blue eyes, light-brown hair; born Chicago, Ill.; plumber; joined May 6, Santa Fe; single.

WELLER, Samuel M., San Antonio; pvt., F Troop; joined May 19, San Antonio.

WELLS, Joseph Ogden, St. Joseph,

Mich.; pvt., D Troop; 21, 5 ft., 9⅛ ins., dark, brown eyes, brown hair; born St. Joseph; student; joined May 5, Guthrie; single; sick in line of duty.

WELLS, Thomas J., Santa Fe; pvt., F Troop.

WENTWORTH, S. Conduit, Santa Fe; cpl., F Troop.

WERTHEIM, Adolph S., San Antonio; pvt., F Troop; joined May 19, San Antonio.

WESLEY, Frederick C., Santa Fe; sgt., E Troop; 37, 5 ft., 6⅜ ins., light, blue eyes, light-brown hair; born Bangor, Me.; printer; joined May 3, Santa Fe; married; wounded in action July 1.

WETMORE, Robert Charles, Montclair, N.J.; pvt., L Troop; joined July 9, Santiago.

WETMORE, Starr M., Newkirk, O.T.; trumpeter, D Troop; 25, 5 ft., 7 ins., fair, light-blue eyes, light-brown hair; born North Cohocton, N.Y.; baker; joined May 5, Guthrie; single; wounded in action July 1.

WHALEN, F. G.; pvt., A Troop.

WHEELER, Frank G., Chautauqua County, N.Y.; pvt., H Troop; joined June 13, Tampa.

WHITE, Harry C., Somerville, Mass.; cpl., A Troop; 27, 5 ft., 4¾ ins., fair, light-blue eyes, dark-brown hair; born Somerville; electrician; joined May 3, Whipple Barracks; single; wounded in action July 2.

WHITE, Lyman E.; pvt., G Troop; joined June 27, Santa Fe.

WHITNEY, Forest, Artesia, S.D.; saddler, A Troop; 24, 5 ft., 6 ins., fair, blue eyes, light-brown hair; born Green Lake County, Wis.; saddler; joined May 2, Whipple Barracks; single; sick in line of duty.

WHITNEY, Schuyler C., Pryor Creek, I.T.; pvt., L Troop; 29, 5 ft., 7⅞ ins., dark, blue eyes, black hair; born Nemaha, Kans.; stonemason; joined May 14, Muskogee; single; wounded in action June 24.

WHITTAKER, George C., Silver City, N.M.; pvt., B Troop; joined July 2, Santa Fe.

WHITTINGTON, Richard, Gallup, N.M.; pvt., G Troop; 25, 5 ft., 9⅜ ins., fair, brown eyes, light-brown hair; born Charleston, W.Va.; joined May 3, Santa Fe; miner; single.

WICKHAM, Patrick, Socorro, N.M.; pvt., H Troop; joined June 28, Santa Fe; barber.

WIENTGE, Frederick W., Santa Fe; 1st lt., I Troop; joined May 10, Santa Fe; died of typhoid.

WIGGINS, Thomas W., Bertram, Texas; pvt., B Troop; 30, 5 ft., 7½ ins., fair, light-blue eyes, dark-brown hair; born in Florida; cowboy; joined May 2, Whipple Barracks; single; wounded in action June 24.

WILBERG, Axel E.; pvt., K Troop; joined July 14, Washington, D.C.

WILCOX, George B., Prescott; 1st lt., B Troop; 34, 5 ft., 10¼ ins., fair, blue eyes, brown hair; born Addison, N.Y.; farmer; joined April 30, Whipple Barracks; sick in line of duty.

WILEY, Harry B., Santa Fe; pvt., F Troop; 21, 5 ft., 5⅛ ins., light, brown eyes, brown hair; born Orleans, Neb.; butcher; joined May 6, Santa Fe; single.

WILKERSON, Wallace W., Santa Fe; pvt., B Troop; joined June 23, Santa Fe; sick in line of duty.

WRIGHT, Albert P., Yuma, Ariz.; pvt., C Troop; 39, 6 ft., ¾ in., fair, light-blue eyes, dark-brown hair; born Fairfax, Va.; cowboy; joined May 2, Whipple

Barracks; single; wounded in action June 24.

WRIGHT, Clarence, Springer, N.M.; pvt., G Troop; 28, 5 ft., 11⅜ ins., light, blue eyes, light hair; born Lafayette, Ga.; railroad man; joined May 5, Santa Fe; single.

WRIGHT, Edward L., Guthrie, O.T.; pvt., D Troop; joined May 19, San Antonio.

WRIGHT, George, Madrid, N.M.; pvt., E Troop; 23, 5 ft., 5⅞ ins., dark, blue eyes, dark-brown hair; born Fort Scott, Kans.; miner; joined May 4, Santa Fe; married.

WRIGHT, Grant, Cold Springs, N.Y.; pvt., H Troop, trans. K Troop May 16; 29, 5 ft., 3¾ ins., dark, blue eyes, brown hair; born Cold Springs; soldier; joined May 5, Washington, D.C.; single.

WRIGHT, Hugh B., Las Vegas; sgt., E Troop; 23, 5 ft., 11 ins., light, blue eyes, light hair; born Bowling Green, Ky.; express man; joined May 5, Santa Fe; single.

WRIGHT, William O., Pawnee, O.T.; pvt., D Troop; 39, 5 ft., 9½ ins., dark, blue eyes, dark hair; born Rice County, Minn.; ranchman; joined May 5, Guthrie; married; wounded in action July 1.

WYLIE, John B., Fort Bayard, N.M.; sgt., H Troop; 42, 5 ft., 4½ ins., fair, blue eyes, brown hair; born in Indiana; soldier; joined May 6, Santa Fe; married.

WYNKOOP, Charles W., Santa Fe; pvt., E Troop; 27, 5 ft., 11¼ ins., light, blue eyes, red hair; born Stanhope, Pa.; tinner; joined May 3, Santa Fe; single.

WYNKOOP, Harman H., Santa Fe; cpl., E Troop; 25, 5 ft., 11½ ins., dark, gray eyes,

dark hair; born Harrisburg, Pa.; printer; joined May 3, Santa Fe; married; wounded in action July 2.

WILKENS, George W., Vinita, I.T.; pvt., L Troop; 21, 5 ft., 7¼ ins., dark, blue eyes, brown hair; born in Canadian District, I.T.; farmer; joined May 14, Muskogee; single.

WILKINSON, Samuel I., Cincinnati, Ohio; pvt., H Troop; joined May 25, San Antonio.

WILLARD, Wallace B., Cottonwood, I.T.; farrier, A Troop; 28, 5 ft., 10 ins., brown eyes, brown hair; born Sacramento, Calif.; cowboy; joined April 30, Whipple Barracks; single.

WILLIAMS, Arthur E., Las Cruces, N.M.; cpl., H Troop; 23, 5 ft., 11⅜ ins., dark, brown eyes, dark-brown hair; born Bell County, Texas; clerk; joined May 4, Santa Fe; single.

WILLIAMS, Benjamin H., South McAlester, I.T.; cpl., M Troop; joined May 14, Muskogee.

WILLIAMS, George W., Ardmore, I.T.; pvt., M Troop; joined May 14, Muskogee.

WILLIAMS, Hiram E., Raton, N.M.; pvt., G Troop; 28, 5 ft., 7½ ins., dark, blue eyes, light-brown hair; born Memphis, Tenn.; laborer; joined May 5, Santa Fe; single.

WILLIAMS, Maynard R., Fairland, I.T.; pvt., L Troop; 26, 5 ft., 6½ ins., dark, dark-brown eyes, dark-brown hair; born Carroll, Iowa; cowboy; joined May 14, Muskogee; single; sick in line of duty.

WILLIAMS, Thomas C., Santa Fe; pvt., E Troop; 40, 5 ft., 9 ins., dark, blue eyes, dark hair; born Hocking County, Ohio; miner; joined May 3, Santa Fe; single.

WILLS, Thomas J.; pvt., F Troop; joined June 28, Santa Fe.

WILSON, Charles A., Colorado Springs, Col.; pvt., I Troop, trans. Hosp. Corps., June 7; joined May 19, San Antonio.

WILSON, Charles E., Boulder, Col.; pvt., H Troop; 23, 5 ft., 9¼ ins., ruddy, blue eyes, light hair; born Boulder; farmer; joined May 4, Santa Fe; single.

WILSON, Frank M., Guthrie, O.T.; pvt., D Troop; 22, 5 ft., 9¼ ins., dark, brown eyes, black hair; born Evansville, Ind.; furrier; joined May 5, Guthrie; single.

WILSON, Harry W., Tampa; pvt., F Troop; joined June 8, Tampa.

WILSON, James E., Madrid, Mo.; pvt., L Troop; 21, 5 ft., 8¼ ins., dark, blue eyes, dark-brown hair; born in Louisiana; cowboy; joined May 14, Muskogee; single; sick in line of duty.

WILSON, Jerome, Chloride, Ariz.; pvt., A Troop; 25, 5 ft., 6 ins., fair, light-brown eyes, light-brown hair; born Grayville, Ill.; cowboy; joined May 2, Whipple Barracks; single.

WINN, Arthur N., Muskogee; pvt., L Troop; 20, 5 ft., 7¼ ins., fair, blue eyes, dark-brown hair; born Westfork, Ark.; joined May 14, Muskogee; single.

WINTER, John G., San Antonio; pvt., F Troop; joined May 19, San Antonio; wounded in action July 1.

WINTER, Otto R., San Antonio; pvt., F Troop; joined May 29, San Antonio.

WISENBERG, Roy O., Raton, N.M.; pvt., I Troop; joined June 29, Santa Fe.

WOLFE, John W., Ardmore, I.T.; pvt., M Troop; joined May 14, Muskogee.

WOLFF, Frederick W., San Antonio; pvt., D Troop; joined May 27, San Antonio.

WOOD, Leonard, Cape Cod, Mass.; colonel; 37, 5 ft., 10 ins., light, blue eyes, light hair; joined Washington, D.C.

WOOD, William D., Bland, N.M.; pvt., G Troop; joined June 23, Santa Fe.

WOODIN, Frank A., Phoenix; cpl., C Troop; 24, 5 ft., 8¾ ins., fair, light-blue eyes, flaxen hair; born Skyland, Neb.; clerk; joined April 30, Whipple Barracks; single.

WOODWARD, John A., Taylor, Texas; pvt., D Troop; 18, 5 ft., 9⅞ ins., dark, dark-brown eyes, black hair; born Bexar County, Texas; horse dealer; joined May 5, Guthrie; single.

WOODWARD, Sidney H., Kingman, Ariz.; pvt., B Troop; joined June 27, Santa Fe.

WOOG, Benjamin B., Washington, D.C.; pvt., M Troop; joined June 20, Muskogee.

WORDEN, John Lorimer, New York City; pvt., K Troop; joined May 24, San Antonio; sick in line of duty.

WORMELL, John A., Phoenix; pvt., C Troop; 21, 5 ft., 7¾ ins., fair, light-brown eyes, dark-brown hair; born Phoenix; rancher; joined May 1, Whipple Barracks; single.

WRENN, Robert D., Chicago, Ill.; pvt., A Troop; joined June 4, Tampa; sick in line of duty.

YANCEY, Kyle, McAlester, I.T.; pvt., M Troop; died of typhoid at Tampa July 5.

YOUNG, Howard G., Washington, D.C.; pvt., I Troop; joined May 19, San Antonio.

YOUNG, James E., Los Angeles, Calif.; pvt., K Troop; joined May 19, San Antonio.

YOUNG, Samuel, Caddo, I.T.; pvt., M Troop; joined May 14, Muskogee.

YOUNG, Thomas H., Phoenix; pvt., B Troop; 25, 5 ft., 5½ ins., fair, light-blue eyes, dark-brown hair; born Lancaster, Ky.; salesman; sick in line of duty.

YOUNGER, Charles, Winslow, Ariz.; pvt., C Troop; 22, 5 ft., 8¼ ins., fair, dark-brown eyes, dark-brown hair; born Dominion, Texas; fireman; joined May 1, Whipple Barracks; single.

YOST, James G., Prescott; blacksmith, C Troop; 25, 5 ft., 6¼ ins., fair, light-blue eyes, light-brown hair; born Eldon, Iowa; cowboy; joined May 1, Whipple Barracks; single.

ZIGLER, Daniel J., Como, Mont.; pvt., E Troop; 21, 5 ft., 9¾ ins., dark, blue eyes, dark-brown hair; born in Oregon; cowboy; joined May 3, Santa Fe; single.

WHERE THEY WERE FROM

STATES

Alabama (admitted to
Union, 1819) 15
Arkansas (1836) 14
California (1850) 42
Colorado (1876) 24
Connecticut (1788) 3
Delaware (1787) 1
Florida (1845) 17
Georgia (1788) 10
Illinois (1818) 81
Indiana (1816) 28
Iowa (1846) 42
Kansas (1861) 52
Kentucky (1792) 18
Louisiana (1812) 16
Maine (1820) 3
Maryland (1788) 7
Massachusetts (1788) 25
Michigan (1837) 21
Minnesota (1858) 3
Mississippi (1817) 6
Missouri (1821) 63
Montana (1889) 1
Nebraska (1867) 8
New Hampshire (1788) 5
New Jersey (1787) 12
New York (1788) 90
North Carolina (1789) 6
North Dakota (1889) 3
Ohio (1803) 46
Oregon (1859) 3
Pennsylvania (1787) 45

Rhode Island (1790) 3
South Carolina (1788) 5
Tennessee (1796) 17
Texas (1845) 127
Utah (1896) 5
Vermont (1791) 4
Virginia (1788) 15
Washington (1889) 1
West Virginia (1863) 10
Wisconsin (1848) 16
Wyoming (1890) 3

TERRITORIES

Arizona (1912) 35
Indian 103
New Mexico (1912) 120
Oklahoma (1907) 12

FOREIGN COUNTRIES

Alsace 1
Australia 1
Canada 10
Denmark 1
England 13
Germany 14
Ireland 5
Monaco 1
Russia 2
Scotland 7
Sweden 5
Switzerland 2
Wales 1

OCCUPATIONS OF ROUGH RIDERS

Accountants	1	Editors	1
Actors	2	Electricians	4
Architects	1	Engineers	12
Army	29	Expressmen	1
Artists	2	Farmers	53
Assessors	1	Farriers	10
Associated Press	1	Firemen	9
Attorneys	16	Florists	2
Bakers	5	Football players	10
Bandmasters	2	Foreign Legion	2
Barbers	6	Furriers	2
Baseball players	7	Gardeners	3
Bicyclists	1	Golfers	5
Blacksmiths	17	Grocers	2
Bookbinders	1	Guards	1
Bookkeepers	2	Half-milers	1
Brakemen	1	Harnessmakers	1
Bricklayers	2	High-jumpers	1
Brickmakers	1	Horse dealers	1
Bridge builders	1	Hotel clerks	2
Butchers	8	Hotelkeepers	1
Cabinet makers	1	Hunters	6
Car inspectors	1	Indian agents	1
Carpenters	13	Insurance agents	3
Car repairers	1	Internal revenue agents	1
Cattlemen	14	Ironworkers	1
Chaplains	2	Jewelers	2
Cigar makers	1	Jockeys	1
Civil engineers	1	Journalists	3
Clerks	44	Judges	1
Coaches	2	Justice Dept. agents	3
Collectors	1	Laborers	34
Conductors	2	Lawyers	16
Confectioners	1	Linemen	1
Congressmen	4	Liverymen	2
Contractors	3	Locksmiths	1
Cooks	13	Locomotive engineers	2
Coopers	1	Locomotive firemen	1
Cowboys	160	Machinists	6
Crewmen	4	Mailmen	2
Cuban insurgents	3	Manufacturers	1
Deserters	7	Marshals or sheriffs	8
Detectives	1	Mechanics	2
Druggists	3	Merchants	3

Miners	87	Salesmen	5
Ministers	5	Scouts and Indian fighters	5
Moulders	1	Sculptors	1
Musicians	14	Sheriffs or marshals	8
Navy	3	Shoemakers	2
Newsdealers	1	Singers	2
Newspapermen	11	Song writers	1
Nurses	1	Speakers of House	1
Nurserymen	2	Stage drivers	3
Orators	1	Steeplechase riders	1
Packers	2	Stenographers	2
Painters	6	Stock exchange	3
Pharmacists	1	Stonemasons	2
Photographers	1	Students	26
Physicians	8	School superintendents	2
Planters	1	Surveyors	2
Plasterers	1	Teachers	15
Plumbers	8	Teamsters	13
Policemen	6	Telegraph linemen	3
Polo players	15	Telegraph operators	3
Postal clerks	1	Telephone operators	1
Printers	14	Tennis players	4
Prospectors	6	Tinners	3
Railroad men	31	Traders	1
Ranchers	44	Trainmasters	1
Rangers	2	Trappers	8
Real estate dealers	2	Veterinary surgeons	3
Reporters	11	Watchmakers	4
Recorders	1	Weather observers	1
Saddlers	11	Yachtsmen	2
Sailors	3		

INDEX

Texas, 20, 56, 127
"Texas" (horse), taken aboard *Yucatan,*
71; on march, 121
Texas (ship), 206
"There'll Be a Hot Time in the Old Town
Tonight," popular, 78; played at Dai-
quirí, 100; sung at San Juan, 165
Third Brigade, 1st Division, 60
Third Brigade, 2nd Division, 60
Third Regular Cavalry, in 1st Brigade,
Cavalry Division, 60; 177, 180, 263, 264,
266, 270
Thirteenth Infantry, 73, 254
Thirty-fourth Michigan, 198
Thomas, Judge John R., 37
Thomas, John R., Jr., lieutenant in Rough
Riders, 37; wounded, 131
Tiffany, William, Jr., prominent, 27; Hig-
gins rides, 40; buys cigar, 64; reports to
Parker, 197; commands sharpshooter de-
tail, 224; visits Morro Castle, 254; re-
mains in Cuba, 262; death, 271
Tod, Garfield A., 39
Tomlinson, Leroy E., sick, 85; 117
Toral, Gen. José, sent flag of truce, 207;
refuses to surrender, 208; messenger
shown camp, 220; asks permission to go
to mountains, 220; repeats request, 225;
asks third time, 226; given deadline, 227;
229; asks further delay, 237; attends conference, 238; 239, 240, 241; ready to surrender, 242; sword delivered, 243; sur-
renders, 243
Torrey, Judge Jay L., asks authority to
organize cowboy troops, 17; organizes
regiment, 17; regiment remains in U.S.,
48
Trail of the Lonesome Pine, 169
Treaty of Paris, 267
Truce, begins, 207; ends, 229; renewed,
233
Tucson, Ariz., 155
Twenty-first District Republican Association, 8
Twenty-second Infantry, 121
Typhoid fever, spreading, 85; Tomlinson
succumbs to, 117; 222; three cases discovered, 228; Shafter alarmed by, 239;
special camp, 241; 258, 268

Uniforms, cavalry fatigues, 3; arrive at
San Antonio, 34; troops without, 49
United States, declares war on Spain, 15;
unprepared for war, 16; Cervera's fleet
feared, 22; 50, 155, 236, 241, 245, 252,
259, 261, 262
United States Congress. *See* Congress

Valencia County, N.M., 21
Van Horn, Col. J. J., 60
Vermont, 26
Vernon, Lord, 89
Virginia, 5, 90, 177
Vixen, 98, 206, 245
Vizcaya, 207
Von Sternberg, Baron Hermann Speck,
suggests Rough Riders, 8; 9, 15

Wadsworth, Craig, leader of cotillions, 5;
rides at San Antonio, 33; at Knicker-
bocker Club, 269
Wagner, Arthur Lockwood, commands ad-
vance, 108; suspicious of Wheeler, 115
Wallace, Alexander H., 180
Walsh, Sgt. George, 264
War Department, training camps in South,

16; order on troop strength, 21; aban-
dons attack plan, 22; 29, 41, 193, 203,
211, 256; urges Shafter to move camp,
259; 260, 261
Warren, Senator Fracis, 17
Washington, George, 89
Washington, D.C., 8; Roosevelt returns to,
11; Roosevelt meets Wood at, 13; Shafter
at, 22; 34; confusion, 43; 57, 60, 63, 65,
75, 98, 169, 192, 193, 203, 211, 225,
227, 228, 233, 238, 239, 240, 241, 252,
256, 258, 268, 281
Washington *Evening Star,* 203
Washington *Post,* 52, 65, 207; editorializes
about Roosevelt letter, 61; 268
Wasp, 90
Wells, Joseph Ogden, tells of meeting
Westerners, 32; diary at Harvard, 32;
writes about rations, 73; writes of voyage, 79; enjoys listening to Westerners,
82; describes shelling, 99; describes Cuban women, 110; describes march to
Siboney, 111; diary entry, 117; moving
camp, 148; expects battle, 162; Grimes's
battery, 171; in trenches, 195; digging
bombproof, 211; writes men worn out,
218; surrender, 241; has oatmeal, 242;
reports surrender, 245; writes army must
move, 259; gets dysentery, 260; goes into
Santiago, 262; departure, 263
West Indies, 78
West Point Military Academy, Wheeler attends, 18; Brodie graduated from, 24,
55, 73, 129, 135, 162, 177, 188
West Virginia, 266
Weyler, Gen. Valeriano, 11
Whalen, F. G., 262
Wheeler, Annie, 272
Wheeler, Lt. Joseph W., 268
Wheeler, Maj. Gen. Joseph, made major
general, 18; arrives at Tampa, 52; visits
Rough Riders, 53; conducts inspection,
57; heads Cavalry Division, 60; 69;
writes about voyage, 80; writes in diary,
84; records course, 85; makes last entry
in diary, 85; to land second, 91; 92;
comes ashore, 103; scouts, 105; fails to
get message, 110; orders Rough Riders
to move, 110; always on move, 113;
holds conferences, 115; decides on reconnaissance, 117; to pull fast one, 118;
approves battle plan, 122; curiosity starts
battle, 125; agrees to ask reinforcements,
131; "damn Yankees on run," 136; com-
mended, 119; angers Lawton, 145; ex-
plains action, 146; fever attacks, 157;
takes medicine, 160; Sumner replaces,
162; watches battle action, 182; against
withdrawing, 201; illness reported, 203;
asked about truce, 207; sends truce
party, 208; 224; requests Rough Riders
to handle pack trains, 236; attends conference, 238; named to surrender commission, 240; 241, 253, 256; ordered to
move, 259; 263; talks of Civil War,
264; at Montauk Point, 265; Mrs. Logan
greets, 266; in Washington, 268; given
Montauk Point command, 268; tent
blown down; 270; 271; announces President, 272; farewell address, 275; son
drowns, 275; 276
Wheeler, Thomas, 275
Whipple Barracks, volunteers march from,
23; 39, 264
Whitney, Caspar, 198
Whitney, Schuyler, wounded, 128; 158

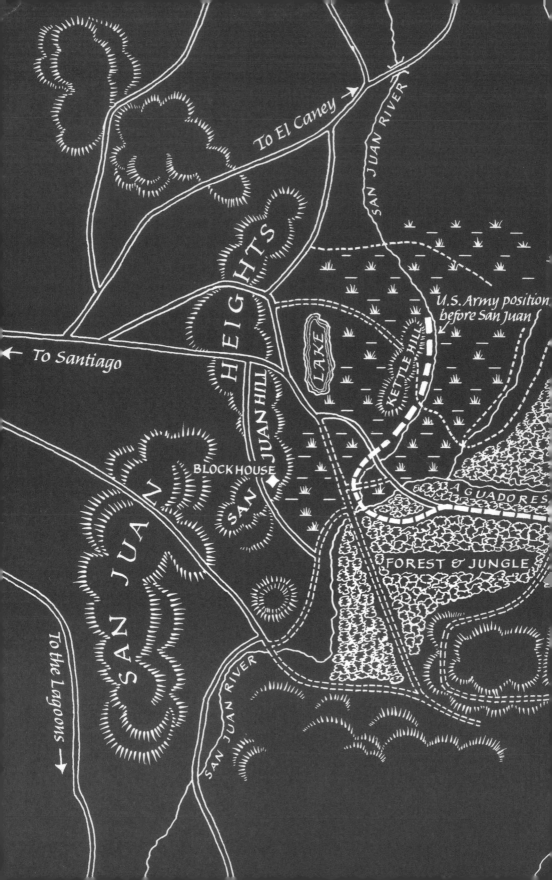